REISCHAUER

The Nature and Truth
OF THE GREAT RELIGIONS

The Nature and Truth
OF THE GREAT RELIGIONS
TOWARD A PHILOSOPHY
OF RELIGION

By

AUGUST KARL REISCHAUER

CHARLES E. TUTTLE COMPANY
TOKYO, JAPAN & RUTLAND, VERMONT

Representatives
For Continental Europe: BOXERBOOKS, INC., Zurich
For the British Isles: PRENTICE-HALL INTERNATIONAL, INC., London
For Australasia: PAUL FLESCH & CO., PTY. LTD., Melbourne
For Canada: m.g. hurtig ltd., Edmonton

Published by the
CHARLES E. TUTTLE COMPANY, INC.
of Rutland, Vermont & Tokyo, Japan
with editorial offices at
Suido 1-chome, 2-6, Bunkyo-ku, Tokyo

PRINTED IN JAPAN

FOREWORD

IN CONNECTION WITH THE PUBLICATION BY THE
Charles E. Tuttle Company of Dr. A. K. Reischauer's new book, *The Nature and Truth of the Great Religions*, I have been asked by Dr. E. O. Reischauer, the author's son and now American Ambassador to Japan, to write a foreword to the work. The primary reason why I have been entrusted with this honor is, I believe, because I am one of his former students and hence am well acquainted with the author's personality, thought, and academic background. Therefore I have accepted this task with pleasure, as it gives me the opportunity to reaffirm my respect and gratitude toward Dr. A. K. Reischauer.

After reading the proofs of the book which the publisher kindly sent me, I saw my task as a threefold one: first, to introduce the person and the career of the author; then to tell something of the background of the book, how it was prepared and finally produced in this form as the result of the author's concentrated studies over a number of years; and finally, to mention some of the special characteristics which distinguish this book from other publications in the field.

Dr. August Karl Reischauer was born on September 4, 1879 on a farm near Jonesboro in southern Illinois. After graduating from Hanover College in Hanover, Indiana, and from McCormick Theological Seminary in Chicago, Illinois, he came to Japan in 1905 as a missionary of the Presbyterian Church in the U.S.A. He was an educational missionary, teaching at Meiji Gakuin in Tokyo until 1930. At first he taught Philosophy, History, and German in the College Department, and then Theology and the History of Religions in the Theological Department. During this period the writer of this Foreword was Dr. Reischauer's student, and later had the privilege of being associated with him as a colleague at the same institution, and also at Japan Theological Seminary. Besides his teaching Dr. Reischauer took an important part in the founding of Tokyo Woman's Christian College, and served as the Executive Secretary of the Board of Trustees of that college. He and Mrs. Reischauer were also instrumental in the founding of the Japan Oral Deaf School. As a Presbyterian missionary he belonged to the "second generation" of missionaries, succeeding such well-known "first generation" figures as Dr. James C. Hepburn and Dr. William Imbrie. Dr. Reischauer became the senior member and leader of the Presbyterian missionaries of his period. He worked in Japan for about 35 years, and left because of the condition of Mrs. Reischauer's health. His work in Japan was related primarily to Meiji Gakuin and Tokyo Woman's Christian College. His eldest son, Dr. Robert Reischauer, a professor at Princeton University, met his death in Shanghai and was buried in the Tama Cemetery near Tokyo.

For his contributions to Christian education in Japan, Dr. Reischauer was awarded the decoration of the Third Order of Merit by the Japanese government. Tokyo Metropolis also honored him by giving him the title of honorary citizen. He is now living in Belmont, Massachusetts, in good health.

A few words about the background of this book would be in order. This is by no means the product of hasty work, but rather the outcome of many years of study and preparation. I feel that this book represents the findings of the author's painstaking, life-long work. From his experiences as a missionary in Japan, he came to conclude that there were two elements of particular importance to the mission task in this country. In the first place, he held that it was urgently desirable to find some way to coordinate and unify the activities of various existing theological institutions, in order to improve their academic standards. Secondly, he felt that it was important in a place like Japan for foreign missionaries to study the nation's traditional culture and religions, in order to have sufficient knowledge and understanding of the most effective and relevant ways of carrying out Christian evangelism. This second element led Dr. Reischauer to make special studies of Japanese Buddhism. The method he used for his study was to get help from his Japanese students for reading the original documents. In this way he read the classical works of Japanese Buddhism, taking notes on them and translating some of the more important documents. He published some of the results of these studies in *A Catechism on the Shin Sect*, and *Genshin's Ojo Yoshu*. *Studies in Japanese Buddhism* (New York: Macmillan, 1917), based on a series of lectures delivered at New York University, is his best-known work, and is very highly regarded both in Japan and abroad. This book has been used here in Japan as a textbook in various Buddhist universities. Dr. Reischauer also read a paper on "Christianity and Northern Buddhism" at the Jerusalem Conference of the International Missionary Council in 1928. In the field of the scholarly study of Japanese Buddhism, Dr. Reischauer has been the West's pioneer scholar.

After his return to America, Dr. Reischauer was called by Union Theological Seminary in New York City to be a lecturer in the History of Religions, filling the important chair in that subject as a successor to Professor Hume. He accepted this call and continued his work there for nine years, until 1952. The contents of this present book are to my mind based primarily on these lectures delivered at Union. I am certain that this book's author is a competent and highly-gifted scholar in the history of religions, who can deal with this difficult subject with great skill.

Lastly, I should like to comment on some of the special characteristics of this book. As the title indicates, this book is not a theological treatise which is solely concerned with Christian faith and thought alone, but rather a book of a wider outlook which deals with various religions. The author takes up Judaism, Islam, Hinduism, Buddhism, Chinese and Japanese religions, as well as Christianity. This field of the history of religions has been rather unfavorably treated for some years in theological circles because of Barthian influences, but a change in the theological climate has been going on, and studies in the history of religions are now well received everywhere. Thus the publication of this book is quite timely and will, I believe, be favorably received both by Christian and by non-Christian scholars.

There are various methods of approaching the study of the history of religions. One method emphasizes historical facts rather than the thought structures of religions. However, Dr. Reischauer's book is concerned primarily with the thought and philosophical framework of religions. Philosophy has been the author's major interest ever since his college days. He taught philosophy, theology, and the history of modern theology at Meiji Gakuin. He has continued this line of interest throughout his life. In the present book also, this bent of the author is clearly seen in the whole course of his discussion. Both the nature and the truth of the great religions are treated from this viewpoint. In fact, the concepts of God, the good life, and the destiny of individuals are the three main interests and focal points from which he views the religions he deals with.

Finally, I wish to call attention to another important characteristic of this book. As the above-mentioned three main interests indicate, the author has always taken his stand on the faith and the thought of Christianity. Although this book deals with the nature and truths of various religions, and is thus a book in the field of the science or the history of religions, its underlying theological basis is that of Christian faith. This may seem to some readers as an unfavorable characteristic, but to my mind it is a welcome and valuable feature of the work. Nowadays we have many theologians in the narrow sense, that is, those who write only on one aspect of Christian theology. But theological faculties have for many years suffered from the lack of highly-qualified Christian scholars who can write competent works on the history of other religions from a Christian viewpoint. The present book surely hits the mark here. To my mind, this volume will not only be well received by Christian theologians, but also by scholars of other religions as well.

HIDENOBU KUWADA, PH.D
President, Tokyo Union Theological Seminary

CONTENTS

INTRODUCTION

THAT RELIGION IN ONE FORM OR ANOTHER has played a tremendous role in the life of mankind no competent student of history can seriously question. It is, however, quite another matter to assess accurately the place religion occupies in the life of the modern world and to state what in even the essentials of the major religions can have any real meaning for modern man.

On the one hand, there can be little doubt that for many, religion is less central than it was to past generations. Much that in the past was sought primarily through religion modern man seeks without any particular connection with his faith. This is especially true of things that are so essential for man's physical life and well-being and for which he turns largely to modern science and technology. So much is this the case that the sphere of religion seems to be shrinking as modern science and technological developments expand their sway and increasingly engage man's interests and activities. In fact, many seldom give religion any serious thought or dismiss it as something that belonged rather to the childhood of the race and thus to be out-grown. And there are, of course, the Communists and kindred spirits who scorn religion as being little more than wishful thinking, or an opiate for the ignorant masses to keep them content with their miserable lot in life while dreaming about a future life in some heavenly realm that religion promises. This attitude towards religion is characteristic not only of many in the Western world but also of many in Oriental countries. They too, are more interested in the good and better life which modern science and technology can provide than in the religion of their fathers. They may not openly repudiate their religious heritage; they are rather indifferent towards it and give it little thought.

Now while this attitude towards religion has become rather wide-spread in recent years throughout the modern world there are, on the other hand, some indications that the tide may now be turning in favor of a renewed interest in religion. This seems to be the case especially in the United States and also, though to a lesser degree, in Europe and in certain Oriental lands. Just what the reason or reasons for this renewed interest in religion may be is rather difficult to state.

In the Western World there is, to be sure, the continuing reliance on science and technology for the things needed to provide the good life in the here and now, but many are beginning to realize that our boasted "economy of abundance" made possible by modern science is not all that is needed for the good life of man. There are some things that are quite essential for the truly good life which modern science and technology can not provide and for which man must look to other sources. This fact is being specially high-lighted in the very field in which modern scientists have achieved their most remarkable success, namely, in nuclear physics. That the use of atomic energy which science now makes possible can bring untold blessings seems quite certain, but it is equally certain that the terrible nuclear weapons which have already been developed could bring mass destruction, if not universal death, unless man can learn to live at peace with his fellow men. It is the leading scientists themselves who hold that no adequate counter weapons of defence can be invented and that man must renounce all wars and settle his differences by peaceful means. This means, of course, that there must be mutual trust and confidence that agreements made in the interest of peace will be kept. But this, in short, requires a real regard for moral and spiritual values such as the major religions of mankind have always stressed.

It is especially the Western World's conflict with the Communists who scorn all religion and moral values that leads many to take more seriously again our moral and religious heritage. Many now realize that much of what is best in the life of the free world and that has been taken for granted all too esaily as being just a natural part of civilized man's life is fundamentally grounded in Western man's spiritual heritage, namely, in the Judeo-Christian religious heritage. If, then, we would preserve this type of life it becomes necessary to take this heritage more seriously again. This is particularly the case with religion's emphasis on the worth and sacredness of the individual human being, the very basis of man's freedom but also the very thing Communism ignores or scorns. And again, religion's emphasis on truth and truthfulness in man's relationship with his fellow men as over against the "Big Lie" repeated incessantly till it seems to be the truth, is another reason why many in the Free World are giving their religious heritage more serious thought today.

In Oriental countries where there seems to be a sort of "resurgence of religion", as mentioned above, the reason for this seems somewhat different. It is probably more a phase of the new nationalism than an actual renewed interest in the age-old religions. When a people become nationally conscious they think not merely about their present status and hopes for the future but they also take pride in their cultural and spiritual heritage that has been handed down from the past. To be sure, they may be quite ignorant of what this spiritual heritage really is, and undoubtedly it needs to be restated in more modern terminology to give it any real meaning for the present generation; but even though this is the case the fact remains that there is a renewed interest now taking place in at least a few of the countries of Asia.

In this connection it should be added that in the Western World there is not only a renewed interest in the Judeo-Christian religious heritage but also some interest in the major religions of the Orient such as Islam, Hinduism, Buddhism and their modern variants. So much is this the case that leading magazines find it worthwhile to publish articles on these religions. In the past, only a small circle of scholars showed any interest in these religions but today others are joining the ranks, for with our growing world-wide contacts it is only natural that more and more Westerners should want to know something about the cultural and spiritual heritage of others. Is there anything in this heritage which is more or less consonant with that of the Western World and which might be a real asset in building a better world? Such questions are peculiarly pertinent to-day in the Free World because of its deadly conflict with Communism.

It is, however, not merely the conflict with Communism that makes it important for people of the Western World to know something about the spiritual heritage of other people. The importance of this existed long before Communism arose. In fact, any Westerner who is really concerned with building a better world should not only be well grounded in his own cultural and spiritual heritage and which has stemmed so largely from the Judeo-Christian religion, but he should also have a real understanding of the ideals and spiritual values by which people of other faiths live. In the past very few Westerners, even among those who lived and worked with other peoples, showed any interest in the latters' culture or religion. All too many have been totally indifferent, if not actually scornful of this heritage. They have usually regarded their own civilization as so superior that they had really nothing to learn from others. It is, of course, this attitude of "superiority" which so many Westerners have shown that has been so bitterly resented, and it is high time that they take a little more interest in the cultural and spiritual heritage of other people.

Now whatever the reason for this apparently renewed interest in religion may be, it could work out to the best interests of the modern world not only in matters that are distinctly spiritual but also in the common things of life. This would be especially the case if this interest led to a clearer understanding of what are really the great essentials of religion as over against secondary things or things tied up with religion that are a positive hindrance to the better life and that clutter up even the major religions of mankind. That is really what constitutes a major problem facing men of religion today, namely, to set forth more clearly what the great essentials of religion really are and to formulate these essentials in ways that can have real meaning for modern man who lives in a world that in many ways differs rather radically from the world of his ancestors and of traditional religion. This is so much the case that the very language of traditional religion is often quite meaningless to men of the modern world however much it may have meant to past generations or however much of essential truth it may have expressed. And if that is the case in the Western World where modern science has had its development over a rather long period and where it brought about the great changes in man's life gradually, it is even more the case in the Orient and other parts of the world where the impact of modern science and technology has recently become cataclysmic and where, therefore, it is even more difficult for the present generation to find any real meaning in its religious heritage.

Thus any one who is really seriously concerned with religion and what it can and should mean in man's life is faced with two major problems as is indicated in the very title of this volume. The first is to determine as far as possible the real nature of religion. The second is concerned with what is true and valid in religion. We shall, therefore, take up in Part I the Nature of Religion as this can be most adequately seen in what the major religions of mankind have to say in their great essentials, especially in what they have to say about the Divine or Ultimate Reality on which man feels himself dependant about the Good Life of man in the here and now, and about any Future Life or the destiny of the individual human being. In Part II, The Truth of Religion, we shall try to present what can be accepted as essentially valid in the various teachings of these major religions.

AUGUST KARL REISCHAUER

The Nature and Truth
OF THE GREAT RELIGIONS
❧ TOWARD A PHILOSOPHY
OF RELIGION

PART ONE
THE NATURE OF RELIGION

❧ Introduction

ANYONE WHO SEEKS TO KNOW THE REAL NATURE OF RELIGION is met first of all with a bewildering variety of admittedly religious phenomena. There is such a thing as "the varieties of religious experiences," and these varieties are even greater than what William James exhibited in his well known volume of that title. And still greater than the variety of religious experience is the variety of external expression, for religious experiences which in their inner meaning may be much alike often find widely differing outward expression owing to the cultural differences of the individuals concerned.

A second and even greater difficulty in understanding the nature of religion stems from the fact that religion is frequently rather paradoxical in its expression. "Religion appears as pervading the entire life of a social group and hardly distinguishable from it, and at the same time appears as a sacred institution and ritual holding itself apart from all that is profane. It takes the form of a priestly caste which stones all prophets, and the form of prophetic leaders who harass the priests and cause their downfall. It worships fecundity, and exacts celibacy. It is now an affair of the state and again it is utterly supernatural and other-worldly. It may smile upon all the arts, or it may sternly break images and whitewash frescoed walls. It consists now in the punctilious observance of rituals, now in a prudential and urbane philosophy, and now in fervent apocalyptic hopes. It may be bound up with all the idiosyncracies of a racial culture, or it may expand itself to include in its ideal the whole of humanity." (Lyman—*The Meaning and Truth of Religion* p. 51).

It might be said that no one religion stands for all these paradoxes at one and the same time or in the minds of the same individuals; but it is true that both sides of these paradoxical expressions have been definitely associated with each and every one of the major religions of mankind.

A

Probably the real explanation of these apparently contradictory characteristics stems from the fact that religion in all its forms represents, on the one hand, man's relationship with his natural environment while, on the other hand, man feels himself also related to a superhuman and divine world which he discovers gropingly as being both continuous with his natural world while yet somehow transcending it. It is therefore rather to be expected that in religion man should both affirm and deny his natural life. How much or how little he will affirm or deny depends largely upon what conception he has of the divine and transcendental world.

Now while it is true that religion in its various historic manifestations has presented a bewildering variety of beliefs and practices which often seem quite paradoxical in expression and meaning it is also true that there are certain characteristic traits which have persistently recurred down through the centuries even under widely varying cultural conditions from which one can determine fairly accurately the nature of any given religion and the elements in it that have had and may continue to have real meaning for human life.

What are, then, these characteristic traits or elements which in one form or another have persistently found expression in the major religions of mankind?

There is first of all what might be called a fundamental assumption which religion always either implies or definitely affirms. It is the assumption or belief that the world of our ordinary sense-experience is not the whole of reality but that there exists also a super-sense world which is equally real if not the deepest aspect of reality. In this all religions, and for that matter, all more or less idealistic philosophies are in substantial agreement and stand in rather sharp opposition to every materialistic or mechanistic interpretation of human experience.

While religion in all its major forms either implies or definitely affirms the existence of a super-sense world which is somehow continuous with man's world of sense-experience while at the same time transcending it, this in itself does not tell us much as to the nature of that transcendental world. Religion is always something a little more specific and at least the major religions of mankind have always tried to come to closer grips with that aspect of reality.

We might say in a summary way that in religion man's interests revolve around two foci. One of these is the very core of that transcendental world itself, namely God or the Divine. The other focus is man's own life and especially what is the truly Good Life and what is required to achieve it. And the Good Life is usually represented in its double aspect, namely the Good

Life in the here and now, and the Good Life beyond the present life or the destiny of the individual.

It goes without saying that the conception of the two great foci around which man's interests in religion revolve are closely related so that the conception regarding one conditions that of the other. In other words, man's conception of the divine and transcendental world determines in a large measure his conception of the Good Life and how it can be achieved; while, on the other hand, what he experiences in his quest for the Good Life influences his conception of the Divine or the Ultimate Reality on which he feels himself dependent. It would seem, then, that for an understanding of religion's real nature one must know at least in general outline what the major religions of mankind have had to say on the three main subjects mentioned above, namely, God or the Divine and Ultimate Reality, the Good Life in the here and now, and the Future Life or the Destiny of the Individual.

In presenting the views of the great religions on each of these three subjects we shall in each case begin with what Christianity has had to say since this is probably most familiar to the average reader of a volume in the English language. This is followed by the two other great monotheistic faiths, namely, Judaism and Islam, which have been rather closely associated historically with Christianity and which also have much in common with it in the great essentials of religion. Just because of this latter fact we give relatively little space in stating the essentials of Judaism and Islam. We turn then to the major religions of India and East Asia—Hinduism, Buddhism, Confucianism, Taoism and their modern versions. We give comparatively more space to these religions, both because they are so little known in the Western World and also because they differ considerably from the great monotheistic faiths in even the great essentials of religion while at the same time they have also much in common with them, especially in some of their modern forms.

Now while the elements which the major religions of mankind have in common may seem to make it comparatively easy to know the real nature of religion as a whole, the differences they exhibit in even the great essentials create a real problem. The problem pertains not only to knowing what really constitutes the essentials of religion but even more as to what is true and valid in any and all religions.

THE GOD-CONCEPT IN RELIGION

RELIGION in every form, as we have said, involves a belief in a super-sense, super-human and divine world. However uppermost may be man's interest in himself and in finding a better life, in religion he seeks this better life in relationship with his god or the divine. What, then, does religion mean by the divine or god? This is our first major question to answer, for even the great religions of the world with all they have in common differ considerably in their answers.

As we said above, we shall take up first what Christianity and the other major monotheistic faiths have to say and then proceed with other faiths in which the god-concept is quite varied and in some aspects differs rather widely from the usually accepted personalistic concept found in the great monotheistic faiths.

A: I THE GOD-CONCEPT IN CHRISTIANITY

WHATEVER else may belong to the cardinal elements of the Christian faith, at the center of this faith is God usually conceived of in terms of ideal and perfect personality. The Christian philosopher as well as any really intelligent Christian believer realizes, of course, that God as the ultimate Reality and the creative source of all existence must be infinitely more than what man experiences even on the highest levels of spiritual personality so that the conception of God as the Supreme and Perfect Personal Being may inadequately express the full nature of the Divine. In fact, there are many expressions in the Bible as well as in the theologies, hymns and other forms of Christian literature which imply, if they do not directly affirm, that no conception which the mind of finite man can form fully expresses what God is in all his being. But in spite of this inadequacy of each and every concept of the divine which man can form Christianity, nevertheless, has always held to this personalistic conception as the most adequate. Any attempt to find a super-personalistic concept usually ends either in a sub-personalistic concept or becomes so vague in meaning that it ceases to be of any help in vital religion. Thus when some modern philosophically minded theologians speak af God as "Being Itself," "Pure Being," "Being as Such" and then add that this is all that the mind of man can formulate about God as the Ultimate Reality that is true and that all other concepts are merely symbolic expressions which in a measure point towards the truth they may be essentially right if by that they mean what we have already mentioned above, namely, that God in his full being transcends even the highest conception the finite mind of man can formulate. But it should be added that to speak of the Divine in terms of such abstractions is not very helpful as is all too clear from the history of some of the major Oriental faiths in which philosophers have used this vague language about the nature of the divine or ultimate reality for upwards of two thousand years. The result has usually been that the average believer has been left to himself and that he has usually thought of his god or gods all too much in terms of his own little image, rather than in terms of spiritual personality raised, as it were, to perfection and infinity.

Christianity is often spoken of as an Ethical Monotheism and as such it links up definitely with the older ethical monotheism of Judaism with its great prophets proclaiming the righteousness of God who demands of man that he lives his life in terms of moral values. However Christianity with all its links with Old Testament Religion revolves even more around the person of Jesus Christ and derives its conception of God from him in a double way. It makes Jesus' own conception of God normative and at the same time sees in Jesus Christ himself the supreme and unique revelation so that it becomes an axiom in Christianity that the "High and Lofty One who inhabits eternity, whose name is Holy," as Isaiah put it, is like Jesus Christ. Even though God is the ultimate ground of all being expressing himself in Nature as a power which at times may seem wholly indifferent to moral values or human interests, Christianity has always maintained that this Power is, nevertheless, like a good and loving father caring for his children as Jesus represented Him to be and that this love of God is supremely expressed in Jesus Christ himself. In so far as Christian monotheism is definitely bound up with the person of Jesus Christ its emphasis is somewhat different from the older Judaic monotheism and it differs even more from other monotheistic faiths such as Islam and the older Zoroastrianism even though fundamentally these great faiths are in substantial agreement in holding that at the heart of all reality is the Infinite and Eternal Being thought of in terms of spiritual personality, i.e. God as the infinite Mind and sovereign Will working creatively in all things and through all things with a purpose which it is man's highest interest to know and with which it is man's chief duty to relate himself.

While there is thus a characteristic Christian conception of God running through all forms of historic Christianity which differentiates it somewhat from the conceptions in the other monotheistic faiths it must be added that there is at the same time a considerable variety of conceptions in different periods of Christian history and among different branches of Christianity. It is impossible to give here all the fine shades of differences but a few major variants should be noted in briefest outline.

The major differences have revolved around two main problems. One of these deals primarily with the relationship of God to the natural world; the other concerns itself more with the question as to the real place and function of Jesus Christ as a revelation of God. The two are more or less interwoven since to the normal Christian view God is seen as being somehow in the natural order as its creative source and sustaining power even though he is supremely known or experienced through his self-revelation in Jesus Christ.

1 *God and the Natural Order.*

CHRISTIANITY, like its parent Old Testament Faith, accepts the view expressed in the opening lines of Genesis as normative for God's relationship to the natural world, or the cosmos, namely, that "in the beginning God created the heavens and the earth." In other words, God is the Ultimate Reality and all things owe their origin and continuing existence to Him. It is evident from the New Testament record that Jesus himself, in perfect harmony with Old Testament religion, regarded the natural world as God's world. While he himself seemed to have a direct awareness of God, the Heavenly Father, he nevertheless saw God also in Nature about him. In his parables he drew heavily upon Nature to teach spiritual truths. The lilies of the field and the birds of the air spoke to him of the Father's wisdom and protective care. However realistic Jesus was regarding moral evil in human life he did not regard physical nature as inherently evil but looked upon it as essentially good and as God's handiwork. The so-called Apostles' Creed also affirms a belief in "God the Father Almighty, maker of heaven and earth." This affirmation had to be made early in Christian history because there was a trend towards a view which regards the physical world as inherently evil and therefore as not being God's good world. That Christianity was greatly influenced by this view is shown by the whole monastic system which early became a marked characteristic and remained so all through the Middle Ages and even colored the Christian conception of God and his relationship to the natural world far down into modern times. The first reaction against this essentially un-Christian view came in connection with some of the mystics of the later Middle Ages. To be sure, most of the mystics insisted on the immediacy of their experience of God and held that the way that leads to this experience is one that turns inward and away from the external world since this latter was regarded as an obstacle blinding man's true vision of the divine. Thus Thomas á Kempis states the attitude of this type of mystic when he says, "Blessed are the eyes which are closed to the outward objects, but intent upon inward. . . . Shut the doors of your senses that you may be able to hear what the Lord God speaks within you." But some mystics and especially Francis of Assisi, though they, too, claimed a direct awareness of God or experienced God supremely in their communion with him through Jesus Christ, nevertheless saw him also in the beauty and the goodness of the natural order. (See, The Canticle to the Sun—Francis of Assisi.) Then with the rediscovery of Aristotle, the philosopher of the natural world, Christianity again looked upon the natural world as an expression of the power and wisdom of God as well as the means through which he exercises his general providence towards mankind. Probably in no Christian writing is there a more serious attempt to harmonize the various ways in which man can find God or the way God deals with man than in the great system of Thomas Aquinas which is accepted to this day as a more or less official interpretation of the Christian view by Roman Catholics.

At the time of the Renaissance, Europeans turned with passionate zeal to the beauties and pleasures of the natural world but this was often a mere sensuality rather than a finding of the divine in the natural world. The Protestant Reformers sought, therefore, to purify Christianity of this by turning man's attention again to God's demands for righteousness and his grace in Christ Jesus. They held that the true Christian serves God through the ordinary pursuits of life, and to that extent they recognized God's presence in the natural order; but with their strong emphasis on man's sinful nature they often seemed to deny that God is really in the natural order and especially did they deny that man can have anything like a real knowledge of God solely through his experience of the natural world. The early Humanists and later the Socinians marked the beginning of that emphasis on man's natural ability and his capacity for finding God through his experience of the natural order which characterizes so much of modern Christian thought. This became more characteristic of Christianity in the Rationalistic Movement of the seventeenth and eighteenth centuries. Rationalists had much to say about Natural Religion by which they meant that God expresses himself in the natural order and that man through his unaided reason can have an adequate knowledge of God. Many of them saw in Christianity but a re-affirmation of "Natural Religion" and they regarded the revelation of God in Jesus Christ as but a confirmation or a clarification of what all men might know of God through their ordinary experience of life and the natural world. It was during this period that Christian apologists developed most persistently their philosophical arguments for the existence of God, especially the so-called Cosmological and Teleological arguments which led to the conclusion that God can be known through the natural order and that man through his own unaided reason can know God as the Supreme Intelligence working for rational and good ends. God's requirements of man, they held, was a life of righteousness, the norm of which was in man's own nature even though some held that this needed clarification and confirmation through such a revelation as God has made of himself in the historic Jesus.

In the Romantic movement and especially in the poets of that period we have a further affirmation of God's presence in the natural order though man's awareness of the divine, it was held, came primarily through feeling and aesthetic appreciation rather than through his rational processes. With some this became virtually a Nature Mysticism or a sort of pantheism though on the whole the older Christian view prevailed so that most Christians, even in this period, saw in the beauties of Nature God's handiwork as the Psalmists of Israel had done. This position found expression philosophically in the so-called doctrine of God's Immanence in nature. To safeguard this from leaning too much towards pantheism and nature mysticism the immanence theory was balanced by the doctrine of God's transcendence by which is meant that while Nature is somehow the expression of God's power and wisdom, God is nevertheless not merely the sum total of the natural order but is other and more than that and does not depend for his existence upon Nature but forever transcends it.

In the Kantian philosophy and in much of the Christian thought that bases itself on the Kantian insight doubt is thrown on the possibility of man's knowing God through Nature or the process of thought that deals with the physical world. The famous arguments for the belief in the existence of God advanced by the Rationalists, namely, the Ontological, Cosmological and Teleological arguments, were rejected as no longer valid. Instead of man's approach to the divine and ultimate reality through reason and the physical world which it was held is the peculiar sphere in which the rational faculty operates most successfully, Kant and his followers substituted man's moral intuition. Religion, it was held, does not deal primarily with the natural world or God as revealed in Nature but rather with moral values. Through man's consciousness as a moral being he gains a sense of freedom and of belonging to a realm which transcends the physical world and through this he obtains his deepest insight into the nature of God and the noumenal world.

In Schleiermacher's thought religion becomes a direct consciousness of God through our feeling of dependence upon a power other than ourselves. It is significant that in so far as this feeling of dependence is a sort of "creaturely feeling," i.e. a sense of one's dependence for one's very physical existence upon God as expressed in Nature, Schleiermacher's conception of the divine is virtually pantheistic, whereas when he deals with man's inner and moral life the feeling of dependence becomes "das fromme Gefühl," a consciousness of man's need for help in his moral struggle such as Christianity claims to give through Jesus Christ. In this latter context Schleiermacher's conception of God is definitely in terms of ideal personality.

The Kantian-Ritchlian interpretation of religion, linked with the rediscovery of the historic Jesus who all through the Middle Ages and late into the modern period had almost disappeared from the Christian's horizon, gave renewed significance to Jesus Christ as God's chief revelation of himself, both in the capacity of setting the pattern for the ideal moral life and as the dynamic through which man is enabled to achieve the good life. If religion deals primarily with ethical values then, of course, God's supreme revelation of himself can not be through physical nature which seems rather indifferent to such values but only through an ideal ethical personality such as is found in the historic Jesus. This marked in many ways a real return to New Testament Christianity but unfortunately it was a bit one-sided in that it virtually implied that God can not be known through the natural order and thus it created a deep chasm in the life of the modern man with the realm of physical nature on one side and man's moral and spiritual values on the other side, the former being assigned to science and general philosophy and the latter made the distinctive sphere of religion and in fact the only sphere in which religion should function. This division became all the more accentuated by the progress of the physical sciences in the latter half of the nineteenth century and especially in consequence of the materialistic and mechanistic interpretation which many scientists and pseudo-scientists gave to the evolutionary process of the natural world. Where Jesus had seen the hand of God in the natural world many Christians during the latter part of the nineteenth century tended ever more towards a view which sees God only in moral values. From this situation developed the conception of "a good but finite" God who is working for moral and spiritual ends in a universe which is indifferent to such values if not positively hostile to them. Jesus was regarded as the supreme moral figure in human history and as such the supreme revelation of God but this was accompanied by a haunting fear that the physical cosmos which began to loom bigger and greater in the modern man's consciousness is really like a monster, self-running machine which however wonderful it may be has really nothing to say about the God of religion or the spiritual values with which religion is supposed to concern itself. This resulted in reducing modern Christianity so largely to a mere activity and emphasis on immediate and so-called "practical values" including, to be sure, ethical values but with the fear that perhaps our ethical values are mere utilitarian rules for playing the game of life but not really grounded in God or ultimate reality. This carried with it the thought that belief in God which has always been so central in Christianity is perhaps little more than a subjective creation of man's own desires. This whole trend in modern Christianity found its extreme expression in the newer Humanism which tries to hold on to the moral values for which Christianity has characteristically stood but which virtually eliminates the god-concept and even the question as to the objective grounding of moral values beyond the merely human sphere. While comparatively few modern Christians take this extreme position of the Humanist it remains true that a very large percentage of modern Christians seem exceedingly hazy as to their belief in a God or as to moral and spiritual values being grounded in God or the ultimately real. Modern science has been immensely successful in dealing with the physical world and in enriching that aspect of man's life. This very success has increased the authority of the scientist not only in his own legitimate sphere but in any sphere concerning which he might care to speak. The result has been that modern leaders of religion in Christendom have been anxiously awaiting the latest interpretation of life's values and meanings from the lips of the physical scientists. Though modern Christianity has theoretically continued to hold the view that God has revealed himself supremely through Jesus Christ, actually many a modern Christian has been looking more to what science had to say about human life and its meanings than to what Jesus had to say about the Heavenly Father and his ideal for man's life. As long, therefore, as scientists gave on the whole a rather mechanistic interpretation of reality it is not strange that those who looked to such scientists as the supreme authority should have become increasingly hesitant about God or all spiritual meanings.

It should be clear that a Christianity like this is something very different from the religion of the New Testament. While it may still accept Jesus as the supreme pattern for the ideal human life it certainly is far removed from the real Jesus, central in whose consciousness was the living God, the Heavenly Father, and who saw in the natural world God's good world. The brotherhood of mankind which modern Christianity preaches as central to true religion and which it links up with Jesus as the finest representative of the spirit of true brotherhood is only half of the true Christian position, and the lesser half at that, for the brotherhood of man which Jesus proclaimed had as its carrying ground the Fatherhood of God; and it may well be questioned whether the former can be fully realized without the latter. And even if it were possible to achieve a universal brotherhood this would still leave unanswered the deeper questions of human life, namely, questions as to life's ultimate meanings and man's relationship to the heart of ultimate reality. These are questions which religion rightly asks and to which it seeks an answer.

Fortunately for modern Christianity and for religion in general modern science to which religious leaders have been looking with such anxiety for the latest interpretation of life's values and meanings, is now giving through some of its greatest authorities an interpretation of even the physical world which is miles removed from the deadening materialistic or mechanistic interpretation of a few decades ago. In fact, some of our leading astro-physicists speak of the nature of the physical universe in terms which seem far more akin to mind and things spiritual than to the old-fashioned materialist's "mere matter and force." There is a reverent attitude towards the nature of reality and an appreciation of its spiritual aspects and deep mysteries requiring a different approach from that of the physical scientist. With this goes also a recognition on the part of such scientists that moral and spiritual values must be sought primarily in moral and spiritual beings like man rather than in physical nature as such. These values, it is realized, find their clearest expression in great ethical personalities; and Christians would hold, supremely so in the historic Jesus. Thus there is even among leading scientists who deal primarily with the physical world a return to a position which is far more congenial to the spiritual values and meanings for which Christianity has characteristically stood.

In the so-called Neo-orthodoxy modern Christianity turns sharply against the whole trend which has been making religion primarily man's quest for spiritual values and a possible discovery of the divine through his ordinary experience of the natural world and instead there is a strong affirmation of the thought that true religion is above all else man's response to God's revelation of himself, not God's general expression of himself in the natural order but a direct self-revelation. In other words, in true religion God takes the initiative and man becomes aware of God and gains his deepest conviction about spiritual values and meanings just because God speaks to him. And it adds most emphatically that God has spoken to man supremely and uniquely in Jesus Christ. It is this above all else which not only gives man his conviction as to the objective reality of God but also reveals to him what God is and what he requires of man. But this brings us really to the second major question over which Christians have differed considerably in their interpretation, namely: the place and function of Jesus Christ as the revelation of God.

2 *The Place and Function of Jesus Christ as a Revelation of God.*

Christianity has usually held that Jesus Christ somehow stands in a unique relationship between God and man. This has been most succinctly formulated in the two titles that have been given him, namely, the Son of Man and the Son of God, expressions that have been used down through the centuries but with rather widely differing meanings.

Early Christians experienced in fellowship with Jesus the reality of God. It is clear that central in Jesus' own consciousness was God the Heavenly Father. This was so real that somehow God became real to those who came into close contact with Jesus. Furthermore the personality of Jesus, his character or the quality of his life deepened this impression and it seems quite plain that even during Jesus' ministry some showed an attitude towards him that was virtually one of worship such as man gives only to deity.

Then it would seem that the first major controversy about Jesus within Christianity arose not because of any denial of his unique relationship with God but rather because some questioned his true human nature. Thus the so-called Apostles' Creed found it necessary to affirm that Jesus lived a real human life among men. After Christian thought had come under the dominance of the Greek "essence philosophy" with its sharp distinctions between the divine and the human "essences" and when some were insisting that Jesus was above all else the ideal Son of Man, the church expressed its conviction (Nicene and Athanasian Creeds) that Jesus was somehow more than man and "one in essence" with God, the Father. This then raised the question as to how Jesus could be both divine and human and yet be a united personal being since the two "essences" were regarded as almost antithetical in nature. An official answer to this perplexing question was attempted in the Creed of Chalcedon but this creed had to be cast largely in mere negatives or at best in paradoxes; and down to the present Christians differ considerably in their views of Jesus Christ even though the question is no longer formulated in terms of the old Greek "essence philosophy." Real differences prevail even when there is general agreement that Jesus Christ is somehow the supreme revelation of God. Some stress the thought that Jesus represents a divine initiative and that in him God has spoken in a unique way to man, whereas others see in Jesus above all else the supreme Son of Man who has most successfully found God in his quest and who reveals to others what he has found.

It is well to remember that all through the Middle Ages this question seldom emerged for the simple reason that the historical Jesus had almost disappeared from men's consciousness and only the sacramental Christ was in the picture. The divine was conceived of as mediated to man primarily through the sacraments and through the church itself regarded as a divine institution standing between man and his God. Religion was thus not a fellowship with God through the Jesus Christ of the New Testament record but more a feeling of mystical union with the divine and of being in right relationship with the divine because of the implicit obedience to the authority of the church as a divine institution and accepting as true and valid whatever the church proclaimed as such. The feeling of mystical union arising from the sacraments was itself perhaps less spiritual in import than what is implied by the term of mysticism and the whole trend of spirituality was often towards an externalization bordering on a crass materialism. It was in protest against this externalization that the real mystics of the later Middle Ages fought with their emphasis on the immediacy of man's experience of God. The majority of mystics found this immediacy in connection with and through Jesus Christ and because of this they were Christian mystics and differed somewhat from mystics in general; that is to say, though they insisted on a direct awareness of God they had in Jesus Christ their objective reference and so avoided what is often little more than a mere subjectivism. This meant that while God was to them ever more than any language or concept can express, they nevertheless conceived of him in the typically Christian way, namely, as ideal personality; and they regarded the ethical life as the supreme way that leads to God for to them Jesus' words, "Blessed are the pure in heart for they shall see God" were axiomatic.

In the Protestant Reformers we have a continuance of the mystics emphasis on the individual's direct experience of God, but they were more insistent on the thought that this is possible only as man comes to God through Jesus Christ; and Jesus was interpreted above all else as being the unique Son of God who by his death on the cross made atonement to a righteous God for the sins of the world. The first step in true religion, it was held, must be an experience of God's forgiving love in Christ Jesus. Only then was it possible for man really to commune with God in prayer and grow into an ethical personality after the pattern set in the historic Jesus and through the dynamic which the risen Christ or the Holy Spirit supplies. Both Greek Orthodoxy and Roman Catholicism would in general accept this view of Jesus though each would have a little different emphasis and approach. In Greek Orthodoxy there is perhaps less emphasis on the ethical aspect both in the conception of God as the ideal personality and in the ideal for man's life as revealed in the historic Jesus. Roman Catholicism, while agreeing fully with the Protestant view as to the character of God and God's grace through Christ as the divine atonement for man's sin, differs as to the way this grace is mediated by stressing more the place of the church as a divine institution which stands between God and the individual and through which God's grace is mediated.

Now these differences between the major branches of Christendom while real are, after all, not so very great. Greater differences have developed in more recent years and find their sharpest formulations in the views of so-called Confessionalists and Fundamentalists, on the one hand, and in those of the various types of Liberals, Radicals and Humanists, on the other hand.

The whole movement in the modern world which has expressed itself in the development of the physical and social sciences has led the modern man, as we have already seen, to think of the world and human life as a long evolutionary process. While it is admitted that in this process there are new beginnings and that the "abrupt," "discontinuous" and the "unusual" has its place, nevertheless the emphasis is overwhelmingly on the thought of a real "continuity" in all reality. Thus even though the whole evolutionary process of the natural world and human history may be regarded as some-how the expression of a divine activity it is nevertheless maintained that this takes place according to certain laws and in an orderly sequence in which what goes before has a close causal connection with what follows. The mood or mental attitude which this creates in the modern man has had a determining effect on the interpretation of the place and meaning of Jesus Christ as God's revelation of himself. In short, it has resulted in accentuating the thought that Jesus belongs to the evolutionary process and is continuous with man in his upward striving. Though the historic Jesus may still be given a unique and central place in the total picture, the center in which he stands is nevertheless regarded as continuous with its surroundings; and thus if other great figures in human history are to be looked upon as pioneers in man's upward struggle for the good life and for God then Jesus, too, it is felt, belongs here rather than standing alone as an absolutely unique "irruption" of the supernatural and the divine into human history. This, in general is the position of Liberalism though there are many shades of differences some of which would accept also the view that though Jesus is continuous with man he yet transcends man but would leave unanswered as to just how or how much he does so.

Over against this position we have the position of the Confessionalists, Fundamentalists and other Conservatives who continue their emphasis on the absolute uniqueness and finality of God's revelation of himself in Christ Jesus. However much they may agree with the Liberals in accepting the whole evolutionary process of the natural world and human history as a fact of God's operation and however ready they may be in linking the historic Jesus on the one hand with man's quest for the good life through God, they would nevertheless insist that the major fact about Jesus Christ is that he transcends the human and represents in a unique and authoritative way God's self-revelation to man.

This position finds strong reinforcement as we have said above, in Neo-orthodoxy and similar movements with their tremendous emphasis on the thought that what God does for man is the determining factor in all true religion. Man's quest for the good and better life and his upward struggle through general culture, even his moral achievements, are regarded as secondary and as having significance only in so far as through them man makes his response to God's initiative. God, his sovereign grace and unique revelation of himself in the historic Jesus and his continued special revelation of himself to the individual upon the basic revelation in the historic Jesus Christ—these are regarded as the great essentials of religion. Everything else of real value must be built on these initial facts.

But while there are these deep-going differences in historic Christianity in regard to the conception of God, his relation to the natural world and the way he reveals himself to man, there is nevertheless on the whole a substantial agreement on one fundamental thing, namely, that at the heart of the Christian faith is a belief in the living God who is the holy and perfect personal being and who has come near to man in a supreme way through the historic Jesus Christ. Or if this is stated from the standpoint of Liberalism, Christianity holds that through Jesus Christ man gains his supreme insight into the nature and character of God as well as the supreme revelation of what the good life of man might be and the dynamic for achieving that kind of life.

Possibly the differences within Christianity on these major problems will enable us to understand better the nature of other religions, thus bearing out the truth of Harnack's dictum, "Wer diese Religion Kennt, kennt alle."

This fact, if no other consideration, should justify the amount of space we have given to the Christian conception of God in a volume which deals with such a comprehensive subject as the nature and truth of religion.

A: II THE GOD-CONCEPT IN JUDAISM

NEAREST to the Christian conception of the Divine is that of Judaism. One can speak in many ways of the two religions as the Judaeo-Christian Religion. In fact Judaism is the first religion which can be spoken of as an out and out ethical monotheism and Christianity is in this respect largely a continuation of the older faith. It has always maintained that God, the Heavenly Father, who was central in the teachings and consciousness of Jesus, is the same as the God of Moses and the great Old Testament prophets. Jesus did not come to tell of another God but rather "to fulfill the Law and the prophets." And Paul, in attempting to explain to his people what in Old Testament Religion was of merely provisional or temporary significance and what was of permanent value for the new faith centering around the person of Jesus Christ, always stressed the thought that the God and Father of the Lord Jesus was none other than the God proclaimed by the fathers and prophets of Israel. Thus in a real sense Judaism and Christianity are in agreement in their god-concept and much of what we have said as to the Christian view of the Divine could be repeated here as equally true of Judaism. In both religions the very core of man's spiritual life is his belief in the One and Only God who is the creative and controlling power of all existence and with whom man can come into personal relationship.

On the question of God's relationship to the natural order Judaism has consistently affirmed its belief that Nature is God's creation and as such is inherently good. The opening chapter of Genesis not only states that "in the beginning God created the heavens and the earth" but also adds that "God saw that it was good." The Psalmist stresses Nature's wonders as a revelation of God when he says that "the heavens are telling the glory of God; and the firmament proclaims his handiwork." This conception of the natural order as being God's creation and therefore inherently good has been so much the case that Judaism as a religion has been quite "this worldly" in its emphasis. It has almost always stressed the belief that man is to find the good life in the here and now whatever else might be added regarding life's ultimate meaning and the individual human destiny. In this regard Judaism stands in rather sharp contrast with most of the other major religions with their characteristic "other world" emphasis. To be sure, this belief that religion should concern itself with helping man find the good and better life here and now has become quite characteristic of all religions of the modern world, for modern man feels that if religion has any real value in its teachings it must help man in his quest for the good life in this world. But while this has become quite characteristic of all religions today, this was not true in the past. In the past, most of them placed far greater emphasis on saving man out of this "evil world" than on helping achieve the good life in this world. That has been especially the case with Indian religions, as we shall see below. But even Christianity, with all its agreement with Judaism that this world is God's creation, has often put far more emphasis on saving man from this "evil world" into the heavenly world than on building God's kingdom in this world. This was especially the case when the monastic ideal was accepted as the truest type of the Christian life and when the withdrawal from the world was regarded as almost essential for the deepest spiritual life and commitment to God. Of course, as intimated above, modern Christians, like other modern people, have become rather "this worldly" in their interests, probably too much so. And there is all too little emphasis in modern Christianity on life's ultimate issues and meaning. But be this as it may, the point is that whatever may be the emphasis in other major religions today, Judaism has almost always stressed the thought that this is God's good world and that it is the place where His kingdom is to be established.

Now while Judaism has always believed that this world is God's good creation and therefore as one way in which God reveals himself to man, it has put greater emphasis on God's revelation of Himself in human history. Judaism is the world's oldest Ethical Monotheism and this means that man knows God primarily in terms of ethical values and moral ideals. It is not so much through intellectual speculations about the nature of the physical world that man comes into close relationship with God but rather through moral intuition and the awareness of ethical values and ideals. The great figures in Judaism have been its prophets and seers—men who had an awareness of God's holiness and who proclaimed God's moral law and His righteous judgements over all men. While most of these prophets directed their message first of all to their own people they nevertheless held that the core of their message was equally valid for all people. Israel as God's "chosen people" was chosen for a great mission to the rest of the world. To be sure, these prophets expected their people to occupy "the promised land" and to live at peace with their neighbors, but when they so often proved unworthy of God's favors and suffered the consequences of their unfaithfulness the prophets saw in their afflictions the just punishment of God. The people who invaded their land and those who drove them into exile were seen by the prophets as God's instruments. Not that these peoples were more worthy than the Israelites, for they, too, were seen as wicked and in consequence were in turn destroyed, but they were nevertheless seen as under God's control and as his instrument for carrying out his justice. If Israel seemed at times to be even under greater condemnation than other people it was because their prophets expected more of them. They had been instructed in the ways of Almighty God and as His "chosen people" they should have lived up to their high calling. Instead of that they repeatedly forgot their God and turned in worship to the gods of their neighbors, the gods represented by idols made of wood and stone. This, the prophets felt, was Israel's chief sin. Over and over again they reminded their people that the God of Israel is not simply one of the numerous tribal gods made in the image of little man, but that He is the One and Only God who created the world and who rules over the affairs of all men. "Ask of me, and I will make the nations your heritage, and the ends of the earth your possession" (Psalm 2:8). And again we read in Ps. 22:27, "All the ends of the world shall remember and turn unto the Lord, and all kindreds of the nations shall worship before Thee." Isaiah predicts that "the earth shall be full of the knowledge of the Lord as the waters cover the sea." Jeremiah believed that the time would come when it would not be necessary to say to one's neighbor or brother, "Know the Lord, for they shall all know Me from the least of them unto the greatest of them." And Malachi, one of the last of the Old Testament prophets, saw the time coming when the One and Only God, whom the people of Israel all too frequently forgot, shall become the God of all nations, "for from the rising of the sun to its setting Thy name is great among the nations."

It is beliefs about God and worthy conceptions of the Divine such as these that has made the great monotheistic Faith of Judaism a religion that has universal validity. It is quite true that in Judaism, as in other great religions, the essentials are often embedded in other elements which do not have universal validity. In fact, Judaism as a religion has perpetuated many things which may have had real meaning for the Jewish people or may still be of some value to them but which do not and can not have much meaning to others who have had a different history. We mention this simply to stress all the more that in what are really the great essentials of religion and which can have universal validity, Judaism has much to offer and above all in what it has to say about God and His moral law.

Perhaps at this point something further should be said about the prophets who were so certain that they spoke on behalf of the One and Only God. How did they conceive of their own relationship to God? One thing is clear, as we have just intimated, namely, that they felt certain that they were God's spokesmen. "Thus saith the Lord," and statements of similiar import, were used to introduce their message to the people. They were not speaking by reason of their own authority, or as superior men, but only because they felt quite certain that they had God's message to proclaim. No claim did any of them make to be in any way superhuman or divine beings, for they had a keen awareness of God's holiness which makes Him far other than sinful men like themselves. They were only God's human instruments through whom His will was made known to their fellowmen.

Now it is especially at this point that we have one of the major differences between Judaism and Christianity. While Christianity accepts the great teachings of the Old Testament prophets and the above interpretation of their relationship to God, it sees at the same time in Jesus Christ something more than a prophet and one who is the very Son of God. Judaism, on the other hand, denies the validity of this view about Jesus and at most accepts him simply as one of the later prophets. It regards Christianity as a kindred Faith and may even take pride in the great success Christianity has had in winning the millions all over the world as believers in the One and Only God who rules over the affairs of man, but the Christian belief in Jesus Christ as the incarnate Son of God it definitely does not accept as valid. Even when Christian apologists point to certain passages in the Old Testament that mention Judaism's hope in the coming of the Messiah, Judaism refuses to see in Jesus the fulfillment of this hope but rather continues to look to the future for such fulfillment.

As a matter of fact this persistent belief in a Messiah has been given various interpretations by Judaism. Usually the Messiah is seen as a superior human being who under God's guidance is to restore the rightful heritage of the Jewish people. Sometimes he is seen as rather superhuman if not actually divine, but even then the kingdom he is to establish is an earthly kingdom; and here we have again that characteristic "this worldly" emphasis of Judaism mentioned above. Then again the Messiah hope is interpreted as a glorious period of Jewish history and without its centering in any particular person as the Messiah. It is rather the Messianic era to which Judaism should look in hope. And some would say that Judaism as a religion, especially the elements in it that have universal validity, such as its belief in the One and Only God, is destined to play the Messianic role not only for the adherents of traditional Judaism but for all mankind. This is especially the view of Reformed Judaism. While some of the more conservative elements may still look for the restoration of Judaism in terms of its old ideals, including the return to the sacred soil of Palestine, these more liberal adherents of the Faith are quite content to be loyal citizens of the countries in which they live and take their deepest satisfaction in having the great essentials of their monotheistic faith become more and more meaningful to their fellow-citizens and to the rest of mankind.

It is, however, not merely these more liberal elements of present day Judaism that would make the great essentials of their monotheistic faith meaningful to other people. Down through the centuries there have always been those who realized that faith in the One and Only God proclaimed by Judaism must rest on broader foundations than those characteristically stressed by ancient seers and prophets of Israel if such faith is to be really meaningfull to others. This was markedly the case after Judaism's contact with Islam. Leading thinkers found it increasingly necessary to give reasons for their faith in the One and Only God who is not only the God of Israel and revealed through Israel's long and varied history, but also the God who rules over the affairs of all mankind and who as the Ultimate Reality is the source and creative power of all existence. These thinkers made various approaches and came up with differing answers but they usually were definitely monotheistic in their god-concept. A good representative of such thinkers was Maimonides of the twelfth century who in an appendix to his commentary on the Mishna of Sanhedrin gives his various reasons for his faith in God. He does not merely assume that the One and Only God known to Israel is the creator of the universe and rules over all existence, as did the Old Testament seers and prophets, but he gives various reasons for his faith. He thus discusses among other things God's existence, unity, incorporeality, eternity, omniscience and why worship is due to him alone. He naturally does not omit the typical Jewish emphasis on God's revelation of himself through the natural order and in the moral law given to Moses and to succeeding prophets.

As we said above, these thinkers came up with somewhat differing answers but what they had to say about God usually cast in personalistic terms even though they saw him as the Ultimate Reality who in his full being transcends man's finite understanding. An outstanding exception to this characteristic monotheistic god-concept was that of Spinoza whose view was virtually pantheistic. Naturally, modern leaders in Judaism, like men of other faiths, are re-thinking their philosophy of life and in this they not only give due place to what the great thinkers of past ages have had to say but they also would include the light which modern science throws on their problems. Many feel that the god-concept in traditional religion has perhaps been cast all too much in terms of man's own little image. In place of the cock-sureness of little minds we need to be a little more modest and reverent before the mysteries of Nature and to God as the Ultimate Reality. In the words of Job: "Can you find out the deep things of God? Can you find out the limits of the Almighty?"

However, it must be added that in trying to understand the mystery of Reality, the mystery of God as the creative and sustaining power of all existence and thus in forming a god-concept that has real content and meaning, no concept seems more adequate than the more worthy formulation of the monotheistic concept as found in the Judaeo-Christian religion.

III THE GOD-CONCEPT IN ISLAM

FROM CHRISTIANITY and Judaism one passes naturally to that other great monotheistic faith that has built in some measure on both, namely, Islam. Muhammad, the founder of Islam, may not have had access to the sacred scriptures of these older faiths but it seems quite clear that he came into contact with both Jews and Christians and so could have learned from them about their religions. In fact, in the *Qur'an* one can find frequent mention of Old Testament figures and also of Jesus. What is more significant is that Muhammad evidently regarded both Old and New Testaments as revelations from the One and Only True God. Thus we read in Surah XLII:13. "God has ordained for you that religion which He has already commended to Noah, Abraham, Moses and Jesus." And again in Surah II:136 the Qur'an makes the fuller statement showing Muhammad's attitude towards Judaism and Christianity: "Say: We believe in Allāh and that which He revealed unto us and that which was revealed unto Abraham, and Ishmael, and Isaac, and the tribes; and that which Moses and Jesus received, and that which the Prophets received from their Lord. We make no distinction between any of them, and unto Him we have surrendered." Even Islam's most sacred shrine, the Kaaba of Mecca, is represented as having been built originally by Abraham and Ishmael (Isma'il); and Abraham is quoted as saying: "Our Lord, make us Muslims unto Thee and of our seed a nation of Muslims" (Surah II:128). Jacob, Moses and the disciples of Jesus are also pictured as having been good and true Muslims.

From these and similar references in the Qur'an it should be clear, then, that Muhammad looked upon both Judaism and Christianity as faiths kindred to his own and as based upon real revelations from the One and Only

True God. However, it is equally clear that while Muhammad regarded these older monotheistic faiths as based upon divine revelation he maintained that he himself had received the more complete and final revelation which is for all men, including Jews and Christians. In fact, he maintained that Jews and, perhaps, even more the Christians of his time were not true to their own faith and that they were guilty of "adding gods" to the One and only God, the greatest sin man can commit. Muhammad, therefore felt that it was his own great mission in life to proclaim again the great essential of true religion, namely, that there is but One God, the God Allāh. On almost every page of the Qur'an one finds this affirmation of faith, and every true Muslim is expected to bear witness daily to such a faith. As the "Word of Witness" puts it: "I witness that there is no God but Allāh and that Muhammad is His Prophet." From the minarets of mosques all over the Islamic world sounds forth daily the call to the worship of Allāh, the One and Only God. Five times each day Muslims are expected to pray to their god and to repeat several times the words of the first surah of the Qur'an which reads:

> In the Name of God, the Merciful, the Compassionate
> Praise belongs to God, the Lord of all Being,
> the All-merciful, the All-compassionate,
> the Master of the Day of Doom.
> Thee only we serve; to Thee alone we pray for succour.
> Guide us in the straight path,
> the path of those whom Thou hast blessed,
> not of those against whom Thou art wrathful,
> nor of those who are astray. (ARBERRY TRANSLATION)

The invocation standing at the head of this first surah stands also at the head of all but one of the other 113 surahs that make up the Qur'an. And there is hardly a single paragraph of the Muslim's Bible which does not in one way or another remind the believer of his One and Only God. All the resources of the Arabic language are used to make real to the believer what and who God is; also how man is utterly dependent upon God for life and all that life has in store for him. Adjectives are piled upon adjectives to describe God's attributes. These are usually the attributes of a personal being but they at the same time convey the thought that God is infinitely above man and in many ways completely transcends man's nature and man's comprehension. While man can know much about God through his growing knowledge of the world in which he lives, since the world is God's creation, man's saving knowledge of God can come only through God's special revelation of Himself. And the most complete and final revelation, as stated above, is in the words of the Qur'an, which is a copy of the Eternal Word of God in heaven.

This tremendous emphasis on faith in the One and Only God which one finds on the pages of the Qur'an is further stressed by Muslims in what are called the Six Articles of Belief. These are: 1.Belief in Allāh as the One and Only God. 2.Belief in Angels as God's messengers. 3.Belief in Sacred Scriptures as the Revealed Word of God with the Qur'an as the supreme and final Revelation. 4.Belief in Prophets and Apostles of God with Muhammad as the greatest. 5.Belief in God's Day of Judgement. 6.Belief in the Destiny for good or evil of all men.

It should be clear, then, that Muhammad had a deep sense of the reality of the One and Only God and of God's sovereign power over man and all things He has created. And it is equally clear that he had a sincere conviction of having been called of God to proclaim His will for man and the impending judgement over his people for their sins, especially the sin of worshipping false gods and idols. How Muhammad came to this conviction may be difficult to know but one can hardly question that he was sincere about the matter or that, at least at the beginning of his ministry, he spoke as one who was certain that he had a mission to proclaim what God had revealed to him. That is why the Qur'an is regarded by all orthodox Muslims as being not merely words written by a man who was more or less inspired but as the very Word of God coeternal with God Himself.

It must, however, be added that this belief in the Qur'an as God's final revelation and the conception of the Divine as recorded in the Qur'an have been variously interpreted in the course of Islamic history. Rather early was it realized by the more thoughtful that many passages in the Qur'an needed interpretation to make them applicable to the practical problems of life. And further was it realized that there were many problems which Muslims must face and for which the sacred scriptures had little or nothing to say. That is one reason why Muslims, with all their reverence for the Qur'an as a Divine Revelation, have looked to other sources for guidance. They looked first of all to authoritative Tradition, the *Sunnah*, which were believed to contain much about how Muhammad himself and his associates faced such problems. There are extant six collections of Islamic Traditions, two of which are specially valuable in that they contain historical, doctrinal, ethical and other material including legal matters. Most of this material has more bearing on the Islamic conception of the Good Life which we present in a chapter below but it also throws some light on the God-concept since everything in the life of a religious man is related to God as its center.

It is, however, not simply the early Islamic Tradition that influenced the interpretation of the essential teachings of the Faith. As Islam spread beyond its original home an increasing number of its leaders and thinkers were men who had been under other religious and cultural influences which inevitably affected their interpretation of the Islamic Faith. To be sure, this outside influence is seen most clearly in the interpretation of Islamic Law and it resulted in the development of four major schools of Jurisprudence differing considerably from each other, but it had also its effect on the great essentials of the Faith, including the conception of the Divine.

As we pointed out above, the Qur'an in speaking of God and His attributes uses many different terms. These seem to range all the way from a rather crude anthropomorphism ascribing to God typically human qualities to an absolute transcendentalism which makes the Divine so wholly other that no term taken from human experience and that has a positive content can be applied. Most of the early converts accepted without further thought the definitely personalistic concept of the Divine which is so characteristic of most parts of the Qur'an as it is of the other great Theistic Faiths. There were, however, some real differences even among the early converts who thought more deeply on the matter. Some of these were not willing to accept the Qur'an as Divine Revelation on merely the authority of its author however much they admired its contents. They felt that man must use his own reasoning powers even in dealing with what is supposedly a revelation from the Divine. In fact, it was these early Rationalists, the *Mu'tazilites*, who first pointed out that some of the passages in the Qur'an in speaking of God, the Infinite and Eternal, use language that was all too human in content to be appropriate. They maintained that God as the Absolute and Ulimate Reality is so wholly other than man and his world that only negative terms or terms that suggest the completely transcendental nature of God are appropriate. This is, of course, the opposite extreme of the anthropomorphism which the Mu'tazilites condemned. The best service which these rationalists rendered to the Islamic cause was that they opened the door to outside influences which had a wholesome effect. We refer specially to the rich content of Greek philosophy which Islamic scholars made more and more their own and for several centuries preserved this heritage when it was being neglected and forgotten by Europeans. Such great philosophers as al-Farabi (d. 950) and Ibn Sina (Avicenna d. 1037) were devoted students of this foreign material and made it really their own. As good Muslims they had inherited the belief in the One and Only God who created the universe and whose sovereign power controls all men and their destiny but they felt that this should be stated in more philosophic terms and so they turned to the philosophy of Plato and Aristotle, and even more to Neo-Platonism. Without going into details as to the results they achieved it is perhaps enough to say that their conception of the Divine as the first cause or in similar abstract terms was not very helpful to the average believer. And when some of these philosphers stated the relationship between God and His creation in virtually pantheistic terminology it ran absolutely counter to Islam's tremendous emphasis on the great distance that separates the One and Only God from finite and sinful man and all finite creatures. It is, therefore, quite natural that the more orthodox theologians and philosophers bitterly opposed such interpretations and that the views of such a great leader as al-Ghazali (d. 1111), who himself had been a rationalist but who had rejected the rationalists' interpretation, should have become the prevailing orthodox interpretation. While al-Ghazali admitted that man's reason and his experience of the natural world had their place in true religion he, nevertheless, maintained that Allāh, the Creator and Sustainer of the universe so completely transcends man's reason and the world in which man lives that he can be known adequately only as He has revealed Himself from time to time and supremely in the Qur'an. This became and remained the orthodox God-concept in Islam and its theologians, like most Christian theologians, hold that God is somehow immanent in the universe as its creative and sustaining power while at the same time He transcends it and thus is more and other than His creation. How this doctrine of immanence and transcendence can be fully reconciled remains for orthodoxy in both Islam and Christianity much the same sort of problem.

It was not only the Rationalists and the philosophers who had come under more or less foreign influences that raised problems for Islamic orthodoxy. In fact, almost immediately after Muhammad's death problems arose in connection with choosing his successor as head of the theocratic state which he had set up during the closing years of his life. When Abu Bakr was chosen, his first great task was to bring the various Arab tribes that had fallen away under his control as head of the state. Islam, within a few years, was developing into an expanding empire which not only held sway over the various Arabic tribes but an ever incresing number of converts who lived in the various parts of the defeated Byzantine and Persian empires. Many of this ever growing host undoubtedly were interested in the religion of the Prophet as an ever-expanding and victorious world empire rather than as a

Kingdom of God and things spiritual. Under these conditions it was only natural that the heads of Islam tended to be primarily political heads rather than spiritual leaders. To be sure, they carried on their world conquest in the name of religion, and they claimed the right to rule over other peoples in the name of Allāh, the One and Only God who foreordains all human events. In fact the Islamic doctrines of predestination and foreordaination early became ruling concepts not only in regard to the individual believer's life and destiny but also for the life and destiny of the nation and empire. These doctrines rose first not as abstract doctrines of Islamic theology but out of practical problems pertaining to men's relationships with their fellow-men. For these and other similar reasons it is, therefore, quite natural that, as we suggested above, some of the early heads of Islam were worldly rulers rather than spiritual leaders even though they claimed to rule in the interest of the one and only true religion and as ordained for that high office by God.

There were, however, many pious believers who were not satisfied with this trend and with such an interpretation of the Caliph's or Imam's true function. They wanted the successors of the Prophet Muhammad to be primarily spiritual heads. Some even held that in order to make sure of a worthy successor he should be chosen from among the family or tribe of Muhammad. It was beliefs and feelings such as these which led to the choice of Ali, a cousin and the son-in-law of Muhammad, in 656. This led to a serious conflict and a deep split which has continued down to the present, namely, the division between the Sunnites and the Shiites, the two major branches of the Islamic Faith.

We are not here concerned with the details of this conflict and the resultant division but simply with the difference between the two in regard to their God-concept. The Sunnites are usually spoken of as the orthodox branch of Islam and it is true that in their God-concept they follow more nearly Muhammad's teachings as found in the Qur'an. The Shiites, while accepting the Qur'an as God's revelation, at the same time look to the Imam, or head of Islam, as being both the political and spiritual head. In fact, the Shiites believe in a succession of Imams who are not only authentic interpreters of the Qur'an but through whom further revelations are made. There are really various conceptions of the Imam. Some see in him little more than a prophet of God such as Muhammad regarded himself to be. Others hold that the Imam, while being human, is nevertheless sinless and thus an ideal spiritual head. Still others tend to see in him an essentiallydivine being. This latter conception pertains especially to the so-called "Concealed Imam," the *Madhi*, who is to come and who will establish God's kingdom on earth in all its fullness and grandure.

Then further, in connection with the martyrdom of Ali and of his son Husain who succeeded Ali as Imam of the Shiites there developed a sort of Redeemer idea, thus establishing a further close link between the infinite God and finite sinful man.

In these and other similar views about the relationship between God and man Shiites differ considerably from the more orthodox Sunnites and from the characteristic conception found in the Qur'an. However, in spite of these differences both Shiites and Sunnites may be said to be essentially monotheistic in their God-concept. Allāh is for both types of the Islamic Faith the One and Only God even though the two differ somewhat in their views as to how the Infinite and the Eternal reveals Himself and mediates His sovereign will and grace.

There is, however, a type of the Islamic Faith which differs rather radically in its God-concept from the characteristic monotheistic conception, namely, Sufism. Sufism has found various expressions all over the Islamic world but it is essentially an ascetic mysticism with a God-concept that is virtually pantheistic. Like most types of mysticism Sufism stresses man's essential unity with God instead of that wide gap between the Infinite God and finite man which is so characteristic in orthodox Islamic teaching. It may seem strange to find such a wide difference in the very essentials of religion as exists between Sufism and the other main forms of the Faith. The fact is that while Sufism is regarded as a form of the Islamic Faith, it is fully as much an expression of other influences, especially Neo-Platonic and Indian, as it is strictly Islamic views.

As we said in our opening paragraph, Muhammad drew on both Judaism and Christianity in formulating his own views of what constitutes religious essentials. It was from these older monotheistic faiths that he obtained his conception about the One and Only God as over against the polytheistic faiths that prevailed among the Arabs of his day. However, it should be remembered that by the time of Muhammad Christianity itself had been influenced by Neo-Platonism and that this had affected many Christians in their views of God and man's relation to Him. In short, it gave rise to a strong ascetic trend expressing itself in a monastic type of life and also in a mysticism in which man feels his unity and essential oneness with his God. It should also be remembered that Muhammad at the beginning of his career had stressed the impending judgement of God and that this tended towards an other-worldliness rather than things of this world. Like many Christians, many of the early Muslims believed in the imminence of the great judgement day which would bring to an end the present world order and usher in a new spiritual order.

Now while Muhammad had preached an impending doom he himself soon became so involved in his conflict with his opponents and with his growing power as a political leader that his message became less other-worldly in its emphasis and more on Islam as a theocratic state foreordained to rule over others. It was against this trend that some of the more pious believers such as the *Kharijites*, "Come-outers" began to protest; and this movement may be said to mark the beginning in Islam of the ascetic type of life and the spirit of other-worldliness. Then later as Muslims came more and more into contact with other peoples and cultures many were influenced by Christian ascetics who, as stated above, had themselves come under the influence of Neo-Platonism with its trend towards an ascetic mysticism. Then in the course of time Muslims came more directly under the influence of Neo-Platonic philosophy as we have pointed out above.

But it was not only Neo-Platonic influences that gave rise to Sufism and to its development into an ascetic mysticism with its pantheistic God-concept. Sufism is probably also the product of direct Indian influences. That this is, of course, the case with Sufism in India no one questions. We wonder whether it is not also true that Plotinus and Neo-Platonists general-ly were under Indian influences far more than is generally recognized.

But be this as it may, it can not be questioned that in Sufism we have a tremendous change in the God-concept and also in man's own true relation-ship with the Divine from what one finds in the Qur'an and in typically orthodox teachings. Instead of the latter's strong emphasis on the distance that separates the One and Only God from finite, sinful man Sufism sees man in his true being essentially one in nature with God; and where Muhammad taught the one straight path to the One true God Sufism holds that "the ways to God are as many as the souls of men."

But in spite of these and other variants in historic Islam this faith has on the whole stood very characteristically for a rigid monotheism in which God is conceived of in terms of ideal personality raised to an infinite degree and known supremely in his revelation of his sovereign will through great prophets and most authoritatively in the words of the Qur'an.

IV THE GOD-CONCEPT IN HINDUISM

IN HINDUISM the God-concept is undoubtedly more varied than in any other religion. Almost every conception of the divine that has found expres-sion in all the other religion of mankind has its counterpart in Hinduism.

Hindu scholars often quote from the Vedas a statement to the effect that "Reality is one; sages speak of it in different ways." They take pride in Hinduism's tolerance of widely different views in even such fundamentals of religion as the God-concept; and as a recent writer has put it: "Hinduism achieves unity in diversity by cherishing the many ways in which men have represented and worshipped the various aspects of the Supreme Spirit." (D. S. Sarma in "The Religion of Hindus" p. 11). Even if one confines oneself to the main stream of India's sacred literature one is faced with this bewildering variety of concepts of the divine and man's relationship to the divine as will appear from our brief outline below.

One naturally begins with the Vedas which Hinduism to this day regards as its most sacred literature, at least in theory, whatever God-concept some modern Hindus may hold. In the earlier portions of the Vedas the God-concept is not unlike that of the early Greeks. It is a lusty polytheism with two major types of deities. On the one hand are the Nature gods—the gods of the sky, the sun, mountains, streams and other major objects of nature which seem to shape man's life and destiny. On the other hand are gods who seem rather human in origin, such as great warriors and illustrious ancestors. Some are a mixture of these two types and again some are deifications of abstract qualities. Almost all of them are patterned rather closely after man's own image. But while the Vedic deities are "all too human" there is, nevertheless, in Vedic religion an awareness of the superhuman Reality on which man's life is dependent and with which he must come to terms if he would have life at its best.

To mention but a few of the seventy odd deities in the Vedas, there is first of all Indra to whom about a fourth of the Rig Vedic hymns are dedicated. In Indra the Aryan hosts saw above all the god of war "without whose aid men conquer not in battle." He is also spoken of as "chief god" and as being "beyond the other gods in wisdom." "Both heaven and earth bow down before him." But in spite of these more worthy ascriptions Indra is all too frequently seen in terms of the lusty warrior "famed as Soma drinker" enjoying his cheering cup after victory in battle.

Another major Vedic deity to whom about 200 hymns are dedicated is Agni, the god of the sacred fire which carries the worshipper's sacrifices and prayers to the gods. Agni is a sort of priest among the gods and as medicator between men and their gods seems nearer to the worshipper than other deities. Also as god of the hearth he is the special guardian of the home and the family. "The worship and the sacrifice, guarded by thee on every side go straight, O Agni, to the gods." "So like a father to his son be easy of approach to us, Agni. For weal abide with us" (Rig. Veda I.1.). In the worship of Varuna, "the All-Seeing" or "Far-Seeing One," Vedic religion attained its noblest conception of the divine and approached most nearly that of the great monotheistic faiths. Varuna is given other names such as "Imperial Ruler," "Sovereign of the Universe," "the Mighty Lord on High" and similar terms conveying the thought that he alone rules over the world in general and over human life in particular.

> *Wherever two together plot, and deem they are alone,*
> *King Varuna is there, a third, and all their schemes are known.*
> *The earth is his, to him belong the vast and boundless skies,*
> *Both seas within him rest, and yet in that small pool he lies.*
> *Whoever far beyond the sky should think his way to wing,*
> *He could not there elude the grasp of Varuna, the King.*
>
> (ATHARVA VEDA IV. 16. 1)

Varuna as Lord of Nature and the Moral Order not only watches over man's life, it is also to him the repentant sinner must turn for forgiveness and help. "If we have sinned against the man who loves us, have ever wronged a brother, friend or comrade, the neighbor ever with us, or a stranger, O Varuna, remove from us the tresspass." (Rig. Veda V. 85.)

It must, however, be added that few of the Vedic hymns are dedicated to Varuna and that he gradually faded from the religious picture as a deity. On the other hand the conception of a universal order of things associated especially with Varuna was one which increasingly occupied the thinkers in subsequent Indian religion. In fact, much of Indian philosophy revolves around the concepts *Rita, Dharma,* and *Karma,* a sort of Cosmic Principle or Law manifesting itself in three major ways or aspects, namely, in the laws of Nature, in the Moral Order and in a semi magic power associated with sacred things and acts such as the sacrifices and prayers offered to the deity. Practically all leading Indian thinkers accepted the view that all things are subject to a Cosmic Law or Laws but they have disagreed as to whether this Cosmic Law as such is absolute and ultimate Reality or whether it is rather the way in which Divine and Ultimate Being controls all things. It should be further observed that in connection with the worship of Varuna we have also phases of the God-concept which in later Hinduism became so characteristic. Thus in the line quoted above: "Both seas within him rest, and yet in that small pool he lies," we have virtually the Panentheistic and the Pantheistic God-concepts which almost always find an echo in Hindu theology even where the major note may be more nearly Theistic. That the Divine is somehow a Unity, however varied may be the gods of popular religion, finds expression in the lines: "They call him Indra, Mitra, Varuna and Agni . . . To what is One, the poets give many a name." (Rig. Veda I. 164. 46). Another indication that the Vedic poets were struggling with the problem as to what is the Ultimate Reality is found in the Hymn of Creation (Rig. Veda X. 129) in which the author speaks of "That One alone breathed windless by itself. Than that, forsooth, no other thing existed." And then he proceeds to speculate about the origin of this world:

> *Who knoweth it, forsooth, who can declare it here*
> *Whence this creation has arisen, whence it came?*
> *The gods came hither by this world's creation only;*
> *Who knoweth then, whence this creation has arisen?*
> *Whence this creation has arisen, whether*
> *It has been made or not: He who surveys*
> *This world in highest heaven, he maybe knoweth,—*
> *Or, it may be, he knoweth not.*

Thus while there is here an affirmation that at the beginning there existed "One alone" and One "who surveys this world in highest heaven" there is, nevertheless, a serious doubt as to whether this "One" created this world or even knows how it came into existence. Evidently "the gods" of popular religion can not be the creators of this world for they themselves are seen as coming into existence in connection with the creation of the universe.

In a late Vedic Hymn (Rig. Veda X. 121) dedicated to "The Unknown God" we read: "In the beginning there arose the Golden Child (Hiranya-garbha)" who "alone was the Lord of all that is. He established the earth and this heaven. . . . He who gives breath, he who gives strength, whose command all the bright gods revere, whose shadow is immortality, whose shadow is death . . . . He who alone is God above all gods." This "Unknown God" is finally identified with Prajapati, "the Lord of creatures." Now while Prajapati received some attention in subsequent Hinduism and in the older Upanishads is represented as one who teaches his creations—gods, men and demons—the cardinal virtues, the truth about Brahman as the Ultimate Reality and the true nature of the self (atman) as essentially one with what is ultimately real, he nevertheless gradually fades from the religious life.

In fact, as the Vedic period passes over into the age of the Brahmanas, Upanishads and the Great Epics practically all the Vedic deities, including even such major deities as Indra, Agni and Varuna, fade out; but, strange to say, two of the very minor early deities gradually gain ascendency, namely, Vishnu and Rudra-Shiva who became the great deities respectively of the two major divisions of later Hinduism, namely Vishnuism and Sivaism. This was, however, a gradual development in the religion of the Hindu masses and was paralleled by many doubts and earnest searchings on the part of the more thoughtful as to the true nature of the Divine and Ultimate Reality.

This quest for what is the deepest reality and what is man's relationship to this Ultimate Reality or the Divine, finds its chief expression in the Upanishads and the subsequent philosophical speculations of the so-called Six Orthodox Schools (Darsanas) professedly based upon the Upanishads and Vedas, with the Brahmanas providing a sort of link between the earlier Vedic religion and the Upanishads.

Let us, therefore, first take a brief glimpse at the Brahmanas' contribution to the God-concept of Hinduism. The term "Brahmana" means "an explanation" or "learned utterance" and in the Brahmanas these explanations center primarily around the sacrifices and the associated prayers and rituals, including above all else the belief in a magic power inherent in these and especially in the "mantras" or magic texts uttered by the priests as they conducted the ceremonies. As these ritualistic observances grew in elaborateness it was natural that only those who knew how to conduct them correctly were qualified. In fact, the slightest error in the ritual, it was believed, would result in a curse rather than a blessing. One result of this emphasis on ritual and the power of the officiating priests who knew how to conduct the ceremonies correctly was that the very gods to whom the offerings were made were over-shadowed by the officiating priests who claimed to be gods themselves. "Two kinds of gods there are," says the Satapatha-Brahmana, "the gods are the gods, and the learned and studying Brahmans are the human gods... the two kinds of gods transfer him (the worshipper), when they are satisfied into the blessedness of heaven." And as it was the priests who really decided whether the sacrificial offerings and presents were satisfactory, they became even more important than the deities. We thus read further: "the Brahman descended from a *Rishi* indeed is all the deities;" and the Code of Manu, after affirming that "a Brahman, be he learned or unlearned, is a great deity," concludes that "the Brahman is the highest deity."

From such statements one might conclude that this type of Hinduism either lacks all worthy conceptions of the divine or has an exaggerated opinion of man. Both are really the case but they must be seen in the light of two basic concepts which were gaining almost universal acceptance if they would be understood right. These two concepts are the Karma concept and the Rebirth or Transmigration of Soul concept. The Karma concept means that the law of cause and effect is operative in the life of all beings, whether human, sub-human or super-human, and is really one aspect of the Cosmic Law mentioned above. According to this Karmaic Law man by his thoughts and deeds is constantly shaping his own fate, for Hinduism subscribes most decidedly to the belief that "Whatever a man sows, that he will also reap." Only in Hinduism this Karmaic Law is seen as operative in the life of all beings, including even the gods themselves. And further, in Hinduism this Karmaic Law is linked with the Rebirth or Transmigration of the Soul concept so that every human being in his present life is what he is because of the type of life he lived in a previous existence; and the type of life he now lives will inevitably determine his next kind of incarnation.

Now while these two concepts pertain primarily to human life it should be obvious that they have definite bearing also on Hinduism's God-concept since even the gods are under the Karmaic Law; and also because if man is largely the architect of his own life and destiny it would seem that any help from the gods would be quite secondary. Furthermore, since both man and his gods are seen as under a common Karmaic Law and so may rise or fall in the scale of beings there is really very little distinction between man and his deities. It is thus not strange that in the religion of the Brahmanas the gods were more or less over-shadowed by their human priests, and that these Brahman priests made claims to superiority over all other humans. This latter however belongs more to what we shall discuss below in the section on the Good Life ideal rather than the God-concept though it should be added that the Caste concept, based as it supposedly was on the Karma concept, was believed to apply even to the gods so that they were seen as ranking according to a caste system.

Now while the Karma and the Rebirth concepts became ruling concepts in Indian thought and have continued as such down to the present, the conception of the divine underwent various modifications from time to time. In fact the gods of the masses and popular religion were all too human to be taken very seriously by the more thoughtful as may be seen from the main trends of thought in the Upanishads and the subsequent philosophical speculations professedly based on the Upanishads. Here we have a search for what is more ultimately real than these all too human gods, a quest for what is ultimately real and true, a longing for a life that is eternal and free

C

from the endless cycle of rebirth into this evil world. This quest is well summarized in the lines:

> *From the unreal (asat) lead me to the real (sat)!*
> *From darkness lead me to light!*
> *From death lead me to immortality!*
>
> (BRIHAD. 1.3.28)

Over and over again and on varying levels of human experience these Upanishad thinkers sought to know what is truly real both in the world without and within. First we have various cosmogonic speculations. Some said: "In the beginning this world was just water." (Brihad.5.5.1.). Others said: "Verily all things here arise out of Space. They disappear back into Space, for Space alone is greater than these. Space is the final goal." (Chand. 1.9.1). Again some thought of ultimate reality in more abstract terms such as "Being" and "Non-Being." "In the beginning this world was merely Non-Being. It was existent. It developed into an egg." (Chand.3.19.1). From this "cosmic egg" the world was then somehow developed. This was countered by those who said: "In the beginning my dear this world was just Being, One only without a second. . . . How from Non-Being could Being be produced?" (Chand.6.2.1-2).

In one passage Yajnavalkya, the philosopher to whom much of Upanishad thought is attributed, is represented as answering a string of questions put to him by a clever woman who began with the statement: "Since all this world is woven warp and woof, on water, on what, pray, is water woven warp and woof?" The answer is: "On Wind." The questions and answers then proceed mentioning element after element, the moon, the sun, the stars and following these with such major Vedic deities as Indra and Prajapati, finally giving Brahma as the ultimate reality from which all things come. But when asked how Brahma came into existence, the philosopher is a bit annoyed and replies: "Gargi do not question too much, lest your head fall off. In truth you are questioning too much about a divinity about which further questions can not be asked. Gargi do not over-question." The text adds: "Thereupon Gargi Vacaknavi held her peace," but we are not told whether she was really satisfied with the philosopher's answers. (Brihad 3.6).

In another passage this same Yajnavalkya, in answer to a similar string of questions, speaks of "the Inner Controller" in all things who is always more and other than the object controlled. In fact, he speaks of him in more spiritual terms. "He is the unseen Seer, the unheard Hearer, the unthought

Thinker, the ununderstood Understander. Other than He there is no seer. Other than He there is no hearer. Other than He there is no thinker. Other than He there is no understander. He is your Soul, the Inner Controller, the Immortal." (Brihad 3.7.23).

In much of Upanishad thought the quest for Ultimate Reality turns inward and the nature of the divine is formulated largely in terms of man's own spiritual nature though at the same time the physical world is usually seen a being somehow a manifestation of this Ultimate Spiritual Reality usually spoken of as "Brahma" or "Brahman." Verily this whole world is Brahma. Tranquil, let one worship It as that from which he has come forth, as that into which he will be dissolved, as that in which he breathes. (Chand.3.14.1).

Not only does man himself come forth from and return to Brahman "all creatures here, my dear, have Being as their root, have Being as their abode, have Being as their support .... That which is the finest essence—this whole world has that as its soul. That is Reality (satya), That is Soul (Atman). That art thou." (Chand.6.8.6).

The various finite beings, to be sure, have their differences and will continue in successive rebirths to show such differences, but they, one and all, owe their existence to this Ultimate Reality for "that which is the finest essence—this whole world has that as its Soul. That is Reality. That is Atman. That art thou." In seven different illustrations this central truth is stated, always ending with the statement: "That which is the finest essence —this whole world has that as its Soul. That is Reality. That is Atman (Soul). That art thou."

Now while in this repeated statement man is said to be one in nature with Ultimate Being and Ultimate Being is spoken of as "Atman" (Soul) or as "Brahman Atman," some Upanishad philosophers, nevertheless, point out that such conceptions of the Divine and Ultimate Being are only approximations to the truth and that Divine and Ultimate Reality so completely transcends man and his understanding that no terms can express the full truth and so one can only add to such affirmations a series of negations in the hope of thus reaching a truer understanding. "That Atman (Soul) is not this, it is not that (neti, neti)." (Brihad 3.9.26). And to express the thought that Brahman as the "inner soul" of all finite beings is not only immanent in them but at the same time transcends them, we have such statements as:

All beings are one-fourth of Him;
Three-fourths, the immortal in the sky. (CHAND.3.12.6)

As the one fire has entered the world
And becomes corresponding in form to every form
So the Inner Soul of all things
Is corresponding in form to every form, and yet is outside.
As the sun, the eye of the world,
Is not sullied by the external faults of the eyes,
So the one Inner Soul of all things
Is not sullied by the evil in this world, being
external to it. (KATHA 5.9, 11).

As a rule Upanishad philosophers speak of Brahma or Brahman in terms of an Impersonal Spiritual Reality rather than Personal. There are, however, some passages which definitely speak of the Divine and Ultimate Being as "the Person (Purusha)."

Higher than the Unmanifest, however, is the Person, (Purusha)
All-pervading and without any mark whatever.
Knowing which, a man is liberated
And goes to immortality.
His form is not to be beheld
No one soever sees Him with the eye.
He is formed by the heart, by the thought, by the mind.
They who know that become immortal. (KATHA 6.8-9).

It is, of course, this conception of the divine as Personal Being which is always prominent in the religion of the masses but even the philosophers, who rightly reject the all too human gods of popular religion, must ever and again ask themselves whether there is any truer and more adequate conception of the divine than one that is expressed in terms of man's own spiritual nature; i.e., if one would formulate it in more or less positive terms and not rest content with such abstractions as "Being "and "Non-Being." The Upanishad thinkers struggled with this desperately and it is not strange that they did not always agree. It is also understandable that subsequent philosophers and theologians whom we meet in the so-called Six Orthodox Schools (Darsanas) which professedly are based on the Vedas and Upanishads should come up with rather widely differing conceptions in their God-concept and the nature of Ultimate Reality. Let us, therefore, turn briefly to what the more important of these "Orthodox schools" have to say on the subject.

Two of these schools—Nyāya and Vaiseshika—are of minor significance for the God-concept of Hinduism since the first is primarily a system of logic and dialectics while the second is more concerned with the analysis of the basic elements in nature. However, in so far as they deal at all with the God-concept both accept an essentially theistic view.

Mīmāmsā, which is probably the oldest of the Six Schools, seeks primarily to interpret the Vedic texts which deal with the sacrificial offerings and other duties of the pious. It sees in the Vedas themselves a manifestation of the Cosmic Law to which all things are subject. While Mīmāmsā accepts the common belief in innumerable souls and the doctrine of Rebirths it denies the existence of a supreme spirit ruling over this world since it regards the Cosmic Law as supreme and ultimate.

Most important of the Six Schools is Vedānta. As the meaning of the name Vedānta implies, it seeks to determine the "end results of the Vedas." The Vedānta scholars realized that the Vedas and Upanishads give various interpretations of even such basic matters as the nature of the Divine or Ultimate Reality and man's relation to the Divine, and they make an attempt to harmonize these differences in a comprehensive and consistent system. Thus in the famous Brahma-sutra of Badarayana, Brahma is seen as the self-existent Unitary Being from which all individual souls have come and to which they ultimately return. However, these individual souls, while owing their existence to Brahma as Ultimate Being, retain a certain degree of continuing identity even after returning to their source and eternal home. This interpretation may be said to represent the orthodox view of the earlier Vedānta scholars.

After the ninth century the views of Sankara, generally regarded as the greatest of all Vedānta philosophers, became dominant. Professing to interpret Badarayana's views, Sankara nevertheless modified these substantially in the direction of a more thorough going Monistic view. Reality is basically an Absolute Oneness, said Sankara, and the plurality of finite beings as seen by the unenlightened is illusory (māyā). The individual soul when truly enlightened knows its complete identity with Brahman, the Divine and Ultimate Reality. However, even Sankara had to make some concessions to man's ordinary experience in which the self is conscious of a self-identity and as different from other finite selves as well as the encompassing physical world. He, therefore, made a distinction between what he called a "Higher" and a "Lower Brahmā." According to the former Brahmā is Absolute Being, the One and Only Reality, while the pluralistic world of man's ordinary experience is illusory. It is not wholly non-existent but it is not what is seems to be to the unenlightened. That is the meaning of Sankara's famous "advaita" (non-duality) doctrine. The true nature of Absolute Being so completely transcends man's experience as a finite self that it can not be expressed in such terms even though the best approach is through man's inner experience as a spiritual self.

Now according to Sankara's "Lower Brahmā" doctrine, i.e., the accommodation of truth to the level of the unenlightened mind, the Divine may be thought of in terms of a personal god (Isvara) and individual souls and finite beings in general may be regarded as having a certain degree of separate existence and self-identity. The relationship of these finite souls to Brahmā as Ultimate Being may be expressed in various ways though in every form of relationship Brahmā must be seen as the ultimate source from which they come and to which they return, as Badarayana had said. In this accommodation of the doctrine to the unenlightened, there is room for a Pantheistic, a Panentheistic and even a Monotheistic god-idea, and correspondingly different views of man's relationship to the Divine or Ultimate Being. As a matter of fact in the course of time the God-concept in Hinduism tended more and more towards a theistic view though seldom as clear-cut as the view in the great monotheistic faiths. The reason for this trend stems in part from the need of the common man in his religious life for a person-to-person relationship with his god and also from the impact which the great monotheistic faiths had on India; first the impact of Islam and in more recent times the impact of Christianity. Of this development we shall speak a little more fully below.

In rather sharp contrast to Vedānta is the view of the classical Sânkhya School. Sânkhya takes its name from its predilection for enumeration of things, such as the basic elements that constitute the natural world. Original Sânkhya had accepted the Vedānta view of a Primary and Unitary Substance or Being from which all things come and into which all things return, but in the course of Sânkhya's development this view was rejected in favor of a radical dualism of matter and spirit, or rather a Primary Matter (prakriti) and innumerable souls or spirits. This Primary Matter and these innumerable souls are seen as equally self-existent and eternal. Matter and spirits have no common ground and are basically opposite in nature. By some mysterious cause, usually defined as Primal Ignorance, some of these innumerable spirits have become imprisoned by Primary Matter and thus constitute the world of embodied spirits, namely, the human and subhuman beings. Here, too, illusion is at work as in Vedānta, but where in Vedānta the illusion consists in the individual souls regarding themselves

as separate realities rather then realizing their oneness with true and Ultimate Being, in Sânkhya the illusion is that the individual souls regard their
present psycho-somatic life as their true life and that they do not realize that
they are pure spirits and as such have really nothing in common with the
bodily life. In short, the soul should realize its own true nature as an eternally
self-existent spiritual being and thus free itself from the illusion of being
imprisoned in a body or of regarding the psychosomatic life as its true life.

Sânkhya has no place for anything like a Divine or Supreme Being on
which man is dependent since it sees only a plurality of self-existent and
eternal souls on the one hand and Primary Matter equally self-existent and
eternal, on the other hand. However, inasmuch as some of these innumerable
souls are seen as free from bodily imprisonment they serve in a measure as
Divine Beings showing the way to freedom to those that are still imprisoned
in human or animal bodies. As a matter of fact, Sânkhya with all its talk
about eternal and self-existent souls, has really very little to say about these
souls or the nature of the life of pure and free souls. It has much more to say
about Primary Matter and its three qualities (*gunas*) which in varying com-
binations give rise to the varied things that make up the world of man's
experience. In fact, this Primary Matter endowed with these mysterious
gunas virtually takes the place of a deity that creates and sustains the visible
universe; and these qualities of Primary Matter as manifested in man's life
seem more psychic in nature than physical. Thus man, in his present state as
an embodied soul, has really three aspects to his being. There is first the
physical body as such. Opposite in nature to the body is the soul which is
the invisible inner reality and known through a self-consciousness free from
all connection with the physical world. Then there is the "subtle body"
which is really an aspect of Matter but which is the instrument of sense-
perception and all forms of the psycho-somatic life. Now the illusion of the
embodied soul consists in that it regards this psycho-somatic life as its own
true life. Only after the soul shakes off this illusion and realizes that its
true life as pure spirit is wholly other in nature can it regain its freedom as
pure spirit. The first step towards gaining this freedom is to withdraw from
the world of sense-perception and all concepts built on such perception into
a life of pure contemplation. All forms of ascetic discipline also are a help.
And, of course, the greatest help is to accept as true what has been said
above as to the nature of pure spirit and therefore to realize its freedom
even when seemingly still imprisoned in the bodily life.

The type of life just mentioned constitutes the major interest of Yoga
which is the last of the Six Orthodox Schools to be mentioned. Yoga is usually

linked with Sânkhya so that often one meets the term Sânkhya Yoga. As a matter of fact Yoga is primarily a method of salvation rather than a philosophy. It accepts the Sânkhya view of the basic dualism of Primary Matter and Spirit or Spirits. However, in its conception of the world of innumerable spirits it makes room for a Supreme Spirit though this Supreme Spirit is seen more in the role of a Savior who helps the imprisoned souls gain their lost freedom rather than as the Creator and Sustainer of the universe. It should be added that while Yoga is a characteristic form of Hindu soteriology it has at the same time played an equally big role in other forms of Indian and East Asiatic religions, particularly in Buddhism.

Now these various conceptions of the divine and man's relationship to the divine are reflected also in the two great Epics—the Mahābhārata and the Rāmāyana. Particularly is that the case with the Bhagavat-Gītā which constitutes a part of the Mahābhārata and which undoubtedly is India's most popular and influential scripture. However in this popular literature as well as in the Purānas and Agamas the trend is more and more towards a personalistic and monotheistic conception even though there is always room left for other God-concepts. In fact, the God-concept in Hinduism down through the centuries has never been clear-cut and even where it has become predominantly theistic it is usually flanked on one side with pretheistic or polytheistic conceptions and on the other side with post-theistic concepts, namely, views which regard the theistic concept as only an accommodation to man's finite mind but which see in a Pantheism, Panentheism or Acosmic Mysticism the more worthy understanding of the Divine Mystery.

Now since the Bhagavat-Gītā is a sort of synthesis of the Upanishad philosophies and the more popular views of the great Epics and also since it has been such a continuing factor in shaping Hinduism's concept of the divine for all classes it deserves special attention. And the first thing to notice about this scripture is that it is cast in the form of a dialogue between the warrior Arjuna and his charioteer, Krishna, who is really an incarnation of the Supreme Deity. All through this scripture the language is in personalistic terms so that Krishna uses the pronouns I, Me, Mine, even when he speaks of the Supreme Deity in other than theistic terms. The result is that it gives the scripture as a whole a far more theistic flavor than the varying concepts of the divine actually set forth would warrant.

Another characteristic of this scripture which tends to give the God-concept a theistic flavor is that man's salvation is seen in terms of his trust in and devotion to his God rather than in terms of the Karmaic Law. "Fill thy heart with Me, be thou devoted to Me, do thou worship Me and bow down to Me. Thus thou shalt attain unto Me. Truly I promise thee, for thou art dear to Me." (XVIII.65)* This and similar passages setting forth the famous *Bhakti* (devotion to God) way of salvation would seem to make other concepts than the theistic concept rather inappropriate if not impossible.

Then further one finds all through this scripture affirmations about the nature of Divine Being which are definitely theistic: "Knowing Me ... the Supreme Lord of the universe and the friend of all beings, he attains peace." (V.29). "He who knows Me as birthless and beginningless, the Supreme Lord of the Universe, he among mortals is undeluded and free from all sins." (X.3). "As I am beyond the perishable and am above the imperishable, therefore in the world and in the Veda I am known as the Supreme Being. . .He who, free from delusion, thus knows Me as the Supreme Being, he, knowing all, worships Me with his whole heart." (XV.18-19).

But while the Bhagavat-Gītā directly and indirectly reflects a theistic concept it must be added that there is much in this scripture which points to other God-concepts. In fact, one can find almost all the various conceptions of the divine which we discussed above in connection with the Six Orthodox Schools, as well as conceptions of the nature of the human soul as a self-existent and eternal reality which needs no deity.

Thus in the opening chapters where Krishna encourages Arjuna to do his duty as a brave warrior the emphasis is placed on the eternal nature of the soul which is not affected by the death of the body. It is not the comfort that God will take care of him but that man, in his true being, is an eternal soul passing from one bodily existence to another. "These bodies are perishable; but the dwellers in these bodies are eternal, indestructible and impenetrable." (II.18). "This (Self) is never born, nor does It die, nor after once having been, does It go into non-being. This (Self) is unborn, eternal, changeless, ancient. It is never destroyed even when the body is destroyed." (II.20). "As man casts off worn-out garments and puts on others which are new, similarly the embodied soul, casting off worn-out bodies, enters into others which are new." (II.22).

While these and many other passages speak in good Sânkhya style of the eternal nature of the soul and without its dependence upon any Divine and

---

*This translated quotations from the Bhagavad Gītā as well as the subsequent quotations are by Swami Paramandanda in "The Wisdom of China and India" by Ling yutang.

more Ultimate Being, there are many other passages which convey more the Vedānta view and which see in all finite beings, including the souls of men, but temporary manifestations of Divine and Absolute Being. "He who sees Me in all and all in Me, from him I vanish not, nor does he vanish from Me." (VI.30). "There is naught else (existing) higher than I. Like pearls on a thread all this (universe) is strung on Me." (VII.7). The whole of Chapter VIII, entitled "The Imperishable Brahman," pictures the universe as emerging from Brahman and then merging again with Brahman in successive cosmic cycles of time. "At the approach of (Brahmā's) day, all manifestations proceed from the Unmanifested, and at the approach of the night, they merge into that which is called the Unmanifested. O, Partha, the multitude of beings, coming into birth again and again, helplessly merge into (the Unmanifested) at the approach of night and again remanifest at the approach of day. But beyond this Unmanifested, there is another Unmanifested, which is eternally existent and is not destroyed even when all beings are destroyed." (VIII.18-20). Then in a more monotheistic strain we read: "That Supreme Self, in whom all beings abide and by whom all this is pervaded, can be attained by whole-hearted and exclusive devotion to Him." (VIII.22).

Almost the whole of Chapter X, entitled "The Path of Divine Manifestations" is cast in Pantheistic terms according to which all things are parts of the Divine Being but which Divine Being is more than these. Even the gods of the Vedas are but different names or aspects of the One and Ultimate Reality. "O, Arjuna, whatever is the seed of all beings, that also am I. Without Me there is no being existent, whether moving or unmoving.... There is no end to the manifestations of My Divine Power; what I have declared is only a partial statement of the vastness of My Divine manifestation. Whatever Being there is, glorious, prosperous or powerful, know thou that to have sprung from a portion of My splendor. O, Arjuna, what need is there for thee to know these details? I alone exist, sustaining this whole universe by a portion of Myself." (X.39-42). Then in response to Arjuna's request to be shown the Infinite in all its aspects, Chapter XI, entitled "The Vision of the Universal Form," pictures the terrifying aspects of Divine Being which are so terrible that Arjuna begs forgiveness for having made such a daring request and asks the deity to reveal himself again in the more familiar and friendlier form of a loving Personal Being.

Now these varying conceptions of the Divine which are so interwoven in the Gītā and as such achieve a sort of synthesis of the different God-concepts found in the older sacred literature, are also more or less characteristic of subsequent Hinduism though the personalistic and theistic strain is more dominant in the later development. As Sir Charles Eliot has so well stated it: "The striking difference between the earlier and later phases of Indian religious beliefs, between the Vedic hymns, Brahmanas, Upanishads and their accessory treatises on the one hand, and the Epics, Puranas, Tantras and later literature on the other, is due chiefly to the predominance in the latter of the great gods Siva and Vishnu, with the attendant features of sectarian worship and personal devotion to a particular deity." (Hinduism and Buddhism, Vol. II. p. 136). We might add that this characteristic of later Hinduism is particularly true of the religion of the masses. To be sure, even in the older Hinduism the religion of the masses expressed its concepts of the Divine in personalistic terms, usually in terms that were all too human, but in later Hinduism the very prominence of the Bhakti (devotion to God) movement which is such a decidedly person-to-person relationship between man and his deity, bears witness to the dominance of the theistic concept.

Now it can not be said that this was pure gain in Hinduism's development for while the theistic conception of the divine sometimes received a rather worthy formulation as it had in the Bhagavat-Gītā it was nevertheless often formulated in terms which, like the older religion of the masses, was all too much in terms of man's own little image. This was the case in both Sivaism and Vishnuism though in somewhat different ways. Siva is seen more in terms of the natural world, as the creative power and the power which also destroys whereas Vishnu is seen more as the God who helps man especially through his *avataras*, manifestations in terms of human life.

Siva as the creative power in the universe is seen more specifically in connection with animal and human life in terms of sex relationships and thus this power is personified and as such becomes Siva's consort, *Sakti*. Siva's power to destroy is also personified and becomes his consort under such names as Kali, Durga or Mahadevi worshipped by millions as the terrible goddess who often demands blood and must be propitiated with costly sacrifices. As a matter of fact, Siva's consort or consorts with their creative and destructive powers tend to overshadow Siva himself and the cult centering in them has become virtually a separate form of Hinduism with its own sacred scriptures.

This conception of the Divine in terms of the husband-wife relationship finds its expression also in Vishnuism. Thus Vishnu himself is pictured as having his consort, Lakshmi and Vishnu's chief *avataras*, Rama and Krishna, have their female counterpart in Sita and Radha respectively. In the original Ramayana, Rama and Sita are seen as the divine couple setting the ideal pattern for the relationship between man and wife, while in such later versions of the Ramayana as that of Tulsi Das, it is more the relationship of love between God and the human soul. In fact in later Vishnuism, Rama or Ram is the name often used for God rather than the name Vishnu as was so well illustrated by Gandhi's last words, "*He Ram*," "O God" which he uttered as he died at the assassin's hands.

Krishna as the other major *Avatara* of Vishnu is seen at his best in the Bhagavat-Gītā where he is on the one hand the charioteer who admonishes Arjuna to do his duty and on the other hand speaks as the Supreme Deity himself. However, in some of the Puranas, Krishna is depicted not only as the ideal husband with his wife Radha but also as the amorous play-boy sporting with the shepherd maidens (gopis) and even as having numerous wives. He is perhaps most beloved by the masses when depicted as the wonder child.

Now while in later Hinduism and especially in the religion of the masses the God-concept is predominantly personalistic and frequently in terms that are all too human, the more thoughtful continued to seek more worthy expressions. Most of these thinkers accepted the Vedānta philosophy in so far as it laid emphasis on the unitary nature of existence but at the same time they realized that this blank affirmation needed to be given more positive content which would do more justice to man's experience. Sankara, the ninth century Vedānta philosopher, had dismissed the pluralistic world of man's daily life all too easily as illusory (māyā) in his zeal for Ultimate Reality. They also felt that in his emphasis on the transcendent nature of Ultimate Reality or the Divine he did not meet the real needs of the religious life. To be sure, Sankara had spoken of a Higher and a Lower Brahmā and the Latter he expressed in terms of a Personal God, Isvara, but he nevertheless said that this latter God-concept was only an accommodation to man's finite mind and thus should not be treated as true for the fully enlightened. What then is the true conception of the Divine that on the one hand would avoid the anthropomorphic conception so characteristic in the religion of the masses but that, on the other hand, has a little more positive content than the philosopher's Absolute or Ultimate Reality that seemed so bare and far removed from man's practical and daily life?

In short, one might say that the philosophers in later Hinduism in varying ways sought for a middle ground between the extremes of Sankara's Monistic Vedānta which, as stated above, failed to do full justice to the realities of the pluralistic world of man's daily experience and the dualistic Sânkhya philosophy which, on the other hand, had failed to satisfy man's persistent quest for a common and unitary ground of finite and dependent beings. To mention but a few of these philosophers in later Hinduism, there is first of all Ramanuja, (11th century) and his so-called "Qualified Monism." He agreed with Sankara that Brahman as Absolute and Ultimate Reality is the Unitary Ground of all existence but he was not willing to regard the phenomenal world as quite so illusory as Sankara had done. Individual selves and other finite beings are real, Ramanuja maintained, even though they are not self-existent realities in the way the Sânkhya philosophers had said. They are real manifestations of the Divine and Ultimate Being with a certain degree of self-identity. In short, Ramanuja advocates a sort of pantheistic view which regards the individual selves and the physical universe as emanations or embodiments of the Divine.

In the 12th century appeared Nimbarka who in his "Dualistic Monism" carried the conception of the Divine and its relationship to the world of finite beings one step further, giving man and the world in which he lives a greater degree of difference from the Divine Being than Ramanuja had done. In fact, he spoke of three categories of reality: God or the Supreme Self, the individual finite selves, and the physical world. God, the Supreme Self is Infinite and Absolute Being and as such is beyond man's comprehension but he is also the creative and sustaining power of finite beings which are also real and whose relationship to God may be expressed by saying that in Him they live, and move and have their being.

In the 13th century Madhva went even further than Nimbarka had done in regarding individual souls and the physical world as substantial realities different from the Divine. In fact, he virtually endorsed the Sânkhya position holding that they are eternal and selfexistent realities even though they are subject to God or the Supreme Self. While Vishnu as the Supreme Personal Being is not the creator of either the finite selves or Primal Matter (Prakriti) he nevertheless shapes the world from this Primal Matter and controls the life and destiny of finite souls or selves. These souls are seen under three categories: souls that have never been imprisoned in a bodily existence and in their freedom enjoy the bliss of God; souls which are now imprisoned and which can be freed by the help of the Divine, especially by their complete devotion to their God; and souls which once had been imprisoned but which have been freed and are now in full communion with their God.

A fourth scholar, Vallabha (15th century) reverts more towards a Monistic interpretation but differs nevertheless from Sankara's view. Where Sankara held that the Divine as Absolute Being is above all qualifying attributes and the world of man's ordinary experience is illusory, Vallabha held that the Divine or Brahman is the Absolute Reality whose very essence is existence (sat), consciousness (chit) and bliss (ananda) but who also creates and sustains the world of finite souls as well as the physical universe and which therefore are real as such since they are manifestation of the Divine Power. Furthermore, since the natural world in its very essence is Divine because of its origin, man should take pleasure in the bodily life rather than regard the ascetic life as the noblest. It should be added that Vallabha followers sometimes carried this view of the good life to an extreme. They saw in Krishna the ideal for human life; not the Krishna of the Bhagavat-Gītā but rather the amorous Krishna sporting with the shepherd maidens.

In the system of Chaitanya (15th century) and his followers who developed it, the God-concept is essentially theistic, for God is above all else the Perfect Personal Being through whose love and grace man is saved. However it is recognized that God in his full being transcends man's powers of comprehension even though he may be known in part through his creation. The finite selves owing their existence to God as their creator are seen as being both one in nature with the Divine and yet as also different. Even after the finite selves that have been imprisoned in a bodily existence regain their freedom and enter into full communion with God they retain their identity as selves which are God-like but are not completely merged in God as Absolute Being.

The above mentioned thinkers were all worhippers of Vishnu as the Supreme God but similar movements can be found among the worshippers of Siva as the Supreme. In varying ways they, too, sought a middle ground between the Vedānta Monism which in its insistence on the Unitary ground of all existence failed to do justice to the actual world of man's experience and the other extreme of the Sânkhya philosophers which saw in the individual selves and the physical realities surrounding man's life self-existent realities. For the practical religious life they, too, spoke of the Divine in terms of the Perfect and Supreme Personal Being though in stating the relationship between God and man they differed among themselves and expressed views which ranged from an out and out Theism through Pantheism, Panentheism to an Acosmic Mysticism in which the Divine or Absolute Reality so completely transcends man's finite experience and powers of understanding that no affirmations can be made. However, as we said, an essentially theistic God-concept was increasingly recognized as the most helpful in practical religion.

Now this predominantly theistic God-concept in later Hinduism was due at least in part to the impact of the great monotheistic faiths, namely, Islamic religion and, in more recent years, Christianity. Islam's influence is seen most clearly in such figures as Kabir (1440–1518), Dadu (1544–1603) and Nanak (1469–1518). All three were not only Theists but also believed that the one true God of Hindus is also the God of Moslims though known by different names. Kabir with his followers, the Kabirpanthis and Dadu with his Dadupanthis remained within Hinduism even though they looked more to their own inspired teachers (Gurus) than to the sacred scriptures of Hinduism for their authoritative guidance. Nanak, on the other hand, became the founder of Sikhism, a separate religion with its own sacred scriptures and Gurus. Sikhism was influenced by the Moslem faith not only in its God-concept but also in its view of man's relationship to his fellowman, stressing as it did the equality of all men before the One and Only God and thus running counter to Hinduism's age-long caste system. Under Govind Singh (1469–1539) Sikhism also took on some of the military characteristic of the Moslim world resulting in making the Sikhs into a separate nation within the Hindu world. Even today with the division of the subcontinent into Pakistan and Hindu India the Sikhs belong to neither, whatever the political arrangement might be. However it should be added that on the whole Sikhism is more Hindu than Islamic.

The influence of Christianity on Hinduism in more recent years has been equally great and this influence is continuing. This is seen in regard to the God-concept and perhaps even more in the conception of what constitutes the truly good life. Thus we find the Brahman Rammohun Roy who founded the Brahma-Samaj in 1828 maintaining that in the theistic conception of the Divine, Hinduism, Christianity and Islam are in substantial agreement but that the original literary expression of this great belief is found in the Upanishads. He realized that in the religion of the Hindu masses there is all too much that is unworthy and he made a serious attempt to rid his religion of its multivarious gods and idol worship. His successor in this reform movement, Keshab Candra Sen, sought to make a synthesis of the historic major religions and thus form a World Religion with a belief in One True God and the Brotherhood of Man.

The Arya-Samaj, another reform movement, founded by Swami Dayanand Sarasvati in 1875 is also theistic in its God-concept and as such opposed to other conceptions found in historic Hinduism and especially to the unworthy conceptions found in the religion of the masses. It is, however, less willing than the Brahma-Samaj to see in the Christian conception of God an equally true view for it holds that the One True God has revealed himself in the Vedas alone. Furthermore the Vedas are also the primary source of all knowledge including knowledge of God's creation. Though compelled to admit the Western World's obvious understanding of the things with which science deals it is, nevertheless, maintained that one can find all this in the Vedas when they are rightly understood.

There are a great many intelligent Hindus today who in speaking of the Divine and man's relationship to the Divine use much the same language Christian scholars use. One thinks especially of such men as the great poet Tagore and Gandhi. In much of what such men say about God, man's relationship to God, or the good life the Christian would be in substantial agreement. It remains true, however, that most of the modern thinkers in Hinduism, however much they may use the theistic conception or speak of man's relationship to the Divine as a person-to-person relationship, almost always add that such a conception of the Divine, while most helpful for practical religion, must always be held with reservations by the philosopher and not to the exclusion of other concepts which may be equally valid since any and all conceptions of the Divine as the Ultimate Reality can be only partially true for in its full Being the Infinite transcends man's powers of comprehension.

Perhaps it is best to end this section on Hinduism's God-concept by letting a modern Hindu scholar speak for himself and others like him: "We represent the Supreme Spirit as a person because personality is the most intelligible and attractive concept of which our minds are capable. The Supreme Being is a person only in relation to ourselves and our needs. In Himself He is something above personality. When the sun blazing in the sky can not be looked at by us, we use a smoked glass and then see it as a round, red disk. Similarly, when the Supreme Being in His glory can not be perceived as He is, we perceive Him through our human spectacles and apprehend only some aspects of Him and think of Him as a person. Thus even the highest theism is only a sort of glorified anthropomorphism, but we cannot do without it . . . ." "Accordingly Hinduism as its highest neither rejects theism nor accepts it at the last word in religious philosophy." Then the author harps back to a Vedic statement, "Reality is one; sages speak of it in different ways." He then closes with the summary statement, quoted above, about Hinduism's conception of the Divine by saying: "Hinduism achieves unity in diversity by cherishing the many ways in which men have represented and worshipped the various aspects of the Supreme Spirit." (D.S.Sarma in "The Religion of Hindus" p.11).

A: V THE GOD-CONCEPT IN BUDDHISM

WHILE BUDDHISM in its long history developed various conceptions of the Divine it is, nevertheless, true that the founder of Buddhism, Sakyamuni had very little to say on the subject; at least not in terms which religious thinkers have used down through the ages. He rather scorned the Brahman priests of his day with their elaborate ceremonies and prayers addressed to their gods and he took very little stock in the philosopher's speculations about the Brahman or Ultimate Reality. The one seemed rather futile to him and the other he felt made pretenses to knowledge beyond what man actually has. It is for these reasons that the Buddha has often been regarded as an atheist both by Buddhist and non-Buddhist scholars. However, that would overstate the facts about his real position. He was rather agnostic in such matters since he felt that man does not know enough to make either positive affirmations or firm denials.

Now while the Buddha had apparently little to say about the Divine or metaphysical realities there are, nevertheless, certain assumptions in his teachings which have metaphysical implications and which he held in common with other Indian thinkers of his day. Thus we find that he accepted the commonly held view about *Samsara*, the world of innumerable beings which are ever passing from one stage of existence to another, some lower than the human, some in various stages of human development and some above the human level. All these beings are seen as under a cosmic law, *Karma*, which law the Buddha interpreted primarily in terms of a Moral Order. He was too much of a realist to hold with some of the Upanishad philosophers that this flux of ever changing beings is a mere illusion, *maya*, of the unenlightened mind. He accepted them as real even though they were ever changing from one stage of existence to another in the apparently endless cycle of "birth and death, rebirth and death." Just how this universe came to be what it is he did not pretend to know. "The world of transmigration, my disciples, has its beginning in eternity. No origin can be perceived from which beings start, and hampered by ignorance, fettered by craving, stray and wander."

Even though the Buddha laid no claim to knowledge about the origin of the universe he nevertheless felt that he had found a way that would free man from the apparently endless cycle of rebirth into this evil world. This is succinctly outlined in the so-called "Four Noble Truths" which undoubtedly constitute the very core of his teachings, for their substance is found over and over again in the older records of Buddhism. In the first of these "Four

D

Noble Truths" the Buddha describes the nature of human life as being predominantly an existence of impermanency, sorrow and suffering. In the second he sets forth the basic cause for such a life, namely, man's ignorance and craving for things that can never satisfy and that only produce further cravings that cannot be satisfied. In the third "Noble Truth" he proclaims a message of hope as to the possibility of release from this endless cycle of rebirths. And in the fourth Truth the Buddha points out the way in which man must walk if he would gain his freedom, namely, the "Noble Eightfold Path" of "right views, right aspirations, right speech, conduct and mode of livelihood, right effort, right mindfulness, and right rapture." Most of the Buddha's teachings as found in the canonical scriptures set forth in greater detail what is meant by this "Noble Eightfold Path."

It should be noted that the Path begins with "right views." However important the other steps in the Path are, a true understanding and real enlightenment is basic in the Buddha's teachings. The very term *Buddha* means the "Enlightened One." Furthermore these "right views" revolve largely around the problems as to man's own nature, his present condition and what he himself can do to improve his life and to gain his freedom from this essentially evil world. In speaking of man's own nature the Buddha steered a middle way between those philosophers who, on the one hand, saw in man a temporary emanation from Brahman, the Unitary Ground of all existence, and those other philosophers who, on the other hand, saw man as an eternally self-existent spiritual monad which is forever the same even though it may pass through various embodiments which constitute its temporary imprisonments. As stated above, the Buddha had little or nothing to say about the "Unitary Ground of all existence" or man's relationship to this but he saw man as a finite being subject to change and able to rise in the scale of beings till he gains freedom from rebirth into this evil world and enters the *Nirvana* state from which there is no return. Nothing is said about any help coming from the Divine in this deliverance from the evil world. Every man must work out his own salvation. To be sure, the Buddha, after he had attained enlightenment and gained his freedom, rendered help to his disciples by the truth he taught them and the example he set but in the final analysis every man must, in obedience to the Karmaic Law, save himself. He is the lord of his own life as the Dhammapada so succinctly puts it: "Self is the Lord of self, who else could be lord? With self well subdued a man finds a lord such as few can find." Among the last words the Buddha is said to have uttered on his deathbed were these: "All that is born, brought into being and put together carries within itself the necessity of dissolution."

"It may be, Ananda, that some of you may think the word of the Master is ended. We have no more a teacher. But you should not think thus. The Truth and the rules which I have declared and laid down for you all, let them be the'teacher for you when I am gone." (Mahaparinirvana VI.1) He did not say that he himself would cease to exist but neither did he comfort them with any promise of his continuing spiritual presence with them. The Truth he taught them was to be their sole guide and comfort.

Is, then, the Truth the abiding and ultimate reality in this world of impermanency and ever changing finite beings? If so, does not this imply the existence of something like a Supreme Mind which thinks the Truth? The Buddha apparently was never confronted with the question in this form but he frequently spoke of the *Dhamma* or *Dharma*, Truth as something absolute and not merely what the finite mind thinks. Much is made in early Buddhist thought of *Panna*, or *Prajna*, which is the collective name for the higher stages of the mind which alone can comprehend absolute truth; and this *Prajna* is personified and as such is one source for the conception of the Eternal Buddha or Buddhas so prominent in later Mahāyāna Buddhism.

Then further, the Buddha himself in speaking of the fully Enlightened One and the state into which such a one passes, namely, Nirvana, used concepts which have at least overtones of the Divine even if they differ somewhat from the God-concept in other major religions. In fact, even in early Buddhism, in spite of its emphasis on the thought that every man must work out his own release from this evil world or that every man may become enlightened and so enter the Nirvana state from which there is no return to this evil world, the Buddha is spoken of in terms which make him seem more God-like than merely an enlightened human being. Thus we find these words ascribed to him in the hour of his enlightenment: "I have overcome all foes; I am all-wise; I am free from stain in every way; I have left everything; I have obtained emancipation by the destruction of desire. Having myself gained knowledge whom should I call my master? I have no teacher; no one is equal to me; in this world of men and gods, no being is like me. I am the Holy One in the world. I am the highest teacher. I alone am the *Sambuddha* (Perfectly Enlightened One); I have obtained coolness (extinction of desires) and have attained Nirvana. To found the Kingdom of Truth I go to the city of the Kasis (Benares); I will beat the drum of the immortal in the darkness of this world." (Vinaya Mahavaga I.6.8) It is especially in the words: "in this world of man and gods, no being is like me. I am the Holy One in this world...I alone am the Sambuddha" that the Buddha is seen more in terms of the Divine than as being merely an enlightened human being.

But however little or much there may be in the teachings of the Buddha that is akin to the God-concept in other major religions and however much he may have avoided any discussion of metaphysical problems, including even the Nirvana state into which the fully enlightened enter upon their release from this evil world, it is a fact that Buddhism, especially in its Mahāyāna form, not only developed great metaphysical systems but also various concepts of the Divine, some of which resemble the God-concepts of other major religions. It is impossible to give here all these varying concepts and for our purpose it is sufficient to state in brief outline only the major variants.

One initial difficulty in setting forth Buddhism's conception of the Divine stems from the terminology used by Buddhist writers. Even the term "Buddha" is used with widely differing meanings, especially in Mahāyāna Buddhism. However, in the so-called *Trikaya*, "Three Bodies," doctrine the matter is somewhat explained. In this doctrine we have first *Nirmanakaya*, "Accommodated Body," in which the Buddha is seen as a human being such as the historic Buddha Sakyamuni, the founder of the Buddhist Faith, who through his own efforts attained enlightenment and taught others the way they must follow if they would gain their freedom from the cycle of rebirth into this evil world. As such the Buddha is not regarded as a god but as, nevertheless, superior to the spirits and gods worshipped by the ignorant masses; for all such beings, even though they may be superhuman, are still subject to endless rebirths into this evil world unless they, too, attain enlightenment and enter the Nirvana state as the Buddha had done.

As the second of the *Trikāya* doctrine we have *Sambhogakāya*, "Compensation Body," in which the Buddha is seen as the ideal and perfect Personal Being who is free from all the limitations of finite existence. In some of the Mahāyāna scriptures the historic Buddha Sakyamuni is pictured in terms of such a perfect Personal Being. In other scriptures we read of Amitābha, the Buddha of Infinite Life and Light who has prepared his Land of Pure Bliss for all who turn to him in simple faith and trust for their salvation. In fact, Mahāyāna Buddhism speaks of numerous Buddhas in terms of ideal and perfect Personal Beings who in the Nirvana state are free and beyond all the limitations to which man and other finite beings are subjected.

According to the third aspect of the *Trikāya* doctrine, namely, *Dharmakāya*, "Law Body," or "Cosmic Body," the Buddha is seen as Ultimate Reality or the Absolute and Unitary Ground of all existence. As such Buddha is not a Personal Being but transcends any and every conception which the finite mind can formulate. The term *Dharmakāya* literally means 'Law Body"

and as such may be one way in which to think of the nature of Ultimate
Reality, namely in terms of the "Law of things," but even this is too definitive to be applied to the nature of Ultimate Reality. Some, therefore, speak
of it in paradoxes and in such vague and all-inclusive terms as "Being and
Non-being." But even such terms take what meaning they have from man's
finite experience and are therefore inadequate for representing the true
nature of the Absolute. That is why other philosophers say the last word
on the subject is no word at all and that the truest insight must lead to the
"White Silence of Truth," leaving one free to give it as much or little positive content as one sees fit.

But while Mahāyāna Buddhist philosophers stress the thought that the
Divine as the Ultimate Reality is beyond all conceptions which the finite
mind of man can formulate they have nevertheless sought in different ways
to come to closer grips and have come up with differing answers.

One of the most wide-spread of these is an essentially Pantheistic or
Cosmotheistic conception. In fact, in much of Mahāyāna Buddhism there is
this Pantheistic strain at least to the extent that the various nature gods and
deified humans of the various religions which Buddhism absorbed in its
conquest are represented as local manifestations of the Eternal Buddha or the
Unitary Ground of all existence. Or we might say that this sort of Pantheism
is a working compromise between the philosopher's Absolute or Unitary
Ground of existence and the common man's gods who are cast in personalistic concepts. Only as one understands this relationship can one make sense
of what one finds so characteristic of the religious life of East Asia where
Mahāyāna Buddhism has been more or less dominant and where there seems
to be such a wide gap between the God-concept of the average believer
and that of the Buddhist philosopher. The philosopher usually justifies this
wide difference and his indifference to what the common man thinks about
the true nature of the Divine or Ultimate Reality by the theory of what is
called "Accommodated Truth" which, in short, means that truth must be
accommodated to each man's level of understanding. As the common man
gets more help in his religious life by thinking of the Divine in personalistic
terms, let him do so even if his god or gods sometimes seem more human
than divine. But by the same token of "Accommodated Truth" the more
intelligent can not take such gods too seriously. They hold that even the
more worthy personalistic concepts of the Divine found in connection with
the worship of Amitābha Buddha, of which we shall speak below, should not
be taken too seriously, for these concepts are likewise a form of "Accommodated Truth" even though on a higher level. What the real truth is,

especially the truth about the Divine as Ultimate Reality, no man can fully know and whatever he says about it must be cast in vague abstractions or paradoxes such as the "Unitary Ground of existence," or "Being and Non-being." Even better than this would it be if in a spirit of reverent agnosticism one bowed in silence before the "Mystery of the Divine and Ultimate Ground of all Being."

A second major variant of the God-concept in Mahāyāna Buddhism is that of the Dhyana, "Contemplative," School. In its original Indian form this school turned its search for the Real inwardly and away from the outside world in the belief that what is deepest and truest of man's own spiritual being is at the same time the key to an understanding of Ultimate Reality. "Directly point to the human mind, see one's real nature and become an enlightened Buddha." What one finds by this approach can not be expressed in words, and if it is to be conveyed to others it must be done by a sort of mystical communion of mind with mind. Even though the approach to the ultimately real or the divine is inwardly or through man's own nature as a spiritual, personal being, it does not issue in a personalistic God-concept but stands rather for a mysticism in which the individual feels himself at one with the Eternal and Unitary Ground of all existence. In fact, this type of Buddhism, more than any other, scorns all definitions and specific concepts. If it expresses its conceptions of the Divine or Ultimate Reality at all it will do so in terms that seem not only paradoxical in nature but out and out contradictions.

When this Contemplative School of Buddhist philosophy first reached China it was quite true to its Indian origin and like typical Indian mysticism it held that man must turn away from the external world and seek the Divine or Ultimately Real within his own contemplative soul. However, in its historical development in China Dhyana, (Chinese Ch'an) Buddhism was influenced by the Taoist Nature Mysticism so that it saw the Divine or the Ultimately Real not only in man's own inner being, in good Indian style, but also in Nature, in good Chinese style. Or in other words, both man and Nature have alike their grounding in the Tao, the Way of the Universe. Or in terms of the Trikāya mentioned above, the Divine or Ultimate Reality is "Dharmakāya," "Law Body" or "Cosmic Body" of the Buddha. While as such it is the Unitary Ground of all existence and can be known in part as expressed or revealed in finite beings, in its full nature it forever transcends all definite human concepts.

This affinity of Ch'an (Japanese Zen) Buddhism of East Asia with the Taoist Nature Mysticism and the Japanese love of Nature is, perhaps, seen best in the great Sung painters and their Japanese disciples. In the quietness of monasteries located in the mountains far away from the noisy world some monk artists would feel their own souls attuned not only with the Eternal Buddha but also with the beauty of Nature that surrounded them. And this feeling of oneness within and without they would then try to express on paper or silk scroll with their brushes. The artist's brush seemed the best medium to express this communion with the Eternal for it only suggests rather than explicitly defines the True and the Real. If, however, one does resort to words in dealing with such matters, then it is best to speak in paradoxes, says this type of Buddhism, for only thus can one suggest the way that leads to the Eternal and at the same time leaves each individual free to fill in whatever details he sees fit. He should, nevertheless, realize that while he is free to do this to his own liking, others are equally free to fill in for themselves what suits their needs; and even more, that the Divine or the Ultimately Real forever transcends in its full nature all definitions and specific concepts.

A third and probably the most widely held conception of the Divine among Mahāyāna Buddhists is an essentially personalistic concept. This is seen most clearly in connection with *Amitābha* Buddha (Chinese, *Omito-fu*; Japanese *Amida Butsu*), the Buddha of Infinite Life and Light. Whatever the origin of the Amitābha faith may have been it seems a fact that beginning with about the first century of the Christian era it gradually gained its way, and as Mahāyāna Buddhism spread across East Asia it became more and more the dominant form, especially in the religion of the common people. And what is equally significant is that it is this type of Buddhism which continues to show real vitality in our day when other types have become rather decadent.

In some of the Mahāyāna scriptures it is the historic Buddha Sakyamuni who is seen as an exalted Eternal Buddha but in others he is only the one who taught his fellow men about Amitābha, the Buddha of Infinite Life and Light, and about the "Pure Land" or Paradise which Amitābha has prepared for all who rely upon him in simple faith for their eternal salvation. Thus it is no longer man that saves himself from this evil world by following in the way in which Sakyamuni had walked but rather that man is saved by the mercy and grace of the Eternal Buddha. In the famous Lotus Scripture we read: "Now are the Three Worlds (Past, Present, Future) mine and all living beings in the same are indeed my children. But great and many are their difficulties and it is I alone that can save them." And again it says: "If a man have seven children and one of them be ill, his love, though equal towards all, will go out in a special way to this one. Thus it is with the love of the *Nyorai*; though it is equal towards all beings, it hovers in a special manner over those who are in sin." In the so-called Three Paradise Scriptures which are so widely used by the worshippers of Amitābha the whole trend is much the same and man is taught to look to the Buddha of Infinite Life and Light for his salvation. "My mercy towards all ye heaven and earth-born creatures is deeper than the love of parents towards their children." Also in much of the literature other than the strictly canonical books, one finds an even greater emphasis on the centrality of Amitābha as the Eternal Buddha whose mercy and grace alone can save man.

Probably in no form of the multivarious Mahāyāna Buddhism does the God-concept seem more akin to that of the great Theistic Faiths than in the teachings of Shinran, the founder of the great Shin Sect of Japan. He not only held with other worshippers of *Amida Butsu* that it is the Eternal Buddha who saves all who in simple faith put their trust in his saving grace but that this faith itself is a gift of *Amida*. Many who worshipped *Amida* still felt it necessary to make sure of their salvation by observing certain rules of conduct and especially by repeating over and over again the prayer, *Namu Amida Butsu*, "I adore Thee, Amida Buddha," but Shinran laid the emphasis rather on the sufficiency of a sincere faith which leaves to the Divine Will the outcome. Good works are not a means of earning one's salvation. They are only an expression of gratitude for the heavenly gift. "Whether we are saved because our sins have been blotted out or not we do not know; it is as *Amida* has ordained. We have nothing to do with it; we have but to believe." It may be that Shinran's followers have carried the conception of divine grace to an extreme but certainly in this type of Buddhism one does meet with a conception of both human nature and of the Divine which is very different from that of the Founder of the Buddhist Faith and which is much more like the conceptions of the great Theistic Faiths.

What this faith in Amida, the Buddha of Infinite Life and Light, can mean to the pious Buddhist may be seen best, perhaps, in the following statements. These are not statements by philosophers but by ordinary believers.

"I am weak and sinful, and have no hope in myself; my hope is all in Amida Buddha. I believe him to be the Supreme Being. Because of the wickedness of man, and because of human sorrow, Amida Buddha became incarnate and came to earth to deliver man; and my hope and the world's hope is to be found in his suffering love. He has entered humanity to save it; and he alone can save. He constantly watches over and helps all who trust him. I am not in a hurry to die, but I am ready when the time comes; and I trust that through the gracious love of Amida Buddha I shall enter into the future life which I believe to be a state of conscious existence, and where I shall be free from sorrow. I believe that he hears prayer, and that he has guided me thus far, and my hope is only in his suffering love."

The second statement is found in a letter written from a sick-bed to a friend and reads as follows:

"I have been ailing for several days past, and believing my sickness to be a messenger of death I am filled with joy, trusting myself entirely to His mercies.... The manifestation of the *Tathagata* (Amida) is the earnest and pledge to us of our entrance into Paradise. Why should we doubt?... Should my sickness change for the worse, I shall never see you again in this life. But I shall, of a certainty, see once more, in the Pure Land, all those who are partakers with me in the faith I have in Amida."

In such statements of faith there are some expressions which have a Christian ring and there is no doubt but that in recent years Buddhists have felt the impact of Christianity and other Western influences but the fact remains that the worship of *Amitābha* as the Buddha of Infinite Life and Light is found in some of the older Mahāyāna scriptures which antedate any possible Christian influence. In fact, this personalistic conception of the Divine in Mahāyāna Buddhism runs more or less parallel with similar conceptions in Hinduism. Just as Mahāyāna Buddhism in its Trikāya doctrine speaks, on the one hand, of a "Compensation Body" or Buddha seen in terms of a supreme and perfect Personal Being and, on the other hand, of a "Law Body," or Buddha thought of in terms of the Absolute which is beyond all definitions or human concepts, so Hindu philosophers, as we saw above, spoke of a "Lower Brahma" and a "Higher Brahma," the former being defined in personalistic terms suited for the common man who needs a person-to-person relationship with his God, while the latter stands for the philosopher's Absolute or Ultimate Reality which is beyond all definitions and concepts.

But whatever may have been the origin of the Amitābha type of Buddhism it is true that in it we have on the whole a concept of the Divine which is often not unlike the God-concept in the great Theistic Faiths. Amitābha is the Buddha of Infinite Life and Light, exalted far above man at his best and noblest. Even those who have been saved in Amitābha's "Pure Land" and who are thus free from the evils and limitations of the earthly life, can not be compared with him or spoken of as Buddhas in anything like the same sense in which Amitābha is the Buddha of Infinite Life and Light. They are rather "Saints" who depend upon the Eternal Buddha for their life of bliss. Other types of Mahāyāna Buddhism may still speak of men becoming Buddhas by attaining full enlightenment as the historic Sakyamuni has done but this type of Buddhism tends to assign man a more modest role just because it has a more worthy conception of the Divine. This comes clearly to light in the famous Japanese tenth century work entitled "Collected Essays on Birth into Paradise" which has been widely used by Buddhists and which has made real for them the heavenly life in much the same way as Dante has done for many Christians. This pictures the heavenly life as one in which the saved pass from one state of bliss into another in an ever ascending scale. The higher levels of bliss are described as "the bliss of beholding the Buddha and hearing the Law;" "the bliss of making offerings to the Buddha according to one's heart's desire;" and finally, "the bliss of making progress in the way of the Buddha." In other words, Amitābha is so infinitely exalted above man that even after man has entered the higher levels of the heavenly life his highest "reach exceeds his grasp" and he can thus ever look forward to "the bliss of making progress in the way of the Buddha."

Now that we have pointed out this personalistic conception of the Divine in the Amitābha type of Buddhism and said that in many ways it is not unlike the God-concept in the great Theistic Faiths we must next point out some real differences.

One major difference is that even though Amitābha is seen as the Buddha of Infinite Life and Light who by his grace saves man in his eternal land of bliss he is never spoken of as the Creator of the universe. Where in the great Theistic Faiths it is held that in the beginning was God and that God created the world and sustains it with his power and guides it with his wisdom, the worshippers of Amitābha make no such claim for him. In this respect they, like other types of Buddhists, rather take the universe as given data and do not pretend to know how it came to be or how it will evolve or come to an end. They rather accept the Indian conception of Cosmic cycles through which the universe passes from a state of the Void, into one in which it becomes inhabited by numerous finite beings which are more or less self-existent or mutually determining and which after a long period of development begin to deteriorate and then finally pass back into the Void again. During the period in which the cosmos is inhabited by various finite beings some are humans and super-human beings and among these some may achieve enlightenment and become ideal, perfect personal beings or Buddhas who pass into Nirvana or the Nirvana state which is above all else a state of freedom, i.e., free from all the evils and limitations of this world. And so in the very basic scriptures of Amitābha Buddhism, Amitābha himself is pictured as having first been a human being who finally attained enlightenment and thus became first the *Bodhisattva Dharmakara* and who as such made his famous vow that he would not enter the bliss and freedom of Nirvana until he had prepared his "Pure Land" or Paradise for all who in simple faith put their trust in him. "In obtaining Buddhahood I shall not enter into perfect enlightenment (Nirvana) until all creatures of the Ten Regions (This World) who wish sincerely to be born into my country (Paradise) or who practice tenfold meditation shall have been born there." If it be asked when *Dharmakara* lived, the answer is that it was some ten *kalpas* ago or in the infinite past. A *kalpa* is the length of time required for the cosmos to pass through one of its cycles mentioned above, and according to some such a cosmic cycle requires 1,334,000,000 years. As *Dharmakara* became the Buddha *Amitābha* ten *kalpas* ago he is indeed more nearly eternal than any cosmic cycle but even so he is not seen as the creative source of the cosmos itself. As we said in connection with the *Trikāya* doctrine, *Amitābha* is a form of the *Sambhogakaya*, "Compensation Body," i.e., Buddha seen as an ideal personal being; but even though he is the "Buddha of Infinite Life and Light" he is not the creator of the cosmos or the Ultimate Ground of all Existence. Only *Dharmakāya*, "Law Body" or "Cosmic Body" stands for the Ultimate or Absolute, but Buddha in that sense is not a supreme Personal Being in any such way as we have in the God-concept of the great Theistic Faiths. He is rather beyond all concepts which the finite mind of man can formulate.

To be sure, Christian theologians, as we pointed out above, have also from time to time stressed the thought that God in his full being transcends every human concept and that therefore any personalistic conception, however lofty and satisfying, is likewise too limiting. They have, therefore, resorted to such abstractions as "Being," "Pure Being," "Being as such," "Being and Non-being" or other paradoxical expressions. It is, of course, true that often the personalistic conception of the divine is all too anthropomorphic and that there is room for a conception that points in the direction of the Super-Personal in the sense that God in his full being forever transcends our highest and noblest conception of personality, but there is the danger that in this very attempt to reach a super-personal concept one lapses into the sub-personal or to a conception which is so vague that it ceases to have any real meaning.

Another major way in which the conception of the Buddha Amitābha differs from the God-concept of the great monotheistic faiths is that even though Amitābha is regarded as the Buddha of Infinite Life and Light he is not the One and Only Buddha but must share his glory with other Buddhas, for even the devotees of Amitābha agree with other Buddhists that there are many Buddhas, some would say "as numerous as the grains of sand on the banks of the sacred Ganges." Some devotees of Amitābha would give this belief in innumerable Buddhas a sort of Pantheistic interpretation as when Rennyo, a leading member of the Shin Sect says: "As the body called *Namu Amida Butsu* includes all Gods, Buddhas and Bodhisattvas, and everything good and every good work, what is the use of worrying your mind about various works and things good?" But he then goes on to say that the pious believer in Amida, nevertheless, "worships the deities worshipped by others. Every God and Buddha worshipped by man deserves reverence and worship. Speaking from the standpoint of human expediency, reverence and worship must not be neglected, and much less should the believer in the *Nyorai (Amida)* neglect this duty of mankind."

Thus even in this type of Buddhism with its lofty conception of Amida as the Buddha of Infinite Life and Light and which is in some ways like the great Theistic Faiths in its conception of the Divine there are nevertheless these differences which we have just pointed out. It should, perhaps, be added that undoubtedly many modern Buddhists, especially in Japan, do think of Amida more and more in terms that are like the God-concept of the monotheistic faiths while, on the other hand, Buddhist philosophers and some Christian theologians are not too far apart in their views when they stress the thought that "the Divine Mystery" in all its fullness and true being forever transcends man's highest conception even though a personalistic conception, couched in terms of man's experience on the loftiest levels of his spiritual life, is the most adequate for vital religion.

Another Celestial or Eternal Buddha rather prominent in Mahāyāna Buddhism is *Vairocana*. While he is spoken of in more or less personalistic terms there is little of that close personal relationship between him and the believer that one finds in the Amitābha Faith. In fact, *Vairocana* is more a personification of Absolute Truth which can be apprehended only by the fully enlightened but which illumines all finite minds and, like the rays of a central sun, gives light and life to all creatures. *Vairocana* or *Virocana* is really a Sanskrit title for the sun and is translated into Chinese and Japanese by characters meaning "Great Sun Buddha." On the other hand, *Vairocana* is seen also as the dynamic source and Ultimate Reality from which all finite beings spring and to which they ultimately return. When this thought is stressed we have really a form of Pantheism and also the thought that all men have the "Buddha Nature" as the core of their true being and therefore can become Buddhas when fully enlightened. Not only human beings have this "Buddha Nature" but all beings, or as it is put more graphically, "In every particle of dust there dwells a Buddha."

Vairocana is sometimes linked with four other celestial Buddhas into a pentad in which he is the central figure while the other four rule each over one of the four points of the compass. These five so-called *Dhyana* Buddhas, "Buddhas of Contemplation" have been produced by the contemplation of *Adi-Buddha*, the Original Buddha Spirit. This line of thought seems to be an attempt to state in Buddhist terminology the belief in the Unitary Ground of all existence. It was, however, never held very widely for the more generally held view among Mahāyāna Buddhists was expressed in the *Trikāya* doctrine mentioned above and especially in the *Dharmakāya* concept or Buddha seen as the "Law of all things." As such, the Eternal Buddha is not a personal being but is either super-personal or beyond all concepts of the finite human mind.

We must add a few paragraphs regarding the God-concept in Hinayāna Buddhism which is the type that prevails in Ceylon and in the South East Asian lands.

This is seen best by comparing the Hinayāna views with Mahāyāna's *Trikāya*, "Three Bodies" doctrine. Hinayāna accepts unhesitatingly the first of the three, the *Nirmanakāya* "Accommodated Body" or Buddha seen in terms of human life. It honors the historic founder of Buddhism as the man who in his own strength achieved true enlightenment and who taught others the way of deliverance from this evil world. It agrees also that the historic Buddha in his enlightenment attained the highest level of a personal being and as such entered Nirvana or the Nirvana state. However, since Nirvana is the great Void any being that has entered this state can no longer be spoken of in terms of human experience, not even that attained on the highest levels of spiritual experience. Thus while the Buddha is believed to continue to exist and while the Nirvana state is not an absolute Void, he nevertheless has become very remote and Hinayāna Buddhism has thus little or nothing to say about his continuing spiritual presence with the believer or about any help coming from him in any such way as is found in Mahāyāna Buddhism, especially the type which centers on Amitābha, the Buddha of Infinite Life and Light.

Just because the Buddha in his Nirvana State seems now so remote is one reason why the average adherent of Hinayāna Buddhism looks for help more to other beings who seem more real and who play a more positive role in his life. It should be remembered that original Buddhism believed in the existence of innumerable finite beings ranging in nature from the lowest sub-human up through the human and super-human levels. Further, it was held that all these beings are under the Karmaic Law so that they may move upward or downward in this scale of beings depending upon what type of life they lived in their various incarnations. Only if they moved upward could they approach and finally enter Nirvana or the Nirvana State from which there is no return to this evil world. Now Hināyāna Buddhists on the whole continue to hold this view with fewer modifications than is the case with Mahāyāna Buddhists. Every man must work out his own salvation and there is no help coming to him from the Buddha in his Nirvana State except such help as comes from the truth he taught or the example he set while still in this world. The Hināyāna Buddhist, therefore, turns first of all for the kind of help that is available in the teachings and lives of the monks who are sup- posedly walking in the way of the Master and are teaching the truth he taught. The common believer, therefore, accepts the monk as his teacher and supports him with his alms believing that in doing this he will reap his reward, a reward which not only improves his present condition but also brings him one step further on the road that leads to his ultimate goal, or Nirvana.

The Hinayāna Buddhist, however, sees the goal as being a long way off and believes that before he can reach it he has to pass through many rebirths into this present world. There is little in Hināyāna Buddhism about achiev- ing enlightenment suddenly or through an intuitive flash of illumination. Since the road is long and progress is necessarily slow the believer must make his terms not only with his fellow men but also with other finite be- ings, especially with the various spirits, both sub-human and super-human, both evil and good spirits which he believes have more or less to do with his own life and destiny. In other words, in Hināyāna Buddhism the common believer has still much to do with the spirits and gods of the age-long Ani- mistic and Polytheistic faiths. This holds more or less also in Mahāyāna Buddhism though in the latter these lesser spiritual beings are usually sub- ordinated to a Supreme Being or seen as local manifestations of the Supreme Power or Powers. Thus when one would speak of the God-concept in Hina- yāna Buddhism one must include not only the Buddha or Buddhas existing in the Nirvana State and who are so remote and beyond all human concepts as to their true nature, but also of the various spirits which are believed to determine in a large measure man's actual life as he must live it from day to day.

There is one further word about the Hinayāna conception of the Divine which should be noted if one would have a more complete picture. It is in regard to the Nirvana concept as such. As we said above, Nirvana is spoken of as the great Void, but it is not an Absolute Void. It is, in fact, the truly

Ultimate for the Hinayāna Buddhist and as such is more or less commensu-rate with the Divine in other major religions. The very fact that according to Hinayāna Buddhism man can enter Nirvana or the Nirvana State only through the cultivation of the highest moral and spiritual qualities, would indicate that in so far as we can have any definite conception of Nirvana it must be in terms of man's spiritual life on its highest levels but this concep-tion, the Hinayāna Buddhist will add, must be held as only provisionally true since Nirvana or the Nirvana State is forever beyond any and every concept the mind of man can have. In fact, in Hinayāna the nature of Nirvana or the Nirvana State seems even more transcendental than is the *Dharmakāya,* the Cosmic Law or Law Body in Mahāyāna Buddhism which we saw was the third conception under which Buddha might be spoken of. The reason for this is that the concept of Nirvana as the Great Void derives largely from that characteristic Indian view which regards the things of this world as either illusory or as so incurably evil that they can in no way stand even provisionally for the Divine and Ultimate Reality. On the other hand while the Trikāya doctrine of Mahāyāna Buddhism is also Indian in origin it nevertheless had its major developments in East Asian lands where the natural world is regarded not only as more or less real but also as essentially good so that *Dharmakāya* can more naturally be the Ultimate Ground of all beings, both spiritual and physical, even though in its full nature it forever transcends all powers of the finite mind to comprehend.

While such God-concepts may seem all too vague to be of real help in vital religion it might be well to remember that some Christian mystics, with all their inherited belief in God as the Creator and Sustainer of the world and with all the definitely personalistic God-concept, nevertheless at times spoke of the *via negativa* as the best way leading to an understanding of the Divine or union with Divine Being. These various ways of stressing the transcendency of God may at least be a reminder to the complacent theist that he not belittle God by picturing Him all too much in terms of his own little human image however much a personalistic God-concept may be not only the most helpful but also the most nearly true.

A: VI THE GOD-CONCEPT IN CHINESE RELIGION

CHINA has for centuries been accustomed to think of religion in terms of its *San-Chiao,* "Three Religions," namely, the native Confucianism and Taoism and the imported Buddhism. That is to say, the religion of the Chinese peo-ple as a whole has been more or less of a blending of these "Three Religions;" and furthermore, especially in the religion of the masses, there has always

been a strong admixture of primitive religions whether they nominally professed to be Confucianists, Taoists, Buddhists or what not. It is, therefore,
to be expected that when one deals with the God-concept in Chinese religion one will find it to be quite varied and frequently a strange admixture
of elements that defy all attempts at harmonization.

The oldest and at the same time one of the most persistent God-concepts
is the belief in innumerable spirits, both good spirits (*shen*) and evil spirits
(*Kwei*) with which man has a close intercourse and which in one way or
another shape his life and destiny for good or evil. This conception of the
superhuman world was central in China's ancient religion as this is so clearly
indicated in the numerous bone and tortoise-shell inscriptions found near
the city of An Yang and dating from the Shang dynasty. But while this belief
in innumerable spirits is the very core of China's ancient religions and while
China has since those early days developed its more mature conceptions of
human life and man's relationship to the Divine or Ultimate Reality in Confucianism, Classical Taoism and Mahāyāna Buddhism, this primitive type
of the God-concept has persisted down to the present day and constitutes a
vital aspect of the religion of the Chinese people.

The second major fact about the God-concept in Chinese religion is that
even in pre-Confucian times China had developed other and more worthy
concepts of the Divine, and these have in turn found varying expressions in
Confucianism, Taoism and Chinese Buddhism. Thus in the older literature
such as the *Shih-Ching*, "Book of Odes" and the *Shu-Ching*, "Book of History,"
one finds in addition to the belief in innumerable spirits—nature spirits and
ancestral spirits—a trend towards what might be called Monarchical Polytheism in which *Shang-Ti*, "Supreme Ruler" or "Supreme Ancestor," and
T'ien, "Heaven," are seen as Supreme Beings to which the various nature and
ancestral spirits are more or less subordinated. The term *T'ien* is used more
frequently than the term *Shang-Ti*. Some times the two are used together as
in the phrase *Huang T'ien Shang-Ti*, "Imperial Heaven Supreme Ruler."
Then again the two terms are used interchangeably in the same context.
Undoubtedly the term *Shang-Ti* is more personalistic than the term *T'ien* and
comes nearer in meaning to a theistic conception of the Divine. So much is
this the case that some of the early Christian missionaries who believed that
man's original religion was monotheistic maintained that the worship of
Shang-Ti was a monotheistic faith. This would, however, be an overstatement of the case for while *Shang-Ti* is a rather personalistic God-concept,
Shang-Ti is seldom, if ever, thought of as the creator or ultimate source of the
universe in any such way as the God of the monotheistic faiths. And one

might add that *Shang-Ti* is more of a personification of the power in things rather than a personal Supreme Being who creates and sustains them.

As we said above, the term *T'ien,* "Heaven" was used more frequently than the term *Shang-Ti,* "Supreme Ruler," in pre-Confucian religion and that was even more the case with Confucius and subsequent Confucianism. It was used, however, with varying meanings as Y.L. Fung points out. (History of Chinese Philosophy). He lists five different meanings: (1) Heaven as the sky in apposition to the earth, as in the expression *T'ien-Ti,* "Heaven and Earth." (2) Heaven as a ruling or presiding power, as in the phrase, *Huang T'ien Shang-Ti,* "Imperial Heaven Supreme Ruler." (3) Heaven as equivalent to the concept *Ming,* "Fate or Decree," as found in the statement by Mencius when he says, "As to the accomplishment of a great deed, that is with Heaven." (4) A naturalistic Heaven corresponding more or less to the Western use of the term "Nature." (5) Heaven as the Moral Order. Of these five usages of the term "Heaven" the second and the fifth, namely, Heaven as the Ruling Power or Law of the Universe and Heaven as the Moral Order which sets the norm for man's conduct, are the more characteristic in the Confucian classics and in much of subsequent Confucian thought.

As to what Confucius himself thought about the Divine there is a difference of opinion among modern scholars. Many hold that he had practically nothing to say on the subject and that Confucianism is really not a religion but only a system of ethics. In support of this view they quote certain passages from the *Lun Yu,* "Annalects," such as the following: "To devote oneself earnestly to one's duty to humanity, and while respecting the spirits, to keep away from them, may be called wisdom." (Lun Yu VI, 20)*. "When still unable to do your duty to men, how can you do your duty to the spirits.... Not yet understanding life how can you understand death." (Lun Yu XI. 11 Fung).

Now there is no doubt that Confucius was above all else interested in ethical values and ideals. He had much to say on the problem of man's relationship to his fellowmen. It is also true that he had comparatively little to say about metaphysical matters; at least not in the characteristic language of religion. But, on the other hand, is it equally true that Confucius regarded ethical values and ideals as grounded not simply in human nature as such but rather in the superhuman realm, in "Heaven" or Ultimate Reality. In

*See "History of Chinese Philosophy by Y.L. Fung translated into English by Derk Bodde.

E

fact, he sometimes spoke of the "decrees of Heaven" in a way that is not unlike in meaning to "the Will of God" in the great Theistic Faiths. He was sure that no man could achieve his highest goal unless he ordered his life in accordance with the "decrees of Heaven," for as he says in the closing chapter of the *Lun Yu*, "Without recognizing the ordinances of Heaven, it is impossible to be a superior man." (XX, 3)★ Speaking of his progress he said, "At fifty, I knew the decrees of Heaven." (Lun Yu II. LV. 4 Legge). Furthermore it seems clear that by "Heaven" or the "decrees of Heaven" he meant more than an impersonal Moral Order of the Universe. Thus when misunderstood by others we find him crying out: "Alas! there is no one that knows me." And when his disciple asked him, "What do you mean by saying that no one knows you?" he replied, "I make no complaint against Heaven nor blame men, for though my studies are lowly my mind soars aloft. And that which knows me, is it not Heaven." (Lun Yu IV, 37, 1-2 Fung). Again we read: "If Heaven had wished to let this cause of truth perish, then I, a future mortal, should not have got such a relation to that cause. While Heaven does not let the cause of truth perish, what can the people of K'wang do to me." (Lun Yu IX, 5.3 Legge). He was even ready to let Heaven be the judge of his conduct. "Wherein I have done improperly, may Heaven reject me. May Heaven reject me!" (Lun Yu VI, 26 Legge). On another occasion when asked, "Is it better to pay court to the god of the hearth than to the god of the hall?" Confucius replied: "He who sins against Heaven has no place left where he may pray." (Lun Yu III. 13. 1-2 Fung).

These and similar statements would indicate that Confucius was more religious than some of his modern interpreters hold and that by "Heaven" he meant more than an impersonal Moral Order and something not so unlike to the God of Ethical Monotheism. Even the passages quoted above that according to some prove their theory that Confucius had no interest in the superhuman world and was merely concerned with human ethical relationships, indicate that he believed in the continued existence of ancestral spirits for he speaks of "respecting the spirits." He probably did not worship these ancestral spirits or the various nature spirits, as did the Chinese masses, but he showed due reverence towards them and even encouraged offering sacrifices to the ancestral spirits. He evidently regarded such observances as essential for cultivating the spirit of filial piety which was such a big factor in giving stability to the family system and the whole social structure. When

*Translation by James Legge.

asked what constituted true filial piety he replied: "That parents, when alive, should be served according to propriety; that, when dead, they should be buried according to propriety; and that they should be sacrificed to according to propriety." (Lun Yu II. 5.3 Legge).

But whatever Confucius' attitude towards the common belief in ancestral and nature spirits might have been, that he believed in a moral order which was grounded not simply in human nature but in Ultimate Reality and that his use of the term T'ien, "Heaven," sometimes had the import of a Supreme Moral Being that knows and rules over human life is at least a tenable interpretation. Granted that his conception of T'ien was less personalistic than the God-concept in the great theistic religions, it must, nevertheless, be said that it had rather close affinity with such a concept of the Divine and Ultimate Reality.

Confucius' greatest disciple, Mencius (372–289), was interested primarily in ethical values and ideals. He, too, like his master, saw these grounded not simply in human nature but in "Heaven." In fact, Mencius makes a sharp contrast between those who see ethical values grounded merely in human nature and those who recognize "Heaven" as the true ground when he says: "The men of antiquity cultivated their nobility of Heaven and the nobility of men came to them in its train. The men of the present day cultivate their nobility of Heaven in order to seek for the nobility of men, and when they have obtained that, they throw away the other:—their delusion is extreme. The issue is simply this, that they must lose that nobility of men as well." (Bk. VI, Pt. I, Ch. XVI, 2-3 Legge). In other words, Mencius says that one can not achieve a true nobility of character unless one realizes that the moral life has its ultimate grounding in "Heaven." And this belief must be held not simply as a means to achieving a worthy human end but as a basic belief in what is ultimate. That by "Heaven" Mencius meant more than an impersonal moral order of the universe and something more like a Supreme Moral Being ruling over human life, may be seen in the following statement: "There is an appointment for everything. A man should receive submissively what may be correctly ascribed thereto. Therefore, he who has the true idea of what is Heaven's appointment will not stand beneath a precipitous wall." (Bk, VII, Pt. I. Ch. II, 1-2 Legge). That is to say, man should realize that his life is under divine control or guidance but that he must use his good sense and not "tempt Providence."

The statement by Mencius that "Heaven does not speak" is frequently interpreted to mean that he had no real belief in "Heaven" as a divine power interested in man's life, but the context in which this passage occurs shows most decidedly that he believed "Heaven" speaks through human history and that the rulers of China hold their power only as "Heaven" decrees.

Now while both Confucius and Mencius at times used the term "Heaven" in a way notunlike the God-concept in Ethical Monotheism it must be added that they spoke of "Heaven" more frequently in a less personalistic way and as standing simply for the moral order or in a more general way for the Law of things, whether things spiritual or things physical. It was, however, the Confucian philosopher Hsun-Tzu (298?–238?) who emptied the term "Heaven" or the phrase "Decrees of Heaven" of their religious content and gave them an out and out naturalistic interpretation. Thus he says that man can know natural phenomena but nothing about their metaphysical or noumenal grounding. "The fixed stars make their round; the sun and moon alternately shine; the four seasons succeed one another.... We do not see the cause of these occurrences, but we do see their effect.... The result of all these changes are known, but we do not know the invisible source: this is what is called Heaven. It is only the sage who does not seek to know Heaven." (Hsun Tzu Ch. 17 Fong "History of Chinese Philosphy" 285). It should be noted that he does not deny the existence of "Heaven" as the Ultimate Reality from which all things come but he is quite agnostic on the matter and says the sage "does not seek to know Heaven." He recommends that man limit himself to what he can know and that he make use of the things in the natural world rather than speculate about the nature of Ultimate Reality or look for any help from the supernatural. And he sums it all up by saying: "Thus if a person neglects what man can do and thinks about Heaven, he fails to understand the nature of things."

Now while subsequent Confucianism did not altogether follow Hsun Tzu in his agnosticism and naturalistic interpretation it is true that it had comparatively little to say about "Heaven" or the "decrees of Heaven" except as standing for an impersonal moral order or more generally for the law of things. Confucianism thus became largely a fixed system of ethics grounded almost wholly in man's own nature and taking its norm not so much from "Heaven," as Confucius and Mencius had done, but from what had been the standards of human conduct in past generations. And we might add that since Confucianism had so little to say about the Divine the Chinese masses continued, on the one hand, to worship the innumerable nature and ancestral spirits, and, on the other hand, turned to Buddhism even though this extremely "other-worldly" Indian religion ran counter in many ways to the "this-worldly" Chinese temperament. But before we take up more fully these developments in Chinese religion let us turn next to Taoism, China's other major religion which from about the fourth century B.C. on down through the centuries was a major factor in the life of the Chinese people and see what it has to say about the Divine and superhuman world.

Taoism, of course, takes its name from the term *Tao* which is central in the nobler aspects of its teachings. The term *Tao* literally means "Way," and in early Chinese religion, i.e., before the rise of Taoism as a philosophy, it meant primarily "the way of man" or, in short, the norm of human conduct. However, in the *Tao-Te-ching* and the other major classics of early Taoism the term *Tao* has a more decidedly metaphysical meaning. To be sure, there are varying interpretations of the term even in classical Taoism just as we saw to be the case with the term *T'ien*, "Heaven" in Confucianism; and in later popular Taoism the meaning often differs so radically from the classical meanings that the two have really very little in common. But as we said above, *Tao* in the classics has a metaphysical meaning and stands above all else for Ultimate Reality which in its full nature is beyond all human comprehension and definitions but which is, nevertheless, the source from which all finite things come.

"There is a reality, formless yet perfect. Before Heaven and Earth came into being it existed. Without sound, without substance it stands alone without changing. It is all-pervading and unfailing. It may be regarded as the Mother of all things. We do not know its name but we call it the *Tao*. Attempting to give it some appellation we speak of it as Great." (*Tao-Te-ching* XXV).

"We look at it but do not see it and we call it the Invisible. We listen to it but do not hear it and we call it the Inaudible. We grasp at it but we can not touch it and we call it the Intangible. These three qualities elude our comprehension and hence we blend them into the One." (*Tao-Te-ching* XIV).

Any attempt to describe the real nature of this One and Absolute Reality must end in failure for it transcends all categories of human thought. As the opening chapter of the Tao-Te-ching puts it:

"The *Tao* that may be called *Tao* is not the invariable (or absolute) *Tao*. The names that can be named are not invariable (or absolutely descriptive) names. Non-being is the term given to that from which Heaven and Earth sprang. Being is the term given to the Mother that rears the ten thousand things. Of the invariable Non-being, we wish to see its secret essences. Of the invariable Being, we wish to see its borders. These two together we call the Mystery. It is the Mystery of Mysteries, the Doorway to all secret essences." (*Tao-Te-ching* I.).

"Heaven and Earth and the ten thousand things are produced from Being; Being is the product of Non-being." (*Tao-Te-ching* XL).

Thus while the *Tao* in its deepest nature is wholly transcendental and is therefore spoken of as Non-being, it is, nevertheless, seen as the source of all finite beings and so is spoken of as Being. Non-being and Being are therefore but two aspects of the *Tao*, the former being its nature as the Absolute or Ultimate Reality and the other its manifestations.

Now it is through the Being aspect of the *Tao* and especially through its manifestations in the so-called "ten thousand things" to which man himself belongs that we have at least some understanding of the *Tao*. But where in theistic religions man as a personal spiritual being is usually taken as the best key to an understanding of the Divine or Ultimate Reality and thus the Divine is seen in personalistic terms, in Taoism man, being just one of the "ten thousand things" or finite manifestations of the infinite *Tao*, is no more a key to unlock the mystery of the *Tao* in its full nature than any other finite being. In fact, man as a personal being is usually regarded as a temporary manifestation and as such is subject to changing into some other form of finite being which is equally a manifestation of the *Tao* and equally good. Thus Chuang-Tzu who did more than any other Taoist philosopher to popularize Taoist teachings says:

"To have attained to the human form is a source of joy. But in the infinite evolutions, there are myriads of other forms that are equally good. What an incomparable bliss it is to undergo these countless transitions!" (*Chuang-Tzu* VI.).

In short, then, while the Taoist philosopher sees in the *Tao* the Ultimate Reality and the source of all finite beings he does not think of it in terms of a Supreme Personal Being who with purposeful and creative activity produces, sustains and rules over all finite beings as is so characteristic of theistic religions. There is thus little of the typical theistic God-concept in classical Taoism and instead we have a sort of Naturalism, or rather a Nature Mysticism in which man feels himself somehow at one with Nature and accepts whatever may come to him or whatever may become of him in the "infinite evolutions" through which the *Tao* or Ultimate Reality manifests itself but which nevertheless is more than these manifestations and forever transcends man's powers of comprehension.

It should be noted that this Taoist Nature Mysticism differs somewhat from the typical Indian Mysticism (or the Mysticism found in connection with the great theistic religions). Where these latter usually seek a mystical union with the Divine or Ultimate Reality by turning inward and away from the external world or things material, Taoist Mystics usually seek union with Ultimate Reality by identifying themselves with the natural order in both its physical and spiritual aspects since they regard both aspects equally real and equally a manifestation of the *Tao*.

Now this conception of the *Tao* and man's relationship to it, or this feeling of man's oneness with Nature may satisfy man in certain moods. Perhaps on a beautiful Spring or Autumn day one may "commune with Nature" and rest content with being a part of it or dream about passing from one form of finite existence into another and finding all equally good, as Chuang-Tzu said. Such moods, however, do not last long and life's problems are such that man feels the need of "communing" with something a little more spiritual and personal. Nothing shows the inadequacy of the Taoist philosopher's interpretation of man's relationship to the Divine and Ultimate Reality more clearly than the history of Taoism itself. As a matter of fact, Taoism as a religion of the Chinese people, while not wholly ignoring the concept of the *Tao* as found in the great classics, has for centuries sought a more personalistic relationship with the Divine. The philosophers have been rather vague in what they had to say about the *Tao* and man's relationship to it. That is one reason why the Chinese people either continued to worship the innumerable spirits, both nature and ancestral spirits, or turned for help to the Divine beings of Mahāyāna Buddhism. Thus De Groot is not far wrong when in regard to this continuing worship of nature and ancestral spirits he says that it is "a cornerstone in the foundation of China's religion; it is a doctrine of the Chinese nation, a dogma, an axiom, an inveterate conviction, that the spirits exist, keeping up a most lively intercourse with the living—as intimate almost as that among men. In every respect the intercourse bears an active character. It brings blessings and evil as well, the spirits thus ruling effectually man's fate. From them man has everything to hope, but equally much to fear. As a natural consequence it is around the ghosts and spirits that China groups her religious acts with the sole intent to avert their wrath and the evil it brings and to insure their good will and help." (Religion of the Chinese, p. 32).

This may be an overstatement of the facts about Chinese religion as a whole, for there are other and more worthy concepts of the Divine and man's relationship to the Divine but it is true that this worship of nature spirits and deified humans has continued to be rather prominent from early times down to the present. Even in China's traditional State Religion such God-concepts are conspicuous. To be sure, there have been changes from time to time in this official religion but on the whole it may be said to have always been a sort of monarchial polytheism in which the world of spiritual beings is patterned after the Chinese social structure. Just as at the top of the governmental and social pyramid stood the emperor and below him in ever widening circles and steps were the various state, provincial, village officials and the common citizens so at the head of the superhuman and spiritual pyramid stood *Shang Ti*, "Supreme Ruler," or *T'ien*, "Heaven" and below these Supreme Beings were the various lesser nature spirits and ancestral spirits. Only the emperor was supposed to worship the Supreme Spirits such as the spirits of Heaven, Earth, Sun, Moon and Stars. He worshipped these officially rather than privately and in this worship he represented his people. State, provincial and village officials were supposed to worship the spirits of lesser objects of nature such as mountains and rivers while the average citizen worshipped only the household gods—the gods of the Gate, the Path, the Court and the Hearth. All Chinese, from the emperor down to the lowest citizen were expected to worship their respective ancestral spirits.

It should be added that this traditional State Religion with its gradations of gods naturally meant different things to different individuals. The average person probably took it all quite seriously and saw in these various spirits the powers that rule over man's life. Some of the more sophisticated probably did not take it at its face value but accepted it, or even fostered it, largely as an instrument of state or social control. In fact, in China, perhaps more than in any other land, religion has all too often been used as a mere instrument of state rather than standing in its own sovereign rights and as interpreting the Divine and man's relationship to the Divine.

As we stated above, the Chinese not only continued their age-old worship of nature and ancestral spirits but also turned to the divine beings of Mahāyāna Buddhism for help. In fact, one major reason why Buddhism finally won the allegiance of millions in China and other East Asian lands is just because it had more to say about man's relationship to the Eternal than the native religions. And Buddhism said this in differing ways, for according to its own theory of knowledge the truth about such matters must be formulated in terms suited to the particular level of intelligence of the person addressed. This principle applies especially when it comes to speaking of the Divine and man's relationship to the Divine or Ultimate Reality, for this in all its depths is ever beyond the powers of the finite mind to comprehend fully and even the most worthy conception can be only an approximation to the full truth. Because of this fact, Buddhism has always been quite tolerant of widely differing views regarding even the great essentials of religion and especially in regard to the conception of the Divine.

We have already given in the preceding chapter what the major variants of the God-concept in Buddhism have been as it made its conquests in China and Japan. It is, therefore, not necessary to do anything more here than add a few supplementary remarks.

The first is that Buddhism with its original Indian "other-worldly" emphasis had to restate its message to win the characteristically "this-worldly" minded Chinese. To be sure, as we have just stated above, Buddhism made its appeal to the Chinese and other East Asian peoples just because it had more to say about the Eternal and man as a citizen of eternity than the native religions, but even so it had to say this in terms that did greater justice to the realities of this world and the practical problems which man must face as a citizen of this world. This, of course, affected primarily what Buddhism had to say about the good life ideal but it also affected what it said about the Divine and man as a citizen of eternity. Thus in Chinese and other East Asian Buddhism one major variant of the God-concept is an essentially Pantheistic or Cosmotheistic concept. This concept is more characteristic of East Asian Buddhism than it ever could have been of Indian Buddhism just because Indian thinkers usually treated the natural world as being more or less illusory or as real only in a secondary sense while in Chinese thought in particular and in other East Asian thought generally the natural world is always seen as a part of the real world however much Ultimate Reality in all its fulness and true being may transcend human comprehension.

The second major God-concept which we mentioned in the preceding chapter, namely, that which is found in the Contemplative School of Mahā-yāna Buddhism is a sort of Mysticism which defies all definite concepts but which stresses a feeling of Oneness with the Eternal by turning inward and away from all the distractions of the external world or the world of sense perception. But in its Chinese and Japanese environment this became more and more a Nature Mysticism just because East Asian peoples normally regard the Natural World as part of the Real World even though they would agree that Ultimate Reality or the "Divine Mystery" transcends all that man experiences in his contact with the Natural World.

Again, the third major variant of the God-concept which we mentioned in the preceding chapter and which centers on Amitābha, the Buddha of Infinite Life and Light, became for the Chinese and other East Asian peoples a living reality cast in personalistic terms which man can understand on the highest levels of his own experience as a personal being just because these peoples were not content to let the Buddha disappear into the Great Void of Nirvana. To be sure, philosophers in Mahāyāna Buddhism also spoke of the

Nirvana State as the great Void or of Ultimate Reality in terms of vague abstractions or in paradoxes which to some may seem flat contradictions, but the conception of the Divine which gained real acceptance by the millions of East Asian peoples was an essentially personalistic concept even though the more intelligent realized that the Divine in all its true being transcends all that man experiences on the highest levels of his own finite being.

This insistence on thinking of the Divine in personalistic terms is seen also in the large role which the Bodhisattva concept played in East Asian Buddhism. Even Amitābha, the Buddha of Infinite Life and Light, or Vairocana, that other great Buddha of Mahāyāna Buddhism, seem rather remote however much they are thought of in personalistic concepts, and so many good Buddhists turn rather to one or another of the great Bodhisattvas associated with Amitābha, particularly to Kwanyin (Japanese, Kwannon) for help. In fact, millions of Buddhists see in this most popular Bodhisattva, often called "Goddess of Mercy," a divine being who is a sort of mediator between man and his highest God. They pray to Him or Her in much the same way as some pious Catholics pray to some saint or to the Virgin Mary.

To be sure, in all such attempts to picture the Divine in more realistic ways which are so characteristic of the religions of East Asia, and particularly in the religion of the masses in all lands including India, there is always the danger that the God-concept becomes all too closely patterned after man's own little image, as we have repeatedly said; but it at least has the merit of keeping the concept tied up with the real world in which man must live his life rather than having the concept fade out into vague abstractions or into an even vaguer mysticism which blots out all distinctions.

Now while the native religions of China and other East Asian peoples had their influence on Buddhism along the lines indicated above, Buddhism in turn had an even greater influence on these native religions. Not only did Taoism as a religion of the masses borrow heavily from Buddhism but even Confucianism in its Neo-Confucian form definitely shows Buddhist influences. Neo-Confucianism was in some ways an attempt on the part of Confucian thinkers to counteract the impact which Buddhism had made on Chinese life and thought; but this very attempt showed how much Buddhism was affecting their thinking. Above all else it compelled Confucian philosophers to give more thought to metaphysical problems than Confucianism had done in the past and especially to say more definitely what its own conception of the Divine or the Ultimate Reality is.

Neo-Confucianism thus had a good deal to say about its "Supreme Ultimate" and man's relationship to this. Just as among the Buddhists so among the Neo-Confucianists there were differing views on these fundamentals of religion. Chu Hsi (1130–1200), probably the most influential of the Neo-Confucianists, identified this "Supreme Ultimate" with the "Heaven" of the older Confucianism and maintained that Confucianism had nothing to learn from Buddhism in such matters. However, even he felt it necessary to say more about the Ultimately Real than traditional Confucianism had been doing. He made his approach to the problem through man's own nature as a thinking and rational being and he, therefore, spoke of the "Supreme Ultimate" as a sort of Universal Reason which is immanent in all things. "In every human mind," he wrote, "there is the knowing faculty; and in every thing, there is its reason." He went on to say that if man carried his investigations far enough, all things would become intelligible to him, for all things exist in accordance with rational laws, or they may be said to be an expression of, and to have their grounding in Reason as the "Supreme Ultimate." Chu Hsi did not speak of the "Supreme Ultimate" in personalistic terms other than may be implied by characterizing it as universal and immanent Reason.

It was Chu Hsi's contemporary, Lu-Chiu-yuan and even more Wang Yang-ming (1473–1529) that showed the greatest affinity with Buddhism in their views of what is ultimately real and man's relationship to that Reality. Like the philosophers of the Contemplative School in Buddhism they, too, held that man has an intuitive knowledge and that by a study of the mind rather than external nature he can know the true nature of Ultimate Reality. While they did not define this in personalistic terms they, nevertheless, held quite clearly that man's life is grounded in what is spiritual rather than in the physical and to that extent at least supported a concept of Ultimate Reality which is akin to the nobler concepts in Mahāyāna Buddhism and not unlike views held by some theologians and philosophers in the great Theistic Faiths.

A: VII THE GOD-CONCEPT IN JAPANESE RELIGION

SINCE JAPAN belongs to the great East Asia cultural sphere of which China was the center for centuries much in Japanese religion is merely a variant of what had been first developed in China. Like China, Japan has her so-called "Three Religions," two of which—Buddhism and Confucianism—came from China via Korea and direct, while the third is Japan's native religion, Shinto. With such widely differing religions constituting Japan's spiritual heritage, it is only natural that the concept of the Divine should be rather varied even though the "Three Religions" have been more or less merged over the centuries.

Shinto was originally a naive nature worship to which was added, probably under early Chinese influence, a form of ancestor worship. Any natural object or phenomenon which gave rise to a feeling of wonder, awe and fear was regarded as a *kami*, "deity." Likewise certain humans, such as great heroes and illustrious ancestors, were seen as so many *Kami*. Thus Shinto has traditionally spoken of its *Yao yorodzu no kami*, "800 myriads of gods" and Japan has truly been "the land of the gods." The very name Shinto means "the way of the gods." It was coined after Japan had come definitely under Chinese influence and was used to characterize Japanese religious life by contrasting it with China's spiritual heritage. Where China had its "Middle Way" of the Buddha and its *Tao*, "Way" of Taoist and Confucian thought, Japan had her "Way of the Gods."

After Japan had come definitely under the influence of the higher Chinese culture her political structure gradually evolved into a loosely organized monarchy and at the same time Japan's primitive religion with its innumerable deities and local cults began to evolve into a sort of monarchical polytheism. Thus the worship of *Amaterasu Omikami*, "the Heaven Shining Deity" tended to become more and more dominant, and while it did not replace other and lesser deities, the Sun Goddess nevertheless was being exalted above all other gods. In fact, as the worship of the Sun Goddess emerges into the light of history we find this chief Shinto deity regarded not only as a chief deity but also as the Divine ancestress of Japan's ruling family. It is this conception of the close relationship between the divine world and Japan's ruling family that has played such a big role in Japanese life down to the present day.

Now it is quite possible that if Japan's native religion had been left to its own resources after the initial impact of the higher Chinese culture it would have evolved more and more into a form of monarchical polytheism and then into an essentially monotheistic faith. This rather natural development did not, however, take place for the simple reason that after the sixth century the imported Buddhism began to be more and more the determining factor in Japan's spiritual development and after the twelfth century became not only the religion of the more enlightened but also of the masses. Naturally Buddhism brought in its train not only the higher culture of China but also its own varied conceptions of the Divine, especially the conceptions of Mahāyāna Buddhism which we discussed in Chapter V and to which the reader is referred for a fuller understanding of the God-concept in Japanese

religion. On the other hand, Buddhism with its characteristic Indian tolerance of differing views, including views of the divine, made room for some of
the more popular Shinto deities as so many local manifestations of Buddhist
divinities; for before Buddhism reached Japan it was already making its easy
compromises with the religion of the masses in the various lands through
which it had spread. Thus in Japan, too, Buddhism won its way by absorbing
the native religion and making it a part of its own comprehensive system.

But while Buddhism became Japan's dominant religion and for centuries
embraced Shinto in its all-inclusive fold it never succeeded in actually replac-
ing Shinto. In fact, some Japanese thinkers, out of pride in things Japanese,
began to reinterpret their ancient faith in terms that could be meaningful to
a people that had come so greatly under the influence of the imported Buddhist and Confucian philosophies and religious views. To be sure, in this
reinterpretation of the native faith much was borrowed from both Buddhism and Confucianism but it was nevertheless presented as the true meaning of Shinto conceptions of the Divine; and they even went so far as to
maintain that it was Buddhism that had borrowed from Shinto rather than
the reverse. Then finally in the 19th century Shinto reasserted itself by
breaking away from Buddhism and by forming out and out Shinto sects.
While all these developments in modern Shinto show more or less the influence of Buddhism and Confucianism some of them show also Christian
and other Western influences. This is as true in regard to the conception of
the Divine as in other matters. Thus the "myriads of gods" of traditional
Shinto have largely disappeared and while some remain in one form or
another there is nevertheless a strong trend towards either a Pantheistic or
a Theistic God-concept. At least four of the major modern Shinto sects are
virtually monotheistic in their conception of the Divine and some of the
others are showing trends in that direction.

But whatever may be the future of Shinto it is not likely that it will play
any large role in the modern world and it is not to be compared with the role
which Buddhism has played in the past and may continue to play in the
future, for Buddhism is, after all, one of the great World religions with which
even the modern world must reckon. The importance of Japan in this connection is the fact that it is Japanese Buddhism and particularly the Amitābha (Amida) type which in its conception of the Divine is most like the great
monotheistic faiths that is showing the greatest vitality and that may yet be
a big factor in shaping the life and destiny not only of the Japanese people
but also of other Asian peoples.

A: VIII SUMMARY STATEMENT OF GOD-CONCEPT

IT SHOULD be evident from what we have said thus far regarding the conception of the Divine in the major religions of mankind that this is indeed rather varied. While there are areas in which there is substantial agreement, there are also real differences. Even within what is nominally one and the same religion the God-concept is sometimes far from uniform. This is especially true in Indian religions and in the religions of East Asia with their characteristic tolerance of widely differing views even in the great essentials of religion such as the conception of the Divine.

Now this bewildering array of the God-concept can, perhaps, be more or less systematized and made less confusing by taking the personalistic God-concept of the great monotheistic faiths as a provisional norm. To be sure, there are some differences in the conception of the Divine even among these great monotheistic faiths but there is nevertheless a wide area of agreement. Furthermore, in other great religions which differ more or less in their conception of the Divine from the great monotheistic faiths there are definite trends towards a theistic view as we saw is the case in later Hinduism, in certain branches of Mahāyāna Buddhism and also in other East Asian religions. In a summary way one might say that the theistic view as held by the great monotheistic faiths is flanked on either side with God-concepts that differ from it more or less widely. On one side are the views found in the more primitive religions and which may well be designated as Pre-theistic views because they often tend to evolve in the direction of the theistic God-concept, especially when there is a rising level of intelligence among the adherents of such faiths. On the other side of the theistic God-concept are various views of the Divine which tend to move away from the theistic concept in search of what is felt to be a more adequate view and which therefore may be summarily spoken of as Post-theistic conceptions.

In the Pre-theistic conceptions of the Divine which we have illustrated in the religions of India and East Asia there is a wide range of views. On the lower levels there is the worship of certain natural phenomena and innumerable spirits, both semi-personalized nature spirits and deified humans. This belief in innumerable spirits and deities often evolves into a sort of organized polytheism or so-called Monarchical Polytheism according to which the lesser deities and spirits are seen as subordinated to some major deity though each lesser deity still retains control over its own limited sphere. This stage of development in the God-concept often evolves into a sort of Pantheism according to which the lesser deities which formerly were seen as controlling their own limited sphere now become just so many local manifestations of the Divine. These local manifestations of the Divine are seen in more or less personalistic terms while the all-inclusive Divine Being or Reality is not further defined. Or again, the evolution of the God-concept may result in what is virtually a Theistic conception according to which the Divine is seen in ideal personalistic terms; and what were formerly lesser deities become mere messengers or possibly temporary incarnations of the One Supreme Being.

It should, however, be observed that in Indian and East Asian religions, even when the God-concept becomes virtually Theistic so that man turns to One Supreme Being conceived of in personalistic terms for help, such a Supreme Being is seldom if ever regarded as One who creates, sustains and controls all things in any such way as one finds in the great Monotheistic Faiths. Indian and East Asian religions rather accept the universe as a given fact; or if they attempt to account for its origin, and as being under the power or control of the Divine, they think of the Divine in terms which are best designated as Post-Theistic just because they reject the Theistic view as being philosophically inadequate however much it may be most satisfying to the common believer who needs a person-to-person relationship between himself and his deity.

Now it is these Post-Theistic conceptions of the Divine that need further elucidation than we have given them, for they represent a continuing problem in religion, particularly for those who think seriously about "the Divine Mystery."

There are really two major types of the Post-Theistic God-concept or mode of the God-consciousness, namely, various types of Mysticism and various forms of Pantheism or Cosmotheism.

In Mysticism one can hardly speak of a God-concept for the typical mystic holds that "the Divine Mystery" in its full being forever transcends all human concepts. It is therefore more correct to speak of "the mode of the God-consciousness." What the mystic experiences in his awareness of the Divine can be known according to the mystic only to those who have had the mystical experience. However when the mystic seeks to communicate to others the content of his mystical experience he must inevitably resort to concepts derived from man's ordinary spiritual experience.

There can be little doubt but that the typical mystic's approach to the Divine Mystery is psycho-centric. It is away from the things of sense and the outer world and seeks to penetrate to the inner nature of man's own spiritual being in the hope of finding in it a depth of being which is at the same time beyond the merely human, the depth where the human becomes the divine, or at least the fore-court of the divine. "Sit in the center of thyself and thou seest what is and shall be," says a Sufi mystic. And Catherine of Sienna, though a Christian who presumably accepted as valid God's revelation of himself in Jesus Christ, wrote, "If thou wouldst arrive at a perfect knowledge of Me, the Eternal Truth, never go outside thyself."

While the typical mystic usually seeks the true and Ultimate Reality within his own spiritual being rather than in the outer world and while virtually all mystics insist that the Divine Mystery in its full nature is beyond all human concepts one can, nevertheless, say that there are really two major types of mysticism, namely Personal Mysticism and Impersonal Mysticism.

In Personal Mysticism as exemplified by most Christian mystics the mode of the God-consciousness does not run counter to the personalistic conception of the Divine. Its major emphasis is rather on man's direct awareness of and ecstatic communion with God. To be sure, even Christian mystics characteristically insist that God is infinitely more than what can be expressed by any personalistic concepts or what man experiences on the highest levels of spiritual insight. But this "infinitely more" which the mystic experiences in his ecstatic visions is rather in the direction of an all-comprehensive truth, an all-compelling purity and goodness, and a loveliness of spirit which lifts the human personality above its ordinary experiences and limitations. This type of mysticisms would never reject the personalistic conception of the Divine in favor of any impersonal or sub-personal concept. Even when there is at times a tendency to flirt, as it were, with the irrational this is largely a way of saying that man can not comprehend the full nature of God even with his highest and noblest conceptions rather than that the irrational is the key. And certainly no Christian mystic has suggested that God is to be seen better in the non-moral or the immoral than in the moral, for the words of Jesus, "Blessed are the pure in heart for they shall see God" have always been normative for the most pronounced Christian mystic. And if Christian art is to be trusted it would seem that the beautiful rather than the grotesque or the ugly has ever been regarded as appropriately associated with the Divine. These external expressions of the beautiful are seen as having their full purpose only as they help man in his quest for "the beauty of holiness."

Thus it should be clear that in characteristic Christian mysticism, and we might add, in the mysticism associated with the other great theistic faiths, there is little that runs counter to a worthy personalistic God-concept. It is rather a way of stressing the possibility of the finite human being coming into a close and intimate relationship with his God. However close this relationship may become in the mystic's ecstatic experience it apparently never quite obliterates the distinction between the experiencing human self and the Divine and Eternal Self.

There is, however, another type of Mysticism, namely, Impersonal Mysticism, which rejects the personalistic God-concept as being too limiting or cast too much in man's own little image to express adequately the true nature of the Divine Mystery. While this type of mysticism is equally psycho-centric with Personal Mysticism it nevertheless attempts to pass through this center to a reality beyond and which is so wholly other in its true nature that it can not be defined in personalistic terms. Impersonal Mysticism does not reject the personalistic God-concept on grounds that the physical cosmos is also an aspect of reality, as is the case with Pantheism which we shall consider below, for Impersonal Mysticism is as psycho-centric as Personal Mysticism is and the outer world is the first obstacle to be overcome in the quest for the Divine and the ultimately real. All sense experience and concepts built up from sense perception must be disposed of as much as possible largely by reducing the concrete details of actual sense contacts to abstractions and vague universals thus freeing the mind from all limiting distractions. In man's moral experience likewise man must pass beyond what in his personal relations with his fellow-men is the right and the good to what is Absolute and which as such is really "beyond good and evil." Whether in the realm of the true, the good or the beautiful, this type of mystic may use man's ordinary experience in these fields as a sort of ladder on which he climbs upward and then from the upper rung he leaps with ecstatic vision into the realm of the Divine and experiences what is so wholly other from man's ordinary experience that it can not be expressed in terms of the latter. However, when this type of mystic does attempt to communicate to others who have not had this experience he must naturally resort to concepts that have meaning to them even though such concepts do not adequately express what he has found in his mystical experience. He, therefore, resorts to a terminology which though comprehensive in meaning is also quite vague. The Divine is, therefore, spoken of as "Being" and without any qualifying adjectives such as "Personal" or even "Supreme." Even the term "Being" is often regarded as too limiting and so the Divine Mystery is spoken of as both "Being and Non-Being," or by other terms of affirmation and negation. It might seem that such terms cancel each other and it must be admitted that at times the negation seems like a flat contradiction

F

of what is contained in the affirmation. Usually, however, the negation is intended to convey "the much more" or "the wholly other" than what is conveyed in the affirmation about the full nature of the Divine as the Absolute and Ultimate Reality.

Now this type of Mysticism finds its best representatives in certain phases of Hinduism and also in the Dhyāna School of Mahāyāna Buddhism, as we saw when we presented the major variants of the God-concept of these religions. But it is interesting to note that one finds even among Christian theologians some who speak of God in similar terminology. They, too, seem to feel that personalistic concepts are too anthropomorphic and hence too limiting to convey adequately what God is in his full being and so they speak of the Divine as "Being Itself," "Pure Being," "Being as Such" or simply as "Being" and without any qualifying adjectives. And since even the term "Being" may be too definitive and limiting they speak of God as "Being and Non-Being." We are not here discussing what we regard as the most adequate terminology in speaking of God or "the Divine Mystery" but only pointing out that when Christian theologians resort to the above terminology they are only repeating what oriental philosophers have said about "the Divine Mystery" for upward of two thousand years. And we might add that this vague terminology has not been very helpful to the common believer who needs a person-to-person relationship with his god however much the philosopher may feel that in using such terminology he expresses more adequately what "the Divine Mystery" is.

There is another form of Impersonal Mysticism which we must mention briefly, namely, what we have called Nature Mysticism and which has its best representative in certain phases of Taoist philosophy. We said above that all types of mysticism are psycho-centric. This type of mysticism seems to belie this and to be rather cosmo-centric for it is definitely a feeling of man's oneness with Nature. But even though there is here such an awareness of the external world it nevertheless remains psycho-centric in that it is rather an emotional reaction towards Nature or a mood which reads into external nature much that is purely spiritual or subjective rather than being a truer understanding of the physical cosmos as such. It might be said that this Nature Mysticism is a sort of connecting link between Impersonal Mysticism and the Pantheism or Cosmo-theism which we speak of next.

Pantheism or Cosmotheism is seen best in certain phases of Upanishad philosophy, especially in the Vedānta interpretation of the Upanishads, and in certain branches of Mahāyāna Buddhism. Like Impersonal Mysticism it rejects the personalistic conception of the Divine as being too limiting, but it differs from the latter in what it regards as a more adequate conception. Where Impersonal Mysticism, like all forms of mysticism, tends to eliminate the things of the outer world as obstacles to man's communion with the Divine, Pantheism or Cosmotheism frankly accepts the things of the outer world as being just as truly an aspect of the Divine or Ultimate Reality as is man's own psychic and spiritual nature. However, it would add that the pluralistic world of the ordinary man's experience, i.e., the world as seen by the unenlightened, is not what it seems to be but is largely illusory. The real world as seen by the fully enlightened is a glorious and harmonious Unity. Back of the multiplicity of the phenomenal world is the all-inclusive Oneness of the noumenal world or the world of Ultimate Reality; back of the ever changing and the temporal is the Changeless and the Eternal.

Now while such concepts and terminology may satisfy the philosopher with his quest for the unitary ground of all finite existence it is all too vague in meaning to be of much help in solving man's practical problems of life. It is for this reason that the Pantheistic or Cosmotheistic conception of the Divine seldom, if ever, stands by itself in actual religion, even in the religion of the philosopher. It is almost always linked with conceptions of the Divine that are cast in rather personalistic terms as we saw in our sections on Hinduism and Mahāyāna Buddhism. Thus the outstanding Vedānta philosopher, Sankara with all his monistic interpretation of Brahman as the Ultimate Reality had to speak of a "lower Brahma" cast in personalistic concepts. And Mahāyāna Buddhism, we saw has its *Trikaya*, "Three Bodies" doctrine, namely, *Dharmakaya*, "Law Body" or "Cosmic Body" standing for the all-inclusive Absolute which in its full nature is beyond all human concepts; *Sambhogakaya*, "Compensation Body" or Buddha conceived in terms of ideal personality; and *Nirmanakaya*, "Accommodated Body" or Buddha seen as a historic human being.

In short, the Pantheist or Cosmotheist rejects the personalistic God-concept as being too limiting to stand for the Divine as the Ultimate Reality or the Unitary Ground of all existence but he is nevertheless compelled to resort to personalistic concepts when he would speak of the Divine in a way that can have any real meaning or be helpful in meeting man's religious needs. In fact, as we have seen in connection with both Hinduism and Mahāyāna Buddhism, the Pantheist or Cosmotheist tends at times to speak of the Divine in terms that are all too much patterned after man's own little image. And this suggests that the very attempt on the part of the philosopher to pass beyond even the most worthy personalistic God-concept to a conception which is more adequate and all-inclusive results all too often in a conception of the Divine which is really sub-personal rather than super-personal in meaning.

A third form of the Post-Theistic conception of the Divine finds its expression in what might be best designated as "Reverent Agnosticism." Although we speak of it as an agnosticism it is not the blatantly anti-religious agnosticism which is really a concealed Materialism holding that the Divine which the man of religion seeks to know is unknowable for the simple reason that it does not exist. Reverent Agnosticism is almost the direct opposite of this. Where the former would explain all psychic and spiritual aspects of existence as mere epiphenomena or reduce everything to mere "matter and motion" the latter holds that we do not know enough about the nature of Ultimate Reality, call it the Divine or whatever term you care to use, to say much about it. Even our best understanding of physical nature and our deepest insights into the spiritual aspects of existence, though true enough as far as they go, are only fragmentary bits of truth and far from knowing what is the true and full nature of Ultimate Reality or the Divine Mystery. In fact, says the reverently agnostic philosopher, the larger the sphere of the known becomes the greater is our contact with the Unknown. How, then, can one be so dogmatic in making affirmations about the Divine Mystery as some men of religion are?

Now this spirit of reverent agnosticism has found expression in various ways in connection with the major religions of mankind. Thus e.g. in Indian religions the Buddha felt that the philosophers of his day were talking rather glibly about the Brahman as the Ultimate Reality while the gods of the common masses were seen too much in terms of finite man to be worthy of respect and worship. While the Buddha was not an atheist, as some western scholars have maintained, it is true that he was reluctant to speak about metaphysical realities. Even when pressed by his disciples to answer their questions he usually said that such speculations were unprofitable and really were a hindrance in solving problems nearer at hand, namely the problem of conquering one's lower passions and achieving a truly ethical personality. When he did refer to what lies beyond this life and to what is ultimately real he used the term *Nirvana*, "the Void," as some translate it. *Nirvana* is not an absolute Void, but a reality so wholly other from the world of the unenlightened man's experience that it can not be expressed in terms of that experience. One might, therefore, regard the Buddha as one who was reverently agnostic regarding the nature of Ultimate Reality or the Divine Mystery. Even if it be maintained that he claimed that the fully enlightneed understood, it must be admitted that such understanding could not be formulated in any definite concepts that are intelligible to the average human mind. This hesitancy on the part of the Buddha to say anything more definite on this matter left his followers in a position where they had to work out their own answers as best they could. As we saw in our section on Buddhism, the Buddhist masses usually worshipped gods patterned after man's own nature while the philosophers gave widely differing answers ranging from a definitely personalistic conception of the Divine to one which is so wholly transcendental in nature that it can be spoken of only in paradoxes or in an endless series of affirmations and negations but in which series the negation had the last word over the affirmation; and with some the last word about the Divine Mystery was no word at all but rather "the White Silence of Truth;" or as Nagaryuna felt it, "Silence is the ultimate truth for the wise."

Another way in which this reverently agnostic mood found expression, especially in Mahāyāna Buddhism, was in its theory of knowledge with its emphasis on the relativity of all human truth or what was called "Accommodated Truth." All human truth must be accommodated to the varying levels of human intelligence and especially is that the case in dealing with the Divine. This emphasis, as we saw, resulted in a generous tolerance of widely differing conceptions of the Divine and other essentials of religion but it also led at times towards an out and out agnosticism, while with the more deeply religious it never went beyond a "reverent agnosticism."

One might include also certain aspects of Vedānta philosophy as being reverently agnostic towards the nature of the Divine Mystery. As we saw, Vedānta looks upon the world of man's ordinary experience as largely illusory for what seems to be a multiplicity of differing and conflicting realities, when seen in their true nature are but aspects of an all-inclusive Unity and Oneness. However, the Vedānta philosopher with all his assurance about the Unity of what is Ultimately Real never gets very far beyond this monistic affirmation and so leaves virtually unanswered the question as to the real nature of the Divine Mystery.

In Confucianism and in typical Chinese thought one can find this spirit of reverent agnosticism expressing itself though it differs somewhat from the typical Indian form. The Chinese mind usually accepts the world of man's ordinary experience as real rather than as being largely illusory. While it is realized that this very real world has its cause or grounding in ultimate Reality call this Heaven, the *Tao* or what not, it is felt that man's first task is to master and understand better the things that are nearest at hand rather than speculate too much about the full nature of Ultimate Reality. Frequently in Chinese thought this emphasis on the immediate practical, even when it includes ethical and spiritual values and meanings, is carried to the point where it virtually ignores what is beyond the human sphere and so becomes what amounts to an out and out agnosticism. However, with some, and especially with those who have been influenced by Buddhist thought, it is more of what we have been calling a mood of "reverent agnosticism" towards the "Divine Mystery."

The great Monotheistic Faiths, as we saw, usually state the God-concept in definitely personalistic and positive terms. There are, however, passages in the sacred scriptures of these faiths which also seem to endorse an attitude of "reverent agnosticism" when speaking of the Divine. "Canst thou by searching find God? Canst thou find out the Almighty to perfection?" (Job. 11. 7). And Isaiah writes: "For my thoughts are not your thoughts, neither are my ways your ways, saith the Lord. For as the heavens are higher than the earth so are my ways higher than your ways, and my thoughts higher than your thoughts." God is one who "dwells in thick darkness", says the Psalmist, "clouds and darkness are around him." Paul also warns that man's knowledge of things spiritual is quite limited for "now we see in a mirror dimly". . ."now we know (only) in part." God, he says is One "dwelling in the light which no man can approach unto; whom no man hath seen, or can see." These and similar passages would seem to suggest that man be somewhat hesitant in what he says about God and that an attitude of "reverent Angosticism towards the Divine Mystery" might be more fitting. Undoubtedly there is in these and similar passages in the Bible a warning not to think of God, the Infinite and Eternal, all too much in terms of man's own finite nature. Men of religion need to be reminded that "the high and lofty One who inhabiteth eternity whose name is Holy" dwells "with him who is of a contrite and humble spirit." But while there is this warning it does not mean that the last word about the Divine can only be one that is cast in the language of a "reverent agnosticism." However true it is that God in his full being forever transcends man's comprehension, Christianity and the other great monotheistic faiths maintain with good reason that man can and does have some real knowledge of the "Divine Mystery" and that the most adequate concept of the Divine is in terms of man's highest experience as a personal being.

Now it should be clear from this general survey of the God-concept in the major religions that there are real differences in views though there are also areas of agreement. What is valid in these various views and what in our opinion is the most adequate and valid conception of the Divine will be presented in Part II where we take up the problem as to the Truth of Religion.

SECTION B
RELIGION AND THE GOOD LIFE

Introduction

WHILE BELIEF IN GOD OR SOME MODE OF THE GOD-consciousness is central in all religions there is at the same time a second persistent trait which is equally characteristic, namely, religion's quest for the Good Life. Thus religion may be said to revolve around two foci—God and the Good Life—for religion is above all else a quest for the good life through a vital relationship with the divine world. It is such a quest even in religions which make God's free grace the major factor. Likewise is it such a quest even in the religions of extreme pessimism which regard man's life in this world so hopelessly evil that only a denial of life through a rigorous asceticism is offered as the only way out, for this very denial of life is really a supreme affirmation of man's quest for something better.

Now since in every religion the quest for the good life is through a vital relationship with the Divine it follows that in the different religions the conception of the Divine and the conception of the nature of the good life are most intimately related. The character of one is inevitably reflected in that of the other. But while there is this mutuality between the two it is quite possible for situations to develop in which a rather radical change takes place in man's conception of the good life without there being a corresponding change in his conception of the Divine; especially is this the case where a religion and its associated culture come suddenly under some strong outside influence. Of course, in the long run the ideal of the good life and the conception of the divine must come to terms with each other. Where they do not there will either be a disastrous disharmony in the inner life of man or it will mean that religion has ceased to be very vital.

There are two great factors at work in the modern world which tend to disturb the harmonious relation between man's conception of the divine, on the one hand, and his ideal of the good life, on the other, and which therefore make it exceedingly difficult to know just what the ideal of the good life is in the different religions. One of these factors is the growing independence of modern science and other activities which have the good life as their objective. Formerly all quests for the good life were carried on under the religious ideal and with religion as the motivating power but today both the physical and social sciences are quite independent of religion and while this does not mean that many a scientist who is working for a mastery of nature in the interest of man does not still draw heavily upon his faith in God for support and motivation, it is a fact that much of our modern activity in every land which has as its objective the good and better life in the here and now is carried on quite apart from religion or religious inspiration. Whether mere science in its present form can really achieve the truly good life is another question. In fact, it seems already rather obvious that in spite of the great enrichment in the externals of life which science has made possible there is often an appalling poverty in the inner life. Either science itself will have to augment its efforts and take up more seriously the study of human nature on all its levels and the things essential for the truly good life in all its aspects or it will have to continue to look to religion as its ally since religion, at least in its nobler forms, has always sought to understand man's inner life and provide for its enrichment.

The second factor which tends to disturb the harmonious relationship between man's ideal of the good life and his conception of the divine through which the good life is sought, is the mingling of cultures which formerly had little connection with each other and the development of a common world culture. Not only do men the world over live by the products of our common science, there is also a sharing of other cultural values and so life is becoming more and more the same for men everywhere. For the present this may be still limited largely to the externals of life but this is nevertheless inevitably affecting also men's conceptions of the good life in its inner aspects and then in turn their conception of the divine and man's relationship to the divine. When telephones, radios and television become commonplaces in the temples of Oriental mystics and when long-whiskered seers cleave the sky in swift planes instead of mounting in imagination on mythical dragons the conception of the good life for man and how this is secured is bound to undergo some change.

In discussing, then, the good life in representative religions it should be noted at the outset that the past differences are tending to become less marked. While this does not change the facts of the past it does become increasingly difficult to see these facts as they were, for modern religionists, especially in the Orient, are now busily engaged in reinterpreting the past and reading into it the ideals of the present. This is peculiarly true of the more or less tangible things though perhaps in the inner values of the good life there is a more faithful adherence to the traditional patterns of the various historic religions.

B: I CHRISTIANITY AND THE GOOD LIFE

THE CONCEPTION of the good life in normal Christianity has always centered around ideal personality and those values which enrich the inner life of
the spirit. As we have seen in our discussion of the God-concept, Christianity holds that at the heart of reality is God who is conceived of in terms of
ideal personality and with whom man may enter into personal relationship.
It is therefore a natural corollary that the supreme value in human life should
be seen in the achievement of an ethical and spiritual personality for the
individual and the fellowship of such individuals with each other and with
God. The supreme pattern of spiritual personality is set for the Christian in
the life of the historic Jesus Christ. As Paul put it, the Christian seeks to attain to "the knowledge of the Son of God, to mature manhood, to the
measure of the stature of the fulness of Christ." (Ephes. 4:13). The good life
is not something which the individual is to achieve in an isolated perfection
but only in a life of fellowship, as Jesus himself stated when asked what the
great commandment for human life is. "You shall love the Lord your God
with all your heart, and with all your soul, and with all your mind. This is
the great and first commandment. And a second is like it, you shall love your
neighbor as yourself." (Math 22:37-39).

In Christianity the world itself, with all its good and evil, its joys and
sorrows, is conceived as having its supreme meaning for man as God's way
of developing beings worthy to be called sons of God, "for the creation waits
with eager longing for the revealing of the sons of God." (Romans 8:19).
Even suffering which is such an inescapable part of the life of man is lighted
up by this hope. Not that Nature has no other values or meanings, nor that
all things exist solely for the good of man, for even on this tiny speck of the
illimitable cosmos called the earth "many a rose is born to blush unseen,"
but that which gives supreme meaning and value to the evolution of worlds
as far as man can discover any meaning is the development of spiritual beings who can "think the thoughts of God after him" and who can grow into
the likeness of Jesus Christ who is "the image of the invisible God." Christianity refuses to hold with a Bertrand Russell that "blind to good and evil,
reckless of destruction, omnipotent matter rolls on in its relentless way,"
for it affirms that there is an Omnipotence which is not blind, reckless and
relentless but which is a Supreme Intelligence, working for a purpose and
that this includes man as a spiritual being capable of growing into a son of
the Living God and living in a brotherly way with his fellow-men. Since
this is the supreme meaning of human life it follows that the good life of man

in the here and now stated in general terms can only be that which fits in with this ideal and leads to that goal.

Now while the achievement of a spiritual personality after the pattern set in Jesus Christ constitutes the very core of the good life it is recognized that this is bound up in actual life with other values and meanings which may either help or hinder the attainment of this supreme value. As life is constituted, the inner life of the spirit and all that which goes for its enrichment often finds its best expression in the way man deals with the physical and especially in the way in which he relates himself to his fellowman in both the material and the spiritual goods of life. We shall therefore present the Christian conception of the good life under two aspects or major problems of life. One is the problem of man's psycho-somatic nature, i.e., the relationship between man's bodily life and the life of the spirit, including in the former the physical environment on which the bodily life is dependent. The other is the problem as to the ideal relationship between man and his fellowman. These two problems are naturally not wholly separate in actual life. They are in fact most vitally intertwined, but as in modern thought we distinguish roughly between the physical and the social sciences so we may properly follow this broad distinction here, remembering however all along that they are only two aspects of one and the same problem in actual life and remembering further that life in every aspect must be lived in conscious relationship with God to be truly the good life as Christianity conceives it.

Christian thought has in general made use of the ideology of the ordinary body-spirit dualism though it has usually done greater justice to the essential unity of man's psycho-somatic nature than was done in the concurrent systems of thought. There is, of course, in traditional Christian thought no scientific analysis of bodily functions and the relation of these to man's mental and spiritual life such as is being attempted by modern science. There is rather the clear assumption that the spiritual aspect of human nature is, if anything, the deeper reality and that this is certainly more than a mere epiphenomenon of the physical even though there is usually a high regard for the bodily life and for physical well-being as a real factor of the good life of man as man lives his life in the here and now.

As a matter of fact Christian teaching regarding the relationship between the physical and the spiritual has not been altogether consistent down through the centuries. It has ranged all the way from the extremes of ascetism to the other extreme which makes physical well-being as such the supreme good. It is clear that Jesus himself held no such extremes. True to the Old Testament conception he looked upon physical nature as inherently good. This world, he held, is God's good world. His parables by which he taught the laws of the spiritual world were based largely upon Nature. During his ministry in which he proclaimed the Kingdom of God and His Righteousness he spent much time in healing men's bodies and in ministering to their physical needs. The "abundant life" he came to give certainly included in his mind also physical well-being. There was little if anything in Jesus' teachings of that sharp antithesis between the physical and the spiritual and which regards the one as inherently the enemy of the other which is so characteristic in ascetic religions and dualistic philosophies. The sacredness of the human personality embraced for him also the sacredness of the bodily life, and the ideal of the good life, though conceived primarily in terms of ethical and spiritual values, had nevertheless in it a real place for physical well-being.

But while Jesus regarded physical well-being as a normal part of the good life it is equally plain that in his scale of values physical well-being, however, good in itself, was always subordinated to the higher values of the spirit, the integrity and health of soul, so that when the interests of the two came into conflict, as they often do in actual life, the lesser value had to be sacrificed to the greater. "For what does it profit a man if he gains the whole world and loses or forfeits himself." (Luke 9:25). And of the man who had planned his life wholly in the interest of physical well-being, Jesus represents God as saying, "Fool! This night your soul is required of you; and the things you have prepared, whose will they be? So is he who lays up treasure for himself, and is not rich toward God." (Luke 12:20-21). To be sure, man must have bread to live but "man lives not by bread alone." He needs many things for his bodily life for which he must seek and strive. "Your Heavenly Father Knows that you need them all,"—all the things that answer the questions, "What shall we eat? or What shall we drink? or What shall we wear?" "But seek first his kingdom and his righteousness, and all these things shall be yours as well." (Math. 6:33) It should be noted that even in this statement where Jesus put first things first he did not say that the seeking after righteousness and the higher values of life excludes the lesser value of physical well-being but rather implied that when men really live righteously these secondary values of the good life will follow as a natural concomitant. Of course, that can only be the case when more than a few isolated individuals make righteousness the rule of life. As long as this is not the case the righteous individual will often have to suffer vicariously and forego the lesser good of physical well-being if he would remain true to his ideals. Jesus himself in promoting the higher righteousness sacrificed his physical well-being. "Foxes have holes, and birds of the air have nests; but the Son of Man has nowhere to lay his head." (Math. 8:20) And it was in the interest of the Kingdom of God and his righteousness that he voluntarily laid down his physical life.

It must be added that while Jesus never implied in his teachings that the physical life is inherently evil or the enemy of the spiritual, as is the case in religions which make the ascetic life the prerequisite of spiritual freedom, he did hold most emphatically that the natural physical impulses, if left unrestrained, can easily degenerate into mere sensuality and so become the deadly enemy of the spiritual life. "If your right eye causes you to sin, pluck it out and throw it away . . . and if your right hand causes you to sin cut it off and throw it away; it is better that you lose one of your members than that your whole body go into hell." (Math. 5:29-30)

And Jesus went one step beyond holding that uncontrolled physical impulses leading to sensuality is the enemy of the spirit when he implied that health of spirit is itself a prerequisite for continued physical well-being, or that much of man's physical suffering has its roots in the sickness and maladjustment of the soul. Thus frequently when Jesus healed men's bodies he first sought to heal their spirits. "And Jesus . . . said to the paralytic, My son your sins are forgiven," and after this, "Rise, take up your pallet and go home." (Mark 2:5-11) And again we read, "See, you are well! Sin no more, that nothing worse befall you." (John 5:14) Modern medical science seems at last to take cognizance of the influence which a man's mental and spiritual attitude exerts on his physical organism though naturally the major concern of medical science is with the physical organism, leaving to religion and psychotherapy the problem of the health of spirit.

But while according to Jesus man's physical life is sacred and a part of the truly good life there appeared rather early in Christian history a very different conception of physical nature and its relation to the spiritual life, namely one which regarded the physical as inherently evil and the very antithesis of the spiritual. Even Paul used expressions which seemed to have something of that flavor, especially when he wrote that "The desires of the flesh are against the Spirit, and the desires of the Spirit are against the flesh; for these are opposed to each other." (Gal. 5:17) It is, however, more correct to say that by the term "flesh" Paul meant the uncontrolled physical desires resulting in sensuality rather than that the physical is inherently evil. He regarded the body really as the instrument of the spirit and one that might be used either for good or evil depending wholly upon the character of the controlling spirit. "Do not yield your members to sin as instruments of

wickedness, but yield yourselves to God as instruments of righteousness."
(Romans 6:13).

In the New Testament the term "salvation" is used frequently and while the meaning of this included the good life in the here and now it nevertheless puts the emphasis on the individual's destiny in a future life. In fact, many of the early Christians seemed to believe that the present world order, with its interest in things physical and its emphasis on physical well being, was soon coming to an end and that therefore a Christian should withdraw from the ordinary life of the world as much as possible. It must, of course, be admitted that the life of the world was so largely a life of sensuous indulgence in things physical that Christians could not participate in it if they would be truly "spiritually minded." However, it is equally true that increasingly Christians came under the influence of views which regarded the physical not only as the lesser good but as being inherently evil. It was this view which found its most emphatic expression in the monk ideal and which for centuries was regarded by many as the highest type that a Christian could live.

One can not question that many who followed this ideal and withdrew from life achieved a high level of spirituality but it nevertheless tended towards a rather warped type of life and not wholly the truly Christian way of life. This is shown by the very developments of Christian history during the Middle Ages. Just because all too many spiritually minded Christian leaders withdrew from life in following the monk ideal the church was often left without adequate leadership. And on the other hand it is true that only when the monk ideal was changed from one which required a complete withdrawal from normal life to one which required the monk to go forth and serve his fellowmen both spiritually and physically that such truly great Christians as St. Bernard and St. Francis emerged.

At the time of the Protestant Reformation some of the leaders who had been monks themselves definitely rejected the monk ideal as the highest type of Christian life. It is true that they sometimes used language which seemed to imply that they still believed that the physical is inherently evil. They stressed the doctrine of "total depravity" and man's nature as being wholly "corrupt," but that they did not mean that the physical as such is inherently evil and must be suppressed by a vigorous asceticism is shown by the fact that they took a vital part in normal life and stressed the belief that all walks of life are sacred so that the layman can be just as truly a Christian as the professional priest or preacher.

It goes without saying that in modern Christianity the good life in the here and now includes physical well-being. In fact, the major attack on modern Christianity from within and without is just this that with all its zeal for physical well-being it has not done enough to secure for all classes more of the good things regarded as essential for physical well-being. Thus modern Christian ethics concerns itself almost wholly with man's social relationships rather than with the individuals own inner life and it does so because of its bearing upon the problem of securing for all men their just share of material goods. It is perhaps less certain as to what else should be included in the Christian picture of the good life.

To the extent that modern Christianity insists on physical well-being as a part of the good life, and this not simply for the privileged few but for all, it is certainly in line with the ideal for which Jesus stood. What differentiates this modern ideal from that of Jesus is not that it has too high a regard for physical well-being but that it has often so little to add in the way of things that build up man's life as a spiritual personality.

But the Christian conception of the good life is seen perhaps even better in connection with the problems which constitute man's ideal relationship to his fellow man. How, from a Christian point of view, should one live with one's fellows? Even the ideal of physical well-being depends for its attainment very largely upon the solution of these problems of human relationships. But how much more is the good life in its spiritual aspects dependent upon the relations between individuals and of individuals to society!

It is a striking fact that with all the emphasis in New Testament Christianity on the worth of the individual human personality and on the direct relationship of the individual to his God, the true Christian is never pictured as one who achieves the good life of spiritual personality in isolation from his fellow men but only as he forgets himself and loses his life in the service of others. Growth in holiness and perfection of character is an ideal and a goal but "for their sake I consecrate myself." (John 17:19).

Jesus himself came not as one who preached an individual salvation but as proclaiming the Kingdom of God among men. When asked for a summary statement of the laws of this Kingdom of God he formulated these in the two great commandments. The first was a knowledge of the one true God and loving him with all one's heart, mind and strength. This is a matter of the individual's relationship to his God. But the second he said is like the first in importance and it is, "You shall love your neighbor as yourself." (Mark 12:31) What this second would mean in actual life Jesus illustrated in many of his discourses and parables and above all else did he demonstrate it in the manner of his life and his death. It would mean the golden rule, "Whatever you wish that men would do to you, do so to them." (Math. 7:

12) It would mean the spirit of the good Samaritan who helped a fellow man in dire need even though this other man belonged to a people which despised his own. It would mean a love for others not because they are so naturally lovable or can be expected to love in return but because the Christian has such a high regard for the sacredness of the human personality that he can still see even in the degraded the "image of God" and the possibility of his becoming a true child of God.

It is significant that the first followers of Jesus did not retire from this "evil world" in quest for an individual righteousness but that they formed groups and organized fellowships. These churches were above all else fellowships of those who had experienced a new life in connection with Jesus and with each other. The supreme rule of their fellowship was the new commandment "that you love one another." This is what differentiated their life from the life of others in the community. In Jesus they had somehow experienced God's forgiving love and learned that the truly good life is a life of brotherhood. The impression which these Christians made upon the pagan world is caught in the remark of Peter Maurin, "See how these Christians love one another."

Paul gave the classic statement as to what this kind of love meant by contrasting it with other human values or other elements which properly belong to the good life when he wrote that 13th chapter of First Corinthians. The eloquence of language which is the very acme of human culture; all knowledge, even knowledge of things mysterious and insights that enables one to prophesy what the future has in store; faith and confidence in one's own ability great enough to overcome all obstacles; material goods not only for one's own needs but also to provide the poor—all these things which made up the good life of the cultured Greeks and Romans to whom he was writing and which should be a constituent part of the good life for the cultured man in any land or age, Paul regarded as empty and worthless unless the one who had these things used them in a spirit of love and brotherhood. The world is ever changing in outward things of human culture, said Paul, Tongues shall cease and the knowledge of today shall be made obsolete by the new and fuller knowledge of tomorrow, for all human knowledge is fragmentary and like seeing "in a mirror dimly" but one thing can remain essentially the same under all the varying conditions of human life and in spite of the widest differences in human culture and that is the spirit of love and Christian fellowship, that spirit which enables a man, no matter how much or how little he has, to share with his fellow man. This, according to the true Christian conception, is the very core of the good life. It is the good life in a double sense. It is the only kind of life that gives true satisfaction and it is also the only kind of spirit that enables one to understand the life of others and that provides an adequate motivation of living in such a way as to secure for others also their full share in the good life. This means that no man can find the good life for himself until he finds it in fellowship with others. "For whoever would save his life will lose it." (Mark 8 :35) "Unless a grain of wheat falls into the earth and dies, it remains alone." (John 12:24) The selfish or self-centered life is the dwindling and dying life. Even though love to God is the first great commandment, such love can not be very real without a true love towards one's fellow men. "But if anyone has the world's goods and sees his brother in need, and yet closes his heart against him, how does God's love abide in him?" (I. John 3 :17) "If anyone says, 'I love God' and hates his brother, he is a liar: for he who does not love his brother whom he has seen, can not love God whom he has not seen. And this commandment we have from him, that he who loves God, should love his brother also." (I. John 4:20-21).

But if the Christian can not find the good life for himself by living selfishly, it is equally true, according to the Christian view, that no man can really work effectively in enriching the lives of others and bringing them the good life in all its fulness without this spirit of love and friendship. This is the real import of Paul's classic hymn of love. It is also the central thought in Jesus' way of life. That does not mean that the spirit of love is a substitute for all other qualities or that the good life can be built up by mere "good intentions." Modern science which has so greatly enriched the life of man is not a matter of mere good intentions but of real knowledge and the practical application of such knowledge to human problems. It is, however, equally plain that with all our scientific knowledge by which we are transforming and enriching human life, this in itself has not brought humanity the truly good life. Even in the externals of life the millions will not get their just share until the spirit of brotherhood becomes regnant not only in the relationships between individuals but also in our group relationships and further in our international and inter-racial relationships. Modern science with all its good gifts to man supplies equally well the weapons which in turn destroy both these gifts and man himself. That is the appalling situation facing the world today and it should make the way of friendship and love the only acceptable way for intelligent men. It is perhaps rather generally accepted that the way of friendship and the golden rule is the condition for the good life as between individuals. However difficult it may be to live by the golden rule, enlightened morally minded men everywhere recognize this as the truly good life and the way that will bring to others the fuller life. But this way is not yet widely accepted as the only way in our group relationships and in the relationships between the larger national and racial units. And yet until this way of friendship and love is accepted also as the rule for these wider relationships the Kingdom of God which is a brotherhood of all men can not be fully established. But that is what true Christianity stands for however true it is that very few Christians take this ideal very seriously when national and racial interests seem to conflict.

Thus the Christian ideal of the good life is one which, on the one hand, recognizes the supreme worth and sacredness of the individual human personality and in this sense Christianity stands for individualism. But the Christian ideal is not a self-centered individualism. It rather insists that man is essentially a social being and that the highest human values can be had only in social relationships. These relationships are extended till they include in one great unity all men. This is not a colorless all-inclusiveness. It insists on the supreme worth of the individual and it stands for the family as a permanent social institution holding that a man's first duty is towards those of his own household. It accepts other social institutions including the state as of value for man must live in a vital way locally to live effectively at all. But including all these and transcending them is the Kingdom of God which envisions the life of all men and their right to the good life in all its fulness. Loyalty to this Kingdom of God or this Brotherhood of men may at times involve the sacrificing of certain privileges held by certain individuals, groups or national units just as loyalty to any larger group involves sacrifice for those who compose it. But the bigger fact is not the sacrifice which the lesser unit must make in the interest of the larger unit but rather that the lesser can not find its fullest and richest life until it finds it as a part of the larger unit. Christianity seeks to build up a "social order in which the values of individual personalities and divergent creative abilities are conserved to the full" and made available for the benefit of all. And as these divergent creative abilities of individuals in a given group should be conserved and made available for all so likewise should the racial and national characteristics in so far as they have real value be regarded, not as antagonistic to each other, but rather as complimentary and worthy to be conserved and made available for all. But this is possible only as one rises in one's thoughts and ideals above mere individual, family, racial or national interests. Nothing short of the ideal of the Kingdom of God among men is worthy of man's supreme loyalty and wholehearted effort in his pursuit of the truly good life.

G

The Christian conception of the good life and the possibility of its realization is, however, not adequately stated until it is seen in the light of the obstacles that stand in the way. At this point Christianity has usually been very realistic as to the darker aspects of human life and this realism expresses itself in the conception of moral evil or sin. Sin is a concept that has rather faded from the modern man's consciousness and it is a bit difficult to convey what is meant by it. Modern man seems to be under the spell of a shallow Naturalism which is one of the unfortunate by-products of a pseudo-science that sees life only in two dimensions. This shallow Naturalism seems to glory in the unrestricted freedom of man's natural impulses and uncritically gives the so-called "natural" the right of way in life. Of course, even this sort of Naturalism can not quite close its eyes to the conflict of interests and must make some distinctions in the hierarchy of values but since it recognizes no transcendental norm of the good but derives its norm wholly from man's own natural desires and impulses and since among these it gives the self-assertive and the predominantly physical impulses the deciding vote it can not even understand what ethical religion means by, and much less submit its life to, the judgment of a moral norm that has its reference in a transcendental spiritual life.

Then further, while many recognize the inadequacy of this shallow Naturalism and acknowledge the reality of moral magnitudes and man's capacity for a self-transcendence through which he sees life under the perspective of a transcendent ideal they nevertheless fail to sense what religion means by sin because they see man's failure in achieving the ideal largely in his ignorance about the natural world. And as through science man is achieving increasingly a mastery of the secrets of Nature it is blithely assumed that such progress is itself the achieving of the good life.

Now all ethical religions, and Christianity in particular, refuse to subscribe to this shallow optimism which sees in man's ignorance the only cause of his failures. Ignorance is, of course, one of the factors and progress in knowledge is one of the steps towards the good life but such knowledge must include also an understanding of man's real nature. And any serious wrestling with the problems of human nature sooner or later will be confronted with the fact of moral evil or sin. Ignorance is a factor in moral evil for the human personality is a unity but moral evil can never be reduced to mere ignorance. It is more an expression of the will aspect of the human personality and there is something about it that can only be described as a "corruption of the moral will" and which keeps a man from living up to the ideal as he sees it, even the low ideal of the morally unenlightened. In a word, the obstacle that stands in the way of the good life is not primarily a lack of knowledge as to what might constitute the good life but an unwillingness to follow the ideal even when it is seen. It is a failure of the moral will. The good life is dependent above all else upon what Kant called "der Wille zum Guten." In fact, Christian psychology holds that only as one wills to do the good can one really know what the good is. "If any man's will is to do his will, he shall know," said Jesus. (John 7:17) Just because the good life in Christianity is conceived so largely in terms of ethical values, is why it becomes supremely a problem of the moral will. Naturally if the content of the good life is primarily a physical good, such as the physical sciences make possible, then the chief key for opening the doors to it is the cleverness of intellect which masters the secrets of Nature. However even on this level the good life is possible for the many only as the cleverness of intellect is wedded with a good will.

We have already seen in connection with the body-spirit problem that the normal impulses of the physical life when unrestrained can easily become mere sensuality and as such the deadly enemy of the life of the spirit. This is one aspect of moral evil and it can only be dealt with as an enlightened moral will becomes master of these natural impulses. That is why the ideal of self-control has ever been stressed in ethical religions. But an even more serious aspect of moral evil centers in the problems connected with man's relationship with his fellow man and in that characteristic of the "natural man" expressing itself in self-assertion, self-centeredness, self-interest and downright selfishness which runs counter to the spirit of unselfish love that we have designated as constituting the very core of the good life. Thus moral evil is, on the one hand, a life of mere sense-indulgence as over against the life of spiritual personality. It is, on the other hand, living both the life of the body and the life of the spirit in a self-centered and selfish way rather than in a spirit of love. Therefore all that hinders man from living out the ideal of the good life of love and fellowship is moral evil or sin, according to the Christian view.

It would take us too far afield to attempt here any detailed list of moral evils. The Sermon on the Mount is the Christian classic in which Jesus himself sets forth the ideal of the good life and the moral evils that stand in the way of achieving it. In the latter he makes clear that moral evil is not simply a matter of the grosser sins of the sensuous life but also a matter of the refined sins of the spirit. Thus not merely murder but all anger and hatred, not mere open adultery but every lustful glance, not mere crude blasphemy and coarseness of language but every departure from straight forward speech of Yes and No, is moral evil. The higher righteousness for which he stood requires that the "eye for eye" justice be replaced by patience and generosity, that the natural love for friend and kindred be raised to the level of love for the enemy and those who have no natural claim on one. Even the "tax collectors" and "Gentiles" love their friends. What is required is that "You, therefore, must be perfect, as your heavenly father is perfect," for "he makes his sun to rise on the evil and on the good, and sends rain on the just and the unjust." (Math. 5:45).

But this higher righteousness which enables one to love even one's enemy is impossible, according to the Christian view, unless one has undergone a profound change in spirit, a change so profound that it is often spoken of as the "new birth" or as Jesus put it when he said, "unless one is born anew, he can not see the Kingdom of God." (John 3:3) It is only after the love of God "has been shed abroad" in man's heart that this is possible. Or as John put it, "Beloved, let us love one another; for love is of God, and he who loves is born of God and knows God." (I. John 4:7) By this love is meant not simply that upward reach in man's aspirations for the true, the good and the beautiful but rather that downward reach that would lift others and that is possible only to those who themselves have experienced a love that has lifted them high above the plane of mere self-interest and self-centeredness which is so characteristic of the natural man.

Thus while Christianity holds that God as the creator and sustainer of the natural order bestows elements of the good life it insists that the truly good life in its inner and spiritual aspects is a matter of God's special grace through great spiritual personalities and supremely through Jesus Christ. It is through Jesus Christ that God deals with man's sin which is the chief obstacle standing in the way of the good life and also through him that he bestows the good life in its fulness. Thus Jesus Christ "saves from sin" and brings the "life abundant," the "life eternal." Just how Jesus Christ helps man in this double way finds different formulations in Christian thought. It would take us too far afield to give even in outline these formulations. They fall roughly under two major types.

One type starts with the fact of sin and sin conceived not merely as ignorance of what the good life might be but more as a rebellion of will against the good will of God and as setting up man's own desires and self-centered interests as normative Thus sin is not merely an obstacle to the good life which might be removed through enlightenment gained either through man's own experience or through a special revelation but it is more an attitude of mind and an act of will involving guilt and deserving punishment at the hands of the Holy God. Therefore in the forefront of this line of thought stands the necessity of an atonement for man's sin as the prerequisite of God's forgiveness and the restoring of the right relationship between man and God without which there can be no really good life. This atonement for sin, it is held, can not be made by sinful man himself but had to be made by God himself through his Son Jesus Christ; and therefore at the heart of the Gospel message is the message of God's forgiving love in Jesus. The beginning of the good life is then a repentance for sin and an acceptance of forgiveness mediated through Jesus Christ. Being thus brought into right relationship with the Holy God man can then grow into the likeness of the pattern set by Jesus. And Jesus not only sets the pattern but also becomes the dynamic through which man can do what in his own natural strength he could not do, or as Paul put it, "It is no longer I who live, but Christ who lives in me." (Gal. 2:20).

The other major type of Christian thought setting forth the way God helps man achieve the good life through Jesus Christ, while recognizing the reality of sin and even the guilt aspect which requires God's forgiveness to set things right, puts in the forefront man's own quest for the good life and sees in Jesus Christ above all else one who alone has successfully achieved the truly good life and shown the way to others. He came to bring man "the life abundant," the "life eternal." Central in his consciousness was the Heavenly Father and he lived the life of perfect love towards his fellow men. By the winsomeness of his life and the compelling beauty of the life ideal he holds out, Jesus draws men to himself, inspires them and imparts to them the dynamic that is needed in their upward struggle for the good life of moral and spiritual personality. Through fellowship with Jesus man gains assurance of the reality of God and comes into communion with Him and thus is lifted above himself and enabled to live a life which in its spiritual quality far transcends what man in his own strength could achieve.

While in the first view Jesus Christ is above all else God's only begotten Son through whom his forgiving love saves man from sin and builds him up in holiness, the second view sees in Jesus more the supreme Son of Man who himself lived the perfect life of conscious communion with God and of love to man and who by that type of life helps man come into that same fellowship with God and men. These two views have, of course, large areas in common but it is true that they differ rather widely from each other in the general approach they make. The first gives Jesus an absolutely unique place in human history, especially in the matter of the significance of his death as an atonement for the sins of the world and as the prerequisite for restoring the right relationship betweeen God and man without which there could be no truly good life, or to use the older terminology, no real "salvation." The second also insist on the supreme significance of Jesus in human history but it tends to place him simply at the upper end of the scale of great spiritual personalities among men rather than in a category wholly unique. While he is regarded as indispensable for bringing man the truly good life in its highest form this view is less emphatic in holding that "there is no other name under heaven given among men by which we must be saved." (Acts 4:12).

But as we said, both views have large areas in common in their conception of the positive content of the good life and even as to Jesus being both the pattern and the dynamic through which the good life is achieved. They would also agree in including the rich content of our modern culture as a part of the good life though they would regard this as belonging more to the periphery rather than to the very core. The core of the good life must ever be the inner life of spiritual personality lived in conscious communion with God, the Great Spirit and Father of our spirits, and in loving fellowship with our fellow men.

B: II JUDAISM AND THE GOOD LIFE

IN JUDAISM, as in Christianity, the conception of God and the good life for man are intimately bound up with each other. In fact, it is an Old Testament tenet that "man is made in the image of God" and that since God is "the Infinite One who inhabiteth eternity and whose name is Holy" man can not come into satisfactory relationship with him or find the truly good life except on a basis of personal righteousness.

The good life thus rests first of all upon a belief in and knowledge of the living God. The great commandment of Judaism which Jesus also accepted and quoted from Deuteronomy is, "Hear, O Israel, Jehovah our God is One God; and thou shalt love Jehovah thy God with all thy heart, and with all thy soul, and with all thy might." (Deut. 6:4-6) And the first of the Ten Commandments which were calculated to regulate the good life for the Israelite begins with the reminder, "I am Jehovah, thy God." Old Testament religion after a long effort to find a satisfactory relationship between man and God through a system of offerings and sacrifices so characteristic of most religions, reached its noblest conception of what the true relationship must be to secure the good life in the great declaration of the prophet Micah, "He has showed you, O man, what is good; and what does the Lord require of you but to do justice, and to love kindness, and to walk humbly with your God?" (Micah 6:8) In fact, the main burden of the message of the great prophets was just this, that Israel as a people can never find the good life except on a basis of man's righteous dealings with his fellowmen and by remembering that the ways of righteousness are grounded in the character of the Eternal.

For centuries in the religion of the Israelites the individual seemed to be regarded as of little significance. Man's relationship to his god was a relationship *en masse*. Israel as a people was Jehovah's chosen people and the business of keeping Jehovah's favor and so securing national safety and prosperity was committed to a priesthood which as such represented the people and performed their routine duties by offering the prescribed sacrifices and by conducting the ritualistic services, but with comparatively little regard for the character of the actual lives of individual men. But with the rise of the great prophets religion became primarily a matter of ethical values and ethical relationships. The good of the nation continued to receive the chief attention rather than merely the good of isolated individuals but it was seen with increasing clarity that national health and strength rest in the last analysis upon the character of individuals and the relationship that these individuals sustain to each other and to society as a whole. This relationship, it was seen, must be first of all one of justice and more than mere justice. There must be added the "love of kindness," that surplus of magnanimity of spirit which is the very foundation and content of the good life among men.

This conception that the good life of the individual and the nation rests ultimately on ethical relationships was open to a double interpretation. One was that ethical values and relationships are merely instrumental in character and that the real content of the good life consists of other things such as physical well-being, general cultural values, national prestige and political power. From this followed the thought that the ethical life of the individual must inevitably bring its reward in health of body, wealth and such aspects of the good life. The corollary of this latter was that if a man does not have these good things of the physical life, it is a sure proof that he is not really a "good man" at heart though outwardly he may be conforming to the prescribed ethical code. The book of Job is, of course, the great classic that deals with this point of view and that undertakes to show that it is essentially wrong, for while the author admits that it is generally true that the righteous life has its rewards in physical well-being, prosperity and honor among men, it is by no means the case that misfortune and physical suffering are a proof of secret sin and unrighteousness but rather that the righteous may at times be called upon of God to suffer. And the author of Job rose to the further conception that even though the righteous man may suffer the loss of all material goods and the respect of his fellow men he can nevertheless have the supreme satisfaction of life which comes from the integrity of soul and being right with God, the righteous Judge of all men.

In Isaiah, this conception is carried one step further in the doctrine of the Suffering Servant, namely that misfortune and suffering may not be merely the lot of the innocent and guiltless but that it is through the vicarious suffering of the righteous one or the righteous few that the good life for the many is often achieved.

The second interpretation of ethical values in their relationship to the good life was, then, that ethical values are not merely the necessary foundation for the good life of the individual and the nation in the matter of material goods but that it is in the ethical and spiritual life itself that man finds the deepest joy and satisfaction. It is especially in some of the Psalms that Old Testament religion reaches this higher level on which it is seen that moral character is not a mere means to an end such as physical well-being for the individual and prosperity and power for the nation but that it is in ethical and spiritual values that the highest content of the good life for man consists. It is on the one hand a consciousness of a satisfactory relationship to God which is described as "Blessed is he whose transgression is forgiven, whose sin is covered. Blessed is the man to whom the Lord imputes no iniquity, and in whose spirit there is no deceit." (Ps. 32:1-2) It is, on the other hand, an actual delight in God's moral law. "The law of the Lord is perfect, reviving the soul; the testimony of the Lord is sure, making wise the simple; the precepts of the Lord are right, rejoicing the heart; the commandment of the Lord is pure, enlightening the eyes; . . . . More to be desired are they than gold, even much fine gold; sweeter also than honey and drippings of the honey comb." (Ps. 19:7 ff.)

Since righteousness is the very core of the good life it follows that the chief enemy of the good life is moral evil. The conception of sin as a wrong relationship between the individual and his God finds, perhaps, its supreme expression in the Psalms, especially in Psalm 51 where the penitent sinner cries out, "Against thee, thee only have I sinned and done that which is evil in thy sight . . . . Create in me a clean heart, O God; and put a new and right spirit within me." And the conception of sin as a wrong relationship towards one's fellow men finds repeated expression in the message of the great prophets who were ever demanding social justice.

But while in Judaism the good life is conceived primarily in terms of ethical and spiritual values it is not with the thought that these values stand in opposition to other values such as physical well-being, material goods, general culture, national strength and prestige or whatever else may make up the good life of man in this world. In fact, Judaism is "this-worldly" in its emphasis rather than "other-worldly" and so it stands decidedly for all that builds up the life of man as a citizen of this world. Not that the hope of a life beyond is absent but the good life is first of all a life in the here and now. Even though its core must be spiritual and express itself above all else in ethical values and righteous relationships between man and his fellow man, such a life is expected to have as its natural accompaniment the things needed for the life of this world. It is in the long run the righteous and not the wicked who "is like a tree planted by streams of water, that yields its fruit in its season." (Ps. 1:3) "I have been young, and now am old: yet I have not seen the righteous forsaken, or his children begging bread." (Ps. 37:25) And it is not merely the righteous life of the individual that has as its natural accompaniment the other things that make up the good life of man in this world. It is equally true of the nation for "righteousness exalts a nation; but sin is a reproach to any people." (Prov. 14:34) In fact, the Old Testament has a very modern ring in its emphasis on the thought that the good life must be a good life here and now and that the basis of it must be not only individual righteousness but also social justice on a national scale.

It should be clear that the conception of the good life in Judaism is not essentially different from what it is in Christianity. What differentiates the former from the latter pertains largely to the place of Jesus Christ in the two. Judaism does not, like Christianity, have its chief reference in Jesus as the embodiment of and the dynamic for the good life of man but expresses its ideal in a moral law. Both religions hold that the good life is the life of the good man, and Christianity would add that in Jesus Christ the Christian has not only the pattern of the ideal but also the power through which the ideal is to be achieved. Paul who had been an orthodox Jew before he was converted to Christianity expressed the difference by saying: "The law of the Spirit of life in Christ Jesus has set me free from the law of sin and death. For God has done what the law weakened by the flesh could not do; sending his own Son in the likeness of sinful flesh." (Rom. 8:2-3) Paul held that through Jesus he not only experienced God's forgiving love which to him was essential for peace of conscience and without which there could be no truly good life for the morally awake, but also that in fellowship with the living Christ he was somehow enabled to live the life of the spirit in a way that had not been possible for him as an adherent of Judaism. We are not here pronouncing judgment as to the validity of Paul's differentiation between the two faiths but we give it simply as a classic expression of what is a characteristic difference between these two religions both of which conceive of God and the core of the good life of man primarily in terms of ethical and spiritual personality.

B: III ISLAM AND THE GOOD LIFE

IN ISLAM, as in Christianity and Judaism, the conception of the good life is bound up with the conception of God but in a rather different way. Though Islam conceives of God in terms of ideal personality it does not stress the thought that the good life for man consists above all else in his growing into the likeness of God or in likeness to one who is the supreme revelation of God's character. Islam places such a tremendous emphasis on the "distance" that separates the omnipotent God from all creatures that the thought of finite man becoming in any real way like God or even the thought that any being could reveal the true nature of God in terms of human life is usually regarded as blasphemy. The good life of man consists first of all in knowing God's absolute sovereignty over human life and in submitting implicitly to God's sovereign will. "Islam" means "submission." "Your God is the one God. To Him therefore surrender yourselves." (Qur'an 22:35) Religion to the good Muslim is above all else the "creaturely feeling," the "feeling of dependence" and the unquestioning acceptance of what God in his wisdom has foreordained. To know that "naught shall befall us, save what God has written down for us," (Qur'an 9:15), is the truly good life. Even when one's life is in danger there is the assurance that "It is not for any soul to die save by God's permission, written down for an appointed time." (Qur'an 9:139).

While this absolute dependence upon God's sovereign will is in many respects like the conception of God's providence in Christianity and Judaism it tends in some cases to become a sort of fatalism which cuts the nerve of all human endeavor. "*Mā shā Allāh*" and "*In shā Allāh*" are characteristic expressions on the lips of Muslims and while they literally mean "What God has willed" and "If God wills" respectively they all too often mean to the one who utters them, "It can't be helped."

However on the whole Islam, in its conception of the good life, stands for an active attitude and for making the best of life in opposition to whatever hinders. While man's first duty is to submit to the inscrutable will of God it is nevertheless believed that this will is a good will as man conceived the good and that this has been revealed to man through Muhammad, the Prophet of God, and is recorded in the Qur'an, the very word of God. Muhammad early organized a sort of theocracy with himself as God's viceregent upon earth and who was guided in leading his followers into the good life by appropriate revelations given from time to time to meet the practical situations as they arose.

Muhammad's conception of the good life was in many respects a considerable advance over the ideals of his day and environment in that he strongly resisted the coarser moral evils of his people. He borrowed from both Judaism and Christianity and patterned his ideal for the good life more or less after these older faiths which he greatly respected, but the unbiased critic would probably admit that he did not add much to this moral and spiritual legacy of the race and that often, in the interest of what seemed a practical expediency, he fell below the latter. It is one of the tragic facts of Islam that its founder, who so emphatically claimed to speak for the Holy and Omnipotent God, himself gradually deteriorated in character and that he was not a more worthy embodiment of the ideals which he proclaimed.

While the norm of the good life is set in the Qur'an it is nevertheless true that since Islam regarded the good life as being first of all a matter which pertains to the here and now this religion was ready to appropriate whatever it found along the road in its world conquest, particularly in the externals of life and general cultural values. The "Word of God" recorded in the Qur'an found its "interpreters," and as is well known from the history of religion in general, this allows usually a wide latitude of meanings and so makes room for many things new and things different as time goes on and a given religion spreads among peoples of varying cultures. Even the Sunnites, the orthodox branch of Islam which continued to regard the Qur'an as the final revelation of God, had various schools of orthodox interpretations which made it possible for good Muslims to cling, on the one hand, to the teachings of the Qur'an regarding the ideals of the good life but which, on the other hand, made room for many things never mentioned in the Qur'an but which seemed desirable as elements of the good life for man. If this sometimes included contradictory elements it should be remembered that Muslims are not the only ones who have tried "to carry water on both shoulders." The great Shiite branch of Islam was from the beginning less bound to the moral and spiritual level of the Qur'an and in its doctrine of the *Imam* it had a natural door opened for new ideals of life coming in from time to time as new situations were faced or as it became desirable to appropriate other and higher values in life. It is a fact that as Islam which had its rise in southern Arabia came into contact with the higher culture of peoples that were conquered by the Islamic hordes, it borrowed more and more from these higher cultures and not only assimilated it but also made important contributions.

During the Middle Ages when Europeans were neglecting and had forgotten much of the rich Graeco-Roman cultural heritage, it was Islamic scholars who not only helped preserve it but also made their own contributions. This was especially true from the ninth to the eleventh centuries. Such great centers as Baghdad, Damascus, Cairo and major cities in Spain brightened the world with a galaxy of stars, not only in the field of religious and philosophical thought, but also in mathematics, astronomy, history and general literature. It is not too much to say that Islam at that time stood in the forefront of Western civilization.

Islam played a big role not only in its contact with European and North African peoples but also with peoples and cultures of Central Asia, India and South East Asia. To this day many of these peoples are as loyal Muslims as are the inhabitants of the Arabian Peninsula, the original home of the Islamic Faith. In fact, in some of these countries Islam has so completely dominated all phases of life that seemingly little of the older cultural heritage remains. It should, however, be added that especially where the Shiite type of the Islamic Faith prevails this older heritage has been assimilated and reinterpreted rather than completely replaced.

In the case of Indian Islam the situation is somewhat different. While the first contacts with India were made by Muslim merchants who in connection with their business bore testimony to their faith in Allah as the One and Only God, Islam became a real factor in Indian life only after a succession of military invasions and occupation. Beginning in the latter part of the tenth century, this went on until it reached the height of its power and influence under the great Mogul dynasty (1525–1857). But even though India, and especially North and Central India, came under the dominance of Islamic rulers, India's agelong spiritual heritage had fully as much influence over the conquering Islamic hordes as the latter's faith had on India. As we pointed out in our presentation of the Islamic God-concept in India, Sufism has a great following. The Sufi type of Islam is not only more pantheistic in its God-concept than theistic but it also interprets the good life ideal much more in terms of Indian ideals than in typically Islamic ideals. Where the latter is usually quite "this worldly" in emphasis and calls for an active participation in the natural life of man as a citizen of this world, Sufism finds the good life more in withdrawing from the world and in an ascetic mysticism.

It should, however, be added that while the Sufi type of Indian Islam reflects the characteristic Indian attitude, other phases of Indian Islam have remained rather true to orthodox teachings. This is not only true of the

God-concept which has remained definitely monotheistic and which has strengthened the theistic strain in later Hinduism and Sikhism, but it has also been the case in the emphasis it has placed on the believer's participation in the practical problems of life and interest in things that are essential for the good life in the here and now. It is also this type of Indian Islam which has been a political force for centuries and which in our time has continued its influence sufficiently to bring about the division of the Sub-continent into the two states of Pakistan and India.

It is probably true that Islam as a whole has been more adept in borrowing and assimilating things from other religions and cultures than in producing values from its own resources. It may also be true that in the expansion of this religion into other lands, particularly lands where a higher stage of culture prevailed, the result was not infrequently an actual destruction of values which should be a part of the good life for all men. But even though this is true, Islam must be reckoned as one of the great world forces which in spite of this disturbing influence, and sometimes because of this, has had a vitalizing effect on the civilizations of great sections of the human race and helped the millions on the whole to a better life.

In at least two or three ways has this religion promoted the good life for its followers. First by its unflinching adherence to and incessant proclamation of its great teaching about the One God who is the sovereign lord of all life it has not only given the individual human life a worthy center and meaning, but it has also been a cohesive force binding men together for a great purpose and thus giving real drive to the lives of men in large units. Granted that this was often perverted to unworthy ends, at least on its higher levels this religion has borne witness to the essential unity of mankind.

The natural corollary of the Oneness of God and the unity of mankind is the fundamental equality of all men and races before God. And this means, or should mean, a real democracy of spirit in the relation of men to each other. Islam has as one of its great appeals just this spirit which has pervaded it wherever it has gone in its world conquests. However ruthlessly some of these conquests might have been, it should be noted that they were not motivated usually by any sense of racial or national superiority but rather by the belief that the Islamic Faith in the One and Only God who rules over the affairs of men should be made known to all men for their own good and their eternal salvation. In fact, Islam has been in many ways quite effective in its mediatorial function between different races and cultures. In areas where it was accepted the conquered peoples were usually regarded as the equals of their conquerors and were soon given a share in the affairs of state and other interests. In fact, in a country like India, with its age-old caste system, Islam's belief that all men are equal before God became a real factor in breaking down the caste system and in promoting a more democratic spirit.

It is, of course, true that this basic belief in the equality of all men before Almighty God is not always carried out in actual practice. Even to this day some Islamic areas recognize human slavery as legitimate. And it is also true that perhaps nowhere in the modern world are the things needed for physical well-being so unequally distributed as in some of the Islamic countries, and most of all in the very land where Islam had its birth and early development. But in spite of these glaring defects it must still be said that Islam, in its basic teachings and in its higher ideals, stands definitely for real spiritual democracy among men.

Another characteristic influence of Islam on the lives of its adherents has been what one might call "the naturalization of religion." The daily call to prayer may for many mean little more than routine of habit but still it has served to remind not only the pious but also the average believer that no man is really self-sufficient but that he is dependent upon God and that he can find the truly good life only at His hands. Even though the actual content of the good life for the average Muslim may be far too much a matter of material goods and not on a very high ethical and spiritual level, it still remains a fact that Islam has succeeded remarkably well in naturalizing the religious consciousness and in making religion a matter of man's daily life and interest.

Now these rather strong points of the Islamic Faith have at times their reverse side which are not so admirable. The very strength of faith in the One and Only God has often given this religion a hardness and spirit of intolerance, for it is all too easy to substitute for the truth that God is One the thought that only one's own conception is true and that all others that differ must be treated as completely false and the enemy of the truth.

To mention but one more of the strong points of the Islamic Faith which has its reverse side: The sovereignty of almighty God, which assures the believer that nothing can befall him which is not ordained of God and so gives a sense of security in life, can also be given a rather fatalistic interpretation. As we said above, "Mā shā Allāh" and "In shā Allāh" are frequently on the lips of Muslims and they usually mean to the one who utters them that he is at the mercy of blind fate rather than in the hands of the merciful God. In fact, as one surveys the modern Islamic world one wonders whether it is not this rather fatalistic attitude towards life that has become dominant and that this explains, in a measure at least, why so many of the Islamic lands belong to the backward and underdeveloped areas of the modern world.

But be this as it may, the Islamic world is beginning to take a more active attitude towards life again and towards the problems involved in building the good life of man in the here and now. And it is interesting to note how this modern awakening is bound on the one hand to the old ideals of the Islamic Faith and on the other hand seeks the good life quite apart from these religious beliefs and ideals, if not in actual opposition to them.

We can give but a few outstanding examples of this twofold trend. There is first the case of modern Turkey. As is well known, one of the consequences of World War I was the dismemberment of the Turkish Empire which up to that time had more or less perpetuated the old Islamic institution of the Caliphate, a sort of Theocratic State in which the Caliph was regarded as being both the head of the state and the head of religion. But what was even more significant was that the surviving smaller Turkish State in 1924 abolished the Caliphate and made itself into a modern state in which religion and matters of state are strictly separated. To be sure, the Islamic Faith continues to be the religion of the vast majority of Turkish citizens, but even so, modern Turkey as a state is no longer identical with Islamic religion as such. And that this is not merely a change in name but a real change is indicated by the fact that modern Turkey is more closely affiliated with the free countries of the Western world than with its fellow-Islamic neighboring countries. While this does not necessarily imply that Islamic religion is no longer a factor in building the good life of Turkish citizens in the here and now, it does indicate that the Turkish people are ready to cooperate with peoples of other faiths in building a better world.

Another example in which one can see the big changes that are taking place in the Islamic World and particularly the changing relationship between religion and the state in their common quest for the good life in the here and now, is that of the United Arabic Republic under the leadership of Nasser. In founding this republic out of some of the fragmented parts of the old Turkish Empire, Nasser as a good Muslim makes his appeal on more or less religious grounds. In fact, in his bitter opposition to Israel he seems to make religion a major issue. But even so, he does not propose to establish anything like the old Islamic Caliphate. His ambition is rather to unite as many Arabic peoples as possible into one modern state. So much is this the case that at times he seems to forget his Islamic Faith altogether, as when he looks for help to atheistic Communists.

These and many other examples that we could give from the modern

Islamic World seem to indicate that while there is a real awakening taking place today so that Islamic peoples are beginning to play a bigger role in life than they have been for some time it seems to be less motivated by religious beliefs than was the case in the past, even though some of the leaders make their appeal on more or less religious grounds. All this is but another way of saying that in the Islamic World today religion tends to become more of an instrument of state than as standing in its own sovereign rights as it did in the days of its founder and also during subsequent periods of Islamic history. This is not to say that modern Islam stands alone in this respect, for it seems equally true of some of the other major faiths of mankind.

B: IV INDIAN RELIGION AND THE GOOD LIFE

IN INDIAN RELIGION the Good Life ideal, like the God-concept, has varied down through the centuries although it is true that there has usually been an overwhelming emphasis on man's natural life being so incurably evil that the only way of achieving the truly good life is through a vigorous ascetic discipline and a withdrawal from the world.

In Vedic religion which reflects the life of the conquering Aryan hosts as they swept in successive waves down from the North West ever further across the country, the conception of the good life was cast largely in terms of physical well-being and whatever is needed for the bodily life. The gods themselves were pictured as lusty warriors enjoying a stiff fight and after victory the "cheering bowl." They looked to their gods to help them secure what was needed for the good life in the here and now such as numerous cattle and good pasture lands, abundance of food, health, long life, strong sons to help in the work of the day and victory over their enemies, those dark-skinned natives whom they gradually forced further and further south or made into servants. The Vedas record their prayers to their "god of the white" for help against those of a "dusky hue" and with "low noses." This help they expected to receive in exchange for the sacrifices they offered to their gods as is so cryptically expressed in their prayer, "I give Thee, Give Thou me." In short, the Good Life concept in much of Vedic religion centered largely on material goods rather than on moral ideals and spiritual values. It should, however, be added as we pointed out in our discussion of the God-concept in Vedic religion that the worship connected with Varuna did stress moral attributes and tended to make ethical values the core of the truly good life of man. But it must be also added that this trend in Vedic religion never became dominant and that the god Varuna faded from the religious picture. It would take too much space to trace in detail the gradual change in the conception of the good life that took place in the evolution of Indian religions as the Vedic religions evolved into the religions of the Brahmanas, Aryanyakas, Upanishads, Jainism, Buddhism and the subsequent various and conglomerate Hinduism. But a most marked change came gradually over the life of these lusty Aryans as they settled down in their new home with its warm and enervating climate, its fertile low lands watered from the distant perpetual snows of inaccessible mountain peaks, its periodic floods and droughts, its quick and luxuriant growths and its rapid decay and certain death. Marked as became their change of color of skin, this was far less significant than the change that came over their spirit and in their conception of human life and what constitutes the good life for man.

The life of action began to slow down, as it were. It was their lusty activity which in the first place enabled them to push back and subdue the older inhabitants. It was not, as formerly supposed, that these Aryan invaders represented a higher civilization, for it is rather certain now that the original inhabitants of the Indus valley represented a higher culture than their conquerors. The invaders were physically more vigorous, better fighters and as such were able to replace others and appropriate for themselves what they found. This sort of thing has repeatedly happened in human history and the physical superiority that expresses itself in military conquest does not at all mean superiority of culture. But be this as it may, the fact remains that in the course of the centuries these vigorous Aryans were themselves conquered or at least underwent a very profound change. Their blood became thinner, as it were, and coursed less vigorously through their veins. Doing things became more difficult and seemed less necessary or desirable. Mere activity gave way to thinking about activity and then more and more to meditation as such.

And as these now thoroughly acclimated Aryans meditated about human life, its values and meanings, they became more and more impressed with the evanescence and vanity of life. How quickly the vigor of youth begins to ebb and sickness, old age and death set in! How much of life, even the happiest life, is mingled with sorrow and suffering! How insecure is the very foundation of man's physical life, and how utterly futile and vain are most men's activities, ambitions and hopes! Is life as most men live it really worth living? Can a man find a type of life that is worth while? Why does man cling so tenaciously to life when so much of it is but sorrow and suffering? What is the real cause of human suffering? Is there a way to stop it, or a manner of life that enables one to be indifferent or superior to life's vicissitudes and trials? And if life is incurably

H

evil, is there a way out and is there, perhaps, a truer life beyond this present? These are some of the questions that thoughtful Indians began to ask with increasing persistency. The unquestioning acceptance of life and the vigorous pursuit of things that make for physical well-being, for prosperity, power, honor, prestige and such things gave way to a great doubt about this sort of "good life," and this doubt turned man's quest in another direction. This other direction may be indicated by saying that it was on the whole away from the outer and the physical life and towards the inner and spiritual, away from the emphasis on the here and now and towards the emphasis on the super-temporal and the eternal.

This change of emphasis as to man's true nature found expression in two great concepts which we have already mentioned in connection with the God-concept and which for upwards of two thousand years have been truly ruling concepts affecting all Indian thought and consequently also the good life ideal. One of these is the so-called Rebirth or Transmigration of the Soul concept. The other is the Karma concept, the cosmic law of cause and effect operative in the life of all beings.

According to the Transmigration of the Soul belief, man is essentially an eternal spiritual being that is born again and again in this world. According to the Karma law the individual in a real way shapes his own life and destiny by the type of life he lives in every rebirth so that his present life and his lot in his present life have been conditioned by the type of life he had lived in a previous incarnation, and the type of life he now lives will determine the nature of his next incarnation. In each stage of his existence the individual has a certain degree of freedom so that he can move upward or downward in the scale of beings and therefore in his next incarnation be born either as a more superior human being and under more favorable circumstances or, if he now lives an evil life, be reborn as an inferior human being and under less favorable circumstances, or even as a sub-human being.

Then further, this belief that one is born again and again into this world and that the nature of one's life and lot in life in each successive rebirth is in large measure conditioned by the type of life one has lived in the preceding existence, was related to a third major concept which has had a tremendous effect on the Indian good life ideal, namely the concept of Caste. The caste system according to which society is divided into different groups, each group being given a certain standing in the social scale and with its definite rights and privileges in the upper groups and its limitations and handicaps in the lower groups, rests upon the belief that the inequalities in human society are basically a just reward for each individual's own doings in his previous existence. If some are born with superior natures and under favorable conditions it is because they have earned this in their previous existence; and by the same Cosmic justice those who are born with inferior natures and under less favorable circumstances likewise receive in this life what they deserve. As we said above, the individual being in each stage of existence has a certain degree of freedom and so can change his lot in the scale of being, thus moving either upward or downward in the scale in his successive rebirths, but it is a slow process to rise in the scale especially for those who occupy the lower rungs on the ladder. On the other hand, those who occupy the upper rungs on the social ladder now, while life for them is pleasant and while they have greater opportunities in further improving their natures and their lot so that in their next rebirth they might rise even higher in the scale of beings, are nevertheless warned that unless they are ever alert and live in accordance with their best and noblest insights and motives they will sink in the scale of beings and in their next rebirth find themselves occupying a lower level of life and under less favorable circumstances.

Now while in Indian religions the more thoughtful were in general agreement that the truly good life consists primarily of things spiritual rather than mere physical well-being and all that makes for such well-being, they nevertheless differed rather widely as to just what is the nature of the spiritual and also as to how the good life in terms of things spiritual is to be achieved.

The most complete break with the Vedic conception of the good life is, of course, the ascetic ideal which has been one of the most persistent traits of Indian religions from ancient times down to the present. This ideal rests on the view that the physical life or physical well-being is not only far from constituting the essence of the good life but that in its very nature it is often the enemy of the spiritual and the truly good life. In increasing numbers the more thoughtful began to retire from the normal life of the world and became hermits in forests and caves, seeking for quietness and peace of soul, for freedom from the "bondage of the flesh" and the entanglements of human relationships, for security and permanence in a world of change and uncertainty.

Jainism is the oldest of these post-Vedic religions surviving to this day in which the spirit of asceticism found perhaps its extreme expression. The founder, Mahavira, is represented in the sacred scriptures as having renounced the world in fulfillment of a prenatal vow. "I shall for twelve years neglect my body." (S.B.E. 22:200). The true Jain monk reduces the physical

to the barest minimum and regards death by starvation as a supreme a-
chievement of the spirit. "Alone, living on allowed food, he should wander
about . . . . He should beg food. A wise man should not care whether he
gets alms or not." (S.B.E. 45:12-13). Not only is the good monk indifferent
to food and all that makes for physical well-being, he is equally indifferent
or superior to all human desires, even such as are usually regarded as noble.
"A monk who loves not even those who love him, will be freed from sin and
hatred." (S.B.E. 45:32). "By conquering love, hate and wrong belief will he
cut off the fetters of *Karma*." (S.B.E. 45:184) i.e., the fetters that bind one to
this evil world. Of course, the ordinary layman does not live up to this ideal
of vigorous asceticism and makes concessions to the bodily life and the
normal life of man as a citizen of this world, but nevertheless the truly good
life held up to him is one he can attain only as he becomes willing to pay the
price of ascetic discipline even though he may delay this until after repeated
rebirths into this world.

In the philosophy of the Upanishads, especially as interpreted by the
Sankhya School, the ascetic life finds due recognition as a means by which
man can attain the truly good life and it is even given a metaphysical basis.
As we saw in connection with the God-concept, Sankhya stands for a radical
dualism. Reality consists of two basically opposites. On the one hand there
is *Prakriti*, the Primary Matter which is the source and cause of all material
forms of existence. On the other hand is *Purusha*, Spirit, or rather the innumerable spiritual beings. Man in his present existence is a combination of
these two opposite realities and that constitutes the tragedy of his life, for he
is a spirit which is now imprisoned in a physical body and which in his
unenlightened state thinks of his psycho-somatic life as constituting his true
life whereas his true life is purely spiritual. Just how and why man as spirit
became imprisoned in a bodily existence is not further explained except to
say that it was due to some Primal Ignorance. But whatever the cause of this
imprisonment, it is possible to gain freedom by becoming enlightened and
seeing things as they really are. When fully enlightened man realizes that his
true life is not the bodily life or the life of sense-perception and all the concepts built upon such perception. In fact, he will realize that even now and in
spite of his apparent imprisonment in a physical body he is not really imprisoned, for the sense life to the enlightened spirit is only like the reflection
of a red Hisbiscus flower in a white crystal. The redness does not really alter
the nature of the white crystal even though it seems to do so, and the enlightened spirit can even now realize that in its true nature it is unspotted
purity and free in spite of the fact that it may seem enmeshed in the evils of

the sense-life. Thus the good life in the here and now is one which realizes what the spirit is and which dwells on pure thoughts untroubled by and indifferent to the clamorings of sense desires. As we saw in connection with our discussion of the God-concept, Sankhya does not recognize the existence of any supreme being or God but only innumerable spirits and, therefore, the emancipation from the bondages of the physical world must be achieved by each individual spirit's own unaided efforts except such help as may come from the example of other spirits who have achieved their freedom or from spirits who have never been imprisoned in a bodily existence.

According to the Vedanta School, which is the most typical representative of Upanishad thought, the Sankhya interpretation of human nature and the good life ideal is an extreme view and does not do justice either to man or to the nature of what is truly real. Vedanta holds that man in his true being is one in nature with what is ultimately real and what constitutes the inner nature of all beings. It makes room for what we experience through sense-perception and what we speak of as physical and therefore it does not scorn our psycho-somatic nature in the way that the Sankhya School and the extreme forms of asceticism do, but it nevertheless maintains that man is basically a spiritual being, one in nature with the Eternal and Unitary Ground of all existence. In fact, it speaks of the Eternal and the Ultimately Real in terms of the Spiritual Self and therefore also interprets man's own true being and what constitutes the truly good life in spiritual terms. The wide chasm that seems to separate the spiritual and the material aspects of existence which Sankhya stresses and which therefore results in its radical dualism, Vedanta explains by saying that the pluralistic world of physical phenomena as seen by the unenlightened is really illusory (Māyā) but when seen as it really is it becomes but an aspect of the Unitary Ground of all existence which Unitary Ground in its full nature transcends all finite concepts but which man nevertheless knows best in terms of his own spiritual being. Hence the good life consists primarily in man's awareness of his union with the Eternal Ground from which he comes and to which he returns. There are different interpretations given as to this union with the Eternal, whether the individual spirit loses his identity as a separate individual spirit or whether it is more of the nature of a communion between two kindred spirits. Frequently the figure of the wave and the ocean depths is used. As the wave rises temporarily on the ocean's surface and is separate from other such waves and even partly separate from the ocean but sinks again into the ocean depths so is the finite spirit of man. In any case man is not a self-existent being but owes his being to the Eternal Ground of all being and he returns to that source and therefore the truly good life is one lived in that assurance. While still a citizen of this world man may take an active part in the life of the world enjoying the physical life and all that makes for physical well-being but he should not become too much absorbed in such a life since it is only temporary and does not constitute his true life. Man is rather a citizen of eternity and his true life is more the inner life of the spirit rather than the present bodily life. He is, as we said, one in nature with the divine or unitary ground of all beings and therefore his life is secure no matter what may happen to him in this present life. To know this and to rest in that conviction is the very heart and substance of the truly good life.

In Yoga, which is also one of the more important orthodox schools based on the Vedas and Upanishads, the quest for the good life is most decidedly away from the outer world or the sense life and a turning to the inner life of the spirit. As a first step in that direction Yoga resorts to the ascetic discipline since it sees in the sense life a real obstacle that must be overcome before the spirit can find its own true nature and enter into communion with other free spirits. What the real content of such an inner life may be cannot be expressed in terms of man's ordinary life and can be known only to those who have had the experience. In any case it is a life free from the "bondages of the flesh" and all the anxieties that is the lot of the unenlightened in this world.

In Indian Buddhism, too, the ascetic ideal has played a big role in the quest for the truly good life. Tradition has it that the Buddha himself started his quest by retiring from the world and living the life of the hermit. For six long years he lived as an ascetic, carrying this to the point where his tortured body almost surrendered to man's last enemy. And while the Buddha gave up the life of extreme asceticism in favor of the Middle Way, the way of moderation which lies between the extremes of asceticism and sense-indulgence, he is nevertheless often spoken of in the sacred scriptures of Buddhism as the "Great Ascetic." There is no question but that the monk ideals, so prominent in Buddhism all down its long history and especially in early Indian Buddhism, is a most natural development of the Buddha's central teachings about human life. The older sources make it plain that the monk with his begging bowl and depending upon alms was a characteristic figure in this religion. Then the first of the so-called "Four Noble Truths" of Buddhism is the truth that human life is predominantly a life of sorrow and suffering. "Now this is the Noble Truth as to suffering. Birth is attended with pain, decay is painful, disease is painful, death is painful. Union with the unpleasant is painful, painful is separation from the pleasant and any craving unsatisfied, that too, is painful. In brief, the five *skandhas* ("aggregates" or the conditions of individual human existence) are painful." It is not simply that suffering is the predominant characteristic of human life but that it is inherent in the very conditions of individual existence, according to the Buddha. He believed with others of his day in the cycle of rebirths and so the major emphasis of his teachings was on living a type of life which would break this endless cycle and free man from this essentially evil world. "Just as, ye monks, the great ocean has but one taste, the taste of salt, just so, ye monks, has this teaching and regulation only one taste, the taste of release." (Vinaya, Cullavaga IX; 1, 4; Udana V. 5).

Now while the Buddha's major emphasis was on a type of life that would ultimately free the individual from the dread cycle of rebirth into this evil world he nevertheless had also much to say on how one can live the good or better life in the here and now. In fact, the way that leads to ultimate freedom and bliss is the Middle Way and this is above all a way of moral living in the here and now. If the first of the Four Noble Truths as stated above is the truth that life as most men live it is one of suffering and sorrow and if the second truth is that this has its origin and cause largely in man's "craving thirst" or "sensual delights," it is possible to bring that sort of life to an end, said the Buddha in his third of the Four Noble Truths, by walking in the way outlined in the fourth Noble Truth, namely the way of "Right views, right aspirations, right speech, conduct and mode of livelihood, right effort, right mindfulness and right rapture." What this means is given in greater details in the Buddha's recorded conversations with his disciples and other individuals including some of India's rulers and potentates as well as in his discourses delivered before larger groups. Thus by "right views" he meant especially views that are free from all superstitions and delusions. "Right aspirations" are such as are worthy of an intelligent and morally upright man. "Right speech" requires that one be truthful, open and withal kindly in what one says. A man of "right conduct" is peaceful, honest and pure in heart while "right livelihood" requires that in making one's living one does not bring hurt or danger to one's fellow man. "Right effort" above all calls for self-control, self-discipline and self-culture. "Right mindfulness" means to be active and alert in one's thought life. Mental torpor or a vapid dream life, the Buddha regarded as a chief hindrance to the truly good life. "Right rapture" is the consummation of life and can be achieved only through a life of meditation. It leads to the Nirvana State of mind which is the highest goal one can achieve. Nirvana is the great Void, especially the extinction of earthly desires, but it is not an absolute Void. What its real content is the Buddha hesitated to say. It is the state into which one passes after being freed from the cycle of rebirths into this evil world. Since the way to win that freedom is living one's present life in accordance with the highest moral ideals and spiritual insight one might well assume that such values carry over into the Nirvana state although the Nirvana State or Parinirvana may transcend all that one experiences in this life even on the highest levels of moral and spiritual living.

In any case, according to the Buddha, the truly good life in the here and now is one of spiritual insight and moral conduct. In so far as his teachings promoted that type of life they certainly promoted the good and better life in the here and now even though the Buddha's major objective for himself and for his fellowmen was to break the cycle of rebirth into this essentially evil world and to gain the unhampered freedom of Nirvana.

In passing it should be observed that when Buddhism spread beyond India, and especially to China and Japan, its conception of the good life was considerably modified in the direction of giving greater recognition to the natural life of man as a citizen of this world. We shall speak of this more fully below in connection with the good life ideal in those countries.

As to just how man is to achieve the good life either in the here and now or in the world beyond, it is quite clear that the Buddha laid the emphasis on the individual's own effort. As we saw in our discussion of the God-concept in the Buddha's teachings, he had very little to say on the subject and, therefore, little or nothing about anything like "divine grace" or help coming from the divine in man's upward struggle. He gets help by the truth taught him by others, by their noble example and their sympathy but basically each individual must be his own savior. In some branches of later Mahāyāna, especially in Amitabha Buddhism with its essentially personalistic conception of the divine there is a decided emphasis on help coming to man from the divine in his struggle for the good life as we shall see in connection with Chinese and Japanese religion.

Although in much of Indian thought the conception of the good life has usually turned man's attention away from the outer world and towards the inner life of the spirit, it was necessary after all to give some place to the life of the "natural man" or man as a citizen of this mundane sphere. This practical compromise found its classic expression in the Bhagavad Gita and that is at least one major reason why this scripture has been so popular. According to this scripture the good life consists, on the one hand, in the assurance that man in his own deepest nature is a spiritual being and that all the sufferings and vicissitudes to which the bodily life may be subjected can not really destroy him. But on the other hand, it recognizes the fact that as long as man is a citizen of this world he must take a share in the work of the world and do his duty in whatever station in life he may find himself. The good life in the here and now, in short, is a life devoted to God and spiritual ends while doing the work of the world faithfully and in a spirit that is not too much attached to earthly things. "He who does all his work for my sake, who is wholly devoted to me, who loves me, who is free from attachment to earthly things, and without hate to any being, he, O son of Pandu, enters into me." (XI: 55)

One of the major problems with which this scripture deals is the problem caused by human strife and war. What attitude should a man who lives for ethical and spiritual values take under such conditions? In a question of this sort one has an acid test of how a spiritual ideal works in a realistic world; and in the Bhagavad Gita we have one of the first great attempts at answering this question. The answer given is quite in line with the whole spirit of the scripture. On the one hand it affirms that as man is essentially a spiritual being death on the battlefield is not real death since the spirit lives on. It adds the further assurance that there is a higher power which shapes the destiny of all men and that the individual can rely on this power for his own good. On the other hand, it insists that each man must do his duty in life if he would find true satisfaction even though such duty involves taking part in the bloody struggle of the battlefield. Of course, strife and war are evil and the good life is one of peace and friendly relationships but under present conditions the best one can do is to do one's duty even though this may involve actions that seem contrary to spiritual ends. Such an answer may not be adequate but it is the sort of practical compromise which many an idealist, ancient and modern, has often made.

Much of what we have said thus far about the good life ideal in Indian religions is true only for the more thoughtful and spiritually minded. In the religion of the Hindu masses the conception of the good life centers much more in material goods and the things that make for physical well-being. It is just because the masses have so little of this world's goods and the things needed for the bodily life that these things loom so large in their imagination. In fact, much in their religion is concerned with obtaining the favor of the gods and their help in securing more of the things needed for the bodily life and its pleasures. To be sure, the masses may do honor to their holy men who have forsaken the world and its pleasures, and they may even regard the ascetic type of life as an ideal which some day in a future rebirth they will make their own, but for the present they would rather have a little more of this world's goods and the things needed for physical well-being. So much is this the case that even their conception of the heavenly life has been cast more in terms of the physical life and its pleasures than in spiritual terms.

There is now a great change coming over the life of India's millions and this is affecting the conception of what constitutes the good life in the here and now. Even the most under-privileged classes are awakening to the possibility of having a larger share in the good things of life. The age-old caste system which in the name of religion had condemned millions to a life of poverty and want and which the upper castes and privileged classes had often used to justify the terrible inequalities in life, is now being seriously questioned, and even attacked by government decree. Of course, anything so deeply rooted in the religious and cultural heritage of a people as the caste system cannot suddenly be cancelled out by mere official decree but the fact remains that the Indian people today no longer meekly accept the social stratification with its attendant injustice that the caste system involved and are demanding a fairer distribution of the good things in life including especially the things needed for man's life as a citizen of this world. This does not necessarily mean that India is turning its back on the best in its spiritual heritage but it does mean that the sharp antithesis between the physical and the spiritual so characteristic in Indian religious and philosophical thought in the past is now being seen as an extreme if not an actually false view of man's nature and of what constitutes the truly good life. It remains to be seen how this change in Indian thinking will affect Indian religion. There are some indications that many of the intellectuals who are so enraptured with what modern science can do in the way of providing the things needed for the bodily life and in building up the national life, scorn their own spiritual heritage; not only those aspects of that heritage that are now seen to have been extremes or false but even what is of permanent value in helping man achieve the truly good life. How far this trend will go remains to be seen but it seems quite certain that whatever the good life ideal in the future will retain of the best in India's spiritual heritage it will also have to hold out a real promise that man's needs for the present life will be met more adequately than they have been in the past.

B: V CHINESE RELIGION AND THE GOOD LIFE

THE DOMINANT conception of the good life in Chinese religions and philosophies stands in rather sharp contrast with what is so characteristic in Indian religions. In a word, Chinese thought is predominantly "this worldly" in its emphasis, and the good life is above all the natural life of man as a citizen of this world. And since the natural life is so obviously grounded in the physical aspect of Reality the good life must include physical well-being as one of its characteristics whatever else it may include. There is, to be sure, the spiritual aspect to man's true being and the good life ideal must therefore also make provision for this. However, these two aspects of man's psycho-somatic nature are not regarded in Chinese thought as being necessarily in conflict with each other as is so often the case in Indian religions. In the life of the normal man they should rather function harmoniously and in such a harmony man can have the good life on all its levels. There is thus little in Chinese thought that regards the physical world as inherently evil and the enemy of the spiritual or as illusory. Where that sort of conception is found it is largely the result of Indian influences which came in through Buddhism.

Now while Chinese religion in its two major forms of Taoism and Confucianism sees the good life as one in which there is this harmonious functioning of the physical and spiritual aspects of man's being, there is, nevertheless, a wide difference between Taoism and Confucianism as to just how such a life is to be achieved in actual practice. In a summary way it may be said that whereas Confucianism puts its emphasis on a well regulated life in which every individual knows exactly his place in the social structure and carefully observes all the rules prescribed for him, the Taoist wants to live his life in complete freedom and unhampered by any rules and conventions of an organized society. It has been cleverly said that the Chinese are Taoists by nature and that is why they have needed the Confucian discipline down through the centuries.

But to take up more specifically what Taoism and Confucianism respectively mean by the good life and how they would achieve it, let us first see what the former has to say on the matter.

In speaking of Taoism we have in mind here Classical Taoism rather than the later popular Taoist religion which is a mixture of various elements including much that is borrowed from other sources, especially from the age-old popular religion and from Chinese Buddhism. In classical Taoism the good life is one that is lived in close communion with Nature of which man is an inextricable part. As we saw in the section on the God-concept, Taoism is a sort of Nature Mysticism and man, when he is true to himself, stays close to Nature or to the eternal *Tao*, "the Way" of all things. He finds the good life in living the natural life simply, quietly and free. It is a life free from all strife or feverish effort to achieve success in competition with others. It is also free from all rules and regulations imposed from without. If man would have such a good life let him take his norm from Nature writ large or the *Tao*, "the Way" of all things which works silently and achieves its ends apparently without any effort. "The *Tao* never does, yet through it every thing is done." (Tao-Teh-Ching XXXVII Lin Yutang).* Thus man, too, achieves most, not by any calculated effort that might impress others, but by quietly being something and above all by remaining true to his inborn nature. "He who conquers the world often does so by doing nothing." (Tao-Teh-Ching XLVIII Lin Yutang).

A key word in the Taoist philosophy of life is *Wu-wei*, literally, "not doing." This, of course, means "not over-doing" or going to feverish extremes in trying to accomplish one's purpose. "The sage discards the excessive, the extravagant, the extreme." (Tao-Teh-Ching XXIX).† "Fill to the very full and you will wish you had stopped in time. Temper to the very sharpest, and you will find it soon grows dull. When gold and jade fill your hall, it can no longer be guarded. Wealth and place breed insolence that brings ruin in its train. When your work is done, then withdraw. That is the *Tao* of Heaven." (IX Ibid)

The virtues stressed in Taoist thought and sometimes called the "three jewels" are gentleness, frugality and humility. "The sage putting himself in the background, is always to the fore. Remaining outside, he is always there. Is it not just because he does not strive for any personal end that all his personal ends are fulfilled?" (VII) Ibid. "He does not show himself; therefore he is seen everywhere. He does not define himself; therefore he is distinct. He does not assert himself; therefore he succeeds. He does not boast of his work, and therefore he endures. He does not contend, and for that very reason no one under heaven can contend with him." (XXII Ibid). "Just because he never at any time makes a show of greatness he, in fact, achieves greatness." (XXXIV Ibid). "What is noble makes inferior position its root. What is high makes lowliness its foundation." (XXXIX Ibid).

The Tao-Teh Ching sums up its ideal for man's life and conduct by saying: "To those who are good (to me) I am good; and to those who are not good (to me) I am also good; and thus (all) get to be good. To those who are sincere (with me) I am sincere; and to those who are not sincere (with me) I am also sincere, and thus (all) get to be sincere." (XLIX).

These and similar virtues in which the emphasis is more on what one is than on what one does, constitute the very core of the good life according to classical Taoism. This ideal of life holds good not only for the individual as such but also for the social structure and for the nation. The natural man does not need any elaborate rules to guide him in relation to his fellowman.

---

*"The Wisdom of China and India."
†"History of Chinese Philosophy," by Y.L. Fong.

He is better off and more likely to be good to his fellowman if left free to follow his inborn nature. Social conventions and governmental rules and regulations tend to make matters worse. In fact, the good Taoist holds that what is called Civilization is really a mark of degeneracy.

"The more prohibitions there are, the poorer the people become. The more sharp weapons there are, the more prevailing chaos is in the state. The more skills of technique, the more cunning things are produced. The greater the number of statutes, the greater the number of thieves and brigands. Therefore the sage says: 'I do nothing and the people are reformed of themselves. I have quietude and the people are righteous of themselves. I deal in no business, and the people grow rich by themselves. I have no desires and the people are simple and honest by themselves.'" (LVII) Lin Yutang.

It may be that this Taoist ideal of life is valid only for a rather primitive stage of society and when man still lives close to nature and in the wide open spaces has ample room rather than for the type of life man lives in more crowded communities which would seem to make certain rules and regulations rather necessary, and yet this Taoist ideal of freedom for the individual awakens a response even in the modern man's soul. The proliferation of rules and regulations and our ever expanding governmental bureaucracies and correspondingly heavier taxes, makes one wonder sometimes whether we might not learn something from the Taoist sage. The Washington wit who said "It is fortunate that we do not have as much government as we pay for," would make a good Taoist.

The Taoist with his passion for freedom and the simple life not only rebelled against all rules and regulations imposed on the individual by organized society but he sometimes carried his protest to the point where even the higher ethical teachings such as Confucianism stressed in what it had to say about righteousness, justice, benevolence and all that was covered by the term *Li*, "Propriety," were seen as a degeneration of true virtue and as a misunderstanding and loss of man's inborn *Tao* nature. "Therefore:

After *Tao* is lost, then (arises the doctrine of) Kindness.
After Kindness is lost, then (arises the doctrine of) Justice.
After justice is lost, then (arises the doctrine of) Propriety. (Li)
Now propriety is the thinning out of loyalty and honesty of heart, and the beginning of the chaos." (XXXVIII) Lin Yutang.

Perhaps it should be said that this was not a scorning of the basic Confucian virtues but rather of the conventional forms of these virtues and especially the Confucian emphasis on Propriety and what is proper. This with some seemed to take the place of what is inherently true and good.

There is another aspect of classical Taoism's concept of the good life that deserves mentioning beyond what we said above about Taoism being in essence a sort of Nature Mysticism and in which man finds the truly good life through his communion with Nature. This is found especially in the writings of Chuang-Tzu. Chuang-Tzu made much of the thought that man is by nature one in essence with the eternal *Tao* and that he should live his life in full realization of this fact and so find a sense of peace and security amid all changes to which human life is heir. The fact that man's present life seems so limited and so ephemeral or transient should not disturb one since man in his true being is grounded in the eternal *Tao* and therefore all change, including even what we call death which seems to end man's life, is, in fact, only a transition from one form of existence to another form. To be sure, when one experiences the joys of this present human life it is only natural that one should cling to such a life and to want it prolonged but there are other forms of existence, Chuang-Tzu points out, which are also good since they, too, are equally an expression in finite form of the infinite and eternal *Tao*. Thus in the passage already quoted in connection with the God-concept he says: "To have attained the human form is a source of joy. But in the infinite evolution, there are myriads of other forms that are equally good. What an incomparable bliss it is to undergo these countless transitions!" (Chuang-Tzu Ch. VI) Fung. "When we come, it is because we have the occasion to be born. When we go, we simply follow the natural course. Those who are quiet at the proper occasion and follow the course of nature, can not be affected by sorrow or joy. These men were considered by the ancients as people who are released from bondage." (Chuang-Tzu Ch. VI) Fung.

Chuang-Tzu carried his Nature Mysticism to the point where he saw man's life completely at one with the Universe and its source, the eternal *Tao*. "The universe and I came into being together, and I, and all things therein, are One." And one who realizes his oneness with the universe or rather with the eternal *Tao* of which the universe is only a partial and temporary expression, can indeed rest assured that nothing can separate him from the Eternal *Tao* in which he shall have life forever more. "Having the vision of the One, he was then able to transcend the distinction of past and present. Having transcended the distinction of past and present, he was able to enter the realm where life and death are no more. Then to him the destruction of life did not mean death, nor the prolongation of life an addition to the duration of his existence . . . . To him everything was in destruction (transient), everything was in construction (i.e., recreated in other forms of existence). This is called tranquility in disturbance. Tranquility in disturbance means perfection." (Chuang-Tzu Ch. VI) Fung.

It must be added that this speculative Nature Mysticism is often more of the substance of which dreams are made and should not be taken too seriously or literally as Chuang-Tzu himself pointed out when he wrote: "How do I know that the love of life is not a delusion? How do I know that he who is afraid of death is not like a man who was lost from his home when young and therefore does not want to return?... How do I know that the dead will not repent of their former craving for life? Those who at night dream of a banquet, may the next morning wail and weep. Those who dream of wailing and weeping, may in the morning go out and hunt. When they dream, they do not know that they are dreaming. In their dream they may even interpret dreams. Only when they are awake they begin to know that they dreamed. By and by comes the Great Awakening, and then we shall find out that life itself is a great dream." (Chuang-Tzu II.) Fung.

Classical Taoism, especially as formulated by Chuang-Tzu, was a bit too much the dreamer's philosophy of life to be taken very seriously by the "this worldly" Chinese however much its emphasis on freedom and the untrammeled life made its appeal. It is for this reason that in popular Taoism in subsequent centuries the emphasis was placed frequently on the prolongation of human life. Taoists were always in quest of the Elixir of Life looking for some element that would magically make man immortal. Even emperors were known to turn to such Taoist magicians in spite of the protests from their Confucian officials; and some were even reported as coming to an early death as a result of partaking of some magician's Elixir of Life.

As a religion of the masses Taoism had little to say about the philosopher's eternal *Tao* but turned more to various popular deities for help in finding the good life in the here and now, while in matters pertaining to man's eternal destiny it borrowed extensively from Buddhism, especially the Amitābha type with its rather personalistic conception of the Eternal Buddha. In other words, Classical Taoism's conception of the Eternal *Tao* and its Nature Mysticism gave way to a more personalistic conception of the divine and correspondingly the good life ideal tended to be interpreted more in personalistic values instead of a feeling of oneness or communion with Nature. However it must be added that even with this change popular Taoism, like Classical Taoism, saw the good life of man in terms of the natural life and not as being so wholly different that the natural life must be denied or repudiated, as is so characteristic in Indian religions.

When we turn now to Confucianism for its conception of the good life we find that, like Taoism, it sees the good life in terms of man's natural life as a citizen of this world; but where Taoism lays stress on the free and untrammeled life of the individual, Confucianism puts its emphasis on the well-regulated life. The Taoist ideal of freedom is based largely on the individual as such and takes little cognizance of his relationships with others, whereas Confucianism always thinks of the individual in his relation to the social structure. Granted that a few recluses, living their solitary life in some mountain vastness, may be left free to live as they see fit, that is not the way most civilized human beings live their lives. They live rather as members of families, as neighbours in local communities and as citizens of a nation or state. It is, therefore, necessary, says the good Confucianist, and to the best interest of all that every one know his place in the social structure and what is expected of him so that there may be harmony and all share in the good life.

Confucianism has, therefore, much to say about its Five Relationships. These are the relation of Father-Son (or Parent-Child); Ruler-Minister (or Ruler-Subject); Husband-Wife; Elder-Younger Brother; Friend-Friend. In each of these relationships, except the Friend-Friend, the first member in the bracket has precedence over the second member and, in fact, some times there is added a sixth bracket to stress this, namely, the Superior-Inferior relationship. Whatever place an individual may occupy in these various relationships he must know what is expected of him and faithfully do his assigned duty. Little is said about the individual's rights as compared with the emphasis on his duties. However, every one does have the right to expect that the other member of the particular relationship do his duty also.

Now while Confucianism sees the good life largely in terms of the well-regulated life and one in which each individual does what is fitting to his station in life, it may well be asked as to what more specifically constitutes the actual core of the truly good life?

The answer to this question is found primarily in what Confucianism has to say about ethical values and meanings, for Confucianism at its best is concerned with just such values and meanings. To be sure, the good Confucianist sees man, as we said above, as a citizen of this world and so physical well-being and all that is essential for this is a part of the good life, but man is not a mere animal and the core of the full and truly good life must ever be far more than merely a comfortable physical life. In fact, when a man is true to himself and seeks the good life in terms of moral values and meanings he may under certain circumstances be called on to give up his bodily life; or as Confucius put it, "Do not seek life at the expense of *Jen*, ('Virtue'). Some even sacrifice their lives to complete their *Jen*." (Lun Yu XV. 8) Fung. Thus while Confucianism lays great stress on a well-regulated social order and while it sees moral values and obedience to the moral law as instrumental in building such a social order it at the same time holds that moral ideals are not mere means to some other end but that living one's life in conformity with such ideals constitutes the very core of the good life. This is so because moral values and meanings are not mere rules invented by man to regulate human society. They are rather man's awareness and understanding of the eternal Moral Order and as such are authoritative for every human being no matter what particular place in the social structure he may occupy. It is true that Confucius had comparatively little to say about the Divine, as we saw in our section on the God-concept, and so there is also little in his teachings about man's relationship with the Divine or the good life being one of communion between man and his God, as is so much the case in some religions: but Confucius, nevertheless, was quite positive about the reality of the moral order and "the decrees of Heaven." No one, he maintained, can become really a true and superior man unless he lives his life in conformity with the moral law, or as he put it: "Without recognizing the decrees of Heaven it is impossible to be a superior man." (Lun Yu XX. 3.1) Legge. And as he says further; "The superior man holds three things in awe: He holds the decrees of Heaven in awe; he holds the Great Man in awe; and he holds the precepts of the sages in awe." (Lun Yu XVI. 8) Fung. These three constitute a unity but they are arranged in a definite sequence in their relationship. There is first Heaven or the Decrees of Heaven as the ultimate norm for human life and conduct. Second is the Great Man who in his life embodies this norm and as such sets the example for others. And third are the sages who formulate various precepts based upon the lives of Great Men who in the past had embodied Heaven's decrees.

If it be asked who this Great Man is or who these Great men are, it must be said that Confucius' answer is not too convincing. He speaks of certain great men of the past, great rulers such as Yao and Shun, but these are rather shadowy figures and the ideals which they supposedly embodied are largely Confucius' own conception of what should be the norm for human life. In other words, Confucius himself had a deeper insight into what constitutes the ethical values and meanings and how living by them man can have the truly good life than did those ancient rulers whom he idolized. While he laid no claims to being an embodiment of his ethical teachings he may, nevertheless, be regarded as one who thoroughly believed in their validity for all men and as constituting the very core of the truly good life.

I

What, then, are the ethical ideals and values of Confucius and Confucianism when stated more specifically?

The key word in Confucius' ethical teachings is the word *Jen*, "Virtue." *Jen* stands for the basic stuff of the all-rounded moral character. Like the term "Virtue" it is a bit hard to define just because it includes so much. It is clear, however, from many passages in the Confucian classics that a man of *Jen* must be all-rounded in his moral perfection. Thus when Confucius was frequently asked by his disciples what he thought of certain individuals who were noted for one or more noble qualities such as wisdom, courage, loyalty, purity, etc., he usually replied that so and so is a good example of this or that particular quality of character but not of the all-rounded character which the man of *Jen* represents.

Now while *Jen* stood for the all-rounded virtuous life and so included all moral qualities there are, nevertheless, certain qualities which are more central than others. Among these more basic qualities are such as uprightness, sincerity, earnestness, courage, loyalty, respect, modesty, kindness, magnanimity, love and wisdom. Such qualities must be kept in balance, as it were, for the Confucian Great Man or Superior Man is not only one whose character is built of the basic stuff but he is also a man of good manners who does not go to extremes nor violates the rules of propriety.

"The superior man in everything considers righteousness to be essential. He performs it according to the rules of propriety. He brings it forth in humility. He completes it with sincerity. This is, indeed a superior man." (Lun Yu XV. 17) Legge.

"Where the solid qualities are in excess of accomplishments, we have rusticity; where the accomplishments are in excess of the solid qualities, we have the manners of a clerk. When accomplishments and solid qualities are equally blended, we then have the man of Virtue." (Lun Yu VI. 1.6).

"To be able wherever one goes to carry five things into practice constitutes Virtue. They are respect, magnanimity, sincerity, earnestness and kindness. With respect you will avoid insult; with magnanimity you will win over everyone; with sincerity men will trust you; with earnestness you will have accomplishment; and with kindness you will be fitted to command others." (Lun Yu XVII. 6) Fung.

The man of Virtue not only tries to be perfect himself but also seeks the welfare of others. "For a man of Virtue is one who desiring to maintain himself sustains others, and desiring to develop himself, develops others. To be able from one's own self to draw a parallel for the treatment of others, that may be called the way to practice Virtue." (Lun Yu VI. 28) Fung. Or to express this more succinctly, we have what is sometimes called the Confucian Golden Rule. "What you do not want done to yourself, do not do to others." (Lun Yu XV. 23) Legge. The substance of this occurs frequently in the Confucian Classics. In fact, when Confucius was asked, "Is there one word which may serve as a rule of practice for all one's life?" he replied, "Is not reciprocity such a word?" Then he added, "What you do not want done to yourself, do not do to others."

Perhaps this principle of Reciprocity lacks something not only in that it states the Golden Rule in negative terms but in that the individual who lives by it has a right to expect others to treat him as he treats them. To be sure, Confucius held that if they failed to respond in the same spirit one is not absolved from doing what is right and just but one need not go too far in the matter. Thus when Confucius was asked, "What do you say concerning the principle that injury should be recompensed with kindness?", he replied, "With what, then, will you recompense kindness? Recompense injury with justice and recompense kindness with kindness." (Lun Yu XIV. 36) Legge.

While Confucius thus set limits to what is required of the virtuous man in his treatment of others he, nevertheless, maintained that the life of virtue is the supreme good and, as we have pointed out above, he held that a man in pursuit of such a good life may under certain circumstances surrender even life itself. And furthermore, even though one should have to surrender life itself in order to be true to one's ideals, one may, nevertheless, rest assured that no real harm can come to the man of Virtue. "Virtue is more to man than either water or fire. I have seen men die from treading on water and fire, but I have never seen a man die from treading the course of Virtue." (Lun Yu XIV. 34) Legge.

Confucius and Confucianism, while having much to say about the good life for the individual in terms of moral values, have even more to say about social ethics and the good life made possible by a well-regulated society. In fact, down through the centuries it was the Confucian social ethics that gave stability to the family, the local community and the state. The chief requirement for any one serving as a government official was that he be well grounded in the Confucian ethical teachings. To be sure, the basic moral qualities for which the term *Jen* stood, held for any and every individual, no matter what particular place in life he occupied, but it was regarded as specially important that those in positions of leadership be grounded in what constitutes the basic stuff of character. This is the case because Confucianism lays so much stress on a well-regulated society as essential for the good life of the individuals that make up that society; but such a well-regulated society is possible only as individuals faithfully carry out the responsibilities that pertain to their particular place in the social structure. "Let the ruler be ruler, the minister minister, let the father be father and the son son." (Lun Yu XII. 11) Fung.

In the opening section of the Confucian Classic called the Great Learning and which later Confucianists often regarded as the best introduction to the essential Confucian teachings we read: "The ancients who wished to illustrate illustrious virtue throughout the kingdom, first ordered well their states. Wishing to order well their states, they first regulated their families. Wishing to regulate their families, they first cultivated their persons. Wishing to cultivate their persons, they first rectified their hearts. Wishing to rectify their hearts, they first sought to be sincere in their thoughts. Wishing to be sincere in their thoughts, they first extended to the utmost their knowledge. Such extension of knowledge lay in the investigation of things." Legge. Then the text proceeds by stating the substance of the above in reverse and then adding: "From the Son of Heaven (Ruler) down to the mass of the people, all must consider the cultivation of the person the root of everything besides. It cannot be, when the root is neglected, that what should spring from it will be well ordered." Thus however important a well regulated social structure, in which every individual knows his place and does what is his particular duty, may be, in the last analysis it is the moral qualities of the individuals that make up any given social organism that is most important and that constitutes the root of the good life. Whatever else Confucius had to say about the good life and how it may be achieved, this emphasis on the moral qualities of the individual is central.

In Mencius the Confucian teachings regarding the truly good life had na interpreter second in importance only to Confucius himself. In fact, much of what down through the centuries has been accepted as classic teachings owes fully as much to Mencius as to Confucius. Like Confucius, Mencius stressed the moral life as the very core of the truly good life. He also laid equally great emphasis on the well regulated society from the family unit up to the all inclusive nation or state. But while he remained true to these great essentials of the master's teachings and wanted to be regarded merely as one who transmitted them, Mencius, nevertheless, gave them his own interpretation and added some things new.

First of all, in presenting the moral life as the core of the truly good life, Mencius laid greater stress on man's inborn goodness than Confucius had done. Man's moral life is thus seen as a development of man's true nature rather than as something extraneous or something "fused into us from without," as Mencius put it. "The tendency of man's nature to good," he says, "is like the tendency of water to flow downwards. There are none but have this tendency to good, just as all water flows downwards." (Bk. VI, Pt. I, Ch. II) Legge. Mencius speaks of this inborn goodness as the "four beginnings." These are: sympathy for one's fellowman who suffers; a sense of shame and dislike for what is mean and wrong; modesty and yielding to others instead of self-assertion; and, in a summary way, a real sense of the distinction between right and wrong. "Since all men have these four beginnings in themselves," Mencius says, "let them know to give them their full development and completion, and the issue will be like that of fire which has begun to burn, or that of a spring which has begun to find vent. Let them have their complete development and they will suffice to love and protect all within the four seas. Let them be denied that development and they will not suffice for a man to serve his parents with." (Bk. II, Pt. I, Ch. VI.) Legge It should be noted that Mencius does not maintain that man is born with a fully developed moral character but only that he has capacities which can be developed until he becomes the all-rounded man of character.

This view of man's true nature was challenged by some of Mencius' contemporaries, for in his day many of the so-called Hundred Schools of Philosophy were flourishing and represented a great variety of views about man and everything else. When it was pointed out that few men manifested these noble qualities with which Mencius claimed they were endowed, he naturally had to admit that this was the case but he, nevertheless, maintained that this was due to the fact that so many fail to develop their inborn nature and so gradually lose it. And the chief reason why men lose their inborn goodness is the unfavorable conditions under which they are compelled to live their lives. It is this fact that leads Mencius to discuss the nature of the social structure and what is needed to improve it.

In Mencius' conception of the ideal society and government so essential for the good life of man there is quite a departure from what Confucius had to say on the subject. Where the latter seemed to be concerned primarily with restoring the old order with its hereditary rulers and its hierarchical structure of society in which the lower strata served the upper strata and in turn received a sort of paternal protection, Mencius was more interested in a government which had as its chief purpose the welfare of the people. It is the people and their welfare for which governments exist and the ruler derives his authority to rule only by faithfully carrying out Heaven's mandate to rule in the best interests of his subjects. "The people are the most important element (in the state); the spirits of the land and grain are secondary; and the sovereign is the least." (VII. b. 14 Fung). In fact, Mencius goes so far as to say that if the deities to whom the people offer sacrifices do not send their blessings the people have a right to give their devotion to other deities; and if rulers have grave faults and do not rule in the interest of the people they should be dethroned.

Mencius believed in the hereditary principle for the ruling family and also that a ruler must have a mandate from Heaven to rule. Like Confucius, he pointed to such great figures of the past as Yao and Shun as Sage-Kings or ideal rulers who had a mandate from Heaven to rule and who in their personal character were embodiments of the all-rounded moral life. With such rulers all goes well, for the people naturally obey their every command as "the grass bends to the wind that blows over it." But what happens when rulers are not such perfect embodiments of moral qualities? Mencius had to admit that some of the descendants of the perfect ancient rulers were rather inferior and yet they continued to rule. "That the sons of these rulers were some inferior and some not inferior; this was of Heaven, and not something which could have been brought about by man." However, Mencius adds that when hereditary rulers become too inferior and evil they lose their mandate from Heaven; and the proof that they have lost it is the fact that the people have turned against them. In discussing this matter with his opponents who wanted to know how Heaven's mandate is given to a ruler, he admitted that "Heaven does not speak," for in Confucianism there is little or nothing corresponding to divine revelation in the great theistic religions, and some of Mencius arguments may sound a bit like reasoning in a circle; and yet Mencius was certain that the moral order is an eternal reality and that Heaven does speak in the great events and trends of human history so that no government can long endure which departs too far from what is right and what is to the best interests of the people governed.

Whatever may be true of the social structure and government under which man lives and however much this may condition man's life for better or worse, Mencius stoutly maintained that the truly good life is achieved only in terms of the moral life, and as one lives in harmony with Heaven's decrees and accepts what comes to one in the course of doing one's duty in life. "To dwell in the wide house of the world, stand in the correct position in the world and follow the Great Way (Tao) of the world; when having obtained one's desire (to hold office) to practice one's principles for the good of the people; and when that desire is disappointed, to practice them alone; when riches and honor can not make one dissipated, poverty and mean condition can not make one swerve, and power and force can not make one bend oneself: these are the characteristics of the Great Man." (III. b. 2. Fung) But it is not only in living the moral life in the service of one's fellowmen, the truly good life is one that also knows itself grounded in Heaven and in what Heaven ordains. "He who exercises his mind to the utmost, knows his nature. Knowing his nature, he knows Heaven. To keep one's mind preserved and nourish one's nature is the way to serve Heaven. To be without doubleness of mind, whether one is to have untimely death or long life; and having cultivated one's personal character to wait with this for whatever there may be; this is to stand in accord with Fate (*Ming*) (VII. a. 1, Fung) In fact, Mencius maintains that one can achieve the truly good and noble life only as one makes one's relationship to Heaven primary as we pointed out in connection with the God-concept.

Now while the Confucian teachings regarding the truly good life of man both as an individual and as a member of society were transmitted down through the centuries it must be added that sometimes they were given an interpretation that differed considerably from their original meaning. Thus, e.g., Mencius' teachings regarding the inborn goodness of human nature as well as his emphasis on man's relationship to Heaven were often ignored or even challenged. Men like Hsun-Tzu flatly denied man's inborn goodness and said that "the nature of man is evil; his goodness is only acquired training." If men were left to follow their inborn nature the result would be confusion and a state of violence. "Therefore," reasoned Hsun-Tzu, "the civilizing influence of teachers and laws, and the guidance of the rules of proper conduct (*Li*) and standards of justice (*I*) are absolutely necessary. Thereupon courtesy results, culture is developed and good government is the consequence. By this line of reasoning it is evident that the nature of man is evil, and his goodness is acquired." (Ch. 23. Fung, Hist. of Chinese Philosophy p. 287).

Regarding Heaven and the view that man finds the truly good life only as he feels himself in harmony with Heaven and Heaven's decrees, Hsun-Tzu held that man knows really nothing about Heaven or any metaphysical reality that may lie back of the phenomenal world of man's experience, as we pointed out in connection with the God-concept. And where Confucius and Mencius had stoutly maintained that the very core of the truly good life of man is a life lived in obedience to the moral law and in the awareness that the moral law is grounded in the Eternal, Hsun-tzu saw the moral law as a mere means to an end. In fact, he regarded it more as mere rules for the game of life which when properly observed will result in an orderly society and so make possible the things needed for a prosperous life. Little or nothing is said about moral values and ideals, or finding in these the very core of the truly good life of the individual human being.

This trend given to Confucianism by Hsun-Tzu became even more pronounced in the teachings of Han-fei-Tzu and the so-called Legalists. As the term Legalist implies, they had much to say about Law and a well regulated or controlled society but nothing about an eternal moral order or a moral law written in the heart of every human being, or about the individual find ing the truly good life only as he lived true to it. In fact, the Legalists rejected all concepts of moral good. They scorned all thoughts regarding the inherent rights of the individual or that government must concern itself primarily with the best interests of the people. Law to the Legalists meant arbitrary laws imposed by powerful rulers and deriving their authority, not by any mandate from Heaven or from the essential rightness of their content, but rather from the power of the ruler to impose his will on his subjects. Any thought that the ruler should in his own personal life set a noble example of moral conduct and so win the admiration and loyalty of his subjects was dismissed as impractical. The average citizen was regarded as stupid and depraved and therefore had to be controlled by strict laws. He could be counted on to obey these laws, not out of any desire to do what is right and in conformity with the moral order, but wholly because he feared the punishment that any infraction of the ruler's laws would bring. As Han-fei-Tzu put it, "Power is the means for gaining supremacy over the masses . . . . His (Ruler's) power enforces his strict teachings and nothing that he encounters resists him." (Han-fei-Tzu Ch. 48 Fung p. 320). Or as he says in another place, "This is the way whereby ignorant people will fear the penalities and not dare to speak, while learned persons will not dispute over anything." (Ch. 41 Fung p. 323). Any thought of teaching the people the great moral ideals of their forefathers or developing their inborn noble qualities which Mencius stressed was scorned as out of date. "In the state of the intelligent ruler, there is no literature of books and records, but the laws serve as teachings. There are no sayings of the early kings, but the officials act as teachers." (Ch. 49 Fung p. 323). One might think that these are quotations from some modern Communist writer but they come from the China of the third century B.C.

In accordance with the Legalist's conception of government, Shi-Huang-Ti, founder of the Chin dynasty ordered in 213 B.C. the burning of the Books, especially the Confucian Classics. He also put to death numerous scholars and condemned thousands to forced labor on the Great Wall. While his dynasty which he had expected to rule for thousands of years was soon overthrown by the Han rulers who were rather favorable to the Confucian teachings, it is, nevertheless, true that the Legalist's conception of government had in many ways a lasting influence on Chinese life. Even after the Confucian teachings were accepted as basic for the training of government officials and the Confucian ethics became more or less normative for the life of the individual, the family and the wider circles of the social structure, Chinese government in its dealings with the people always retained traces of the Legalist's imprint. It practically always claimed the right to control every aspect of the citizen's life. Little or no place was given to the individual's inalienable rights and all too often citizens were treated as mere pawns to be pushed about as the authorities saw fit. This rigid control was not limited to economic and political matters which belong more naturally to the sphere of government supervision but it frequently was extended to include also man's spiritual life. Thus the government often saw fit to interfere in religious matters. There was little thought of religion as standing in its own sovereign rights but it was regarded all too much as a mere instrument of state. And when religion's emphasis tended to run counter to what government officials regarded as of primary importance for their this-worldly objectives, religion was not only strictly regulated but even persecuted and suppressed. This was specially true in the case of Chinese Buddhism. The Buddhist monk ideal and Buddhism's other-worldly emphasis ran counter to the characteristically this-worldly emphasis of Chinese thought and it was therefore not strange that sometimes Buddhist monasteries were destroyed and their inmates forced to return to secular life.

It may seem a bit strange that a religion like Buddhism with its characteristic Indian other-worldliness should have made any appeal whatsoever to the this-worldly minded Chinese and it might be well here to give the main reasons why it nevertheless did win its way into the hearts of millions of Chinese and other East Asians.

We have already shown in the section on the God-concept that Mahāyāna Buddhism gave a more satisfying answer regarding man's relationship with the divine than either the native Confucianism or Taoism had done. This has bearing not only on the individual's ultimate destiny but also on his conception and realization of the good life in this world. With its emphasis on man as a citizen of eternity and not simply as one who spends a few fleeting years in this world of sorrows and suffering, Buddhism gave greater scope to man's aspirations. It made ethical ideals and values not a mere set of rules for regulating human relationships, as Confucianism in its traditional form often did, but instead a self-discipline which opens the way to greater freedom.

In the second place, Buddhism was the vehicle of another great civilization which enriched China in various ways. China was rather prone to regard itself as the one great Civilized land which had nothing to learn from her barbarian neighbours. And in fact it is true that China's closest neighbors were inferior in many ways and added little or nothing to China's cultural heritage but rather were themselves greatly influenced by it. However with the introduction of Buddhism China came into contact with India, a land with an advanced civilization and with aspects of this civilization which could supplement and enrich China's own. It was Buddhism that made the contact between these two great centers of Civilization with the result that much of India's spiritual heritage gradually became a part of China's. Thus, e.g., in the field of literature, Buddhism brought into China an enormous amount and ranging in content from deep philosophical speculations to popular folk tales. Upwards of 6000 new terms had to be added to the Chinese language to express what was new in this importation. Also in the field of the fine arts Buddhism enriched Chinese life both by what it brought in from without and what it developed in China after it had gained a real footing. It is therefore not so strange that this Indian religion with its predominantly other-worldly emphasis nevertheless made its appeal; and from about the fourth to the ninth century became in many ways the dominant influence in Chinese life.

It should be added that this Indian religion gained its hold on the Chinese not only because it enriched China's life in various ways but also because it gradually adapted its message more and more to its new environment so that it took on a Chinese coloring and even underwent a real change in some of its inner content. Where in its Indian setting Buddhism had much more to say about "release from this evil world" than about making this world over into a better world, in China the emphasis tended to be more on what constitutes the core of the good life in the here and now. Of course, even in India the religion of the Buddhist layman had gone a long way in that direction and had come to terms with man's natural life as a member of the family and the individual's participation in the life of the community, but Indian Buddhism continued to hold up the monk ideal as the highest and stressed the thought that even the layman must some day, perhaps in his next incarnation, choose the life of a monk if he would climb up the ladder that leads out of this evil world and finally reach the top from which there is no return. In China, on the other hand, the monk ideal was held in less esteem even by good Buddhists. To be sure, when old age comes on and man is about to leave this world the quiet life of the monk in his mountain retreat might be the better life; or in times of great social upheavals or when one has failed in achieving success in the normal life, retirement to some monastery can be a real comfort and peace. But ordinarily the Chinese, even as good Buddhists, see the good life more in terms of the family life and in having a real share in the natural life of man as a citizen of this world. That is one reason why it became the custom in Buddhist families with only one son that the son could not become a monk, at least not until after he had raised a family and had a son who could assure the family's continuity and future welfare. In fact, this conception of the good life as centered in the family life had such an effect on Buddhism that even monks could become family men.

With this adjustment to the Chinese temperament which Buddhism gradually made, it can be understood why the severe measures, which officialdom sometimes took to suppress it as a subversive influence, could not be carried too far and were usually of short duration. To be sure, Confucianism continued to be the dominant influence in the government even though Buddhism or a Taoism strongly influenced by Buddhism became the religion of the Chinese masses and had even a great following in the upper classes of society including court circles. As the dominant influence in government circles Confucianism, particularly the traditional Confucianism which laid more stress on a strong government to which the citizen must give unquestioning allegiance than on what it owed to the citizen in the way of providing him with the good and better life, naturally saw in Buddhism an influence that was rather subversive because of its predominantly other-worldly interest. Even though Buddhism in China, as we have just said above, gradually accepted much of the Confucian ethical teachings as its own and in other ways came more or less to terms with the characteristic this-worldly Chinese temperament, it nevertheless continued to be suspected by Confucian trained officialdom. Had the Confucianism of Chinese officialdom been better grounded in the real teachings of Confucius and Mencius, especially in their emphasis on moral ideals and values as grounded in an eternal moral order rather than as being mere rules for regulating the social structure, Buddhism might have been seen in a better light and its major emphasis accepted as supplementing the true Confucian heritage. As a matter of fact that is what in a sense did finally take place in spite of officialdom's opposition to Buddhism. In saying this we have reference to the developments in Neo-Confucianism which from the eleventh century onward became dominant.

Neo-Confucianism arose in the first place in opposition to the growing influence of Buddhism on Chinese life but it saw the chief cause of this growing influence in the failure of traditional Confucianism as represented in Chinese officialdom to be fully true to its own spiritual heritage. It, therefore, undertook to restore the pure and undiluted Confucianism of Confucius and even more of Mencius. However, in this effort it had to take cognizance of Buddhism with its hold on millions of good Chinese citizens. Therefore in restating what is the pure and full teaching of the Confucian Classics, Neo-Confucian scholars unwittingly betrayed how even their thinking on the great essentials of religion and philosophy was influenced by Buddhist thought. Thus we find them making a serious attempt to give Confucian teachings a deeper grounding in metaphysical reality than traditional Confucianism had been doing. They were, of course, right in saying that according to the Confucian Classics ethical ideals and values are more than mere rules for maintaining a well regulated society and that they have their grounding in an eternal moral order which remains the same even though conditions under which men live may change from time to time. That is to say, while the specific laws made by governments may change from age to age because of these changing social conditions, the moral principles on which laws should be based remain ever unchanged. However, in stressing this basic concept of moral law as found in the Confucian Classics, Neo-Confucian scholars often used terms and concepts which are more akin to Buddhist than to Confucian thought.

Thus Neo-Confucianism, as we pointed out in connection with the God-concept, spoke of a "Supreme Ultimate" (Tai Chi), an obscure term found in the *I Ching*, and made it into a sort of unitary ground that lies back of the old *Yin Yang* dualism and all phenomenal pluralism. In developing their conception of this "Supreme Ultimate," or this noumenal reality underlying all phenomenal existence, much more use was made of Buddhist concepts and terminology than of what is found in the old Confucian heritage. Even Chu-Hsi who maintained that he was following only the thoughts found in the Confucian Classics, shows this Buddhist influence. While in good Chinese style he held that the good life of man must be in terms of what he experiences in this world, especially the life of reason and understanding more fully the things of the natural world, he nevertheless saw all truth grounded in metaphysical reality and as transcending in its absoluteness the powers of the finite mind to comprehend fully. Much of what he says in this connection sounds more like Buddhist philosophy than anything Confucius or Mencius had to say. Then further, while Chu-Hsi as a good Confucianist was interested in government and in applying the Confucian ethics to social problems in a practical way he nevertheless made a study of the Classics and all learning much more of a personal problem or an effort at attaining true enlightenment. This, too, gave more of a Buddhist than a Confucian slant to his thought.

It is however in Wang Yang-Ming (d. 1529) and his influence on subsequent Neo-Confucian thought that one can see most clearly how Buddhism, especially the Ch'an type, affected Neo-Confucianism. For Wang the external world, always so important in Chinese thinking, became rather secondary as compared with the inner world of the spirit. He held quite definitely that by a study of the mind rather than the external world man can know best the true nature of Reality. Not by an eager quest to understand things, but by quiet meditation and through an intuitive insight man can apprehend what is most deeply true and real. This does not mean that one who has thus found in the depths of his own inner being the key to what is true and real, will therefore withdraw from the active life or find the good life only in quiet meditation. Far from that sort of dreamer's world, Neo-Confucianism of this type had much to say about the life of practical action, or rather the proper relationship between knowledge and action. Even though the deepest knowledge of the true and the real is gained by concentrating on the inner life and often comes in a flash of intuition, one who has attained such insight must nevertheless express it in terms of practical action. And he must do so because this insight into what is most profoundly true and real is not so much in terms of mere reason as it is an awareness of moral magnitudes. And moral man who knows what is truly good and real can not but act out the good if he would be true to his own deeper self and to what is ultimate. Though the Neo-Confucianists did not use any term that is quite like Kant's "Categorical Imperative," much of what they had to say about the relationship between knowledge and action has this flavor. As we saw above, traditional Confucianism often used the Confucian teachings as a mere instrument of state. While the ordinary government official was required to have a knowledge of the Confucian Classics there was no way of knowing whether in his own inner life he lived by the Confucian ethical ideals except by the sincerity he showed in his actions. Even then he may in his practical actions follow a course prescribed by authority rather than what in his own inner life he really believes, but where that is the case there is no longer anything that is moral or truly good however much such actions may seem to be in the interest of the government and the people. In the last analysis the Wang Yang-Ming type of Neo-Confucianism, however much it may be interested in training men for government service, is nevertheless more concerned with true enlightenment, i. e., the moral enlightenment of the individual who lives out in practical action the moral values and ideals he knows from his own inner life to be valid and grounded in what is ultimately real and true. Now while this emphasis in Neo-Confucianism is compatible with what Confucius himself had to say it is nevertheless more akin in many ways with Buddhist thought and that is one reason why especially the Ch'an type of Buddhism sometimes sponsored Neo-Confucianism.

Perhaps we have said enough to show that in the course of the centuries there was a mutual influence between Confucianism and Buddhism especially in regard to the good life concept. In fact, Taoism must also be mentioned in this connection for it both influenced and was influenced by both Confucianism and Buddhism so China for centuries has had its "Three Teachings" and most Chinese have sought the good life under the guidance of all three.

Now while Chinese religion as a whole has been enriched by elements from all three of the above mentioned major faiths and while in the course of the centuries the basic differences between the three had been more or less reconciled so that most Chinese lived under the guidance of the "Three-Teachings" it is also a fact that in recent years religion in China seems to have lost its former hold; especially is that the case with the younger generation and many of the intellectuals. This loss of influence pertains especially to what religion has to say about the good life in the here and now. It is understandable that Buddhism with its predominantly other-worldly interests or Taoism with its vague Nature Mysticism and its dream world should be regarded as rather impractical for meeting the problems of modern life. But why should even Confucianism which for centuries had been the main force in regulating and guiding the life of the family, the local community and the relationship between the citizen and his government, be also regarded as no longer relevant and as out-moded by so many?

One reason is undoubtedly the fact that Confucianism with all its interest in promoting the good life of man in the here and now always directed men's minds towards the past and saw the good life largely in what past generations had supposedly accomplished rather than pointing towards a better future. As long as China was obviously superior to her neighbors in general culture and the thing that make for the good life this reference to past a-chievements was rather convincing. But for more than a century now the Chinese have come more and more into contact with the Western world and a civilization enriched by what modern science can provide for a good and better life. As a result of this China is seen now by many Chinese themselves as a backward country and it is perhaps only natural that some of them should blame especially Confucianism just because of its traditional glorification of the past.

As a matter of fact Chinese patriots and intellectuals have tried in various ways to account for their country's present backwardness as compared with the Western World. At first they claimed that Western civilization was at present superior only in the externals of life, such as modern science can provide, but that in real culture and things spiritual China's great heritage remained supreme. Like other Asians the Chinese joined in what has become a trite boast that the West is materialistic while the Orient is spiritually minded. While such a claim may sound rather plausible in a land like India with its traditional emphasis on "other-worldliness" and on "release from this incurably evil world" as the highest goal of religion, it is not too convincing to the Chinese who have always been so decidedly "this-worldly" minded and have sought the good life fully as much in physical well-being as in things purely spiritual.

A second explanation advanced by Chinese apologists was that China's present backwardness is due to the neglect of true Confucianism. True Confucianism provided for the good life on all its levels and all that is needed is to return to the real teachings of Confucius and Mencius. There is, of course, some truth in this and it is a point that had often been stressed by Neo-Confucianist long before China came into contact with the Western world. Then further, it can be claimed that until quite recently China, with her Confucian heritage, was fully as advanced in its civilization as any of the Western peoples. And while it is true, the apologists proceed, that China is at present a little backward as compared with the Western world, this is only a temporary lapse and one from which the country can soon recover and thus resume her honored role which she has played for so many centuries.

Now this line of reasoning may satisfy the pride of those well grounded in China's cultural heritage or the older generation which lives more in terms of the past than the present, but it is not very convincing to the younger generation and the more progressive elements who have come into living contact with the Western world and have had a glimpse of what modern science might do in the way of enriching man's life. In fact, they have become quite impatient with those who keep stressing China's past glories rather than doing something about their country's present backward condition. And it is for this reason that they are quite ready to listen to any one with a definite program for solving present day problems, particularly their country's economic problems.

Now it is this situation which has opened the doors to Communism in present day China. It should be noted that the Communists have wasted little time in talking about China's past glories, especially not the Confucian heritage. In fact, they have singled out Confucianism as the chief culprit and cause of China's present backwardness. Taoism and Buddhism are dismissed scornfully as being an opiate that would keep the common people satisfied with their miserable lot in life by promising them a happy life in the next world. But Confucianism the Communists realize has been a large factor in shaping China's life over the centuries and therefore they center their attack on it and blame it for present day conditions. More specifically, Confucianism is condemned as responsible for China's stratified social structure and for having championed always the interests of the upper strata, the gentry-literati, at the expense of the common people. Secondly, Confucianism is condemned for its exaltation of the older generation at the expense of youth. The age-long ancestor worship which has been such a characteristic of Chinese religion is seen by the materialistically minded Communists as a major obstacle to progress and things new. Then a third count against Confucianism is that in so many ways it has always kept men's minds fixed on the past rather than on the present and the future. There has been all too much glorification of what role China has played in the past and this has been a major reason why China has been so backward. To be sure, Chinese Communists take pride in their country's great history but they are quite realistic about their country's present backwardness and so they would put greater emphasis on what China can become in the future than on the past and especially on a future in which the common people who make up the real China will come into their own. They frankly admit that Western nations are at present superior to China in the things that modern science and industry make available for the good and better life, but this is only temporary and can be soon changed for the better. In fact, Chinese Communists, like their European predecessors, maintain that while Western countries are at present more advanced in many ways than China, only those that accept the Communist ideal of a classless society will be able to maintain their place. Capitalistic countries are much like Confucian China has been, namely, geared to the interest of the privileged class rather than the common people; they are like a pyramid standing on its apex but Communist countries rest on the broad foundation of the common people or rather a classless society.

That this line of thought has made its appeal first of all to the common masses is only natural. It is interesting to note that Communism gained its first real hold, not primarily on the city proletariat as was the case with orthodox European Communism, but on what Mencius called "the country-men" i. e., the ignorant peasants living in the villages and constituting about 80% of the total population. By confiscating the holdings of the rich landlords and distributing the land to the impoverished peasants, Communism seemed to prove its contention that it has above all the interests of the common people at heart. Even non-Communist observers were rather favorably impressed with this program and spoke of it as an agrarian reform. Closely connected with this was the change in village government by which the age-long rule by village elders was replaced by young Communists who were eager to follow the Party line. On the higher levels of government which had in recent years been largely in the hands of Feudal Lords and their willing tools, the gentry-literati, Communism has been making greater use of younger intellectuals who are products of modern schools, many of whom come from the less privileged classes and as such see in Communism's program the promise of a better future.

In these and other ways Communism has gained a real hold on China. Whether Communism will continue this hold and so gradually make China over into its own image or whether it will itself be greatly modified and perhaps be brought more into line with the best in China's great cultural heritage remains to be seen. There are some things even in the areas in which Chinese Communism has had its measure of success that must raise doubts as to its claim of standing for a better future. Thus its early agrarian reforms which seemed to do so much for the landless peasants were soon cancelled out by forcing all into Collectives and then into Communes in which the workers are treated more like slaves than free citizens. This new system of Communes may result in increased production and the worker may be led to feel that he is now working and making his sacrifices in the interest of his government which constantly assures him that in the future things will be better but he may nevertheless have his doubts as to whether that better future will come in his own time. Then in regard to Communism's offering greater opportunities to the younger generation there must be doubts in the minds of many as to whether this is all to the good. Even though it be granted that the Confucian teachings regarding the family and the relationships between youths and their elders was rather lopsided and slanted in favor of the older generation it is nevertheless a fact that it gave remarkable stability to the Chinese social structure. With all its defects this system is far

K

superior to what Chinese Communism is trying to put in its place when it openly encourages children to turn against their parents and praises them as being great patriots for doing so. Surely a system that undermines the family unit can never build a solid nation or state. Even Russian Communism has discovered this.

But an even greater doubt as to Communism being the real "wave of the future" arises in connection with its claim that it is above all the champion of the common man. Granted that the old order in China, as in many other lands, was geared to the interests of the privileged upper classes and that it is high time that the common man have a bigger share in the good things of life, there are two things about Communism which make any thoughtful person question whether Communism is really the champion of a more just and better system. One is that Communism breeds an even more ruthless ruling class than the old order which it seeks to replace ever did. And the other is that while Communism has so much to say about the welfare of the common man or the people it has absolutely no regard or respect for the individual human being. Instead of being the "wave of a better future," in this respect it is painfully like China's Legalists of the third century B.C. The Legalist, too, had no regard for the individual human being as such only in so far as he was an obedient slave to his government. Nor did they have any room for the moral law by which the individual lives his own inner life in freedom. Only the law imposed by government decree and backed by power, had any place in their system.

It is considerations such as these that should make any intelligent Chinese or any other student of human history realize that however much the Chinese Communists may accomplish in the way of bringing to their people the better life in terms of what modern science and industry make possible they can never give them the truly good life unless they have a greater respect for the individual human being and the moral values and ideals by which man can truly live. Sooner or later even those who are now so favorably impressed with the Communist program of doing something positive about their country's backwardness and improving its economic condition, will realize that man, just because he is man "does not live by bread alone." Whether that means that the Chinese people will then turn again to Confucianism and their other age-old spiritual heritage remains to be seen. That there is much in the best of this heritage that is of permanent value cannot be questioned by any fair-minded student. It is, however, quite likely that this heritage will be reinterpreted and modified by the influence of the Western world's spiritual heritage and so bring it more in line with what might be called our developing common World Culture, especially in matters pertaining to the good life in the here and now.

B: VI JAPANESE RELIGION AND THE GOOD LIFE

As WE SAW in connection with the God-concept, Japan belongs to the great cultural sphere of East Asia of which China had usually been the center for centuries and until rather recent times. It is therefore, quite natural that the good life ideal in Japanese religion should have much in common with that of China, especially in so far as this ideal was shaped by Buddhism and Confucianism.   However, it must be added that while there has been a tremendous influence on Japanese life from the neighboring continent down through the centuries, Japan has usually modified what she has borrowed from others before accepting it fully as her own. Furthermore much of the best in the spiritual heritage of East Asian peoples is perhaps better preserved in its Japanese form than elsewhere; and it is for these reasons that we must add here a few pages dealing more specifically with the good life ideal in Japanese religion.

Before Japan came so greatly under the religious and cultural influences of the neighboring continent her own native religion, Shinto, was a naive nature worship. The early Japanese thought of their land as "the land of the gods," for Japan is indeed a land in which nature is so wonderful and alluringly beautiful but on the other hand is also a land with devastating storms and shattering earthquakes. Thus in a unique way man's life seems so decidedly conditioned by the forces of his natural environment; and it is perhaps only natural that in early Shinto the good life ideal should have been cast so largely in terms of material goods which these nature gods could give so attractively and which they could also take away so ruthlessly.

Another characteristic of the native Shinto was ancestor and hero worship. Whether this came originally through the early influence of China's ancestor worship is not altogether clear. At any rate it became a marked characteristic rather early in Japanese history and was bound up with the belief that the ancestors of especially the ruling family were the very gods themselves, particularly the Sun Goddess, *Amaterasu Omikami*. It should be noted that in Japanese ancestor worship the emphasis is not so much on what the descendants must do for the welfare of the departed ancestors as on what the guardian ancestral spirits can do for the earthly welfare of their descendants. And it is not so much the welfare of the individual that is stressed but rather that of the family, the clan (in earlier times) and the nation or state (in more recent times). Of course, the descendants must do their share if they would have the protection of these guardian spirits and enjoy the good life on this earth. They must above all else be loyal to their ancestral traditions and heritage. This is, perhaps, the finest aspect of Japan's native religion. With all its naivete and which the Japanese gradually outgrew as they came more fully under the influence of the higher Chinese civilization, Shinto's emphasis on the spirit of loyalty has persisted down to the present and has been a great source of strength even though it be granted that this spirit of loyalty has at times been directed towards unworthy ends. While every Japanese loves his native land because it is his own country and also because of its natural beauty and so in a way may be said to be a worshipper of nature, what is even more characteristic is his pride in *Yamato Damashii*, the Spirit of Yamato (Japan). Loyalty to this national heritage is to him the very core of the truly good life and for which he will sacrifice everything, even life itself. Cast doubt on an individual's loyalty to his country and life ceases to be worth living until he has vindicated it; if need be, by surrendering life itself.

It is, of course, true that in the modern world there is everywhere much made of loyalty to one's country and people. Nationalism and Patriotism are such marked characteristics of the modern man that it is often said that "Patriotism is man's other religion;" with some it seems to be their only religion. However, in Japan this is even more the case and has been so for a longer time. Perhaps it is just because Japan has borrowed so much from others that there is such an over-emphasis on the uniqueness of the "Spirit of Japan" and on loyalty to that spirit as constituting the very core of the good life for every true Japanese.

Now while the native Shinto with its emphasis on the spirit of loyalty to the ancestral heritage has been a factor in shaping the good life ideal of the Japanese it is, after all, not the major force that has shaped this ideal. For upwards of a thousand years and especially since the twelfth century the good life ideal has been shaped more by Buddhism and Confucianism than by Shinto. Buddhism coming into Japan via Korea or direct from China was, as indicated above, the vehicle of the rich cultural heritage of China. At first this importation was accepted wholesale and without much discrimination. This was true of both the various Buddhist sects themselves and what they brought with them. However, in the course of time Japan not only assimilated what she received from the continent but in the process of making it truly her own she modified it in various ways so that even Buddhism itself as it became fully grounded in Japanese soil differed considerably from Chinese Buddhism and even more from original Indian Buddhism. Especially was this the case in regard to what it had to say about the good life of man in the here and now.

To be sure, Buddhism in Japan continued to proclaim its characteristic other-worldly message as it had done in China and in its original Indian home. In fact, it alone gave to the Japanese anything like a satisfactory answer as to life's issue and ultimate meaning. The native Shinto with all its lusty spirit world had really little to say on this point that could have much meaning for the more intelligent, and Confucianism likewise had little or nothing to say to man as a citizen of eternity. It was thus quite natural that Buddhism should have received a hearing by the Japanese as it had by the Chinese because of its other-worldly message. But whereas in China Buddhism won its way into the hearts of the people primarily because of the hope it held out to man as a citizen of eternity, in Japan Buddhism won its way not only because of this message but also because it had a great deal to say as to what constitutes the truly good life of man in the here and now. At first Buddhism did this, as we stated above, by being the vehicle which brought so much of the rich cultural heritage from the neighboring continent .but after Buddhism had become fully grounded in Japan it had its own interpretation of what constitutes the good life of man as a citizen of this world and it formulated this ideal in terms that are distinctively Japanese. This was particularly the case with the so-called sects of the Great Awakening, namely, the two great Amida sects (Jodo-shu, and Jodo Shin-shu), the Zen and the Nichiren sects. Each of these, in its own way, sought to answer the question as to what constitutes the truly good life of man in the here and now.

The first of these, the Jodo-shu, founded in 1175 by Honen Shonin, sees the good life primarily in a knowledge of and trust in the all-sufficiency of divine grace, the grace of the eternal Buddha Amida (Sk. Amitābha). To be sure, man is a creature of this world and as such the good life for him must include physical well-being and the material goods that make this possible. For this reason it is only natural and really necessary that he should take part in the ordinary pursuits of life. However, man is more than a creature of this earth. He is a being with an eternal destiny and so this must ever be his main interest and deepest concern even while he is engaged in his daily tasks of making a comfortable living.

But how is one to live the normal life of a citizen of this world and at the same time make sure of one's eternal salvation? Indian Buddhism had usually answered this question by saying that one must cut all ties with this world as far as possible so as to concentrate on the inner life, and by strenuous effort win one's freedom from the bondages of the flesh and attain the life eternal. Even in China, with all its this-worldly interests, Buddhism characteristically exalted the monk ideal which would deny this life in the interest of one's eternal salvation. As we said above, the Chinese turned to Buddhism largely for what it had to offer to man as a citizen of eternity, while in matters pertaining to the good life of man as a citizen of this world the Chinese looked primarily to Confucianism. In Japanese Buddhism, especially in Amida Buddhism as interpreted by Honen, and perhaps even more as interpreted by Shinran, the founder of Jodo Shin-shu, man's eternal salvation, to be sure, remains a major interest but it is not achieved by man's own anxious efforts. It is rather the gift of Amida accepted in simple faith and trust by the believer. Resting in this assurance of divine grace the believer can live his earthly life joyfully and with confidence. He does his good works not to earn his eternal salvation but rather as an expression of gratitude. In that spirit he can live the normal life of man as a citizen of this world taking a real part in the work of the world and helping his fellowmen build the good life in the here and now though ever remembering that the better life awaits him in Amida's Paradise when his own short span of life in this world comes to an end. To emphasize the thought that the man of religion should live as a normal citizen of this world, Shinran gave up the celibate life of the monk and married. He also dressed more like a layman and in other ways sought to live his religion in terms of man's normal life.

Shinran's bold innovations naturally shocked many of his fellow monks and they saw to it that he was banished to a remote part of the country. This, however, did not worry him and, in fact, he regarded it as rather providential since it gave him an opportunity to spread his conception of true religion without too much interference from the authorities in the capital and other centers of Buddhism. It is rather significant that over the centuries it is this type of Buddhism that has won the greatest following in Japan and that even to this day shows real vitality.

Another type of Japanese Buddhism which sought to link the religious life more definitely with man's normal life as a citizen of this world is the Zen sect which is the Japanese form of Chinese Ch'an Buddhism. In the first place Zen Buddhism as it came into Japan had close affiliations with Neo-Confucianism and as such stressed the thought that the good life is dependent in large measure upon a well-regulated social structure from the family up through the local community and the state. Furthermore, Zen Buddhism sought in its own way to promote the good life in the here and now by its emphasis on an inner life of the spirit which enables one to face the problems and difficulties of life with courage and confidence. Zen Buddhism has nothing to say about divine grace through which man's problems are solved. That solution which the Amida type of Buddhism offered is regarded as a religion for weaklings by the Zen Buddhist. Man must be his own savior and not rely upon another to solve his problems for him. Man can do this when in quiet contemplation he realizes that he has inner resources for solving life's problems, both for the good life in the here and now as well as his eternal salvation. Man has such inner resources, Zen Buddhism holds, because in the depths of his own true being he is akin to and a part of what is ultimately real and eternal.

Although Zen Buddhism lays much stress of the contemplative life it does not say that one should withdraw from the world in any such way as Indian and even Chinese Buddhism had often done. Man must rather take a real part in the work of the world, facing its problems boldly and with confidence. It is this courageous spirit stressed by Zen Buddhism that made its appeal to the Japanese, especially to strong men, including military leaders.

A third type of Buddhism which arose in Japan at the time of the so-called Great Awakening when Buddhism became more or less naturalized in Japan is Nichiren Buddhism. It is the only Buddhist sect in Japan which is known by the name of its Japanese founder which in itself bears witness to the fact that this type of Buddhism was thoroughly naturalized in its Japanese environment. Nichiren's interest in religion was not so much in what religion can do for the individual either in the way of the good life in the here and now or for his eternal salvation, but rather what religion can do for the good of the nation. To be sure, this attitude towards religion was not altogether new or unique for as a matter of fact both in China and in Japan religion has often been regarded more as an instrument of state than as standing in its own sovereign rights; and as we saw above, one reason why Buddhism in China was often persecuted and suppressed was just because Chinese leaders, with their Confucian training, often felt that it was really undermining the foundations of Chinese society and the state with its otherworldly emphasis and its monk ideal which encouraged men to withdraw from the normal life of the world. Now Nichiren did not attack the monk ideal as such but he did insist that religion must concern itself primarily with the welfare of the state and especially with providing a spiritual foundation which unites the people in the interest of the state. But that is just what was lacking in Japan, Nichiren felt. Religion was really dividing the people. Especially was this the case with the new Buddhist sects such as the Amida and Zen sects which were gaining such popularity in Nichiren's day.

These sects were not only dividing the people with their differing teachings but were also perverting the true teachings of the founder of Buddhism, Nichiren insisted. What was needed, therefore, was a return to the true teachings of the historic Buddha and an interpretation of these teachings in a way that assures harmony among all good believers. This alone can save Japan, Nichiren maintained.

As a matter of fact, Nichiren knew very little about the real teachings of the founder of Buddhism and it is rather ironical that instead of bringing about any harmony among Japanese Buddhists he and his followers sowed the seeds of dissension. The main point, however, that we wish to make is that Nichiren Buddhism is but one more example that shows how Buddhism in Japan concerned itself very much with man's problems as a citizen of this world and not merely with the individual's eternal salvation as had been so characteristic of Indian Buddhism and even of Buddhism in the this-worldly minded China.

In our day the Japanese, like so many other people of the modern world, are even more interested in finding the good life in the here and now. They also see the good life very largely in terms of material goods which are so essential for physical well-being and comfortable living. And again, like so many others, they look more to what modern science and technology have to offer along these lines than they do to religion. However, the Japanese are not quite such devotees of modern science as other Asians are since it is to them not so new and they are well enough grounded in science to know that there are aspects of the truly good life of man that science as such cannot provide and that, after all, are the province of ethics and religion.

B: VII THE GOOD LIFE IN RELIGION—SUMMARY

As we have seen, the good life ideal for man as a citizen of this world has found rather widely differing interpretations in the major religions of mankind. Even within what is nominally one and the same religion there have been rather marked differences over the years.

At one end of the scale is the view which is rather pessimistic about the possibility of finding anything like the good life in this world. Man's natural life is seen as so incurably evil that it seems the part of wisdom to withdraw from the world and to concentrate wholly on an inner life of the spirit and commune with the divine or with what is transcendental and ultimately real. At the other end of the scale is the view which sees the good life almost wholly in terms of man's natural life and which has little to say about man's relationship with superhuman realities or about man as a citizen of eternity.

In between these two extremes are the views which in one way or another hold that man should take an active part in the life of the world but at the same time live this life in spiritual terms and with due regard for his relationship with the divine and his own eternal destiny.

On the whole, Indian religions have tended towards the first of these two extremes. They have often pictured this world as so incurably evil that it is impossible to find the good life in terms of man's natural life and instead have held up the celibate monk's life and a rigid asceticism as the only way to find the truly good life. To be sure, there have been other trends in Indian religions; and in the religion of the Indian masses the good life is pictured largely in terms of material goods rather than in spiritual terms, but even so it remains a fact that Indian religious leaders and thinkers have often treated the physical world and man's natural life as evil or illusory and thus the very enemy of the spiritual life and of that which makes man at one with the divine and the eternal.

Chinese religions, on the other hand, have tended rather towards the second extreme view as to what constitutes the good life. Both classical Taoism and Confucianism have regarded man's life as essentially good. As we saw, Taoism stressed man's oneness with Nature and sought the good life in terms of the natural life but living it in freedom and unhampered by man-imposed rules and regulations. Confucianism also saw man's natural life as inherently good but held further that the individual can find the truly good life only as a member of a well-regulated social structure and as each member of the group does his assigned task. Even after China came more and more under Indian influence with the introduction of Buddhism and looked to Buddhism for what it had to say about man's eternal salvation, the Chinese people continued to cling to their belief that man is above all a citizen of this world and that he can find the good life in terms of man's natural life. As we saw, the world-denying life for which the Buddhist monk ideal stood seemed foolishness to good Confucianists and as undermining the very foundations of human society. Of course, there have been some Chinese who accepted the ascetic ideal for themselves and who believed that by cutting all ties with the world they would be on their way to eternal salvation; but it is also true that the type of Buddhism that increasingly gained the adherence of the Chinese and other East Asian peoples was the type that not only promised the good life in the here and now but that even pictured the future life and the heavenly world largely in terms of the good things in man's earthly life.

The great monotheistic faiths have been on the whole less prone to go to either extreme in their conception of what constitutes the truly good life of man in the here and now. On the one hand, they have usually stressed the thought that man and the world in which he lives are the creation of a good and perfect God and therefore it is rather natural to regard man's earthly life as essentially good. Both Christianity and Islam accept as their own Judaism's affirmation that "God saw everything that he had made, and behold it was very good," (Gen. 1:31); or as Psalm 24 puts it: "The earth is the Lord's and the fullness thereof; the world and they that dwell therein." On the other hand, these great faiths, even with their firm conviction that the world as God's creation is essentially good, nevertheless, maintain that the truly good life can never be found merely in terms of man's natural life however successfully he may relate himself with Nature or make use of Nature's gifts. Man is after all more than merely a part of Nature, they hold. He is a spiritual being and as such he can find the truly good life only in spiritual terms and especially in his moral and spiritual relationships with his God and his fellowmen. And it is in this connection that the great ethical monotheisms are perhaps more realistic than the other great faiths of mankind in what they have to say about the real obstacles to man's spiritual life, namely, moral evil or sin. It is not any evil or imperfection in Nature as such but rather something in man himself. To be sure, it may seem rather contradictory to hold, on the one hand, that man and the world in which he lives are the creation of a good God while at the same time affirming that man is a sinful creature. Theologians and philosophers have wrestled with this problem and have come up with different answers. Perhaps none of these quite clears up the difficulties involved; but they usually have at least this merit that they frankly face the problems created by moral evil in human nature and that they insist that the truly good life cannot be had until this evil is somehow conquered and the individual is enabled to live his life in terms of moral and spiritual values. However much man's life may be grounded in Nature or is conditioned by the way he adjusts himself to his natural environment, the truly good life is nevertheless something spiritual and only as man makes this his primary interest can he find it.

Now while the great religions of mankind in one way or another have usually held the view that man is a spiritual being however much he may be grounded in the natural world and that he can therefore find the truly good life only in spiritual terms, it is a fact that modern man has become rather sceptical about religion being much of a help in providing the good life in its physical aspects and especially in the way of material goods and the things needed for physical well-being. For this aspect of the good life which seems so all important to modern man he looks rather to science and technology. In the Western world this has been the case for a century or more and that is one reason why the Western world is on the whole so much more advanced in this respect than other parts of the modern world. As we said before, Oriental peoples have often consoled themselves by saying that the West is materialistic while they are spiritually minded and have produced the great religions and philosophies of mankind. This is, however, no longer very convincing, for it is especially in the economically under-developed countries of the world that there is such a demand today for the things which modern science and technology make possible. Even in India, with all its other-worldly emphasis in the past, there is now this passion for a better life in terms of material goods. In fact, it is in the lands that are backwards in the things that modern science can provide that the Communist jibe about religion being an opiate to keep the underprivileged satisfied with their miserable lot in life hits home with telling effect. And it is in "the spiritually minded" Orient and lands that boast of being the birthplace of the great religions of mankind that so many of the intellectuals and political leaders have turned their backs on their religious heritage as a hindrance to progress and are looking to modern science and technological developments for a solution of their problems.

In short, then, modern man the world over tends to see the good life above all in terms of material goods and the things that make for physical comfort and well-being. And nowhere is this more the case than among intellectuals in the economically underdeveloped areas of the world. There can, of course, be no question about science and technology being most effective in solving man's economic problems. If the increasing millions are to be fed, clothed and housed more decently then men of science and industry must show the way.

But while it should be perfectly clear that modern science and technology are the best answer to man's bodily needs and all that makes for physical well-being it is also true that they can and are being used to destroy these good things on an unprecedented scale as has become all too evident in recent years. That is just the irony of modern life that man's very mastery over Nature's secrets which has enriched human life in so many ways has also produced nuclear weapons which can wipe out these rich gifts and annihilate man himself. Thus modern man, with all his progress in things that make for physical well-being and security of life, now lives in deadly fear of the weapons that his own mastery over Nature has produced. His one and only hope that these weapons in the hand of his enemy will not be used against him seems to be the enemy's own fear of reprisal or the realization on the part of all concerned that an extensive use of nuclear weapons by all parties might well result in universal death. This is not a mere scare on the part of the ignorant masses who do not understand the mysteries of modern science. It is rather the sober opinion of the world's leading scientists themselves. That is why they are taking the lead in calling for an end of all wars and for settling all disputes that lead to war by peaceful negotiations. That means, of course, that men will have to trust each other and place confidence in agreements reached by peaceful negotiations. In fact, it involves what is basically a moral and spiritual solution; something that is not far from the ideal of universal brotherhood of all men or an ideal for which the great religions of mankind have usually stood at their best.

But it is not only that man must turn again to moral and spiritual values if he would be saved from the folly of self-destruction and live in peace. It is also, as we have repeatedly said, that the very core of the truly good life consists of such values and meanings. That is what the great religions of mankind have always said in one way or another and that is undoubtedly a major reason, as was stated in our introduction, why today at least some of the more thoughtful are showing a renewed interest in their religious heritage. And it should be noted that this interest is most pronounced in the very lands where modern science has achieved its greatest success in providing the things so essential for man's physical well-being. That is but another way of saying that however much man's life is grounded in things material and however essential physical well-being is as a part of the good life, if man would have life at its best he must seek it also in terms of things spiritual.

RELIGION AND THE DESTINY OF
THE INDIVIDUAL

As WE SAW IN THE PRECEDING SECTION, RELIGION ALWAYS concerns itself with the good life of man in the here and now, but equally characteristic is religion's concern with the destiny of the individual beyond the present life. In fact, one of the major attacks on religion in the modern world is just this: that it has always been more interested in saving man out of this evil world into a future heaven than in making over this present world into a fit place for man to live in. Be this as it may, it is a fact that in most religions the question as to the individual's destiny beyond the present life occupies a large place. This is so in the very nature of the case, for religion, at least in its more or less mature forms, views man *sub specie aeternitatis*. Just in so far as religion sees in human life something more than the mere sense life, does it seek to answer the question as to what will become of that reality in human nature that is more than the body when the body is dissolved in death. The question as to the survival of the individual is bound up most intimately both with the conception of the spiritual aspect of human nature and the conception of the divine world or the spiritual core of ultimate reality. Thus just because religion stands characteristically for a spiritual interpretation of the nature of human life and for a spiritual conception of the nature of ultimate reality it is a natural corollary that religion should also affirm that the life of the individual does not end with the death of the body.

The conceptions as to the nature of that survival and the grounds for it differ considerably in the various historic religions, just as do the conceptions of the nature of the good life and of the divine. The truth is, as we have already pointed out before, these three cardinal elements of religion mutually condition each other. This is only natural for religion, at least in its more developed forms, recognizes the principle of continuity as does any other serious view of reality. Just as a purely materialistic or mechanistic interpretation of human nature would make belief in spiritual survival after the death of the body an absurdity, so a recognition of the spiritual aspect of man's life as being something more than a product of mere physical forces makes a belief in the survival of this "something more" a rather natural corollary. To what extent such a belief can be validated will concern us in

Part II. Let us here proceed with a brief survey of the conception of survival and ground for it as this is held in representative historical religions.

C: I CHRISTIANITY & INDIVIDUAL DESTINY

THAT CHRISTIANITY stands for a belief in immortality hardly needs to be said. This is one of its cardinal beliefs. And immortality in Christianity always means personal immortality. In fact, the Christian conception of the good life in this world is that it is at the same time the life eternal. It is a life of the spirit and even though it is at present conditioned by the bodily life it is nevertheless regarded as even now transcending the physical and therefore as something which is not necessarily ended with the death of the body.

But in Christianity the belief in personal immortality is based not so much upon the inherent nature of the spiritual self (though this has always been a prominent conception especially after the amalgamation of Christian thought with Platonic idealism) as upon the faith in a Personal God and his concern for his creation. Jesus himself stated the supreme Christian reason for this belief when he said to the Sadducees, "He is not God of the dead, but of the living." (Math. 22:23) If it is reasonable at all to believe in the God of their fathers, as the Sadducees claimed they did believe, then it is equally reasonable to believe that such a God will not write zero at the end of man's life. The sacredness and supreme value of the human personality is a fundamental of Jesus' teaching. This carries with it the thought that such a supreme value in God's universe can not be a matter of a few fleeting years upon earth but that it belongs rather to the eternal realities.

Then, further, the early Christian faith centering around Jesus Christ was above all else a faith in the risen Lord, and linked with this was the conviction expressed in the Fourth Gospel as the words of Jesus, "Because I live, you will live also." (John 14:19) However this faith in the risen Christ may have arisen, that it was the very core of the faith of the apostles and the early Christian church can not be questioned. Nor can it be questioned that this positive conviction about Jesus' own triumph over death was a major factor in giving his followers the assurance that they, too, would not end in the grave but that they would live forevermore. To this was added the belief in the conservation of life's highest values which grows out of the experience of the very quality of life such as Jesus had lived. Eternal life is really a qualitative life according to the New Testament, and those who have experienced this type of life as the truly good life in the present gain through this experience the conviction that such a life must survive the death of the body.

And what was true with the early Christians has been more or less true for succeeding generations of Christian believers. Faith in personal immortality has always been most natural where men have striven earnestly to live the Christ-like life in this world. The two seem to go together. It is true that in Christian history there have been those who have shown a live interest in a future life without a correspondingly deep concern for the Christ-like life in this world. And on the other hand, is it also true that in modern Christianity there seems much more interest in the ethical ideals of Jesus as applied to our social relationships than in the question about the individual's destiny beyond physical death. But even a superficial understanding of the religion of the New Testament would show that these are one-sided views and partial perversions of the true Christian position. Normal Christianity has always stood for the thought that salvation means, on the one hand, a good life in this world which has the life of Jesus as its pattern and dynamic, and that, on the other hand, it means that this Christlike life begun here has its continuation and consummation in the life beyond.

One of the chief difficulties in believing in a personal survival beyond physical death arises from the fact that it is hard to form any satisfactory picture of a personal life that is no longer associated with the bodily life since all our present experience is always somehow connected with the bodily life. This accounts in a large measure for conceptions of the future life that are rather "realistic," not to say materialistic. In Christian literature we have had numerous attempts to picture the heavenly life. Probably a Dante and a Milton have shaped up the average European Christian's conception far more than have the New Testament writings. And it is, perhaps, only natural that modern Christians with their new conception of the universe as presented by modern astronomy and astronomical physics find it impossible to think any longer in terms of the paradises pictured by Dante and Milton and for that reason find it difficult to cling to a faith in personal immortality. Perhaps a return to the New Testament conception of the nature of the future life would present fewer difficulties, for while it is true that some of the New Testament writings would be of little help if taken too literally, certainly the New Testament conception of the future life in terms of a life of spiritual qualities such as we experience even now on the plane of ethical and spiritual personality can still be a true key to our understanding of the nature of the future life. Probably the best summary statement of the Christian conception is that in the First Epistle of John where we read, "Beloved, we are God's children now; it does not yet appear what we shall be, but we know that when he appears we shall be like him: for we shall see him as he is. And every one who thus hopes in him purifies himself as he is pure." This means that whatever else the life beyond may be, it is a continuation of the eternal life begun in this world, i.e., the life of the spirit which is Christ-like in character. That the achievement of an ethical, spiritual personality in this life is a value which is conserved beyond physical death, is the Christian conception. This is the clearest and withal the most reasonable Christian conception of the nature of the individual's destiny beyond the death of the body.

Christianity, however, does not hold that all individuals will necessarily share the same fate. At least is it true that the predominant emphasis has been on the thought that if ethical and spiritual personality is a supreme value that is worthy to survive then the natural corollary is that those who in this world do not seek for such values, or fail to become somehow related with the divine power that develops such values in human life, cannot share in such a destiny; at any rate not immediately after the death of the body. These restrictions as to this happy destiny find expression in Christian thought in various ways such as the doctrine of eternal damnation of the wicked or the eternal death of the same. Then in the Catholic doctrine of Purgatory we have an intermediary state for those who are not yet worthy of the heavenly life but who are nevertheless destined ultimately to share in it. It would take us too far afield to go into further detail on this point. It is enough for our purpose merely to indicate the fact that while the belief in personal immortality is a cardinal Christian belief it is not always affirmed that all men are by nature inherently immortal beings; or if they are, that they all share necessarily in the same happy fate irrespective of the type of life they have lived in this world. It should, however, be added that there is a growing minority among Christians who hold that while the fate of the individual in the future world is in a real measure conditioned by the character of his life in the present and by the spiritual forces with which he has related himself, no such supreme value as any human personality, however low or undeveloped in ethical and spiritual qualities it may now be, can ever become a total loss in a universe where the good and almighty God rules with a loving purpose. In the words of the poet they would hold,

"That nothing walks with aimless feet
And not one life shall be destroyed
Or cast as rubbish to the void
When God has made his pile complete."

C: II JUDAISM & INDIVIDUAL DESTINY

IN OLD TESTAMENT religion there is much less emphasis on the belief in personal immortality than in the New Testament. Where in the latter this hope is repeatedly affirmed directly and even more often implied when not directly affirmed, in the former one finds it mentioned fairly often in the literature of personal religious devotion such as the Psalms and also in the book of Job, but it is not prominent in the historical books nor in the prophetic books. This is, perhaps, natural enough since in the latter books the writers are so largely concerned with the life of social groups and the nation rather than with that of individuals and for this reason also more with the destiny of the nation rather than with the destiny of the individual beyond death. The life of righteousness under a righteous God is the major interest, but it is not so much righteousness in the sense of the achievement of an ethical personality which has supreme worth for the present and as such is conserved in a life beyond as it is a righteousness of a people as a whole which righteousness "exalteth a nation" in its relationship with other peoples.

But while there is this characteristic difference in emphasis between New Testament and Old Testament religions it nevertheless remains true that in the latter there is a definite belief in personal immortality, and like the New Testament faith this is grounded not so much in the inherent character of man's spirit as on the conviction that the God of righteousness and mercy "will not suffer his holy one to see corruption," but will rather show him the "path of life." It is the faith of the Psalmist who said, "Surely goodness and mercy shall follow me all the days of my life: and I will dwell in the house of the Lord forever." Isaiah spoke of God as one who "will swallow up death forever: and the Lord God will wipe away tears from all faces." (Isa. 25:8) And again we read, "Thy dead shall live, their bodies shall rise. O dwellers in the dust awake and sing for joy!" (Isa. 26:19) Daniel sees as the consummation of all things a deliverance of the righteous, "And many of those who sleep in the dust of the earth shall awake, some to everlasting life, and some to shame and everlasting contempt. And those who are wise shall shine like the brightness of the firmament; and those who turn many to righteousness, like the stars for ever and ever," (Dan. 12:2-3) Even the pessimistic preacher who held that life is a vanity of vanities nevertheless wrote as his verdict of life's issues that "man goes to his eternal home. . .and the dust returns to the earth as it was, and the spirit returns to God who gave it," (Eccles. 12:5,7.).

L

Even though it is true that such passages as given above are comparatively few in the Old Testament and that Judaism seemed far more interested in finding the good life in the here and now than in the individual's destiny in a future world, it is nevertheless also true that in the course of the centuries Judaism showed more and more interest in the latter subject. In fact, Israel's bitter experience at the hand of her neighbors, and resulting in exile and dispersion, had a marked effect on Israel's understanding of life's true meaning and issues. Thus while Judaism continued to be rather "this worldly" in its emphasis it gave more and more thought to the future world. Life in this world seemed to be full of injustice and there must be a future life for the individual in which the injustices of this world do not prevail. That this interest had become quite marked by the time of Christ may be seen from the New Testament account of his encounter with the Pharisees and Sadducees, the former holding definitely a belief in a future life for the individual while the latter denied it. And that the Pharisees triumphed over their rivals in this matter is seen in a dictum of the Mishna according to which any one denying the belief in the resurrection of the dead "shall have no share in the world to come."

Then in Judaism's contact with Islam and other faiths it formulated more definitely its essential teachings and included in these essentials the belief in the future life of the individual the blessed life for the righteous and damnation for the wicked in accordance with God's eternal justice. Thus we find among other thinkers the great Maimonides mentioning "belief in reward and punishment in this world and in the life hereafter," and "belief in the resurrection of the dead," as two of the thirteen important articles of Faith in Judaism. In fact, Judaism has for centuries been both "this worldly" and "other worldly" in its teachings even though it is true that on the whole the emphasis has been more on establishing God's Kingdom in this world than on the destiny of the individual in a Future Life.

C: III ISLAM & INDIVIDUAL DESTINY

IN ISLAM the destiny of the individual is of primary concern. However much interest may center on man's life in this world, the ultimate issues of the individual's life are of even greater importance. This is specially true of Muhammad's teachings as reflected in the Qur'an. Over and over again one finds reference to the Resurrection and Judgment Day when God, the righteous judge of all men, shall reward them according to their faith and their deeds. Muhammad frequently speaks of himself as the "warner," one who warns the unbelievers of eternal damnation in hell if they do not repent of their evil ways and turn in faith to the One and Only True God. "They shall make their bed in Hell, and above them shall be coverings of fire! After this sort will we recompense the evil doers." (Qur'an VII:39)

On the other hand the believers and those who do what is right are promised eternal life in Paradise. "But as to those who have believed and done the things which are right (we will lay on no one a burden beyond his power) these shall be inmates of Paradise: forever shall they abide therein." (Qur'an VII:40)

> *Those who fulfill God's covenant, and break not the compact;*
> *And those who attain what God has bidden to be attained;*
> *And are steadfast in prayer; and secretly and openly*
> *Expend in alms of what we have bestowed upon them;*
> *And ward off evil with good—*
> *These shall have the recompense of the Above (Qur'an XIII:20-22)*

This reward in Paradise bestowed by the All-Merciful upon all who do their duty in this life made many a faithful follower of the Prophet ready to forego the good things in this life and even surrender life itself, for death to such is but the door to the presence of their Lord.

> *Thou shalt in no wise reckon dead*
> *Those who have been slain in the cause of the Lord.*
> *Nay, they are sustained alive with their Lord. (Qur'an)*

The actual content of the future life is pictured in terms of what is regarded as good and pleasant in man's earthly life. Thus over and over again Paradise is pictured as a Garden beneath whose trees the rivers flow. Some times the imagery reflects a life of sense indulgence rather than one of ideal spiritual values. However this should not be over-stressed. At any rate in the writings of the great mediaeval scholars the Islamic conception of the future life was definitely in terms of things spiritual. Many of the rather crude and materialistic ideas and practices reflected in the Qur'an were sublimated and made more spiritual. This in turn found expression also in the conception of the future life. Then in Sufism, as we saw in connection with the God-concept, there is quite a different conception of what constitutes the good life in the here and now and this in turn is reflected also in Sufism's conception of the future life. The good life is one of mystic communion with God and the life beyond is a continuation and consummation of such communion. Even in this life the soul may mount the ten rungs of the spiritual ladder and in the future life the finite becomes completely one with the Infinite. And as the conception of God is less sharply Personal than in the Qur'an so also is the conception of man's future state less in terms of a person-to-person relationship between the individual and his God and seems to be almost a complete merging with the Divine. While a certain degree of personal identity remains according to the conception of most Sufi writers, with some at least the individual practically disappears into the all-inclusive Divine Reality. "When the temporal joins itself to the eternal, the former has no more existence. Thou hearest and seest nought but Allah." (Nicholson, Mystics of Islam p. 150)

C: IV HINDUISM & INDIVIDUAL DESTINY

IN INDIAN religions a marked characteristic is, of course, the overwhelming emphasis on "other-worldliness" and a chief problem is always the problem of man's destiny. To be sure, the early religions of the Vedic period concerned themselves largely with the problem of getting on in this world, but after that period religion's chief concern was usually with the individual's destiny beyond this present life.

In every one of the great orthodox philosophies of Hinduism we have an emphasis on man's spiritual nature and on the thought that he is something more than that ephemeral thing known as the bodily life. India has had its materialist, its Nastikas who say "Na asti", "the soul is not," but these have been so decidedly the exception in Indian higher thought that they only help to emphasize the all but universal acceptance of a spiritual interpretation of human life and the belief that man is a citizen of eternity.

As might be expected, in the long history of Indian thought one finds quite a variety of conceptions of both the ground of man's immortality and the content of that state beyond physical death.

Perhaps the form in which the belief in man's survival finds its most common and wide-spread acceptance is the so-called "transmigration of the soul" doctrine. The heart of this belief is that the deepest aspect of man's nature is the psychic or spiritual aspect but that this is somehow associated with a physical organism in successive stages of its existence, the type of the physical organism in each stage being determined by the nature or character of the spirit. Thus the soul of an evil man will be born the next time in a less favored human body and under less favorable circumstances or even in the form of some animal while the soul of a good man will be born under better human conditions or even as a super-human and heavenly being. In popular belief this is usually conceived as a punishment or a reward meted out by the gods, but underlying even the popular belief is the thought that there is an inexorable causal nexus operative in the things of the spirit which manifests itself in a series of physical organisms in an ascending or descending scale. The point to note here is that in this transmigration doctrine the emphasis is on the spiritual aspect of man as the abiding reality while the body is but the temporary instrument or imprisonment of the spirit suited to the nature of the spirit in each stage of its existence. This is regarded, as we have said, either as a punishment or a reward meted out by the divine world or as a natural condition created by the spirit itself in accordance with *Karma,* the inexorable law of cause and effect.

But Indian religions and philosophies find many other ways in which they express the conviction that man is by nature a spiritual being and that the death of the body means but the change from one state of existence to another. In fact, this problem as to man's true nature and his ultimate destiny is the supreme problem of thought in the Upanishads, in Buddhism, in the great epics and then all through the changing forms of later Hinduism and the more recent reform sects.

As is well known, Vedanta in its interpretation of the Upanishads does not only insist that man in his deepest nature is spiritual but that he is identical in essence with the *Brahman Atman,* from which (whom) all things come and to which (whom) all things return. Physical death can then not mean the destruction of the spiritual in man which is the real man. It may lead to a change in outward appearance and in a sense there is an apparent loss of individual existence but in reality it is only a loss of a separate existence which gives way to a closer union of the finite with the Infinite Spirit. It is as when the wave on the ocean's surface sinks back again into the depths from which it had temporarily risen. Though it may lose its identity as a wave which is distinct from other waves like itself, it does not cease to exist when it seems to disappear. As the mystic in his god-consciousness loses all sense of separate existence and feels himself one with the divine so, Vedanta insists, that when man understands his own deepest nature he realizes his identity with the Eternal Being and therefore may disregard as unimportant that experience we know as the death of the body.

According to *Sankhya* the individual soul or spirit is an ultimate reality since Ultimate Reality is a sort of dualism consisting on the one hand of innumerable individual souls or spiritual beings and, on the other hand, of an active material substance or principle. Man's present life is an unfortunate union of these opposites, and the spirit of man is, as it were, imprisoned in the body and the life that has its source in sense impressions. Even in this life man may become sufficiently enlightened to know what his true nature is and that it does not consist of the physical or of the sense perceptions and concepts and ideas built up from sense perception but rather of pure spirit and that state of consciousness which arises when the mind has freed itself from all that beclouds it with sense impressions and the concepts built up on these. It is as if the pure white crystal realized that the red hibiscus flower reflected in its whiteness as red is not really a part of its own nature and can not really affect it even though for the time being the red flower seems to have made the crystal red. And since man's true nature is pure spirit it follows that physical death, instead of marking the death of the spirit, can be only the freeing of the spirit from its prison house. It is freeing it provided the spirit knows its own true nature and does not allow itself through ignorance to become caught again by this other aspect of reality which we experience as physical.

One must, however, turn to the Bhagavad Gita for India's finest expression of the belief in the immortality of the spirit. Here again we have a strong affirmation of the reality of the spirit. The spirit is not set in opposition to the bodily life as we have just seen to be the case in *Sankhya* philosophy for the Gita accepts the bodily life as more or less normal and good. Man is expected to play his role as a citizen of this world in whatever particular state he may happen to find himself placed, but man is at the same time a citizen of eternity and the death of the body can in no wise end the life of the spirit. This thought is brought out in various ways but perhaps most strikingly where Arjuna is told that the foe he may have to slay in battle as a part of his duty to his own people is really not slain since the spirit is the real man and can not be slain with sword or spear. In the words of the Gita already quoted above in connection with the God-concept, "These bodies are perishable; but the dwellers in these bodies are eternal, indestructible and inpenetrable." (II.18) The body is only the garment of the spirit which is cast off when worn out. "As a man casts off worn-out garments and puts on others which are new, similarly the embodied soul, casting off worn-out bodies enters into others which are new." (II.22)

On the other hand, immortality of the individual human being and especially his salvation and release from rebirth into this world is represented in the Bhagavad Gita as something to be achieved by right effort or as a gift of God bestowed on those who are devoted to Him. "Even though constantly performing all actions, taking refuge in Me, through My grace he attains to the Eternal, Immutable Abode." (XVIII:56)

In later Hinduism the conception of man's destiny fluctuates between the traditional Vedanta interpretation according to which man's spiritual nature survives even though it may lose its separate existence by being absorbed back into Eternal Being and the conception of man surviving as an individual spiritual being either because he is inherently an eternal reality or because he is made immortal at the hand of the Divine. In popular Hinduism as represented in the great Vishnu and Siva sects one finds a belief in heavens and hells conceived in very realistic terms. They are filled largely with whatever man desires or dreads in this life and seem little more than a continuation of what man experiences in the present.

C: V BUDDHISM & INDIVIDUAL DESTINY

BUDDHISM, perhaps more than any other form of Indian religion or philosophy, concerned itself preeminently with the problem of man's true nature and the individual's destiny. Unfortunately there is no general agreement among students of early Buddhism as to the real teaching of the founder on this subject. The older views regarded the Buddha as being virtually an atheist and as denying the existence of a real human self; and, of course, if no real spiritual self exists to begin with then there could be no possibility of a spiritual self surviving beyond physical death. As we saw in our discussion of the God-concept there seems room for several interpretations of the Buddha's conception, and the same seems to be the case regarding his conception of man's true nature and the destiny of the individual beyond death.

It seems clear that while the Buddha did not hold the belief in the transmigration of the soul in its popular form he nevertheless did insist in his *Karma* doctrine that there is a "spiritual something" which survives the death and dissolution of the body and which not only survives but causes in turn the assemblage of a new set of five *Skandhas*, aggregates that constitute individual existence. (Bodiliness or Form, Sensation, Perception, Predisposition, Consciousness, i.e., the psycho-somatic being man is at present). In fact, the Buddha represented his own teaching as being above all else a way of life which will guarantee man's "release" from this dread cycle of individual existence and which he regarded as inherently evil. But when that "release" has been gained so that there is no longer any return to this evil world, what becomes of that reality which has thus been released? Does anything survive and what is the nature or state of this?

The Buddha called this "release" or the state of mind that insures such release *Nirvana*. But what does Nirvana really mean? Its primary meaning is "the void" or "emptiness," but does this mean simply that the *Nirvana* state is void of passion and evil, an emptiness of the undesirable things of this life, or is it an absolute void and an emptiness amounting to annihilation?

As a matter of fact Early Buddhism speaks of a *Nirvana* and a *Pari-Nirvana*, the former standing for the state of enlightenment which one may achieve in this life and which frees one from all the distractions and evils that make up the average life of man while the latter means the state of the enlightened one who has passed out from this realm of evil and suffering. The first is easy enough to understand. It is the life that is free from all passions and desires, even the desire for a better life. It is the complete indifference to all existence as we ordinarily experience existence. It is what the mystic seems to experience when he feels himself free from all sense-impressions and all the concepts and ideas built up on the sense life. It is the cessation of the stream of consciousness of the empirical ego. "Thus the wise conduct themselves, they do no longer long for life. Since *Godhika* has torn out desire with its roots he has attained complete Nirvana."

But while the enlightened one is freed from attachment to this world and from the cycle of rebirths into this evil world, what is the nature of his existence when he is thus free? Or does he have existence in any way? This question is a bit difficult to answer. Some passages seem to imply that *Pari-Nirvana* is not a state of total annihilation and that it has a positive content even though this content is wholly void of all that which makes up human life as we experience it now, even void of the higher aspects of our present spiritual life. Other passages are more agnostic in their answer. "As a flame blown out by the wind goes out and cannot be reckoned as existing; so a sage delivered from name and body disappears and cannot be reckoned as existing." And when he was asked, "Has he only disappeared, or does he not exist, or is he only free from sickness?" the Buddha replied, "For him there is no form and that by which they say he is exists for him no longer." And again we read, "No one knows where the fire has disappeared when the descending hammer hits the iron and the spark flies away and is extinguished. Thus no one knows where he has gone who has been fully released, has escaped the bondages of the senses and the stream of lust and who has attained the bliss of *Nirvana*." Such passages are, as we said, rather agnostic. In fact, it would seem that the Buddha looked upon such questions and speculations about the future state as constituting one of the bondages that bind man to this evil existence. "Unwisely does one consider, 'Have I existed in ages past . . . . shall I exist in ages to be, do I exist at all, am I, how am I? This is a being, whence is it come, whither will it go?' Considerations such as these is walking in the jungle of delusions." It would seem that he was not only rather agnostic on this question but that he hesitated to talk about it and even sought to avoid such questions. This attitude of the Buddha apparently left some of his disciples dissatisfied with his teachings as may be seen from the story about *Malunkyaputta* recorded in *Majhima-Nikaya* 63. It is too long to give here in full. This disciple was determined to have the Buddha answer his questions about man's destiny and similar questions which the Buddha had apparently set aside. If the Buddha was unable to answer his questions, this disciple insisted that he should state frankly that he did not know the answer. The Buddha's first reply was that when he preached salvation as a release from suffering (The Four Noble Truths) he did not promise to solve all such metaphysical questions. His second answer was that when this disciple first came to him he had not come on condition that the Buddha would have to answer these questions. And when *Malunkyaputta* still persisted in pressing his questions the Buddha replied with the famous parable about the man who had been shot with an arrow. If a friend should offer to extract the arrow from the wound and heal him, the man would gladly accept and not first ask all sorts of questions as to who shot the arrow, what kind of man he was, what the arrow was made of, etc., before he let the friend pull out the arrow. So is the teaching of the Buddha. He offers to save man from the evils of this life, an existence which is inherently nothing but suffering from which all sensible men will want release whether there is an existence for one who has found release or not. He added that if he first had to explain all these metaphysical problems men would die in their state of ignorance before he could help them and so would not find release. "What did I explain, *Malunkyaputta?* 'This is suffering,' that is what I explained. 'This is the cause of suffering,' that is what I explained. 'This is the suppression of suffering,' that is what I explained. 'This is the way that leads to the suppression of suffering,' that is what I explained. And why was this explained by me? Because this, Malunkyaputta, brings profit and is the beginning of the holy way of life, because it leads to a turning from the world, to passionlessness, to cessation, to rest, to insight, to enlightenment, to *Nirvana*, that is why I explained this."

"Therefore, Malunkyaputta, whatever was left unexplained by me, that leave thou unexplained, and whatever was explained by me, that thou mayest hold fast as explained."

Even though this story may not represent an actual historic incident, that it represents the impression which the Buddha made in such matters upon many of his disciples is safe to infer from the general tone of many of the older records as well as the tone of much in subsequent Buddhist history. We seem nearer right if we hold that the Buddha was rather agnostic than to say that he either positively affirmed or denied the existence of the individual beyond physical death. And yet his agnosticism leaned more in the direction of giving life's content and life's issue a spiritual value and meaning rather than towards a bland and barren nothingness. Thus even in the above quoted passage the Buddha says that the "holy way of life" which he taught not only "leads to a turning from the world, to passionlessness, to cessation, to rest" but also "to insight, to enlightenment, to Nirvana" which rather point to a continuing existence even though Nirvana is void or empty of all that one experiences in the present life. Then if one thinks of the Buddha's ethical seriousness and his emphasis on achieving in this life what amounts to an ethical and spiritual personality it is difficult to escape the conclusion that with all his apparent avoidance of this question of survival he did stand for values in life which are most worthy to survive. At any rate, whatever the Buddha's position was, later Buddhism, especially in its Mahāyāna form as this developed in China and even more in Japan, not only saw in the Buddha a spiritual personality whom physical death could not blot out but also stood more or less clearly for the belief that spiritual personality in general belongs to the abiding realities of the universe. In fact, it was just because Mahāyāna Buddhism had so much to say about man being a citizen of eternity that it won its way into the hearts of the Chinese and other East Asians as we pointed out in dealing with the good life concept and as shall appear below where we speak of the individual's destiny as seen in Chinese and Japanese Buddhism.

It is also true that Hīnayāna Buddhism, as perpetuated in Ceylon and in South East Asian countries, is quite emphatic in its Nirvana concept that the individual human being has an eternal destiny. While the historic Buddha in his Nirvana state seems rather remote and is remembered only as one who in his days in the flesh taught the way of release from the bondages of life in this evil world, nevertheless the Nirvana concept stands for what is ultimately real and therefore for the corollary belief that any one who has attained true enlightenment in this life not only gains freedom from the bondages of this evil world but that he participates forever after in the bliss of Nirvana. Just what the Nirvana state is can not be expressed in terms of man's present life for it is "void" of all that the unenlightened regard as real. It is, however, not an "absolute void" but rather a fullness of transcendental reality. We might add that this is the way the philosophers speak about Nirvana. In the religion of the masses, both in Hīnayāna and Mahāyāna

Buddhism, the bliss of Nirvana is interpreted, after all, more in terms of what man experiences as the good and pleasant in this life.

C: VI CHINESE RELIGION & INDIVIDUAL DESTINY

AS WE SAW in our discussion of the good life, Chinese religious thought is predominantly "this-worldly" in its emphasis. Especially is this true if one regards Confucianism as the characteristic Chinese attitude towards life and its meaning. Confucianism, as has often been said, is an ethical rationalism which seeks to promote the good life of man as a member of the family, the community and the state but shows comparatively little interest in the ultimate destiny of the individual. A long and prosperous life lived in such a way as to command the respect of friend and neighbor and to serve as an example for one's descendants, is the thing above all others desirable. It is realized that this does not altogether satisfy. "But though I live a hundred years, we'll meet within the grave at last." (Shi King 1.10.11.3) There is occasionally an affirmation of a brighter destiny for the spirit than ending in the grave. "All the living must die and dying, return to the ground. The bones and the flesh moulder below and, hidden away, become the earth of the fields. But the spirit issues forth, and is displayed on high in a condition of glorious brightness." (Li Ki 21.2.1)

Then further, even though Confucianism showed very little speculative interest in the individual's destiny, by its exaltation of filial piety as the supreme human virtue, it gave a strong support to popular ancestor worship which usually means a belief in the continued existence of the spirit beyond physical death. Of course, ancestor worship may often mean little more than a belief in an "immortality of influence" or a grateful and sacred memory of the dead but even so it inclines man's thoughts in the direction of a belief that the deepest aspect of human nature is something more than "the bones and flesh that moulder below and, hidden away become the earth of the fields." It is, however, characteristically Chinese that the spiritual reality which does survive seems ever more or less tied to the physical— not in the Egyptian way which sought to preserve the actual body as necessary to the spirit, but by making the burial place of the body so sacred that it must never be obliterated, and this has resulted in making the land of China look like one huge city of the dead whose borders encroach ever more upon the limited fields of the living.

But while Confucianism has shown comparatively little interest in the question of man's immortality, Taoism has concerned itself very much with this subject. The Tao-Teh-ching holds that man in his deepest nature is one with the *Tao*, the Eternal, and therefore the death of the body can not mean the end of him. "Possessed of the *Tao*, he endures forever. Though his body perish, yet he suffers no harm." (*Tao-Teh-ching* 16.2.) "Life is a going forth. Death is a returning home." "Look on death as a going home," said Chuang Tzu. As is well known, the lofty teachings of the *Tao-Teh-ching* did not maintain themselves very long among Taoists. However Taoism in its popular forms kept up a lively interest in the problem of the individual's destiny; in fact, it often became little more than a vain quest for the "elixir of life" which it was hoped would prolong man's natural life and make it as such an everlasting life. Tradition has it that expeditions were sent forth in search of the fountain of perpetual youth and the medicine of immortality. And when this quest proved futile Taoism in conjunction with popular Buddhism developed its beliefs in heavens and hells both of which being conceived in rather realistic not to say grossly materialistic fashion.

It is, however, Mahāyāna Buddhism which gave to the Chinese people the noblest conception of man's ultimate destiny. Whatever may have been the actual teaching of the founder of Buddhism on this subject, the Buddhism which first won the allegiance of China's millions and which continued as one of the dominant currents of life and thought down through the centuries was a religion which interpreted man *sub specie aeterintatis*. Not only did this type of Buddhism have much to say about the Eternal Buddhas of whom the historic Sâkya Muni was but a sort of revealer and teacher, but it also had much to say about man as being in his deepest nature one with the Eternal Buddha and thus a citizen of eternity. In fact, one of the very first scriptures translated into Chinese from the Sanscrit and widely disseminated in various subsequent translations was the Larger *Sukhavativ-yuha* with its message about *Amitabha*, the Buddha of Eternal Life and Light, and about the Land of Bliss which he has prepared for all who put their trust in him. So strongly "other-worldly" was this emphasis in Chinese Buddhism that tens of thousands retired from active life as citizens of this world in order to prepare themselves for the world to come. It was because of this influence that repeatedly in Chinese history the government which was usually under Confucian influence interfered forcibly by destroying monasteries and temples and so compelling the monks and nuns to return to active life and share in the common work of the world. But in spite of these severe measures Buddhism usually regained its hold on the hearts of the Chinese, for in one way or another it gave a more adequate answer to the question about the individual's destiny than traditional Confucianism ever gave. It is also a fact of history that in spite of this deep-seated difference between the native Confucianism and the imported Indian religion Buddhism finally forced upon Confucianism a reconsideration of its own metaphysical foundations as we find this in the famous Neo-Confucian schools. Though Neo-Confucianism did not affirm definitely a belief in the survival of the individual it did provide an interpretation of ultimate reality which was rather favorable to a belief in man's immortality; and in some of its developments, especially in Japan, Neo-Confucianism tended towards a monotheistic conception of the divine and as a natural corollary it gave greater significance to man's achievement of ethical and spiritual personality as belonging to the values that survive.

C: VII JAPANESE BUDDHISM & INDIVIDUAL DESTINY

IN JAPANESE Mahāyāna Buddhism we have an exceptionally strong emphasis on man's survival beyond physical death. The largest Buddhist sect and the one which seems to show most vitality in spreading its teachings today is the great *Jodo Shinshu* with its message about *Amida* (*Amitabha*), the Buddha of eternal life and light and his paradise for all who come to him in simple faith. The older *Jodoshu* which also makes central this teaching is likewise a strong sect. Then almost all of the other greater sects, though they do not stress the gospel of the Buddha of eternal life and light, accept the main teachings of the famous Lotus Scripture which has at its heart the thought that man in his deepest nature is one with the Eternal Buddha and as such is or can become a citizen of eternity. To be sure, neither in these latter nor in the *Amida* sects is there a clear cut affirmation of personal immortality. The concept of personality, as we saw in the section on the God-concept, is regarded as not wholly applicable to the Divine or Ultimate Reality and for the same reason it is not affirmed that the spiritual survival of man is necessarily a personal existence such as finds expression in the doctrine of personal immortality, but nevertheless Japanese Buddhism in general and the great *Amida* sects in particular do affirm that when man dies and the body returns to the dust the real man does not come to naught but that he rather survives in some form of spiritual existence.

In the more or less popular forms of Japanese Buddhism there is not only a belief in man's survival but this is often expressed in terms that are all too "realistic." Perhaps no Japanese religious writing has had a greater influence among the masses than the famous tenth century Essay on Birth into Paradise (Genshin's *Ojo Yoshu*). Here we have a regular Buddhist Dante who gives us vivid pictures of the hells and heavens or the stages through which the soul passes in its long struggles till it reaches its ultimate destiny.

Though Buddhism is often spoken of as a religion of pessimism, and rightly so, it is an interesting fact that in this classic there is not written over the portals of hell as Dante wrote over his, "Abandon Hope all ye who enter here;" for even the worst sinner in the nethermost hell may some day, when he has paid the full price of his evil *Karma*, again turn his steps upward and perhaps at last rise from hell and pass through the intermediary states till he finally plants his feet on the first rungs of the heavenly ladder and by the grace of the Buddha Amida finally arrives in the highest heaven where his greatest happiness shall be in what is indicated by the name of the highest heaven itself, namely, "Making Progress in the Way of the Buddha."

Though Japan owes to Mahāyāna Buddhism its first more or less worthy interpretation of human life, it should be added that Buddhism itself owes to Japan some of its finest developments for nowhere else has Buddhism been as positive in its affirmation of the value of human life and its worthiness to be reckoned as an abiding value. To be sure, the life of the individual is frequently treated as of little significance and as something to be all too readily sacrificed. It is a fleeting thing like the cherry blossom which the midnight wind flings to the ground. However, underlying this attitude is usually the conviction that the individual sustains a mystical union with the ultimately real and that the apparent destruction that comes with physical death is but the means through which the abiding reality of man's life is again somehow united with its ultimate source, however hesitant and agnostic may be the conception of just what that state might be.

C: VIII SUMMARY

IT SHOULD BE CLEAR, then, even from this short outline that religion everywhere has concerned itself with the great question as to man's destiny beyond the death of the body. Just because religion in any form is an affirmation of the reality of the spiritual aspect of human life it naturally affirms also the survival of the individual in some form. But since man is not a self-existent being and in religion recognizes his dependence not only upon his immediate environment but also upon that which he regards as constituting the very heart of reality, it follows that his grounds for hope in survival and his conception of the nature of his future existence are naturally conditioned by his conception of the nature of the divine as the ultimtely real and the way he relates himself in this life to the divine.

What we have set forth thus far gives in bare outline the major traits that have persistently recurred in religion as this has found expression in the major religions of nankind. From this outline it will be seen that there are large areas which at least the more highly developed religions have in common but also that there are real differences. And it should also be clear that even where the higher forms of religion are in substantial agreement in what they affirm as the great essentials there is always about these affirmations an element that belongs decidedly to the realm of hope and questing faith rather than to the field of assured and unquestioned certitude, so that there often runs through the various religions an undertone of a recurrent agnosticism. Thus man in religion as in all his life experience must ever wrestle with the problem of what is really true and essentially valid. We must, therefore, turn in Part Two to what constitutes the real crux of the problem with which a philosophy of religion must deal, namely, the problem as to the Truth of Religion.

AUGUST KARL REISCHAUER

The Nature and Truth
OF THE GREAT RELIGIONS
❦TOWARD A PHILOSOPHY
OF RELIGION

PART TWO
THE TRUTH OF RELIGION

SECTION A
TOWARD A NORM OF TRUTH

IN PART ONE WE SOUGHT TO SET FORTH THE NATURE OF RELIGION without taking up seriously the question as to religion's truth value and validity. We did this by stating the position of representative religions on such major problems as the nature of the super-human world with which man feels himself in contact in religion, the conception of the good life which man seeks through his relationship with the divine world, and finally the problem as to the individual's destiny beyond physical death. As may be observed, we confined ourselves almost exclusively to the more worthy forms of these beliefs and ideas passing by largely the absurdities and superstitious aspects which have often found expression in connection with the different religions and which to this day still constitute a large element of the religion of the ignorant masses in all lands. We pursued this course for the simple reason that a philosophy of religion is primarily concerned not with the vagaries and perversions that have accompanied the development of the religions of mankind, as they have every other development including even science and general philosophy, but rather with those aspects of religion that have persistently recurred and that apparently have had great significance for man's life.

But even though we confined ourselves so largely to the nobler aspects of the different religions it must be clear from even such a brief survey that the answers that the different religions have given to the great questions as to the nature of ultimate reality or the divine, the nature of human life, its meaning, values and destiny, differ considerably and for this reason, if for no other, they can not all be accepted as standing equally for what is valid. Then, further, in the face of the fact that in the modern world religion's interpretation of life's meaning and values is being questioned by sincere and intelligent minds it becomes all the more necessary to examine religion's claim to truth. In fact, the philosophy of religion must make this really its major task. One might leave the problem as to the nature of religion to the two sciences of the History of Religion and the Psychology of Religion but the truth of religion and its claim to insight into life's meaning and values must be the chief concern of the Philosophy of Religion. And this is not a merely academic inquiry but one which should concern every serious minded person, for let it be said at the outset that no honest man wants to have anything to do with religion if it does not somehow stand for a sincere effort to get at the truth about human life. We shall consider below theories of religion which regard religion as a mere subjective whim and a pleasant self-deception. Much in certain religions may be of that nature but even a superficial glance at the survey we have given in Part One should be convincing that religion is usually an honest quest for the truth and the truly good life. A philosophy of religion which fails to recognize this essential sincerity condemns itself as unfit to undertake this difficult task of getting at what is valid in the different religions of mankind.

The moment, however, one assays an inquiring into the truth of religion and its validity for human life one is faced with the problem of an adequate norm of truth. The truth value that one finds in religion depends largely upon the yardstick of truth that one brings to the problem. Two extremes are to be avoided in building up this norm of truth. One extreme is the position that seeks this norm wholly outside of or independent of religion and the other extreme is to allow religion the exclusive right to set up the norm. It is a fact of history that not only have the great religions of the world claimed to stand for the highest truth values but the world's greatest minds which have done so much to build up life's meanings and values have often been deeply religious. In the face of this indisputable fact it would be preposterous to say that religion has no right to be heard in setting up the truth norm by which its own insights are to be judged. But, on the other hand, it should be equally clear that not every insight that the various religions claim to have can be one hundred per cent true and valid and that therefore no one religion and not even religion as a whole can be given the right exclusively to fix the norm of truth by which religion's validity is to be tested and measured. To grant religion this right without any further checks would not only defeat anything like a philosophy of religion at the outset but it

M

would also make it impossible to find a fair norm for judging the respective claims to truth of the historic religions in matters where there are serious differences, for as we have shown, religions do differ rather widely in even the great essentials, not to mention minor and secondary matters. It follows, then, that a norm that is at all adequate and fair must, on the one hand, come from religion itself since deeply religious individuals down through the centuries have so obviously contributed to the world's insight into truth values, but that, on the other hand, this norm must also grow out of the rest of man's experience of reality and from his honest and intelligent quest for the true, the good and the beautiful. In saying this we assume what probably must always remain more or less an assumption, namely, that reality is somehow a unity and that even though we may experience the real on different levels, as it were, the experience we have of one aspect or on one level cannot stand wholly by itself but must be somehow integrated into experience as a whole. Hence the experience that man claims in religion cannot stand wholly alone or be measured as to its validity by a norm supplied wholly from the religious experience itself but must be integrated into the rest of experience and its validity must be checked by the whole field of man's tested experience. In short, then, the norm of truth by which religion's claim to truth values is to be judged must be broad enough to recognize the true on whatever level of reality or of experience it may be found, and hence it cannot be really fundamentally different from the norm of truth by which philosophy measures truth in general. The old dualism which held that a thing might be true in religion even though it is not true in science and general philosophy is impossible as is every other dualism that would separate too sharply the different aspects of reality that man can experience. But at the same time it should be added that a philosophy that would do full justice to religion's claim to insight into truth must be broad enough and deep enough to realize that the methods of approach to reality that for example the physical sciences follow so successfully are not necessarily the only ones open to man and do not yield all that is true and valid in human experience.

Now when stated in this general way it may seem simple enough to get a norm that is fair and adequate for judging religion's truth values. The real difficulty is, however, in coming to more concrete terms as to what is really meant by the real and how man may know the real. It raises, in short, the problem of knowledge itself and this, as is well known, is one of the major problems of philosophy and one, too, on which there is today a wide difference of opinion. In fact, the major controversies in modern philosophy are largely over just this problem—questions as to what is meant by reality, or the object of knowledge and then questions as to the factors involved in gaining our knowledge of the real. Men's attitudes towards religion differ so widely today partly because there is such a wide disagreement among modern thinkers as to what is meant by the real and the true. Possibly there is no final way of settling these controversies about theories of knowledge for the simple reason that every theory of knowledge is more or less reasoning in a circle. One has to posit in a measure the very thing that is to be proved as true and what one posits depends so very largely on one's previous experience and the type of life one lives. The result is that about all that one can demand of any theory of knowledge is that it be at least consistent with itself and withal as comprehensive in the survey of its material as possible.

To the average man the real is first of all that which seems so obvious, namely, the physical world which surrounds him and with which he wrestles for his very existence. He is usually quite certain that he knows this reality beyond a shadow of a doubt no matter how he knows it, for it is too real to be doubted. And it is an interesting fact that the first of the modern philosophical theories of knowledge to emerge after European thinkers began to question the adequacy of the Platonic view of reality and the mediaeval theory of immanental ideas, was that of Locke who held that "nothing is in the intellect which was not first in the senses." This, of course, meant that reality is above all else the physical world that man perceives in sense perception and that all true knowledge, therefore, consists of the concepts and ideas that are built up from sense-impressions that the outer world writes, as it were, upon the mind as upon a "blank tablet." Locke's theory represents a very strong reaction against the older view which had dominated European thought for centuries and which had its chief source in Platonic idealism. To Plato, it will be remembered, the truly real was the realm of ideas and ideals whereas the physical world was real only in a secondary sense since the physical objects were regarded as a sort of imperfect embodiment of universal ideas—ideas embodied in a something, the "me-on" which more or less resists the free and full expression of the ideas as the hard marble expresses in part but also resists the full idea and ideal of the sculptor. Man can know the nature of physical objects because of the ideas embodied in them and because man's own mind and rational nature is akin to and really belongs to the realm of ideas and true being. Sense-perception is, then, not so much a first awareness of physical objects which have a real and independent existence as such, as it is the occasion which arouses in the mind the idea which the object represents and which idea is already immanent in the mind since the mind is itself akin to universal Mind and the ultimately real. This is in substance the position of Platonic Idealism. Perhaps, we should call it rather Idealism. The term Idealism becomes more appropriate when to Plato's conception of the true is added his conception of the good, for both these aspects are represented in his conception of the truly real. It is this aspect of the good which makes Platonic Idealism essentially at one with the systems of all great ethical thinkers such as the great Hebrew prophets, the ethical poets of Greece that preceded Plato and in a large measure one also with the Buddha of India, Confucius of China and others since they saw in moral magnitudes at least one aspect of the truly real if not the deepest aspect of reality.

All through the middle ages, it will be remembered, Realism in philosophy meant that the world of ideas and ideals was regarded as the deepest and truest reality. The so-called Nominalists of the time, in their contention for the substantial reality of individual objects of the physical world, did not thereby deny the reality of moral and ideal values and meanings. The Conceptualists of the later middle ages, harping back to Aristotle's position, seemed to reconcile the conflicting views of the two other schools by granting substantial existence to the individual objects that man experiences in sense-perception but seeing in these the embodiment of general ideas or what later were called the rational laws of Nature. Man can know these objects he experiences through sense-perception because they exist according to certain rational forms or ideas and because man's own mind is akin to universal mind and the ultimately real which expresses itself in the objects of Nature.

It is, perhaps, natural that Christian theology should have for centuries made such extensive use of Platonic idealism in presenting its own thought about God and the world as well as its conception of the good life. Especially when in Conceptualism an apparent harmony had been achieved between the respective claims of the physical aspects of reality and the realm of spiritual values and meanings it seemed as if religion's claim to truth values as measured by philosophy were permanently established.

It might be added that the Platonic-Aristotelian conception of the real finds a close parallel in Mahāyāna Buddhism, if not an actual borrowing by the latter from the former. Here, too, true reality is, on the one hand, the world of ideas and ideals called by one of the Buddhist sects the "Diamond World" since it is unchangeable and permanent, but this true reality finds, on the other hand, its embodiment in the world of concrete objects which though real enough as such are not self-existent, and which are understood in their true nature only as they are seen as localized and temporary expressions of an ultimate reality that is spiritual.

Now, as we have said, European philosophy became increasingly skeptical of the Platonic view of things, especially was this the case as men's minds turned more and more towards the varied and rich content of the physical world which the budding sciences were presenting with ever increasing success. Locke's theory of knowledge registered this changed attitude and interest. From that time on the emphasis was to be more and more on the physical aspect of reality even though it is true that German idealism dominated European philosophy for a long while after Locke's day. Now when Locke held that "nothing is in the intellect which was not first in the senses" he meant to affirm the undoubted reality of the physical world and that human knowledge is built up from man's contact in sense-perception with this aspect of reality. This would not of itself deny other aspects of reality such as man experiences in moral intuition or in his aesthetic appreciation but its effect was to move into the foreground of man's experience that which he knows through his contact with the physical world and which knowledge has since Locke's day become so greatly expanded through the work of the physical sciences. It has even tended to obscure the one datum of certitude in knowledge which Descartes thought he had established beyond a shadow of doubt, namely, the reality of the thinking, or the doubting, self. Of course, Locke realized that the mind is not wholly passive in knowledge even though he spoke of it as a "blank tablet" but the whole trend of his philosophy tended to stress the thought that reality is above all else the physical world and that the content of knowledge is limited largely to what is registered on the mind of this outside world.

It was left to Kant to work out a more comprehensive and better balanced theory of knowledge and one on which most of the subsequent theories have either built or from which they start as a point of departure. As will be remembered, Kant accepted neither Locke's sensational-empiricism nor the older rationalistic systems based upon Platonic idealism but developed a position which seeks to do justice to the truth in each of the contending types of theories. Thus in his Critique of Pure Reason, he showed how knowledge of the external world is really a "construct" in which the "raw material" of knowledge received in sense-perception is shaped into concepts and ideas by the active mind in accordance with its own laws of thought. While Kant agreed with Locke and all theories of sensational empiricism that the mind receives its material of knowledge and does not create this itself, he held that after all the indisputable fact in knowledge is the creative activity of the experiencing mind itself. What man therefore knows in his contact with the objects of the physical world is that these objects are a "source of experience" and that he can know them in the sense of "what they are for him." This much we can know and any theory of knowledge that denies this, i.e. the reality and activity of the experiencing mind which organizes the materials of sense impressions, and the reality of something other than the mind which is perceived in sense perception, would defeat itself. To deny the former would preclude all possibility of what we actually experience in the process of knowledge since it would reduce all knowledge to a mere flux of unrelated sense impressions; and to deny the latter would make all knowledge based on sense perception illusory and empty. Kant summarized this in his well known dictum that "perception without conception is blind, conception without perception is empty."

Now when Kant went on to say that in our experience of the physical world we can know only "what these things are for us" but not what reality in itself-*das Ding an sich*—is, he seems to have shown a rather unwarranted degree of skepticism. At least to the modern mind impressed with the obvious success of the physical sciences in handling the world of physical objects it would seem that if we do not have true knowledge of reality in this way then we have no real knowledge of any aspect of reality. Kant was, of course, right if by that apparent skepticism of sense experience he simply meant to point out the fragmentariness of all knowledge that is based on sense perception. In the very nature of human experience the data in sense perception are always limited and selective. Furthermore each object experienced in this way is only an infinitesimal part of the contingent world to which it belongs and this larger contingent world is present to the mind only in imagination and never as an immediate or direct datum of sense perception. Thus the simplest physical object is never really experienced in all its full relationship to the whole realm of contingent things but is conceived only through the creative imagination of the individual having the experience. And as individuals differ in their range of experience and in the power of their creative imagination by which they assemble the details of the picture as a whole, it follows that probably not two persons have exactly the same knowledge of the outer world and each knows it in a real sense only "what it is for him" and not in anything like an absolute sense. This is a point which modern existentialism stresses. But this fact should not be taken to mean that the same object can not be treated as knowable in essentially the same way by different minds or that the experience of one can not be verified in part by others. As a matter of fact, all common sense experience of the outer world as well as all science which is really only an extension of common sense experience rests on the assumption that there is a large area of experience which is common for all and verifiable by methods open to all. But Kant's position is nevertheless right in so far as he maintained that however large this common element of sense experience may be it is in the very nature of the case always a very small part of the world of contingent things. Instead of calling this knowledge merely a knowledge of the "phenomenal" and not of the "noumenal" world, as Kant did, it would seem more nearby correct to hold that in this sort of knowledge we have a real though only a partial experience of noumenal reality. Of course such knowledge does not cover the whole range of reality. The very fact that this kind of knowledge which we gain best through the methods of the physical sciences is an ever expanding knowledge shows that it only indicates the direction, as it were, of a true experience rather than that it gives us an exclusive and all-comprehensive insight into the nature of the real. In other words, it is to be regarded as one of the true and successful approaches to reality open to man but not necessarily the only approach.

As is well known, Kant did not follow Locke and sensational empiricism in holding that man experiences the real only in the objects known to him through sense perception. Though human experience concerns itself much with what appears in sense perception and with the concepts, ideas, inferences, deductions, and syntheses through which the theoretical reason functions in building up what we call knowledge of the outer world, this is only one aspect of experience. Equally normal and valid data of human experience are such matters as awareness of moral magnitudes, conscience, or the so-called "Categorical Imperative" which control man in his relationship with his fellowmen and which lead him to make ethical distinctions and to follow ideals. In this experience it is not so much the faculty of ratiocination or the theoretical reason that functions, though this is always present in every psychic state, as it is the will aspect of the human personality and primarily what we call the moral will that is in the forefront of consciousness. It is that in man which seeks not so much the factual existence of the sense world as the world of values and ideals that ought to be. This realm of values and ideals, to be sure, has not the same sort of existence as the realm of sense objects but that man seeks and lives by such values and ideals is as true a fact about human experience as are the facts of the sense world. Kant called his critique of this aspect of human experience the "Critique of the Practical Reason", for what man experiences through moral intuition, through his moral choices and conduct is of the very nature of things practical in human relationships. In fact, Kant held that in this realm of human experience man gains his deepest insight into the nature of Noumenal Reality. While in knowledge gained through sense perception man really never gets beyond the realm of contingent things, in moral intuition, Kant held, he gets his only real glimpse of the very heart of reality. This is the case because as moral will man is conscious of himself as an essentially free spiritual being and no longer bound by the limitations of the sense world to which he is subject in his bodily life and of which the body is a closely concatenated and conditioned part. In this inner sense of freedom which is an ultimate datum of human experience and which arises in consciousness in moments of moral choices and in conduct motivated by ideal values man's insight penetrates beyond the realm of contingent things and reaches the very nature of true reality.

Now in this Kantian emphasis on what he called the Practical Reason, i.e., the moral values and ideals known through moral intuition and by which man lives his life in relationship with his fellowmen, we have a reaffirmation of what has been so central in the thought of the great ethical thinkers of all ages. In this respect Kant built on Platonic idealism, on the ethical achievements of the great Hebrew prophets, and he is a kindred spirit of the great ethical teachers of the Orient. He is also definitely in line with the great Christian tradition and with Jesus' own penetrating insight when he declared that moral integrity is a primary requisite for a knowledge of the highest truth. "If any man's will is to do his will he shall know." (John 7:17)

Some ethically minded philosophers since Kant would agree that in man's awareness of moral magnitudes we have one of the ultimate data of human experience beyond which we can not pass through further psychological analysis. Our moral intuition, in other words, is as truly one of the authoritative approaches to reality as any other approach open to man. Kant held that it is the supreme approach and really the only one that gives us a glimpse into the nature of noumenal reality. It is not necessary to go that far, i.e., to hold that it represents man's only insight into the noumenal world, but it is true that much of the best experience of the race down through the centuries, including the tested experience of the present, warrants the validity of the Kantian insight that in our awareness of moral magnitudes and in the ethical ideals that guide man in his quest for the good life we have one of the authoritative data of human experience. However fragmentary this experience may be it can be accepted as true and valid if anything in experience can be so accepted. Of course, it is perfectly true that to one who is insensitive to moral magnitudes it is impossible to demonstrate their reality or validity. To try to vindicate these in terms of something else would be neither convincing nor really valid if convincing, for in their very nature they belong to the most ultimate data of human experience and so are not reducible to lower or other terms.

We shall consider later Kant's philosophy of religion which is based, as we shall see, on the primacy of the moral will. It is enough here to say that while his philosophy of religion is not altogether true to the religious consciousness itself all ethical religions find in the Kantian epistemology a rather congenial atmosphere and staunch support.

Though most theories of knowledge since Kant build on his insight, or at least feel it necessary to reckon with him, they naturally find fault with what might be called his "phenomenality of knowledge." This finds its strongest expression among the modern schools of Realism. Modern Realism is, of course, almost the exact opposite of mediaeval Realism. It starts, in fact, with the presupposition that the real is above all else this immediate world that forces itself upon us in sense perception rather than some realm of ideas and ideals expressing itself imperfectly through the objects of the sense world. In truth, the modern Realist is not much concerned with getting at ultimate or unified reality or with finding any larger values and meanings in things as a whole but rather with what he considers to be the actual and close-at-hand facts of the world in which we live from day to day. Realism is almost a violent reaction against the idealistic and rationalistic systems of the past, including also the Kantian philosophy.

The Realist first of all insists that the objects of knowledge do not depend upon the human mind for their existence. However real the mind may be and however much it may contribute from its own nature and laws in the process of knowledge it still remains true that man as a thinking being is *in* and a part *of* the world rather than that the world is in him or his mind. In all practical human activity we not only assume that a real physical world exists beyond us but that we can produce some effect on it. We must also admit that the physical world extends far beyond our ken and that it has existed long before any human mind apprehended it.

In the second place the Realist holds that however much all reality may hang together in some sort of unity, as all idealists and monists have claimed, it is an indisputable fact that reality consists of many things with real differences between them. These differences must be recognized and not too hastily blended into a harmonious whole.

Then in the third place the method of approach to the real should be by a process of analysis which brings out the actual differences in things whether these differences can later be harmonized into a unitary system or not. The modern Realist, in short, wants to fix man's attention more closely upon the world of sense experience as being at least one real aspect of reality if not the sole aspect. He builds primarily on the physical sciences and Realism as a philosophy seeks to be in fact the philosophy of the physical sciences. It is like every fresh start, almost naively simple though refreshingly honest and frank. Of course, what the modern Realist affirms in the above mentioned main theses cannot be denied. The only difficulty is that the modern Realist is usually too one-sided in his Realism and so instead of giving us a new insight into reality he is in great danger of slipping back into the position of the old-fashioned materialist which mature minds should long since have out-grown. While the Realist is perfectly right in holding that the physical world with all its variety of individual existence is undeniably real and while he is right in warning against a too hasty harmonization and a too all-inclusive unity which is beyond all differences, as idealistic philosophies are all too prone to do in their search for Absolutes, he must be reminded that there is also a mental world with its differences between truth and error, right and wrong, the beautiful and the ugly-all of which belongs also to the real. He must be further reminded that it is only as the creative imagination conceives the Realist's "real world" and brings it together into some sort of unity that we can have anything like real knowledge, not to mention a theory of knowledge. In spite of all this rebellion against idealism of one sort or another, human knowledge has to be a sort of "construct" in which the creative mind plays its part in accordance with its own inherent laws of thought; and idealistic systems have just as good a right to assume that the laws of thought are one with the laws of being as the Realist has a right to ignore this possibility. In fact, unless this is really the case it is hard to see how we can have any knowledge, even of the things that make up our immediate world. To be sure, true knowledge is of the nature of a "discovery" of what is in reality rather than a "reading into things," but there is nevertheless always present the creative element in all knowledge, even in knowledge of the physical world, and this creative element is of the mind itself. As such it bears continuous testimony to the nature of the human spirit as a reality which transcends the merely physical. This fact should always lead the careful student of reality to be open-minded towards other aspects of reality and towards other aspects of the creative human spirit and its needs which do not find full expression in man's experience of the physical world as such.

The fact that human knowledge is fragmentary at each successive stage of its development and that the mind through its creative activity adjusts itself repeatedly at every new onslaught that it makes on reality, finds its clearest recognition among present day Pragmatists. Where the older theories of truth, based largely on Platonic psychology and philosophy, held that an idea is true when there is an exact correspondence between the idea and the given object for which it stands, the Pragmatist insists that man has no way of knowing whether there is such correspondence except by the way the idea functions sucessfully in opening up further experience. And since the history of human experience has been one of change and growth it follows that at no stage of knowledge is there an exact correspondence between the idea and what a given reality might be and that the idea or knowledge at each stage of experience is really only of the nature of an instrument which makes a further successful experience possible and which instrument grows, as it were, at each stage into greater accuracy and range. This view of knowledge frankly abandons all conceptions of so-called Noumenal Reality and Absolutes but confines itself to attempts at an expanding experience along lines open to all who make similar attempts.

Now the Pragmatist is, of course, essentially right in holding that each stage of knowledge is partial and that each stage provides a standing ground from which the active mind projects further experimentation and accepts as only provisionally true such ideas as seem to open up further experience of the real. He is also right in holding that man has no criteria by which to judge the exact correspondence between his ideas and the reality for which they stand except the test of their workability in the long run; and we would add, their self-consistency. Obviously if an idea does not work in actual experience something is wrong either with the idea or with its practical testing; at least that seems to be the case with all ideas concerning physical reality. Probably ideas in the field of mathematical truth and all logical reasoning and deductions have their chief test of validity in their self-consistency and are not dependent for their verification on our experience of physical reality. The old conception of an idea being true when there is an exact correspondence between it and the reality for which it stands, or the conception of an absolute truth, is not quite as meaningless as the Pragmatist would make it out to be. In the Pragmatist's very conception of the instrumental nature of knowledge as a process that opens up an ever expanding valid and progressively true experience there is really implied the ideal of absolute truth, or the exact correspondence between an idea and the object for which it stands. We may never reach the goal of knowledge where there is an exact correspondence between our ideas and the reality for which they stand but the very belief that it is possible to make progress in our knowledge which the Pragmatist affirms, implies most decidedly the existence of such a goal. With this caution we accept the Pragmatist's emphasis on the fragmentariness of all human knowledge and the possibility of a continuous growth, each stage being a new starting point for further adventures into the yet unknown, and testing our projected ideas by the acid test of their workability in practical experience, meaning, however, by "practical experience" that which works in the long run and which does full justice to the whole human personality. It should go without saying that the Pragmatic theory of knowledge does not as such make any precommitments as to what is the truly real. Of course the Pragmatist, as every practically minded man of today, accepts the physical world as real and sees in the methods used by the physical sciences, perhaps, the best example of the working out of his own theory of knowledge. He would, however, also accept other aspects of reality and other methods of approach to reality if these other methods actually succeed in opening up human experience more successfully and produce evidences of other aspects of reality.

Whatever new emphasis in the theory of knowledge the modern Realist or the Pragmatist may make, the Realist can be right only when he is open-minded to reality on all its levels or in all its aspects, and the Pragmatist's "workability" will work only if it takes into consideration the full and all rounded human personality in its contact with the truly real. It is all too easy to let the more obvious aspects of reality crowd out the things that are invisible, or to define the practical too exclusively in terms of sense experience. Even within the field of the physical sciences there are, as it were, various levels of reality, each level demanding a slightly different method of approach and technique though there is such a thing as a scientific approach and technique. Thus the method of the physicist is not altogether adequate for the chemist and the chemist finds it necessary to make a distinction between inorganic chemistry and biochemistry. The biologist, in turn, while building on the findings of the physicist and the chemist, must nevertheless take cognizance of aspects of reality which transcend those found by the latter, and as he ascends in the scale of life he finds himself compelled to take into consideration an increasing number of factors if he would tell us all there is to be said about a physical organism. At the upper end of his problem he finds himself handing his task over to the psychologist, especially when it comes to dealing with human nature. Unfortunately many of our modern psychologists deal with their part of the task entirely too much with the methods of the physicist, chemist and biologists and do not recognize sufficiently that they must use a somewhat different technique if they would do full justice to their part of the problem. There is still much discussion as to whether psychology is or can be a real science. The truth is that it can only be a real science when the psychologist has wit enough to see that he is dealing with an aspect of reality which cannot be adequately handled by the methods of the physical sciences. Of course, he is quite right in trying to find out just what is the physical basis or aspect of the psychic life, or the relationship between these two aspects but, after all, the human mind or spirit is not a mere bit of delicate machinery and thought and other psychic phenomena cannot be reduced to mere glandular activities, brain movements, or physical responses of the nervous system to external stimuli. There is, of course, this physical level to man's life but the psychic level is somehow more than this however intimately the two may be bound up with each other, and any science which fails to recognize this is just that far from being an adequate science. And then within the psychic life of man there is further room for analysis if one would do full justice to the human personality. This further problem may be approached either through an analysis of the inner structure of the human self such as the traditional trichotomy of intellect, feeling and will, or through a survey of man's achievements in the great spheres of science, art, ethics and religion. Either approach will bring to light a rich and varied content of reality which yields itself to our quest best if the methods of our approach are not on a dead level but are really adapted to the nature of the real that we seek to know.

We moderns speak glibly of science and the scientific approach as the one and only way of getting at the nature of reality. We accept nothing as true which has not been "scientifically established." That is in many ways a great gain. But we must be on our guard lest we make our so-called scientific approach too narrow and seek the real too exclusively along preconceived lines of what the real must be. Undoubtedly the modern scientific approach is valid in so far as it first of all stands for a frank and untrammeled observation of reality as it is rather than attempting to read into it things that are not really there and that may be nothing more than the projection of our unwarranted desires. This method is further right when on the basis of continuous and critical observation and experimentation it formulates its general laws and builds up its theories and then tests and checks these by further observation and experimentation. And still further is the scientific method right when even after repeated experimentations, tests and alterations of laws and theories to fit in with all the known facts it holds its latest restatement in a tentative way and with a mind open to yet unknown and relevant things. This is, in short, the spirit and general method of modern science when it is at its best and this spirit and method must be accepted as valid in human experience. It may seem a little disturbing to those who are accustomed to rest undisturbed in the arms of inherited "absolutes" whether these be absolutes of religion, politics, science or what not. It may seem as if such a critical spirit might result in reducing all human knowledge to a mere flux, abandoning apparently at the outset all hope of certitude and pursuing an ever receding, not to say elusive, goal. This is, however, not really the case for with all the change and abandoning of previous positions which this involves and which, in fact, a growing knowledge of reality in any sphere makes necessary, there is nevertheless a nucleus, and an ever enlargening nucleus, which when once achieved remains an essentially permanent possession of the race. This is true in every realm of human experience; in the physical sciences and in the social sciences the latter, for our purpose here, may be regarded as including also art and religion. There are e.g. masterpieces of art which all the progress of civilization somehow still leaves "masterpieces." While these were produced at a certain point in time and space they seem really ageless and universal in their appeal and authority. The same may be said of certain moral and spiritual insights. They belong to all ages and to the race as a whole, and they seem never to be outmoded or superseded by the progress of thought and life. As Professor Hocking has so well said, "The life of knowledge as well as the life of action swings, I believe, in irregular rhythm or alternation between this pole of certainty and the region of exploration, tentativeness, probability, hypothesis." (Types of Philosophy p. 443)

While, we then, accept this characteristic spirit and method of modern science as valid in our approach to reality it must, nevertheless be pointed out that this very spirit and method with its continuous emphasis on critical analysis has its limitations and needs to be supplemented by other methods of approach. Also the very necessity for specialization and concentration on a more and more limited field for the individual scientist makes the typical scientific view rather lopsided. There is real truth in the witticism that "specialization is to know more and more about less and less." What is required is a more comprehensive view of reality than the different sciences tend to give and our critical and analytical approach needs to give way from time to time a more intuitive insight. In fact, the enrichment of detailed knowledge which modern science has given us tends to blind us to the larger meanings and values in reality as a whole. Undoubtedly philosophy and religion in the past made their unities, harmonizations and larger meanings of reality as a whole without sufficient knowledge of the specific content of the real; but modern science, after giving us such rich content of detail, especially of the physical aspect of reality, certainly needs to be supplemented by a more comprehensive view of things and its method of approach needs to be supplemented by other methods and the results of all these approaches to the real need to be more fully harmonized before we can have anything like a true and adequate picture of the real. It still holds good that the fullest understanding of anything consists of more than a mere analysis of its constituent parts or even of an understanding of the exact functions of each part but rather of a synthetic view of things as a whole and a comprehension of its larger meanings. It is an actual fact that even in the field of the physical sciences some of the most illuminating insights have come not so much by a process of patient and critical analysis as by sudden flashes of intuition. This probably means that the given scientist let the details which analysis tends to accentuate to sink out of sight and in a passive and receptive mood allowed the thing as a whole to appear and by so doing he gained his sudden flash of insight. But we need to go beyond this and let the world picture as a whole make its impress and speak of its larger meaning to the whole of the human personality. That is to say, our analytical knowledge of reality which modern science is giving us so effectively needs to be completed by what might be called an "interpretive view of things." Mere interpretation without facts obtained from critical analysis of given segments of the real may be largely a "reading of values and meanings into things." But equally true is it that mere analysis of facts without seeing the details of things in their larger setting and their possible larger meanings is too much like looking at the mere pigments which the artist uses in painting his picture and never stepping back to view the real picture. It has well been said that the modern man, as a result of his scientific training, finds many values and meanings in life but that he no longer finds any larger meanings and values in life as a whole or in reality as a whole. There is nothing which science has authoritatively established that makes this quest for larger meanings and values invalid. It is simply that the characteristic approach made by the specific sciences is not adequate for this comprehensive view of reality and this discovery of the broader meanings and higher values. But that we needs must strive for this should be clear, for it may seriously be questioned whether even the various physical sciences can succeed fully in their own limited sphere without the continuance of the scientist's faith in the essential unity and rationality of the universe. And certainly the social sciences, particularly those which seek to deal with the whole human personality and the relationships of man to his fellow men and to ultimate reality, can never be truly scientific until they take full cognizance of human nature as this has repeatedly expressed itself in religion and in its desire for a comprehensive philosophy of life.

We thus need not only that comprehensive view of the universe which philosophy, basing itself upon the findings of the particular sciences, seeks to give but also an understanding of human nature and its deeper longings and needs as this has found expression in art, ethics and religion. After the physical sciences have given us the fullest account of man's physical organism and after psychology has analyzed the thought processes and exhibited the working of the whole psycho-somatic reality we call man, then we need to see further the real and complete human personality in its true character and as a unity which lies beneath these elements brought out by physical and psychological analysis. This means seeing man in his relationship to other personal beings who are concerned with life's values and meanings, and these values and meanings necessarily include some sort of answer to questions regarding the nature of ultimate reality upon which man feels himself dependent.

These problems as to the true nature of man, problems as to what really constitutes the good life for him and what are the larger values and meanings of life, are the ones with which a comprehensive philosophy must deal and with which religion down through the centuries has concerned itself. The truth value or validity of any given philosophy or religion must be measured largely by the answers it gives to such questions. It can be shown that many of the answers that have been given can not stand in the light of present day knowledge and experience, but equally true is it that some of the more worthy answers that have been given must command the respect of mature minds and sincere seekers after the real. Even though it may be true that no answer given fully meets all the facts of life, the questions which these answers have tried to meet still persist and anyone is free to come forward with a more worthy answer, whether he brings this in the name of science, art, philosophy, religion or without labeling it by any one of these larger divisions of human interest.

As we said above, any and every theory of knowledge is a kind of reasoning in a circle since the very basis from which one seeks to prove the true must be largely posited to start with, and what one posits depends so very largely on what one has previously experienced as real and valid. Therefore it would seem to follow that the theory of knowledge which has the greatest claim on us is one which takes into consideration the whole of the human personality as this is seen both from its inner structure and from its external expression in the general fields of science, art, philosophy and religion. Such a theory of knowledge rests, in short, on a sort of synthesis of human experience. This synthesis of all methods of approach to reality open to man, especially as seen from the inner structure of the human personality, has been well expressed by L.T. Hobhouse when he wrote: "No truth can be final or complete which is not in harmony with the whole of our nature so far as our nature is consistent with itself. It is on each and all of our impulses to think and believe that our knowledge logically rests. And of these none is before or after the other, none is greater or less than the other. Only they must harmonize with one another. And that reality, and only that reality in which such a harmonious whole could find rest, is the only reality which we can logically take as true. Feeling, imagination, emotion, the moral will, thought, all so far as self-consistent, claim a determining voice in the system of belief which we finally accept as the system of knowledge." (Theory of Knowledge p. 620)

To achieve such a synthesis is, of course, not an easy matter. It would be far easier e.g. to set up certain forms of experience as the norm by which the validity of the rest of experience is tested and measured. It is thus quite natural that today when the physical sciences have been so remarkably successful in their particular field their method of approach to the real and their findings should be given such a preponderating voice and should exclude for many all else which does not fit into these molds as not belonging to the real. We shall consider below a number of theories of religion which pursue this course but such a solution really condemns itself by its very narrowness of outlook.

Another way in which a synthesis of human experience is often attempted is by "re-interpreting" the religious experience in terms of something other than what religion claims for itself and thus recognizing truth value in religion only in so far as religon supports the truth gained in other ways. This is exceedingly popular in the modern world for it is now recognized that religion has played a big role in human history and that it still has a place in the life of many. We shall see below how many different forms this "re-interpretation" of religion takes. It succeeds, of course, in achieving a harmony or synthesis of human experience but only so by making religion over into something else than what it characteristically claims for itself.

A third easy way in which a synthesis has been attempted is to divide man's experience into separate and water-tight compartments and so by a neat division of labor avoid the problem of really harmonizing the ap-

N

parently conflicting claims. Thus we had the old dualism of philosophy and religion and the more recent dualism of science and religion, each half of the dualism regarded as standing for truth in its own sphere but without any real agreement in a common truth. This division of labor is defended on the grounds that it grows out of the different aspects of human nature itself such as the familiar trichotomy of intellect, feeling and will. Thus religion is said to be peculiarly grounded in the feeling aspect of man's personality, or that it is primarily a matter of the moral will in contradistinction from science and philosophy which are more an expression of the intellect. Or religion is even more separated from the rest of man's experience and grounded in its own peculiar right which can not be challenged by the rest of experience by saying that it rests on a "religious *a priori*" in human nature. To Kant's well known three *a priori*, namely, the *a priori* of the theoretical reason expressing itself primarily in science, the *a priori* of the moral intuition expressing itself in ethical choices and conduct, and the *a priori* of the aesthetic judgment and appreciation expressing itself in art, there is added this fourth, the religious *a priori* through which religion finds expression and which gives religion its real validity since it is thus grounded in man's basic nature as are science, ethics and art. Now whether religion is grounded peculiarly in the feeling or will aspect of human nature, or whether there is such a thing as the "religious *a priori*" we pass by for the present and simply point out the fact that such a grounding of religion would not in itself guarantee the validity or truth value of religion. The specific things which man claims to find in his religious experience would still have to be checked and tested as to their truth value by integrating these into the rest of man's experience. Of course, religious experience has a right to be heard even in the matter of setting up the norm by which its validity is to be judged, but this can not be pushed to the point in which it can stand so completely apart from the rest of man's experience that it can not be touched or challenged by the latter. To set religion apart in this way might achieve for religion a recognition of immunity from attack but it would always leave religion under the suspicion that it can not stand the critical test of truth. We shall discuss this matter later in connection with some of the post-Kantian philosophies of religion and which attempt just this sort of synthesis of human experience.

Now while the above mentioned three methods of achieving a synthesis of human experience have in them some value they do not really meet the situation. It is, of course, true that the very fragmentariness of human knowledge even at its best makes a complete synthesis of experience impossible.

Likewise is it probably true that man even in his fullest nature can never be an adequate measure of reality on all its levels. There may be aspects to reality which to man must ever be "super-rational" and perhaps even seem "non-rational" if not actually "irrational" even if in the "rational" we include every normal phase of human nature. But in spite of these reminders to keep modest and humble in our search for what is real and true we must nevertheless attempt a real synthesis of human experience on all levels of reality. At any rate, we can not afford to be so narrow in our outlook upon reality as to hold that only that is real which man catches in the network of sense perception even when this is almost infinitely extended through the methods and instrumentalities of the physical sciences. To "re-interpret" religion's truth value in terms of something other than what religion claims does not help much. To be sure, much in religion can be cleared up in just that way for the simple reason that religion is bound up most intimately with what man finds apart from religion, but as long as intelligent and sincere religious men and women insist that they find in religion something more and really something other than what we have ordinarily in the general fields of science, art, and even ethics, then an open-minded philosophy of religion cannot shut its door at the outset against such a possibility. And while the third method of achieving a synthesis mentioned above apparently does full justice to the claims of religion in that it gives it an independent standing it tends to limit religion's claim to truth values to merely such spheres as have not been sufficiently investigated by the critical spirit of science, and it implies further that as science expands its field of inquiry religion must necessarily retreat and perhaps ultimately be limited to the realm of mere values which are largely subjective and which cannot be vindicated as having real truth value.

By a real synthesis of experience, then, we cannot mean any one or all three of these familiar attempts taken together. We mean rather first of all an open mind to human experience on all its levels no matter what these levels are called—science, art, ethics, religion or what not. We would not let anyone of these experiences provide exclusively the norm of truth value for the others. Neither would we let these stand in absolute isolation from each other. We would rather seek to integrate each into experience gained through the others even though it may be exceedingly difficult to see how they can all be harmonized. It is a bit old-fashioned and withal un-scientific to accept as true only what fits in with one's preconceived notions of reality. If experience has taught us anything about reality it is that reality is infinitely richer in content than what any man has thus far fathomed and that all human knowledge is at best only partial. And yet we must hold before us the ideal of completeness and consistency so that all experience of the real will be as far as possible harmonized and made consistent with itself. Without this as a guiding principle the very attempt at a philosophy of religion would have to be abandoned at the outset, for that is what philosophy seeks to be—a comprehensive and so far as possible a harmonized view of man's experience of reality.

To be true to this ideal, a philosophy of religion in its search for an adequate norm of truth must keep its mind open to one further possibility not mentioned thus far. We have been speaking only of man's quest for reality on all its levels and of man's norm of truth growing out of his own nature and from the experience he has of the real. But what shall we say if human experience includes something which is more or other than what man gains through his own quest and is really of the nature of what religion calls a "self-revelation" of the divine? One of the characteristics of religion, especially the great theistic religions, is just this insistence on the reality of a "self-revelation" of the divine. In fact, a very central aspect of at least the great monotheistic faiths is the belief in so-called "divine grace" which means above all else that in religion there is not only man's quest for the good life and for truth but that there is even more marked the element of the given. Religion claims that man not only seeks and so finds but that he also asks and receives, he knocks and it is opened unto him. One may dispute the fact of this given element or the fact of self-revelation of the divine but an open-minded philosophy cannot deny the possibility of this on philosophic grounds. To deny this possibility would be to prejudice the case against religion at the outset. Of course, to affirm at the outset that a self-revelation of the divine is a fact would be to establish at once the very core of religion's claim to truth, namely the truth as to the reality of a divine being who reveals himself to man. Obviously an open-minded and critical philosophy can neither reject nor blindly accept at the outset religion's claim to truth values because it rests on a divine self-revelation. Even if it were accepted that there is such a thing as a divine self-revelation we would still have the problem of deciding as to which of the many claims to divine revelation can be accepted as valid and then further the harmonization of this with the rest of man's valid experience. That this would be a real task is shown by the very fact that the adherents of the same given religion in which there is a claim to revelation have frequently held wide differences of opinions as to just what is meant and as to how it fits in with the rest of experience.

Thus while philosophically there is no *a priori* ground for rejecting the possibility of divine revelation, unless one's philosophy is a closed system and definitely committed to a non-spiritual interpretation of reality, the claim as to the fact of divine self-revelation must be submitted to just as critical a test as any other thing that is claimed in human experience. In truth, just because it is a claim which by its very nature makes it different from ordinary experience is an added reason why it can not be allowed to pass unchallenged by any critical philosophy. But we repeat, for a philosophy of religion to exclude divine revelation as a possibility would be to stultify itself, for let us remind ourselves again that it is the very nature of a true philosophy to seek a comprehensive survey of reality, and if reality should be such that at its very heart is a divine being who reveals himself to man, then this would have to be accepted as a fact; for "*super omnia veritas.*"

Perhaps what we have said thus far is enough to make clear along what lines lies the norm of truth that would be fair and more or less adequate for estimating religion's truth value. As we have said, this norm can be neither wholly independent of religion nor wholly from within the religious experience itself but must grow out of the whole of man's experience no matter how we may divide this or label it for our practical purposes. After all, there really are no such sharp and absolute divisions either in human nature itself as we indicate by our psychological functions of intellect, feeling, will, etc., or in reality in general as we divide it up into such fields of interest as science, art, ethics, philosophy, religion and all the rest. These are but aspects of the human personality and aspects of man's experience of reality and therefore they cannot stand apart in separate entities or in their separate rights, nor can one of them be made the exclusive norm for judging the validity of the others. What we must strive for is a view of human nature which does full justice to it in all its aspects and a view of reality which recognizes it on all its levels.

TRUTH VALUES OF RELIGION
AS SEEN BY REPRESENTATIVE THEORIES

✅ *Introduction:*

A S WE HAVE SEEN IN THE PRECEDING CHAPTER, ANY ATTEMPT TO get the truth values in religion must see to it first of all that the norm by which religion is measured is really adequate. It should be clear from our survey in Part One that religion in its various historical forms is a very complex matter, especially since it is usually closely interwoven with the whole of man's life. Because of this fact there is always the danger that one finds in religion only what one looks for. Moreover, the truth values which one discovers in religion depend not simply upon what religion actually stands for but, perhaps, even more upon the yardstick one uses in measuring the naked truth and that which shades off into merely symbolic truth and on down into the actually false.

Now religion's truth values have been measured by various norms of truth. Some of these, it will be seen below, are entirely too one-sided and not sufficiently grounded in the religious consciousness itself to do full justice to the subject. Others, on the other hand, grow too exclusively from within the religious consciousness to vindicate religion's claim in the arena of man's general experience of reality. Only a norm which grows out of man's whole tested experience in so far as this is consistent with itself can hope to be equal to this difficult task. What this more adequate norm of truth is beyond what we have already indicated in the preceding chapter will be seen as we proceed with our survey and criticism of current theories and philosophies of religion.

Some of the theories current today are little more than modern versions of theories current among the ancient Greeks and Romans as well as Indians and Chinese, for it is not only our age that is critical of religion. In fact, religion has always had its critics and frequently the most severe have been those who in the interest of truth have sought to purge their own faith of all that is false.

It will be remembered e.g. that the early naturalistic philosophers among the Greeks disposed of religion with one stroke as being little more than pious ignorance and gross superstition. Since they gave a wholly naturalistic and materialistic interpretation of human experience religion in any form was regarded as devoid of all objective truth value. Of course, the popular religions of the day were little more than a web of superstitions and things purely imaginary. Whatever elements of truth they contained were usually effectively hidden and so these first Greek scientists with their passion for the real might be forgiven if they saw little truth and meaning in the religions of their day. This same adverse judgment was pronounced upon the religion of the masses by the great ethical poets and philosophers of the succeeding period but they did not thereby deny the reality of moral and spiritual values. In fact, they laid the foundations for a higher type of religion which had a rational content and spiritual meaning for the life of intelligent men. So successfully did they do this that for centuries afterwards many a religious philosophy built on their insight. Then it will be remembered how this first philosophical grounding of a higher type of religion among the Greeks was followed by the Epicurean philosophers who not only rejected the religions of the ignorant masses and that higher type held by the ethical thinkers and idealistic philosophers, but sought to explain how religion arises in the first place and how it is but a product of human fancy, fear, and unenlightened desire. It is especially this latter view which constitutes the germ of some of the modern popular adverse theories of religion which we must consider at some length.

But it is not only among the ancient Greeks and Romans that there was at times a lively discussion of the nature and right of religion. In the Orient, too, keen minds struggled with this problem even before the Greeks did. Some challenged religion in every form while others sought to give it a more worthy content. Thus in India S'akya Muni, the Buddha looked upon popular religion with its faith in gods made in the image of man and with its promises about a happy existence in a future paradise filled with the good things denied man in this life as but a delusion and a snare. He saw in these beliefs the greatest obstacle to the solution of the real problems of life, namely, man's deliverance from the bondages of human passions. In such religions man only deceives himself when he looks to the gods for help in the struggle where there is no other help than self-help and the help that comes from the good example of those who have helped themselves. The religion of the philosopher with its speculations about a transcendental Absolute, the Buddha held, was little more than idle words and pride of intellect which makes a pretense to knowledge of things where there is no real knowledge. Such speculations, it seemed to him, had no real bearing on the practical problems of deliverance from the evils of existence. It is still an open question whether the Buddha's own views of life can be called a religion in the ordinary sense of the term. That Buddhism soon became a religion can not be questioned. But be this as it may, our real point here is that the Buddha was a severe critic of existing religions and from the standpoint of his own norm of the true and the real he condemned the religions of his day as having little claim to truth value.

And about the same time that the Buddha was condemning the religions of India, Confucius was taking much the same attitude towards the popular religions of China though from a very different standpoint. Until man knows more about his immediate problems, the problems dealing with human relationships, he held, it is rather foolish to be talking about gods, spirits and such things. To be sure, in his own philosophy he recognized the reality of moral magnitudes and the grounding of these in a cosmic order but he had comparatively little to say about the transcendental world and the divine which is so characteristic in religions. But again our main point here is not whether Confucius' own philosophy of life can be called a religion or not but rather that from his standpoint he regarded much in the religions of his day as having no truth value.

And while Confucius' ethical rationalism had little place for the characteristic elements of most religions there were other critics who were even more severe in their evaluation of current religions. There were some who from the standpoint of a materialistic monism saw even in the ethical rationalism of Confucius a mere system of utilitarian rules for playing the game of life and who held that any belief that ethical values are grounded in a cosmic moral order as well as all beliefs in the divine and in spiritual values of any sort are just so much "moonshine" and illusion.

In short, then, a critical attitude towards religion's claim to truth values is not altogether a modern phenomenon but one of long standing. And at least some of the adverse theories of religion current today have indeed a long history. This fact does not, of course, prove them right in their estimate. That these theories recur from time to time and that other more or less adverse views of religion have arisen in our time is due to two main causes. One is the simple fact that there is so much in the historic religions which can lay no real claim to truth value and which tends to overshadow that in religion which does have truth value. The other cause is another simple fact, namely, that many critics of religion bring to their task an utterly inadequate norm of truth. This applies not only to theories more or less adverse to religion but also to some which seek to vindicate religion's truth claim but do so on an all too limited foundation.

The order of our presentation of these current theories of religion is briefly the following: We shall first consider those which are almost wholly adverse to religion. Next we shall take up theories which find certain truth values in religion but only by a process of re-interpretation of religion's content. This will be followed with theories which recognize the truth value of certain aspects of religion as set forth by religion itself but which deny other aspects. And finally we shall consider theories which in one way or another seek to vindicate the truth of religion in what religion at its best has claimed as the great essentials. As might be anticipated, no intelligent view of religion taken in all its historic forms could be either wholly adverse or wholly favorable. Only blind prejudice could result in such extreme conclusions.

B: I ALL RELIGIONS FUNDAMENTALLY THE SAME & EQUALLY TRUE

PERHAPS NO THEORY of religion is at bottom more damning to religion's claim to truth than the one which holds that all religions are fundamentally the same and equally true. The advocates of this theory recognize that religions differ in outward form and expressions but they assume that in the inner content all religions are essentially alike and lead ultimately to the same goal.

In the sense in which it is true that all religions worthy of the name stand for the same thing it is so obviously true that it becomes a banality to state it. Of course, it is true that in every honest religion man is seeking for the good and better life either in the here and now or in a future world, and man seeks this better life in religion as a rule through his relationship with the divine and the transcendental world. But that is far from saying that the historic religions are all agreed on what is meant by the good and better life or by the divine in relationship with which man seeks the good life. The higher religions of the world, as we saw in Part One, have much in common so that in many respects their paths do converge as they struggle towards the true and the valid, but in the interest of scientific accuracy it was necessary to point out that even the higher religions such as Christianity, Judaism, Islam, Hinduism and Buddhism differ rather widely in even the fundamentals of religion. In fact, even within what is nominally the same religion great differences appear so that they amount to virtually different religions. This over-generous estimate of religion may be preferable to the old spirit of fanaticism, intolerance and religious imperialism which saw in one's own religion all that is true and valid and in other religions only the false and the perverse. One can also understand why in lands where several religions have come into close contact with each other and where there has been actually much borrowing back and forth, and above all, where religion in every form has usually been subordinated to other interest such a theory should find a ready assent. It lends itself beautifully as a means of harmonizing things in the interest of the state which desires above all things that its citizens dwell together in peace and harmony. But the reverse side of this sweet picture is that such a theory is held largely by those who are really indifferent to religion in any form and who would resent any religion that stood forth vigorously for any view that happened to run counter to the accepted order of things. It is also a striking fact that those who are so glib in their affirmation as to the essential unity of all religions never take the trouble to state very clearly just what religion really stands for. The truth of the matter seems to be that this theory, where it is not a deliberate instrument of crafty statesmen, is but an expression of our modern popular "theory of universal relativity, according to which," as Professor Hocking puts it when speaking of general cultural values, "there are no better and no worse in social orders, but only differences, because the *mores* can make anything right." And so in religion, too, there can be no better or worse but only differences since all are purely relative and equally far from the really valid.

And just as extremes often meet so here, too, this over-generous estimate of religion leads directly to its opposite extreme which holds that because all religions are equally valid and equally relative none can stand for anything that is universally valid or that can approximate the permanently and universally true.

But "total relativity," as Professor Hocking goes on to say, "is so far from reason and common sense as to be totally useless in checking our self-assurance. For by all the gods of all the nations there are a better and a worse in modes of human life; to lose that sense of values in a pseudo-hospitable indifferentism is to lose all capacity to judge and therefore to act. Total relativity is essentially a closet philosophy. While it, i.e. total relativity, is nominally the precise opposite of that cultural self-confidence which makes us so willing to impose our own type upon the rest of the world, it is not different in effect; for it, too, refuses to do the one thing necessary, namely, to discriminate what is universal and what is local in our brand of civilization. For a self-satisfied imperialism, everything in our culture is universal, what is good for us is good for everybody. To the theory of relativity everything is local; there is nothing which is good for everybody. Both are false; but only the latter is futile.

"It is this which makes it so imperative that we, too, should learn to distinguish between Western civilization and civilization." ("Our Western Measuring Stick Carried East" Mag. Asia. Sept. 1931).

What Professor Hocking here says about "Total Relativity" in its aplication to civilization in general is peculiarly true in the field of religion and in the problems of discovering in the historical religions what is universally valid. An all too easy acceptance of the truth value in all religions as well as a too facile rejection of all religions except one's own, or a rejection of religion in each and every form, are extremes to be avoided. However ready one must be in admitting the principle of relativity in all things pertaining to human experience, one must nevertheless insist that not all is on the same dead level but that some views are closer approximations of the truth and the permanently valid than others. This over-generous theory of religion, in the background of which lurks its opposite extreme which sees nothing that is really valid in any religion, must therefore be rejected as too hopelessly shallow to be of much help in our evaluation of religion's truth value.

B: II RELIGION AS A HANG-OVER

PROBABLY the most widely held adverse view of religion is one which sees religion as merely a sort of hang-over from the past, one of those survivals from a more primitive age which for one reason or another continues to hang on but which an advancing culture makes more and more obsolete. It is something from which the more or less enlightened gradually become emancipated.

In the popular form in which this view of religion is held there is no attempt to understand or explain the real nature of religion. It is enough to know that in its very nature it is an expression of a past age and that therefore it can not have any real meaning or value for mature men and women who live in the progressive present and who have their eyes fixed on the better future.

There are several reasons for this wide-spread conception of religion. One is that religion itself has usually magnified its connection with the remote past. It usually claims to stand for "the faith of our fathers known of old," "the faith once for all delivered to the saints." The truth of religion and orthodoxy in religion have usually meant agreement with what was taught by the "church fathers." This is peculiarly the case where a given religion has developed a sacred literature and canonical scriptures. The norm of truth by which the experience of each succeeding generation is measured is thus taken largely from the sacred past. A Confucius compiles the teachings of the wise men of old and his own formulations of these teachings then become the standardized and unchangeable truth for the following two thousand years of Chinese history. A Qur'an becomes the norm of truth for the millions of Islam and however difficult it was to harmonize its teachings with the new truths and higher standards of later centuries the emphasis on the authoritative character of this ancient document remained. The orthodox Pharisee takes from his ancient scriptures the norm by which he judges the radical teachings of Jesus and condemns him because he does not seem to fit into the traditional picture. The Protestant reformers appeal to the early church fathers and the older Bible in justification of their revolt against the evils of the church of their day. And to this day to be "orthodox in religion" means above all else to be in agreement with certain standards of the past.

It is therefore not at all strange that the average man thinks of religion as something which rests largely upon the past for its authority. Now this very appeal to the past was once a real source of strength for religion. In the ages of authority and respect for traditions such an appeal secured a hearing for religion and gave its teachings truth value in the eyes of its adherents. But our age is not such an age. We are living in what is boastfully called the "modern age" and the word "modern" here stands for all that is new and in sharp contrast with all that has come down from the past. And since the new is to the modern mind synonymous with the true and the valid, the old must then mean largely that which has been outgrown. Hence for many, religion has little truth value just because according to its own claims it has such intimate connections with the distant past. This is not only the case with the present generation in Europe and America but, perhaps, even more so with the younger generation of Japanese, Chinese and Asian generally. Religion is to them largely a matter of an outgrown tradition rather than something that might have real meaning for modern intelligent men and women.

But it is not simply religion's own emphasis on its connections with hoary antiquity that handicaps it in getting a fair hearing today. After all, this worship of things that are new at the expense of things that have come down from the past may be only a temporary intoxication of our generation. This very attitude will itself soon belong to the past and perhaps a little reflection will discover that not all that is true is new nor all that is new is true. The real count against religion therefore can not be that it is so largely an inheritance from the past but rather that it has brought down with it from the past so much that can have little meaning or value for the present and the future. The religion of the ignorant masses is so often little more than a web of fantasy and pious superstitions and even the more advanced religions of the world carry along with what has permanent meaning and value an immense amount of useless trappings and things worse than useless and which are a positive hindrance to life. It is this fact about the historical religions which gives the impression that religion stands characteristically for things which do not and cannot have any real place in the life of an enlightened modern man. In short, religion appears as a mere hangover from an outgrown past.

This estimate of religion is, of course, very superficial and unfair for even in the case of the more primitive religions there are some elements of true insight and, of course, the great religions of the world have as their essential core, as we shall see below, the spiritual culture of the race. But it is true, as we have said above, that religion in almost every form is frequently cluttered up with a lot of meaningless rubbish which tends to hide its essential values and meanings.

B: III RELIGION AS A PRIMITIVE PHILOSOPHY OF NATURE

THE VIEW of religion mentioned in the preceding section tells us nothing about its true nature except by way of implication. There are, however, several theories which come substantially to the same conclusion but which attempt an explanation as to why religion is an outgrown viewpoint and must be gradually superseded by a truer insight. Probably the best known of such theories is that of Comte in his Positivistic philosophy. It will be remembered that Comte divided the history of philosophy into three great periods which represent the three successive stages of human development. These are: the religious stage, the stage of metaphysical speculations and abstract rational principles, and finally the stage of the positive sciences heading up in the Positivistic philosophy. In each of these stages man is seeking essentially the same thing, namely, an understanding of the world in which he lives.

In the religious stage, according to Comte, the explanation which man makes is largely in terms of his own nature. He reads himself into things and then he extracts the corresponding meanings and values from things. Thus religion from the lowest to the highest is only a sort of naive anthropomorphism. First this is exceedingly childish and then it becomes more subtle and refined as the higher monothesitic and pantheistic religions are developed, but it is nevertheless all an anthropomorphic explanation of the natural world which though satisfactory for the time being must naturally be out-grown as man advances in intellectual acumen and insight.

In the second stage man has outgrown the distinctively religious type of explanation. He sees that the gods of religion, including even the god of the monotheistic faiths, are but illegitimate personifications of the forces of nature and so he drops his beliefs regarding such beings and instead tries to comprehend nature in terms of general principles and metaphysical ab-stractions. This is the stage of metaphysics par excellence.

In the third and highest stage of man's developing thought life he realizes that reality is too concrete to be understood in terms of abstractions and metaphysical speculations and that the real and final explanation is nearer at hand, namely, in terms of the positive sciences and above all else in terms of the Positivistic philosophy which Comte conceived to be the summation and harmonization of all that man learns through the sciences.

Thus according to this Comtean theory religion is at bottom a sort of philosophy of nature, an expression of man's intellectual curiosity to under-stand the world in which he lives with a view, of course, of adjusting him-self practically to his natural environment. It is man's first attempt and it served a really useful purpose at a certain stage of human development but since it is only a naive understanding of things it must be superseded by a more mature and adequate explanation of reality. Such a more adequate explanation man now has in science and a philosophy based on the sciences and therefore he can dispense with religion in its traditional forms. There is still room for a kind of religion, according to Comte, and his various types of followers, namely the religion of Humanity in which the individual is the worshipper and Humanity the object of his worship. Where traditional religion has usually placed God or the gods in the center of things this reli-gion makes Humanity as a whole its only *Grand Etre* and sole object of worship.

Comte undoubtedly said some very illuminating things in his classifica-tion of the sciences and in his insistence that one of the major problems of philosophy is the unification and harmonization of the findings of the dif-ferent sciences. He was also right in holding that religion has often repre-sented a very naive view of things and that many of the older philosophies were often too much a matter of empty metaphysical speculations lacking in real content because they did not rest sufficiently upon man's concrete experience of reality. But it is equally plain that Comte and his followers do not do full justice to what religion can be and often has been. Nor does he successfully answer the great questions about human life which philosophy and religion have been trying to answer and which persist for all serious minded men.

When Comte says that religion belongs to the childhood stage of human development he falls in line with that popular attitude which thinks of religion as something which man must necessarily outgrow as he advances in maturity of thought. We might suggest that science, too, had its origin in the childhood of the race as did art, ethics and many other things that are characteristically human. And just as art, ethics, science, etc. outgrew their childish forms so did religion. In fact, religion was perhaps earlier in achieving maturity and these other phases of human culture and activity were usually fostered by religion and to this day often draw much of their vitality from religion. While it is true, as we have already said in the preceding section, that religion often clings needlessly to outgrown forms it is equally true that many of the keenest minds and great leaders in human thought and welfare have been deeply religious. And what is also quite contrary to the Comtean theory about the positive sciences superseding the great essentials of traditional religion is the simple fact that to this day religion counts among its devotees some of the world's greatest scientists, and scientists, too, who are not merely religious in the Comtean sense where Humanity becomes the supreme object of worship but rather in the traditional sense where man recognizes that at the heart of reality is a divine and transcendental Being worthy of his worship and on whom he feels himself dependent. An intelligent man today accepts the assured results of modern science but that does not mean that he has to accept all the poor philosophies which have been propounded in the name of science. And this holds regarding Comte's own Positivistic philosophy. He claimed to base it on the assured findings of the positive sciences avoiding all ungrounded metaphysical speculations but as a matter of fact Comte had his own metaphysic and one too which is not very impressive since it was a sort of old-fashoined materialism and mechanistic determinism which in the eyes of the really mature is also more properly listed among the things that are obsolete rather than being the final word as to the true nature of reality.

The simple truth is that vital religion and religion at its best is always more than a mere philosophy of nature, and that reality is more than what is caught in the meshes of the net spread by the positive sciences however much of the real is caught in this way. In so far as Comte had his gradation of the sciences and had placed at the upper end of the scale his "social physics," the science which deals with human conduct, values and meanings he gave partial recognition to this fact. But it is more than doubtful whether in his highest of the sciences he made sufficient room for all that is truly real and valid and for all that the religious consciousness in its noblest forms substantiates. This aspect of the Comtean theory of religion we shall take up later in connection with theories that build partly upon his conception of a religion of Humanity but which develop this more adequately. What we wish to stress here is simply that religion is not a mere naive philosophy of nature which is superseded where modern science leads man to discard his primitive philosophies of nature.

B: IV RELIGION AS A FORM OF WISHFUL-THINKING

A FOURTH MODERN THEORY of religion which is calculated to discredit religion's claim to objective truth values seeks to explain religion as being only a form of wishful thinking growing out of man's capacity for imagining things and especially from his frustrated desires. Where Comte and other rationalistic philosophers regard religion as primarily rooted in man's intellectual curiosity and need for understanding the world about him, this view looks upon religion as being grounded more in man's desires and in his proclivity for creating an imaginary world that fits in better with what he wants of life than does the real world.

It must be remembered that one line of post-Kantian philosophy has been stressing the will aspect of the human personality as the deepest and the very core of man's being. Fichte had reduced the physical world to a mere self-projected area in which the will of man might do battle in the interest of self-realization and freedom. Schopenhauer and a host of subsequent philosophers and psychologists saw as central in man's nature "the will to be," sometimes "the blind will" with the intellect being at best a mere guiding function, and all too often but a servant of man's unwarranted desires. Our reasons for doing things or not doing them, it is held, are largely mere "rationalizations" of our desires. We first want things and then we build up reasons and justifications for such desires in order to make them seem more respectable to ourselves and others. This is, in short, one widely accepted theory of human nature.

Now since religion is recognized as an all but universal phenomenon in human history it, too, must be primarily an expression of this fundamental aspect of man's nature; it, too, must be above all else a product of man's will and desires. It is, however, not so much the product of man's legitimate and rational desires as of man's frustrated desires. As long as man can get what he wants religion does not arise or function. It is only when man is frustrated and when he gets into trouble that he begins to create for himself an imaginary world which fits in better with what he wants than the real world does. The facts of life are often not to his liking. Instead of accepting these as they really are, and as the intellect unbeclouded by blind desire tells him they are, man turns to his capacity for fantasy and imagination and then he begins to see things not as they really are but as he would like to have them. And it is this tendency towards creating in imagination and fantasy a dream world and a world of illusions and delusions that is the substance of which religion is made. In religion par excellence "the wish is father to the thought." Religion is a "reading into things" values and meanings which are not really there. In the language of the street, it is "just kidding yourself." Its promises are but "a bogus check on the future." God or the gods as well as all the transcendental values for which religion characteristically stands are but "Wunschwesen," as Feuerbach so succinctly put it; and religion as a whole is, in short, a mere form of "wishful thinking."

There are two different attitudes towards religion on the part of those who hold that in its very essence it is nothing but a subjective projection of human desires and without any real claim to objective truth value. One is that since religion is in its very nature a self-deception it should be shown up as such and eradicated from human life. This was virtually Feuerbach's position when he said, "I do nothing more to religion than to open its eyes." By this he meant that when the religious man's eyes are opened he will realize that what he had hitherto regarded as realities and truth values are but things which he has himself projected from the realm of his own present desires and needs into the transcendental world. And when he realizes this self-deception religion will naturally cease to have meaning for him.

The other attitude is that even though religion is at bottom only a form of self-deception arising from man's blind desires and misguised self-interest it might still be allowed a useful place in the life of some. Life is, after all, very much what we make of it and the subjective attitude and private whims are a very large factor in even the sanest man's life. If then, religious beliefs and make-beliefs give some people courage to face life's problems and if they give them comfort and peace of mind, why not let them continue to hold such beliefs? Every man seeks happiness in life, and if religious people can get greater happiness by believing what they do, why rob them of this happiness? To be sure, the truly enlightened know that such beliefs are purely subjective and have no grounding in objective reality, but why not let those who can believe do so and thus get real satisfaction and peace of mind? Thus runs this variant of the "Wishful Thinking" theory of religion.

O

It should go without saying that no really honest man will take such a position. If religion is really nothing more than a mirage reflecting only man's blind desires and is not grounded in objective reality it would be only common decency and honesty to tell men so frankly. The Communist position which brands all religion as an "opiate of the people" making men see visions of a world that does not really exist in order to satisfy them with their hard lot in the real world, would be far more honest and honorable.

Now this theory of religion is one of those half truths which can so easily be made to appear as the whole truth. It is a fact that religion is often little more than a grand illusion. What illusions and delusions have not been bound up with man's religious life! Religion has often stood for the grossest forms of superstition and self-deception. The popular shrines of the ignorant masses and the sacred places of even the world's noblest religions are all too often the storehouses of pious frauds. Yes, it is all too true that religion can be at times little more than a web of illusions and superstitions and the very enemy of all sanity and true enlightenment. And we will add that even in religion at its best it is not always easy to draw a clear line between a reasonable faith and mere credulity, between real vision and the merely visionary, between the truly real and the seemingly real.

But while it may readily be granted that religion is often closely bound up with that which is merely visionary and illusory it is simply not true that religion is necessarily identical with these. It might be well to remind ourselves in the first place that illusion is not confined to the religiously minded but that it dogs the footsteps of man quite as frequently in other spheres. Man's undisciplined will and blind desires are equally operative in other fields of interest. This, of course, does not of itself prove that religion may not be illusory but it should at least be a warning to those who so glibly dispose of all religion as a mere illusion for that judgment may itself be one of the worst illusions that befalls man, particularly the man whose yardstick of the real is too naively "realistic."

Then in the second place it must be pointed out that religion can be and often has been the most rigidly honest and persistent struggle against the false and the illusory in the interest of the true and the real. Many of the world's keenest minds and the most conscientiously honest seekers after truth have been deeply religious. In fact, one supreme reason why religion persists among the intellectually honest and mature in experience is just because they are not willing to accept too easily the mere appearance of things but continue their search for the truly real and the permanently valid. It is quite true that some aspects of this truly real and permanently valid may seem as but an illusion and a form of self-deception to those who can sense the real only in the things of sense perception. The whole realm of moral magnitudes and our spiritual values and meanings may seem to have no real objective existence to those who can see the existent only in the tangible and the visible but that does not prove that these things are not real. It may only prove that some are rather dull and insensitive to certain aspects of reality.

At any rate it is an incontestable fact of human history that the ideals and spiritual values and meanings which constitute the noblest aspects of an advancing human culture are at the same time the very core of religion at its best, and these have been achieved and are being maintained to a very large extent by the deeply religious who have wrestled honestly with life and reality and not by those who have been chasing shadows and following mere illusions. Among these ideals and spiritual goods are such as the ideal of truth, goodness, justice, love, friendship, beauty of righteous conduct, sacredness of personality, intellectual and moral freedom, and the whole range of things that tend to make up the life of a spiritual personality. These are the very heart of enlightened religion and it is largely through religion that these have been made the common possession of man's growing culture. It may well be granted that these things are not real in the same way that rocks, shrubs, trees and flowers in the garden outside my study window are real. But even these things take on much of their reality for me because of the thought, love and good taste that went into their arrangement in making them into a garden of beauty. Religion itself has always maintained that "spiritual things must be spiritually discerned," and while faith and imagination may be psychologically the organ through which these intangibles are apprehended, it does not mean that they are made of "Imaginary stuff." They are rather the hard stuff of man's long and tested experience in practical living.

It will probably be granted by all but the hopelessly old-fashioned materialists that in so far as religion stands for ethical magnitudes and for spiritual values that can be tested and vindicated in man's practical life it is not dealing with illusions but with the true realities of which man's higher life is made. It is only when religion proceeds to ground these realities in a transcendental or transhuman sphere that the illusory and unreal aspect of religion manifests itself. This is, of course, the real crux of the problem but we shall postpone dealing with it until after we have considered several other theories of religion which head up in this same problem. Here let it be sufficient to make clear that while religion can often be justly accused of dealing entirely too much with illusions and of indulging in mere "wishful thinking" it nevertheless remains true that religion can also be and often is an intellectually honest and a keenly penetrating search for the true and the permanently valid. And what is more is the fact that historically the world owes largely to men of religion the finest and best things that make up the good life of man. The religious man is not content with things as they are but is ever striving to create a more ideal order. And it is this very belief in the possibility of creating a more ideal order that becomes the driving power in bringing it about. Instead of being a mere projection of our subjective desires ending in self-deception true religion is the belief that this world is not an absolutely closed system of mechanical necessity but rather that it responds to a creative activity directed by intelligence and the guidance of a worthy ideal.

B: V RELIGION AS INSTRUMENTAL

THERE ARE several theories of religion which are closely related to the theories mentioned in the two preceding sections and which may be called the Instrumental Theories. Like the "Wishful Thinking" theory these, too, deny that religion's own inner content represents objective realities but they, nevertheless, see in religion a possibly useful instrument for achieving or conserving certain universally recognized human values, thus linking up with the Comtean view discussed in section III.

In general these "Instrumental" theories build more or less on the pragmatic theory of knowledge. All human knowledge, it is held, is at best only instrumental in character and all truth perceived by the intellect is necessarily relative. It is simply a means by which man handles the practical problems of life and this he does in varying degrees of success. Now religion is just one of these ways of handling our problems and the different religions of the world are variants of this "religious way." Inasmuch as men differ widely in their tastes, their culture, and degree of general development it is quite natural that some should find in religion a certain kind of help in dealing with the practical problems of life which others who have attained a different level of development cannot find. Let, then, religion have its place where it can have a place as an instrument and let that particular type of religion be used which fits in best with the racial characteristics or the degree of development which any given people has attained. It is not religion's own inner content that matters or that has objective value but only what religion helps man achieve in values which are more or less generally recognized as valid.

This "instrumental" theory of religion finds expression more specifically in two major forms, namely, religion as an instrument of state and religion as an instrument of general culture.

That religion has often been used as an instrument of state is a plain fact of the long history of religion and the state. But we must distinguish here between the two different senses in which religion may be regarded as an instrument of state. There is one sense where this is the case which grows out of the intimate relationship that may exist between religion and the state, and where religion becomes such an instrument just because its own main content and the content of the ideals for which the state stands are conceived of as closely related if not actually identical. This is e.g. the case in most of the more primitive religions and the early forms of organized society. A conspicuous example of this almost complete identification of religion and the state so that each is instrumental to the other is such a religion as Shinto and the Japanese theory of the state where the very core and inner spirit of religion is loyalty to the ruler and where the ruler himself is conceived of as divine and the descendant of the divine founder of the state. Also in the pre-Christian Jewish theocracy there was almost a complete identification of religion and the state. Mediaeval Christianity likewise made church and state at least instrumental to each other's welfare even if they were not wholly identical. In fact, wherever religion concerns itself directly with building up the life of man as a citizen of this world it becomes a real instrument of state. But in all such cases religion is an instrument of state because its own inner content is regarded as objectively valid and as standing for those values which are essential to the welfare of the state.

The theory under discussion, on the other hand, denies that religion's own inner content has objective validity and holds that religion is at best only an instrument of state because it may incidentally promote certain values desirable by the state but which values are not inherently a real part of religion. They are mere by-products of religion. Thus e.g. religion may promote the spirit of solidarity in a given group by disseminating certain beliefs which all its adherents have in common. Whether these beliefs stand for objective realities or not matters little for as long as they are accepted as true by the given group they tend to bind the group together and this spirit of solidarity and unity is the real value and one which may come to the good of the given state for the state desires above all else harmony and unity among its citizens. It is said that Napoleon looked with favor upon the Catholic Church, not because he had much interest in the real content of the Catholic faith, but because he saw in the church a great instrument of unity and solidarity on which the state might build its own structure. There are other incidental by-products which religion might promote for the state some of which may even be perverted to such an extent that they run counter to religion's own major purpose. Thus e.g. while it may be true that the leaders of the early Islam's military state accepted for themselves the content of the Faith of the Prophet it is more likely that some of them fostered the acceptance of the doctrine that death on the battlefield leads direct to Paradise because this had as its by-product the making of these Islamic hordes into the world's most fearless fighters. During the World War I some Christian churches of Europe and America were made into effective instruments of state, not through their dissemination of the teachings of the Prince of Peace but because they unwittingly became centers of propaganda of hate for the enemy on both sides. Perhaps the most striking case of how religion may become a mere instrument of state comes from Japanese history of the Tokugawa period when the rulers who were Confucian in faith used the Buddhist priests and temples for which they had little respect as instruments for suppressing Christianity. In other words, here was one religion being used as an instrument of state to suppress another religion by rulers who gave their own spiritual allegiance to a third.

One might go on indefinitely with such examples from every one of the historical religions showing that it is quite true that religion is often little more than an instrument of state whether used for good or evil ends. All too frequently religion ceases to stand in its own sovereign rights and its leaders become mere mouthpieces of the state, and sometimes for purposes which run absolutely counter to what the particular religion is supposed to stand for. But while all this is true it is not true that this expresses the real nature of religion. If religion has at times been reduced to a mere instrument of state it has at other times stood in courageous opposition to the state. It thus depends largely upon the nature of the particular religion and the particular ideal of the state as to whether the two stand in a relationship of cooperation or opposition. To endorse religion, therefore, not because of its own objective truth and life values but merely because of its accidental by-products would be indeed a precarious procedure. Certainly religion itself would decline such a doubtful compliment. It demands rather to be accepted or rejected on the basis of its own inherent content and not because of any accidental by-product that it yields and that might be acceptable as an instrument of state.

Another form of this "instrumental" theory of religion is that which looks upon it as an instrument of general culture. In this form, too, religion's claim to objective truth values is denied but it is conceded that religion has played and may still play a big role in promoting the general culture of mankind as a by-product of its own otherwise misguided purpose.

That religion has been an instrument of general culture is too obvious to be questioned. It is only a question as to whether this has been due to religion's own inner content and purpose or whether this has been merely an incidental by-product, as this theory holds. Probably even the advocates of this view will have to admit that whatever may be the relationship between religion and general culture today or in the future, in the past at least religion was such an instrument of culture largely because its own inner content was regarded as objectively valid and as the very heart of the culture which its adherents sought to promote. This is but another way of saying that until quite recently practically all the great cultures of the world have been religious cultures, or at least cultures in which religion had a normal part. So close has the relationship between the two been that they have often been virtually identical, religion being on the one hand the creative force of a given culture and this culture being regarded on the other hand as flowering out in religion as its highest product. One could give innumerable examples of this close relationship. In fact, religion has been an effective instrument of general culture in a double sense, namely, as a creative force in culture and as a vehicle which has carried the culture of one area into that of another or transmitted it from one generation to the next.

As examples of how religion has been a creative force of culture one has but to remember how in every land most of the arts and sciences of mankind had their birth and their inspiration in an atmosphere created by religion; or if one cares to put the fact the other way around, how the arts and sciences were developed with religious motives and in the interest of religious objectives. Thus the world's best architecture, sculpture, painting, music, poetry, the drama, etc. have been either the product of religion or the servant of religion. One might also cite the fact that philosophy, ethics and the higher ideals and values that constitute one major aspect of any advanced culture were largely the product of religious thinkers, or how the higher religions of mankind have as their own real inner content these ethical values and philosophical meanings. This was true in the great pre-Christian cultures of Babylonia, Egypt and Greece as it was in Mediaeval and later Christian Europe. And what was true in the West was equally true of the great cultures of India and East Asia.

And that religion has been a major vehicle for transmitting culture however produced is equally clear. Thus e.g. it was Christianity which carried the higher culture of the Greeks and Roman to the barbarians of central and northern Europe, and it was the Romans church which carried on when the Roman state collapsed in successive stages of weakness. On an equally large scale in the Eastern world was it the missionaries of Buddhism who carried Indian culture across almost impassable mountains into central Asia and China and then, in turn, the higher culture of China to Korea and Japan. Even in modern times religion has been at least one of the chief vehicles which has carried the culture of one area into that of another. The long line of Christian schools and hospitals stretching across Asia, Africa, South America and the isles of the seas is recognized as having been instrumental in spreading the culture of Europe and North America. And religion has been even more a vehicle for transmitting the culture of one generation to the next. In every land what little effort was made in transmitting the culture of the fathers to their children was largely an effort of men actuated by religious motives and interests. Thus until quite recently all organized education was largely a matter of the church, the synagogue, the mosque and the temple. Only now is the leadership in this passing into the hands of the state and made into a so-called secular enterprise. But even so these enterprises lean heavily upon those motives and inspirations which are peculiarly the product of religion.

It is then a plain fact of history that religion has been a major instrument of culture both in the sense of being a creative force in culture and in transmitting it from one region to another and from one generation to the next. And equally clear is it that in all the great cultures of the past it was firmly believed that the very core of a given religion constituted at the same time the best of the given culture so that this culture was not regarded as an incidental by-product of religion or that religion was looked upon as a mere instrument of culture but as the very source and acme of the best in the associated culture. And it may well be questioned whether religion could ever have served this high purpose if in its own inner content it did not stand for realities and values which are objectively valid.

The theory under consideration, however, denies that religion is valid in its own inner content and holds that its validity is confined to its functional values. Even though it is admitted that in the past there was this close relationship between religion and culture and that religion was regarded as representing in its own inner content the elements that constitute true culture, it is nevertheless held that for men of the present true culture can be had without religion and that where religion does still serve as an instrument of culture it does so not because of its own inner content but in a purely indirect and incidental way.

The truth of the matter is that this theory of religion is again one of those half truths which superficially seems quite plausible. It is essentially right in two of its contentions or implications. The first of these is that however close the relationship between religion and general culture may be, the two are never wholly identical. Religion itself always claims to stand for something more and other than mere culture. Even though this "instrumental" theory does not accept this "something more and other" as valid it at least recognizes that religion itself claims to stand for this. To this extent the theory is right. In fact, it might be added that religion has at times stressed this "otherness" of its own inner content to such an extent that it set itself in open opposition to the prevailing culture. This has been peculiarly the case with most of the great reformers. They have usually stood in opposition to the prevailing culture; not so much because they regarded themselves the advocates of a different and higher culture but because they followed an ideal growing out of their own vivid religious consciousness. This ideal, to be sure, became in turn the driving power for a new and higher culture as it became generally accepted. But the point is that it was not to begin with an element of a given culture but rather an element of a given religious consciousness. Thus there is a good reason for differentiating between the inner core of religion and the elements of an associated or resultant general culture.

But this "instrumental" theory errs when it pushes the distinction to the point where the inner content of religion is regarded as being necessarily without any objective validity and where religion is reduced to the status of a mere instrument which may be incidentally helpful in promoting cultural values. This seems to us a rather perverse view of the nature of reality since it amounts to saying that permanent values can be produced and conserved by forces which in their own inner nature are not objectively real or valid. If it is admitted that religion has been an instrument for promoting universally valid satisfactions in the evolution of the race, as it is admitted by this theory, then it would seem far more reasonable to hold that religion played this helpful role just because in its own inner nature it stands essentially for objective realities rather than to hold that religion has achieved real values merely incidentally or as a by-product of its own purpose.

The other implication of this "instrumental" theory that is essentially right is that it is possible to have a certain kind of culture without religion even though in the past all the great cultures were "religious cultures."

On this point the theory can make its appeal to a fact about the modern world, namely, the growing separation between the elements that make up our common world culture and religion, or at least religion in its organized and traditional forms. As is well known, the different arts and sciences that constitute much of our modern world culture have become more and more independent of religion and they stand now each in its own rights. It seems, therefore, quite possible for a modern man to be a man of culture without being particularly religious. The "unbeliever" is no longer a "barbarian" nor even a "heathen." He is simply a "pagan" and our neo-paganism can be quite cultured.

Now all this is quite true. It is possible to have a culture of a certain type without accepting as valid the particular content of any given religion, for that seems to be exactly the case with many "cultured" people in the modern world. In fact, we may add that there are types of religion which the man of culture may well dispense with. But this is not all that is true about culture and religion. If it may be possible to have real culture without religion it is equally possible to have all the essentials of the highest culture and at the same time be deeply religious. The fact that the arts and sciences are today independent of religion and that they stand each in its own rights does not mean that they now stand in opposition to true religion or that one can not share fully in their spirit, activity and fruits while taking religion seriously.

A second point to note is that the devotees of a refined culture who regard themselves as indifferent to religion's own inner content often do so while holding views of life and life's values which are essentially religious. At any rate, in so far as religion stands for ethical ideals and moral values a culture that accepts these as valid is to that extent in harmony with religion. Whether such ideals and values can be maintained in a society that is irreligious has yet to be demonstrated; at least there is room for a difference of opinion. The point here is simply that a culture which recognizes ethical and spiritual values as valid is to that extent in agreement with what religion in its nobler forms has always maintained.

In the third place it should be noted that while we have spoken of general culture as if this were a clearly defined thing that is not really the case. It is true that there are certain common elements which enter into every culture that is really worthy of the name and also that there is today a tendency towards the development of a common world culture, but in spite of this there are still real differences between cultures. And we question whether the highest spiritual culture can be achieved or maintained apart from those conceptions of the nature of human life and its relationship to ultimate Reality which have been characteristic of the higher religions. By such a culture we mean one which gives great prominence to ethical values and in which the human personality is looked upon as something sacred and as a supreme value. There are, to be sure, many elements that make up our common culture today which are not specifically dependent upon any religious views. This e.g. is the case with that aspect of modern culture which draws its content from the ordinary findings of the physical sciences, though even here it is interesting to note that some of our leading scientists, when it comes to dealing with problems as to the ultimate nature of the cosmos, take an attitude towards the mystery of this aspect of reality that is essentially religious. Still, as we said, one can take part in the ordinary work of the physical sciences and share in their products without any particular religious beliefs or views. When it comes, however, to that aspect of modern culture which deals with the way man lives and ought to live then one has to deal inevitably with the kind of problems which religion usually has made central. As we saw in Part One, one of the major problems of religion is the problem as to what constitutes the good life of man and as to how this is to be attained. The answer which one gives to these questions will make a real difference in the resulting culture. If the answer is rejected which religion at its best has given then the type of life and the general culture will necessarily be different from one where it is accepted and acted upon. One can not simply smuggle into modern culture those desirable ideals and values which in the past have been so intimately bound up with religion and which have been largely the product of religion. Even though ethics stands today in its own rights and is regarded by many as independent of religion there are aspects to the problems of ethics which inevitably raise questions that are fundamentally religious questions, and the answer one gives to these latter questions in turn affects most decidedly the nature of one's ethics. It has yet to be demonstrated that the higher ethical values and the conception of the sacredness of the human personality which we moderns accept so glibly as a natural part of our highest culture can be maintained without those conceptions of human life and its relationship to ultimate reality or God for which the higher religions have contended, or at least views of life which are essentially consonant with the higher ethical religions of the world.

This last point takes us really beyond the problems raised by the "instrumental" theory of religion and over to the problems raised by modern Humanism and a whole series of theories of religion which accept religion in so far as it is an ethical idealism grounded in human nature but which deny religion's validity when it concerns itself about God and the transcendental world. We shall therefore defer our discussion of this aspect of the problem until we come to those theories. Here let it be simply pointed out that if religion is reduced to the position of a mere instrument of culture it might as well be dispensed with altogether. If religion does not stand for any objective realities and any values that are valid in its own inner content and purpose then we question most decidedly whether it can ever serve effectively in producing and conserving values which are not really dependent upon religion. Probably the real reason why the advocates of the "instrumental" theory of religion still want to give it such a place in modern culture is because they have to admit that in the past religion has played such a big role in this respect and they are not altogether certain just what would happen to our higher ideals and the finer things of our culture if suddenly the religious people of the world went on a strike. Perhaps they see what is rather evident to the more thoughtful, namely, that with the weakening of religious convictions among modern men there seems to be also a fading of moral certitude if not an actually growing insensitiveness to moral distinctions. In fact, there seem to be evidences of a disintegration of modern culture just because there is lacking that sense of certitude as to the real validity of those spiritual elements which formerly constituted the very core of our culture and gave it a true unity. Even when the different elements are accepted as valid in their own particular sphere there is lacking a conviction as to whether life itself, however rich it may be in the details of its culture, has any deep meaning and permanent value. And it can well be questioned whether this can be had without religion. (Cf. quotation from Lippmann's Preface to Morals, pp. 235–36). One reason why all over the world today the state is being held up as the supreme authority and the highest value in the interest of which all other values must be sacrificed is because even religion which should concern itself not only with man's human relationships but also with his relationship to ultimate reality and values has been made all too much into a mere instrument of state and general human culture. But if anything should be clear to the thoughtful it is that along that line lies suicide not only for the higher cultural values of mankind but even for the state itself.

B: VI SOCIOCRATIC THEORY OF RELIGION

FROM the "instrumental" theory of religion one passes naturally to the so-called Sociocratic theory which has much in common with the former but which takes one step further in the direction of recognizing the validity of certain aspects of religion. The "instrumental" theory, as we have seen, denies all validity to religion's own inner content but holds that religion may nevertheless promote incidentally certain values which are not inherently religious. Now this Sociocratic theory affirms that religion's own inner content may have real validity provided this content is limited to certain social values and gives up all interest in transcendental realities and divine beings except such as may be retained through an idealizing of the human. The two are thus in substantial agreement in what they deny about characteristic religion. They differ only in that the latter sees more clearly the big role which religion has actually played in the social evolution of the race and in recognizing that the social values for which religion has stood can be rightfully regarded as an essential part of religion and not as a mere incidental byproduct of it.

The Sociocratic theory may be said to have had its origin in Comte's philosophy though it finds its more complete formulation among his disciples, particularly in Durkheim and the whole school of sociological writers such as Levy-Bruhl, Hubert and Mauss. Comte had already shown how the earlier social evolution of the race had taken place in an atmosphere of religion, and while he held that religion's belief in God and its interest in a transcendental world was not permanently valid he regarded even this aspect as provisionally valid or "morally indispensible as long as the true Grand Etre that rules our lives" was not understood. But when man reaches maturity, Comte held, then he knows that the "true Grand Etre that rules our lives" is Humanity itself. This should then be the object of his adoration and the true content of religion should be limited to the sciences, arts and social values and institutions which make up the culture of a scientific age. "Those who would prolong it (i.e. the worship of God) at the present day," he writes, "are forgetting its legitimate purpose, which was simply to direct provisionally the evolution of our best feelings, under the regency of God during the long minority of Humanity." When, therefore, humanity's majority or maturity is reached then man should worship Humanity alone as the "true Grand Etre."

Now Durkheim and his school go a step beyond Comte in that they try to show that it was the social organism itself that constituted the first god of religion. This conclusion is based upon a prolonged study of the life and religion of primitive man, especially of the Australian Bushmen. It is found that among these primitives religion is so completely interwoven with the whole of life that the two are virtually identical. Everything the primitive does from birth to death is controlled by his religious beliefs. Religion is for him not a mere instrument of social control; it is the very content of the life of the social organism. And the conclusion is drawn that religion in its very inner nature is but the response which the individual makes to the dominance of the social organism over him and that the real god of religion is at bottom nothing else than the clan itself personified; or as Durkheim puts it, "the god of the clan, the totemic principle, can be nothing else than the clan itself, personified and represented to the imagination under the visible form of the animal or the vegetable which serves as a totem." Durkheim holds that Totemism was man's first religion and that from this one can therefore determine best the origin and true nature of man's belief in God. Other adherents of the Sociocratic theory however, hold that not only primitive man but even civilized man shows this almost inevitable habit of personifying things and treating these mere personifications as if they constituted real personal beings. Thus E.S. Ames, harping back to Schleiermacher's penetrating definition of religion as being above all else a consciousness of God, defines religion as the "consciousness of the highest social values," and then in turn gives religion an object of worship by personifying these highest social values and substituting this personification for the personal God of traditional religion. He explains just how this takes place and why he thinks it is justified. Writing as a Christian of "the new orthodoxy" in his work of that title he says, "It is not an accident that we think of great social entities as great personalities. Our college is our Virgin Mother to whom we address songs and sentiments of genuine affection. Our city has a personality, photographed and visualized, whenever her honor or ambition is challenged. Each state has an individuality and every nation is personified through a definite face and figure. Is it not just as natural to sum up the meaning of the whole of life in the person and image of God? Seemingly it is quite inevitable. It appears to be the most natural and the simplest way to represent to our minds and wills the moral and spiritual entities of life."

Undoubtedly these writers are right in so far as they contend that all religions from that of the primitive Australian Bushmen to that of the cultured modern man have as their content much that is identical with the accepted social values so that in a real sense religion may be defined as a "consciousness of the highest social values." And it is further true that the individual usually comes into an awareness and acceptance of such values just because he is part of a social organism and that the vast majority of mankind never get beyond accepting such values simply because they are the recognized things of the social group to which they belong. In other words, these values are not accepted in such cases on their own inherent worth as seen by the particular individual but largely because of their place in the general social inheritance. This is, of course, true not simply in religious matters but also in every other phase of human interest. A great many accept blindly for themselves as authoritative whatever is the customary thing for the social organism to which they happen to belong. It is only the few who do their own thinking and who live by an inner rather than an external authority. So we may say that in a real sense the "Grand Etre" that rules many a person's life is the social organism itself.

But this is only a part of the truth. Even the primitive man, though his attitude and feeling towards the social organism is one of almost absolute submission and complete dependence so that he lives and moves and has his being in the life of the clan, must nevertheless realize at times that neither the clan nor the spirit of the clan personified is really the determiner of his destiny but that both he and his clan are in the grip of other forces or of a reality that is more and other than the clan. If it is the personified clan or the group spirit to which he turns in worship and for help then it is this only because he reads into this far more than what the clan actually stands for in his life. That is to say, if the personified clan functions for him as a God-idea it does so only because the primitive includes in it also those other experiences of his surrounding reality which conditions both his own life as an individual and the life of the clan. And what is true for primitive man is even more true for civilized man. It may be granted, as we said above, that for many the "Grand Etre" that rules their lives is the social group to which they belong and that we constantly "think of great social entities as great personalities" and give these our loyalty and devotion. This is peculiarly the case in the modern man's attitude towards his nation. The state is idealized and personified. To live for one's country is for many the highest ideal. As some one has said, "Patriotism is man's other religion" and perhaps for some it is man's only religion. But all this is only half the truth. No social organism, whether it be that of primitive man or that of the modern totalitarian state, nor even humanity as a whole, no matter how many hymns of praise, loyalty and utter devotion we may sing to it, has ever functioned or can ever function fully as the God-idea of religion characteristically functions. Where "patriotism is man's other religion" and especially where it is man's real religion it is so only because such patriotism is more than mere patriotism; it is a patriotism tinged with religion.

Historically human nature has expressed itself in its arts, sciences, philosophies and religions. In all these spheres of interest man has usually had the good sense to know that he himself, yea he and all his human tribe, are only a very small part of reality and that man is in the grip of a reality greater than himself and to which he must seek to adjust himself. Religion has frequently been pathetically inadequate in forming a worthy conception of the nature of that greater reality but it has been essentially right in using the noblest and highest of man's experience as a key. The Sociocratic theory itself really affirms this when it says that valid religion is identical with man's highest cultural values. It errs, however, when it reduces the God-idea of religion to a mere idealization of the human and denies that it stands for any objective reality beyond the human. Of course, it is true enough that man is always limited to the sphere of his own human experience. In the very nature of the case it can not be otherwise. But that is a very different thing from saying that humanity is the only spiritual reality that exists or that has existence for man and so must become the object of his worship. On the physical side man is obviously but a tiny part of the cosmos. Why, then, should we think that on the psychic or spiritual side he is the sole or greatest reality and why should it be regarded as unreasonable to hold that another and greater spiritual reality than man himself or humanity as a whole should exist and have something to do with man's life and destiny? That is what the God-idea in religion has always stood for and such a God-idea has functioned far otherwise than a God-idea can function which has its reference only within the limits of humanity. The simple truth is that man never has been big enough to be successfully a god to himself, and not even humanity as a whole can function as the "Grand Etre" that rules our lives, least of all for an intelligent man.

It is indeed a very strange fact that our age should produce two views of reality which are so wholly contradictory as those which find such general acceptance. On the one hand there is the enlarged view of the physical cosmos which modern astro-physics has given us and which has reduced man and his little speck of dirt called the earth to a mere nothingness. On the other hand is the view which we have discussed above and which makes humanity itself the object of man's worship. It would seem that if man ever needed a god greater than himself it is now when he knows that he lives in a cosmos of almost infinite proportions and baffling mysteries. Perhaps that is one reason why both our leading astro-physicists who look outwardly across the almost limitless cosmos and our keenest seers who look inwardly into man's deep needs and high aspirations agree essentially that at the heart of reality there must be the Infinite and Eternal One—the One whom man may know best in terms of what is noblest and best in himself so that he may address Him as "Thou" and yet who is so infinitely more and other than man that he can but bow before Him in wonder, admiration and worship. To ask man who knows his own littleness, weakness and sin but who also hungers and aspires for the Infinite and the Eternal to worship himself or man in the mass called Humanity, is to ask the absurd and the impossible. At any rate religion has always meant more by its belief in God than simply man's belief in himself. Even the religions which see the divine only in the human do so by ascribing to the human more than what is characteristically human. Religion may have been wrong in much that pertains to its belief in God and the realities that transcend the sphere of the strictly human but certainly it has been essentially right in its assumption or belief that man is only a small part of reality and that his life and destiny are largely conditioned by a reality other than himself and with which it behooves him to come to terms.

B: VII RELIGION AS ETHICAL & OTHER IDEAL VALUES
WITHOUT THE DIVINE:HUMANISM

A THEORY OF RELIGION closely related to the Sociocratic is one which recognizes the validity of religion in so far as it stands for ethical and other ideal values but which regards as invalid all beliefs in a divine and transcendental world. It shows less interest than the former theory in the role which religion has played in the social evolution of the race and so makes little room for things which the Sociocratic theory regards as having had temporary or provisional validity but, on the other hand, it accentuates more the place which the higher religions can have in the life of the modern man in promoting ethical and other ideal values. There are many variants of this theory but all are in substantial agreement in holding that in so far as religion promotes the good life in the here and now by stressing ideal values as grounded in human nature and in man's natural environment it is on solid ground but that religion must give up all interest in a superhuman and transcendental world. Thus the nature of true religion would be confined largely to what in Part One we discussed under the section dealing with the Good Life but that all which we presented in the sections dealing with the God-idea and Ultimate Human Destiny is a misplaced emphasis in religion and essentially not valid.

This general view of religion is widely held in the modern world both in the West and in the East. It is a view which had able representatives also in the ancient world. We can give here more or less specifically only a few outstanding examples.

Perhaps the best representative among American thinkers is Professor

John Dewey as he has set forth his views in the little volume entitled "A Common Faith." Professor Dewey recognizes clearly that religion, in addition to its interest in promoting the good life in the here and now, has always concerned itself with the divine and the transcendental world; and further, that it has made the good life conditioned largely upon man's correct relationship with this superhuman world. But he regards this latter interest as misplaced and so he proposes to "wipe the slate clean" of all beliefs in God, immortality and the transcendental world in general and instead get at the "religious phase of experience," "one that separates it from the supernatural and the things that have grown up around it." (p. 2). In religious experience, he holds, man seeks to orientate himself in the world in which he lives. This means "a better, deeper and enduring adjustment in life," but in place of the superhuman power or powers to which man has sought to adjust himself in characteristic religion, Professor Dewey would put "all the conditions of nature and human associations that support and deepen the sense of values which carry one through periods of darkness and despair to such an extent that they lose their depressive character." (pp. 14–15) Man is thus not solely dependent upon himself but on what is in nature and on his ability to discover and use for his own ends the values that are thus grounded. Instead of depending on Fate, Fortune or Chance, as the irreligious do, or on Divine Providence, as the characteristically religious do, "it is the part of manliness to insist upon the capacity of mankind to strive to direct natural and social forces to human ends." (p. 24) Essential truth is what man works out for himself rather than any truth through divine revelation. "Faith in the continued disclosing of truth through directed cooperative human endeavor is more religious in quality than any faith in a completed revelation.". . . . "It trusts that the natural interaction between man and his environment will breed more intelligence and generates more knowledge provided the scientific methods that define intelligence in operation are pushed further into the mysteries of the world, being themselves promoted and improved in the operation. There is such a thing as faith in intelligence becoming religious in quality." (p. 26)

Though Professor Dewey eliminates from religion faith in God or a transcendental world he nevertheless holds that the natural world of which man himself is a part is so constituted that it contains and supports ideal values or ideal ends for which man in his higher life strives. "I should describe this faith as the unification of the self through allegiance to inclusive ideal ends, which imagination presents to us and to which the human will responds as worthy of controlling our desires and choices." (p. 26) "The reality of ideal ends as ideals is vouched for by their undeniable power in action. An ideal is not an illusion because the imagination is the organ through which it is apprehended. For all possibilities reach us through the imagination." (p. 43) "The reality of ideal ends and values in their authority over us is an undoubted fact. The validity of justice, affection and that intellectual correspondence of our ideas with realities that we call truth, is so assured in its hold on humanity that is it unnecessary for the religious attitude to encumber itself with the apparatus of dogma and doctrine." (p. 44)

It is thus clear that Professor Dewey accepts the ideal values of the higher ethical religions as valid but he maintains that these ideal values do not need their grounding in a divine being to give them permanent objective validity as religion has usually claimed, though he admits that they are grounded not simply in human nature as such but also in nature beyond the strictly human sphere. It is at this point that it seems to us Professor Dewey fails to do full justice to religion at its best and also fails to follow out his own views to their logical conclusion.

One reason he fails to do full justice to religion at its best is because he makes religion stand for that old-fashioned sharp distinction between the natural and the supernatural so characteristic of mediaeval European thought. It is true that religion has sometimes separated reality into two mutually exclusive halves, the natural and the supernatural. This is, however, not always the case for religion has frequently stressed the thought that the natural world is an expression of the divine or that the divine is somehow in the natural world. This is, of course, the case in all pantheistic religions but even such theistic religions as Judaism and Christianity, with their strong emphasis on the transcendency of God, have insisted that the natural world is God's world, that man is as it were "made in the image of God," that there is "a divine spark in the soul of every man," and that however much God may transcend the natural world he is nevertheless also "immanent" in the world. All this should make clear that religion has persistently stressed the belief that ideal values are in a real way grounded in human nature and in the wider nature that surrounds human life so that all Professor Dewey says about man working out the ideal values through an intelligent and scientific approach to his environment can be accepted by an enlightened religion. But religion is not willing to stop where Professor Dewey stops but insists on carrying the inquiry a step further. It holds that these ideal values are not only real and grounded in human nature and that man's natural environment is so constituted that in the long run it supports human life best when lived under the regency of ideals but it would add that such ideal values are grounded also in the very heart of Ultimate Reality. If it is granted that ideal values are real and not mere subjective whims, and if it is further granted that they are grounded not only in human nature as such but also beyond human nature in Nature, then why should it be unreasonable for religion to seek to know the very heart of Reality which is said to support such ideal values, and why may we not conclude that since man experiences these ideal values as objectively real best on the highest levels of his life as a spiritual personal being, and further since these ideal values seem real only to a personal being like man—why, we ask, is it not most reasonable to think of the heart of Reality in terms of ideal personality rather than in other terms or in no terms at all?

Professor Dewey himself halfway recognizes the reasonableness of this position when he says, "There are some persons deserving of more respect who say; 'We agree that the beginning must be made with the primacy of the ideal. But why stop at this point? Why not search with the utmost eagerness and vigor for all the evidence we can find, such as is supplied by history, by the presence of design in nature, which may lead on to a belief that the ideal is already extant in a Personality having objective existence?" (p. 45) Exactly, and why not? Professor Dewey's answer to this query is not very convincing. He raises the problem of moral evil which he feels is inconsistent with a belief in the existence of a good God. In this he points out one of the real difficulties of theistic religion though his own elucidation of the problem of moral evil is even less satisfactory. Certainly this is the case when he goes on to say that a belief in the existence of a Personal God undermines man's own efforts for achieving ideal values. In this oft repeated trite statement he is far from the facts of human history. It is true enough that theistic religions have had their "antinomians" who relied so completely on the "grace of God" that they made little effort themselves but "antinomianism" in whatever form it has appeared has usually been regarded as a heresy in the given religion. It is also true that religion has had its extreme mystics who were so absorbed by their vision of the divine that they forgot the realistic world in which man must live and strive, but it is also true that many more, through their vision of the divine, have gained insight and courage to do the spiritual work of the world. It is an indisputable fact of history that the world's greatest moral heroes and fighters for ideal values have usually been men and women who believed most firmly that these values are grounded not only in human nature but in the very nature and will of God, and that they themselves had a call of God to bring these ideal values to the attention of their fellowmen. Certainly this was the case with the great prophets of Judaism, with Christian apostles and reformers and with many a moral leader outside of these religions. The eleventh chapter of Hebrews is a far more accurate statement of facts than Professor Dewey's account. And surely even Professor Dewey would have to admit that no man has had a greater influence in the realm of ideal values than Jesus of Nazareth. But to think of Jesus and his ideals is to think of one who lived his whole life in the consciousness of God and who had the courage to follow his ideals though they led to the cross because it was, as he himself had said, his very meat and drink to do his Father's will.

Professor Dewey seems to realize that his own position is open to serious objections when he says, "The view I have advanced is sometimes treated as if the identification of the divine with ideal ends left the ideal wholly without roots in existence and without support from existence. The objection implies that my view commits me to such a separation of the ideal and the existent that the ideal has no chance to find lodgment even as a seed that might grow and bear fruit." This objection he answers by saying, "What I have been criticising is the identification of the ideal with a particular Being, especially when the identification makes necessary the conclusion that this Being is outside of nature, and what I have tried to show is that the ideal itself has its roots in natural conditions." What, then, if religion says that "this Being" with whom ideal values are "identified" is in a real sense "in Nature," or that Nature is somehow the expression of Divine Being and that the ideal values which Professor Dewey finds grounded in human nature and in Nature are objectively real just because they have their ultimate source in Ideal and Ultimate Being? In fact, as we said above, it is difficult to imagine how ideal values which man experiences best and only as a spiritual being can have any objective existence beyond human nature unless they are somehow grounded in and identified with the nature of Ultimate Being. Professor Dewey, in the above passage, comes almost to that conclusion but he then backs away from it and proceeds to talk about ideal values as embodied in the lives of great moral leaders. But these great moral leaders in whom ideal values are most clearly embodied have usually been men and women who were most certain that the ideal values for which they strove are achievable largely because they are grounded not merely in the human but in reality beyond the human, in the Divine.

Among modern European philosophers perhaps none stand more definitely for this general view that religion's validity is limited to its ethical and ideal values as grounded merely in human nature than do the adherents of the so-called Marburger School of Neo-Kantians, particularly such men

as Herman Cohen and Paul Natorp. (Cohen's "Religion und Sittlichkeit."
"Der Begriff der Religion im System "der Philosophie." Natorp's, "Religion
Innerhalb der Grenzen der Humanität.") As Neo-Kantians they approach
the problem of religion and philosophy in general from a very different angle
from what is the case with Professor Dewey who is an out and out Pragmatist in his theory of knowledge. Thus where the latter builds wholly on
what man finds in actual experience and where he concludes that ideal
values are real because they obviously influence human life and conduct,
Cohen in particular ignores empirical religion and turns at once to the
Kantian *a priori* to get at the real content of what alone can be valid in religion. "The facts," he says, "can never and nowhere bring forth the concept" of true religion. And in good Kantian style, he turns especially to the
a priori of the moral will as the true religious *a priori* so that religion, or what
can be valid in religion, is wholly identical with ethical values and ideals.
But where Kant had concluded that moral ideals which control human life
and conduct imply the existence of a cosmic moral order and that this implies
the existence of a Moral Lawgiver, Cohen declines to take this latter step.
If religion is to have validity at all it must find this in its ethical ideals and in
the way it promotes these ideals in human life. All interest in metaphysical
reality and all claim to insights into life's meanings and values other than
those which man has in his ethical relationships with his fellowmen must be
given up. "Religion must not be separated from its living connection with
ethics." ("Der Begriff" p. 44) This would, of course be accepted by all
ethical religions. Cohen, however, explains that "all content of ethics is
man and what belongs to him" (Op. cit. p. 44) and he makes no room
whatever for man's relationship to the divine in his ethical life which latter
is naturally always a major factor in the great ethical religions. Cohen realizes that in ethical religions there is always a God-idea bound up with
ethics and that therefore ethical religion is something more than mere
ethics. To conserve this "something more" for his type of religion he offers
what he regards a valid substitute for the God-idea that stands for a real
divine being, namely, a God-idea which is simply a sort of carrying ground
in man's natural environment and man's own nature on which his moral
striving as an individual can rest and which also represents the ideal goal
towards which he struggles. Cohen realizes that if the good life depended
for its realization wholly upon the individual human beings who strive for
it then no truly good life could be permanently built up. The good must be
grounded in something broader and deeper than the mere moral will of
individual man. It must be grounded in Human Nature and Nature at large.

It is this insight that religion stands for according to Cohen. Religion's God-idea means, then, just this assurance "that there is ever present a carrying ground for man's ethical work." (Op. cit. p. 51) And God "is thought of as the goal towards which man's own ethical work is directed." (Op. cit. p. 63) "God does not mean the power on which man can draw for his ethical life but only the example and the goal after which he must regulate his conduct." (Reg. u Sittlichkeit p. 43) Cohen, as a good Jew, claims that this is the real meaning of God in Jewish monotheism. He says, "in the pure monotheism of Judaism the God of grace and forgiveness has only this meaning; a guarantee of the goal, success and victory of man's own ethical self-work". . . . "The transcendence of God means the sufficiency of man in affirming his humanity. In the independence of man's ethical nature is grounded this sufficiency." (Der Begriff. . . . p. 66) In Christianity and pantheistic religions, on the other hand, says Cohen, God is conceived of as a transcendental Being who takes part in man's ethical striving, but this, he holds, is a confusion of thought and vitiates the truly ethical life.

Thus Cohen comes to essentially the same conclusion which Professor Dewey reached though by a very different route. He differs slightly from the latter in that he appreciates more fully the big role which the God-idea has played in ethical religions and so he seeks to conserve it by a reinterpretation but without the idea standing for anything more than ideal humanity and those conditions in man's natural environment which are conducive to the achievement of ideal values. But it may well be questioned whether Cohen gains anything of real value by this specious reinterpretation. Certainly when he claims that this is the meaning of God in pure Jewish monotheism he is far from the real facts. If ethics needs the God-idea to make it adequate for man's deepest needs it will have to be a God-idea which stands for something more than a mere idealized humanity. And if man's ideal values are objectively real and are grounded not simply in human nature but also beyond human nature, as both Cohen and Dewey affirm, then it is certainly more reasonable to hold, as ethical monotheism has always held, that at the heart of this transhuman reality is a moral Being whose nature is best conceived of in terms of ideal personality than to hold this vague conception which fluctuates uncertainly between the strictly human sphere and a something a little more than the human.

Paul Natorp is, perhaps, more clear-cut in his view that religion can be valid only in so far as it limits its interests to ethical and cultural values but gives up all concern about the divine and transcendental world. This appears even in the title of his dissertation on the subject, namely, "Religion within the Bounds of Humanity" and which carries the suggestive subtitle, "A Chapter on the Foundations of Social Pedagogy."

Having in mind the modern critics of religion who attack it on the ground that it concerns itself with the superhuman and transcendental world rather than with the practical problems of life, Natorp seeks to defend religion by insisting that its true nature and interest is virtually identical with whatever promotes man's highest culture and particularly man's ethical ideals and values. He would limit religion's validity to this. "Religion, or what has hitherto concealed itself under this name, is exactly so far to be retained as it remains locked up within the bounds of humanity." (Op. cit. p. 49) He then proceeds to define what he means by Humanity within whose bounds religion must confine itself to be valid. The human is "the full power of human nature in man," i.e. it is more than the power inherent in any individual but rather what is resident in humanity as a whole from the lowest savage up to a Plato and a Jesus. And human culture, too, is an all-inclusive and well-balanced thing. It is "not a one-sided development of the intellectual, the ethical or the aesthetic faculties, much less the mere capacity for physical activity and enjoyment, but the opening up of all the aspects of man's being in their healthy, normal and with all correct relationship to each other so that as far as possible they will mutually advance rather than hinder each other." (Op. cit. p. 1)

Though religion has frequently stood in opposition to human nature and general culture through its concentration on the superhuman and transcendental world, Natorp holds, this was a perversion of true religion and that religion at its best makes "the human, the ethical the very center" of its interest. Though religion is not wholly identical with ethics "it nevertheless grows from the heart of the moral consciousness and retains its connection with this in all its stages. It gains thereby its human, yea superhuman character; and it becomes so much a matter of common human interest that the term God hardly means anything else than the highest human consciousness through which the unity of mankind is realized." (Op. cit. p. 15)

Natorp realizes that religion has frequently stressed the feeling of man's dependence upon a power other than himself, or that religion is a sort of feeling of the finite for the infinite; at least an aspiration for something more than the merely human. He therefore seeks to analyze and explain this feeling, accepting Schleiermacher's view provisionally that religion is grounded primarily in man's feeling. Feeling, he says, is not a faculty coordinate with the powers of knowing, willing and the creative fantasy but rather their common ground. It is the "innerness of the psychic life, the real self-realization of the soul. Knowing, willing, aesthetic fantasy are in comparison only the outward expressions; feeling embraces these more or less, or represents their common root." (Op. cit. p. 27) But while feeling is the common root of all psychic functions, as Natorp holds, there is no object peculiarly apprehended through feeling. It is therefore not a special organ through which man becomes aware of an Infinite Reality that transcends the world of finite things known to the intellect or with which man strives as will and seeks to reshape to his liking through his creative aesthetic faculty. Of course, even in man's ordinary knowing, willing and creative fantasy he seems to reach out beyond what is actually present and existent. This is specially true of man's moral will. "I know what is; I will what is not but what should be." (Op. cit. p. 28) This desire of the moral will for ideal values seems therefore to open the way from the finite human sphere to the transcendent infinite sphere and man may "feel" in this experience that he is thus reaching out for, or is in actual contact with, infinite Being, as religion has often claimed, but this, says Natorp, is where man misinterprets his own inner experience for this apparent "feeling for the Endless" is only man's capacity for "endless feeling." "The Infinite as an object for the feeling does not exist." (Op. cit. p. 39) In so far as religion thinks that it is in actual contact with a real infinite and transcendent object in the religious feeling it takes "a dangerous tendency which falsifies the sense of scientific truth." (Op. cit. p. 40) Also human conduct, Natorp holds, is vitiated if man pretends to step beyond the bounds of finite things. "One can not act honestly over against an Infinite Reality, but only against a finite, since neither the will nor the intellect has at its disposal other than finite powers." (Op. cit. p. 40)

But man's feelings, Natorp proceeds, always seem to demand as their goal "an eternal, blessed communion with the Infinite, with the Divine." (Op. cit. p. 41) From this finiteness of man's nature and yet this apparent feeling for the Infinite arises an inner conflict in man's nature. This conflict can be solved, Natorp says, only if and when we realize that this feeling for an Infinite is really a perversion and an extravagance of feeling. Let man's feeling "fill the bed of the stream of consciousness with its flowing life, but it should not in its exuberance break all bounds and dissipate itself in the wideness of the Infinite." (Op. cit. p. 45) For beyond what man experiences in science, ethics and aesthetic creativeness there is no object he can apprehend. With all his feeling for the Infinite "man can never really step beyond the bounds of the human." (Op. cit. p. 47)

Thus in so far as religion keeps within these bounds and concerns itself with man's ordinary cultural values, i.e. values which can vindicate themselves in man's immediate experience, it is valid. A religion that does this, Natorp proceeds, is really the only kind that can promote the true welfare of man. Where religion concerns itself with the thought of an Infinite Being it rather weakens the bonds between man and his fellowmen for it puts in the foreground the relationship of the individual to a transhuman sphere. "But on the other hand where this interest (in the superhuman) is given up, there still remains an elevation of the soul through its enlargement of itself into the soul of the All; not the all of things but the inner universal in which the all of humanity finds its unity and communion. In place of the transcendental deity appears then humanity itself." (Op. cit. p. 52)

Undoubtedly Natorp makes a strong case for religion's validity in so far as it is identical with the cultural values of mankind and particularly with ethical values. He also shows a keen awareness of that aspect of human nature which expresses itself in an aspiration for a fuller and higher life. In religion man reaches out for something truer, better and more beautiful than on the ordinary level of life. It is a quest for the good life, an endless quest as it were since the goal of man's striving ever advances as he moves towards it. As Natorp puts it, nothing satisfies man but "the eternal, blessed communion with the Infinite, with God himself." (Op. cit. p. 41) Yet in spite of this true insight into the religious consciousness he holds that the religious quest for the Infinite and Eternal One is only a "dangerous tendency" and that religion is valid only in so far as it remains "locked within the bounds of humanity." But if by nature man is such that he is ever questing for the Eternal and the more than human, as Natorp admits, then why is it not more reasonable to conclude from this as Augustine concluded that man is made for God and can not rest until he rests in Him? Just why should man forever remain "locked within the bounds of humanity?" Natorp's solution of the inner conflict in man between what he is and what he aspires to be, namely, by simply dropping out one side, is really no solution. Of course, in one sense man is always limited to the sphere of his own human experience but it is preposterous to say that this must mean that the object of his experience can not be anything beyond the bounds of humanity itself. That is just the very heart of the religious consciousness in all vital religion, that it is an awareness of a spiritual reality other than man himself. Religion may be wrong in this conviction but Natorp has produced no convincing reasons that prove this to be wrong.

Now this general theory of religion finds expression in the modern world far beyond the circles of a few philosophers such as we have discussed above. It is virtually the position of what might be called the religious wing of modern Humanism. Humanism as a whole is far from being in agreement as to what is valid in religion. The older Humanism, it will be remembered, definitely affirmed its belief in God. Its main quarrel with Christian orthodoxy was not at this point but rather over the question as to man's share in the process of salvation and the real content of the good life, stressing as it did man's natural ability over against the doctrine of total depravity and putting a more exclusive emphasis on ethical relations. Modern Humanism moves several steps further away from traditional Christianity and also from the older Humanism. One wing abandons religion and religious concepts altogether, and though it recognizes religion's validity in so far as it promotes general cultural and ethical values it holds that these values can be had better without religion and that therefore they have really nothing to do with it. The other wing which might be called the religious wing not only recognizes religion's validity in the realm of ethical and ideal values but even seeks a grounding for these values beyond the strictly human sphere though it hesitates to formulate this belief in anything more definite than in the language of poetry.

Perhaps the best representative of the first type of modern Humanism, at least among English speaking thinkers, is Walter Lippmann in his well known book, "A Preface to Morals." Lippmann accepts the highest ethical ideals and values which the practical experience of the race has found valid. He would, however, insist that these values are strictly human values and that they are in no way dependent for their validity upon being grounded in a transhuman sphere such as religion and religious metaphysics claim. There is only one unique ideal value of religion towards which Lippmann still casts a longing glance. This is what he calls the "Lordly ideal" of religion. By this he means that synthesis which religion in the past achieved and by which it marshalled the various activities and ideals of men under one supreme ideal and so gave life a unity and a directive goal. Modern Western culture, he says, lacks this synthesis, for with the growing separation and independence of the different arts and sciences, each standing in its own rights and with its own ideals, there is nothing which binds these various interests of the modern man together into an organic unity or that gives life a supreme meaning and dominating purpose. Life has many minor meanings but no one supreme meaning. He writes, "What was happening to painting is precisely what has happened to all the other separate activities of men. Each activity has its own ideal, indeed a succession of ideals, for with the dissolution of the supreme ideal of service to God, there is no ideal which unites them all, and sees them in order. Each ideal is supreme within a sphere of its own. There is no point of reference outside which can determine the relative value of competing ideals. The modern man desires health, he desires money, he desires power, beauty, love, truth, but which he shall desire the most since he can not pursue them all to their logical conclusion, he no longer has any means of deciding. His impulses are no longer parts of one attitude towards life; his ideals are no longer in a hierarchy under one lordly ideal. They have become differentiated. They are free and they are incommensurable. The religious synthesis has dissolved. The modern man no longer holds a belief about the universe which sustains a pervasive emotion about his destiny; he no longer believes genuinely in any idea which organizes his interests within the framework of a cosmic order."

There is no question but that Lippmann in this memorable passage describes accurately the state of many a modern man to whom religion no longer provides a supreme ideal and unifying life purpose. But if that is really the case and if it is impossible for such a modern man to turn back to religion as he understands religion then, perhaps, the only way out for him is to go forward to a religion or philosophy of life which will supply the ideal. Surely it would be difficult to state more emphatically than Lippmann has done the need of finding an answer to what is essentially the religious quest, namely, the quest for the value and meaning of human life. If the answers which religion has given thus far are not wholly satisfactory it would seem rather foolish to abandon the quest for that reason. Even Lippmann admits that the moral ideals and values for which the great ethical religions have stood at their best are valid for human life. Though modern ethical science stands on its own feet and claims these ideals and values as its own and as independent of religion, the fact nevertheless remains, as we have repeatedly pointed out, that the great moral leaders of the race have usually been deeply religious. Since this is so and since according to Lippmann's own confession an independent ethic fails to marshal the ideals of the separate activities of man under one "lordly ideal" or unifying purpose, does this not mean that an ethic without religion or an ethic grounded simply in human nature and not in the heart of Reality or the Divine is only a half-way affair? Why stop at this point and not pursue this quest until we find what ethical religion has always affirmed, namely, that ethical ideals and values are what they are and have their commanding place in man's conscience and life just because they represent an aspect of ultimate reality and are grounded in the very nature of God?

In Johan Bojer's novel, "The Great Hunger" we have an excellent expression of the modern Humanist's view who not only endorses the ethical ideals and values of the higher religions but who also feels the need of a God-idea to symbolize the goal and the achievement of man's spiritual quest even though this "symbolic god" has no objective existence and is only man's own creation. "And more and more it came home to me," says the hero, "that it is man himself that must create the divine in heaven and on earth—that that is his triumph over the dead omnipotence of the universe. Therefore I went out and sowed corn in my enemy's field, that God might exist.

"In the midst of this thraldom he created the beautiful on earth; in the midst of his torments he has had so much surplus energy of soul that he has sent it radiating forth into the cold deeps of space and warmed them with God . . . . So marvelous art thou, O spirit of man! So God-like is thy very nature! Thou dost reap death, and in return thou sowest the dream of everlasting life. In revenge for thine evil fate, thou dost fill the universe with an all-loving God.

"Honor to thee, O spirit of man. Thou givest a soul to the world, thou settest it a goal, thou art the hymn that lifts it into harmony; therefore turn back into thyself, lift high thy head and meet proudly the evil that comes to thee. Adversity can crush thee, death can blot thee out, yet art thou still unquenchable and eternal. . . . .

"She, too, the stricken mother, had arisen up from the ocean of her suffering that here, in the daybreak, she might take her share in the creating of God."

What a magnificent tribute this is to the unquenchable spirit of man! But also how pathetic is such a faith in the spiritual realities of life! On the one hand these spiritual values are recognized as real; in fact, as the great realities for which man must live to be true to his own best nature. But, on the other hand, in spite of this nobility of soul and in spite of man's triumph over "the dead omnipotence of the universe" the last word shall, nevertheless, be spoken by that "dead omnipotence" and the spirit of individual man who has so nobly striven shall be blotted out by death. Only the unquenchable spirit of man as it lives on in the race, only that is eternal. And only that can be the meaning of God, this kind of God whom man himself is creating in his upward march through the centuries.

There is a real flavor of religion in this passage in so far as religion represents man's striving for ideal ends and for securing these values as an ever growing possession of an advancing race, but it falls far short of what religion stands for when it holds that while ideal values cannot be real to man except as he appropriates them through a creative activity of spirit these values are nevertheless not bound up solely with or primarily dependent upon man's activity but rather are grounded in the character and activity of Divine Being. Bojer, in spite of his "great Hunger" for the divine does not seem to get beyond the bounds of humanity itself, as was the case with Cohen, Natorp and the kind of Humanists represented by Lippmann.

But if one wing of modern Humanists accepts merely the ethical values of religion as valid and regards these as merely grounded in human nature there is another wing which sees in religion a little more than that. It, too, puts in the foreground the cultural values of life and particularly the moral ideals and values as the most worthwhile. Religion, to have validity, must stand for these things, and these values must vindicate themselves in the practical tests of concrete human living. They are not seen as values which are brought in from a supernatural sphere through special divine revelation and valid largely because divinely revealed, but they are seen as wrought out by the persistent activities and searchings of man and valid because they are experienced as such in actual life. But this type of Humanism is not quite content to stop with that. Its ethical ideals and cultural values, though thoroughly grounded in human nature and valid because of their practicability in human living, are nevertheless tinged with an awareness of the divine. However in stating what is meant by the divine, this type of Humanism becomes overly cautious and hesitant.

Probably the best example of the type in question is John Haynes Holmes. It is a bit precarious to quote from his writings to get his real views since he himself says that his view changes with his mood and that he prefers the language of poetry to any clear cut theological formulations. In an article entitled "A Humanistic Interpretation of Prayer" (Christian Century Oct. 16, 1929) written "in revolt against the pragmatic type of Humanism which now prevails" and which "cannot pray, cannot worship and cannot sing," Dr. Holmes seeks to show that his type of Humanism can pray, worship and sing. While prayer, according to him, is first of all "the deliberate formulation in our minds of an idea of something that we need or want" and, "the conscious, deliberate direction of our life forces to the attainment of our desires," in prayer we must nevertheless "move out beyond the limits of our own poor strength and rally the universe to our support." And again he says, "it is the attempt to merge our lives in the life of the whole, and therewith identify ourselves with cosmic destiny." If it be asked what the inner nature of the cosmos or ultimate reality might be which determines man's destiny, Dr. Holmes refuses to commit himself to any formulation such as one finds in traditional religious concepts but says he prefers the language of poetry to that of theology. He accepts as a "postulate that the spirit of man is akin to the spirit of the universe in itself as well as in its myriad separate forms, and that 'spirit with spirit can meet,' " but lest this be taken too literally he hastens to remind us that this is only the language of poetry.

In response to a host of critics, some claiming that Dr. Holmes believes in a personal God, after all, and others that it is inconsistent for him to pray since he does not believe in a personal God, he replies: "When I am asked if I believe in God, I am either impatient or amused, and frequently decline to reply. All I know, all I want to know, is that I have found in my relation with my fellowmen and in my glad beholding of the universe a reality of truth, goodness, and beauty, and that I am trying to make my life as best I can a dedication to this reality. When I am in the thinking mood, I try to be rigorously rational, and thus not to go one step farther in my thought and language than my reason can take me. I then become uncertain as to whether I or any man can assert much about God, and fall back content into the mood of Job. When, however, in preaching or in prayer, in some high moment of inner communion or of profound experience with life among my fellows, I feel the pulse of emotion suddenly beating in my heart, and I am lifted up as though upon some sweeping tide that is more than the sluggish current of my days, I find it easy to speak as the poets speak, and cry, as so many of them cry, to God. "But when I say 'God,' it is poetry and not theology."

This is undoubtedly an honest statement and one, too, which describes rather accurately the inner experience of many. It clearly affirms the reality of ideal values as experienced in practical human living. It also affirms that these values are grounded both in human nature as such and in man's environment. It goes even one step further when it affirms a real faith in the Divine even though it is rather hesitant in stating definitely what it means by the Divine and prefers the "language of poetry" to that of theology.

In his autobiography entitled *I Speak For Myself*, Dr. Holmes identifies his type of Humanism more nearly with Theistic religion when he says: "I am a Humanist who finds no contradiction between Humanism and Theism, but sees in the one the fulfillment and completion of the other." In fact, he differentiates his own type of Humanism from the usual type "whose denials are but a feeble echo of the atheism of ancient days. Beginning his religion with man, he ends it in the same place, finding nothing beyond this creature, who lives a few years and dies forever, to kindle his imagination or extend his vision."

It should seem clear, then, that Dr. Holmes' type of Humansim does believe definitely in God even though it prefers the language of poetry to that of theology in formulating its belief. Probably if the slate could be wiped clean of the many dogmatic assertions about the Divine which traditional religions have made and some of which are often all too anthropomorphic in nature these reverently agnostic but deeply religious natures like Dr. Holmes would be less hesitant in formulating their conception of the Divine. But it must be added that just as long as men like Dr. Holmes who claim to believe in God are so hesitant in stating more definitely what they mean by the term "God" just so long will these inadequate conceptions of the Divine prevail in the religion of the masses. And we might add further that in making these more worthy affirmation one need not abandon one's "Thinking mood," as Dr. Holmes suggests, and give way to one's emotions when only the language of poetry is a fit vehicle. A "thinking mood" that tries to be "rigorously rational" may be all too narrowly rationalistic and so miss the true reality which is so central in all vital religion. Nothing short of the whole human personality and the full response that it makes at its best to man's encompassing Reality is adequate.

Now while the general position which we have been discussing above is one which is widely held in the modern Western world it is one which is by no means limited either to the modern age or to the Western world. It is rather a view that has persisted through the ages both in the West and in the East. In Western thought we have close parallels in the religious philosophies of some of the ancient Stoics. Likewise do we find kindred spirits among some of the older Humanists of the fifteenth and sixteenth centuries as among some of the theologians of the seventeenth and eighteenth centuries. All of these were more or less agreed that ethical magnitudes are real and that these are grounded in man's own nature; and further, that man can work out these ideal values through his practical life and human relationships. As to how far these ideal values are grounded in reality beyond human nature and as to the nature of that reality there were varying degrees of hesitancy in their formulations. They usually stopped short of any clear affirmations such as one finds in the great ethical religions with their insistence on the thought that ultimate reality upon which man's life is dependent is best conceived of in terms of ideal personality and that through man's moral intuition he apprehends the ultimate as a supreme Moral Being.

But it is not only in Western thought that religion's validity is restricted largely to its affirmations and promotion of ethical and other ideal values. This view is equally characteristic of much in Oriental thought. It is peculiarly the emphasis of Confucian philosophy and of certain phases of Buddhist thought. It is customary to think of the Orient as the home of mysticism and other-worldliness where men dream about the unseen world and where the world of sense experience is treated as more or less illusory and where practical ethical values are dissolved in the vapors of a vague pantheism. There is some truth to this picture, especially is it true of much in Indian thought where the best minds in their quest for transcendental reality have often shown a supreme indifference to the natural life of man and the things needful for building up the good life in the here and now. But this picture is emphatically not true of the East Asiatic people, especially not of the Chinese. The dominant philosophy of life for the thinking classes of China, from upward of two thousand years, has been the Confucian philosophy and Confucianism in its main emphasis is a kind of Humanism. Its major interest has always been the ethical ideals and values that govern, or should govern, human relationships. These ideals and values, Confucius held, grow out of the practical experience of the race. He had little to say about prophets inspired of God with the visions of a higher spiritual order or about man's primary relationship to the divine, but he had much to say about the good life consisting of ethical ideals and values which the wise men of the past had achieved in their practical human relationships and which should serve as examples for their descendents. Human nature is fundamentally good and if man lives true to his own nature as this is best exhibited in the life of the "Superior Man" he will attain the good life in the here and now. To be sure, in much of Confucian thought the average man hardly comes to his rights since the individual as such has little permanent meaning or value but must fit himself like a cog into the machinery of a well-ordered society. But Confucianism at its best does affirm the objective reality of ethical ideals and values and makes these the very core of the truly good life for man. To this extent it therefore recognizes beyond a shadow of doubt the validity of all the higher ethical religions.

Confucianism goes one step further in the direction of ethical religions when it affirms that the ethical and ideal values that should govern human life are grounded not only in human nature itself but also in what might be called a moral order on a cosmic scale. Man is part of a wider reality and this reality is moral at its core. Is there a supreme Moral Being at the heart of this moral order, or has this moral order a Moral Law-giver, as Kant had reasoned? In answering this question ancient Confucianism, like the modern western philosophers we have discussed above, is rather hesitant if not agnostic. Wherever Confucianism speaks of *Shang Ti*, Supreme Ancestor or Ruler, the answer tends towards an ethical monotheism. And there are also a few passages which seem to indicate that Confucius felt he had a kind of call of God not unlike that of the Old Testament prophets. However the more usual terminology implies rather the belief in a moral order but seems rather agnostic as to whether at the heart of the moral order there is a supreme Moral Being. In fact, Confucius' characteristic attitude was one which avoided as far as possible any definite commitment on metaphysical problems, holding rather that it is more important to get on with the business of practical human relationships than speculating about the real nature of ultimate reality. It should, however, be added that when Neo-Confucianism occupied itself more definitely with the problems of metaphysical reality we find some philosophers clearly repudiating all personalistic conceptions of ultimate reality, while others, especially some of the later Japanese Neo-Confucianists, were virtually monotheists.

If typical Confucianism saw religion's validity primarily in ethical and other ideal values grounded in human nature and in a cosmic moral order but was rather hesitant in going beyond this, the same may also be said of certain phases of Buddhism. That original Buddhism placed a tremendous emphasis on the reality of ethical values no one can seriously question. In fact, the one thing that the Buddha was more sure of than anything else was the inexorableness of the moral law. If there is a law of cause and effect in the physical world it is even more certain that such a law is operative in the moral sphere. There is much in the early literature of Buddhism which gave rise to the view that the founder looked upon the so-called natural world as more or less illusory but there is no doubt about his accepting moral ideals and values as real and the living in accordance with these ideals as the one road that leads out from the world of illusions. To be sure, he did not clearly affirm that the achievement of an ethical personality has survival value nor did he make any clear affirmations as to the nature of Ultimate Reality but he did say most emphatically that the way out from this world of suffering and illusion must pass through this point of the highest ethical values known to man. The *Nirvana* state to which this road leads is such that ethical and all ideal values as understood by mortal man are no longer quite definitive. What his conception of the nature of Ultimate Reality really was is not clear. That he rejected the conceptions of popular religions is plain enough and it is also clear that he did not think very highly of the metaphysical speculations of the philosophers of his day. As we pointed out in Part One, there are several different views among leading scholars as to this point but that we are perhaps nearest to an understanding of his real position if we say that he was reverently agnostic as to the true nature of ultimate reality holding, however, that a life lived in harmony with the highest ethical values known to man indicates at least the direction in which the nature of true reality may be found even though ultimate reality may be such that it completely transcends all that man can experience and know.

In subsequent Buddhist thought the lines diverge rather widely but at least one line is closely akin to the general position under consideration in this section and which sees religion's validity primarily in its emphasis on ethical values grounded in human nature and beyond human nature in man's encompassing reality but which is hesitant in making use of any God-idea or in making any definite affirmations about the heart of ultimate reality other than that its nature transcends all powers of man to know. This phase of Buddhism merged in China with Confucian ethics and so became more this-worldly in its emphasis than original Buddhism had been. That is to say, instead of regarding the ethical life as the supreme road of escape from this world of evil and illusion it sought more to build up the good life in the here and now in good Confucian style. However even this type of Buddhism could not get away from its interest in metaphysical reality which was so characteristic of all Mahāyāna Buddhist philosophy and because of this it in turn influenced Confucian thought in the direction of taking greater interest in metaphysics and which resulted, as we have said, in what is known as Neo-Confucianism. It is through this combination of Buddhism and Confucianism that we get in Chinese and later in Japanese thought the finest emphasis on the reality of ethical and ideal values as grounded in human nature and beyond human nature in a sort of cosmic moral order but which usually stops short at that point or only hesitatingly makes affirmations about the divine. There are, to be sure, plenty affirmations about "the divine in man" and also about the whole of reality being "divine," but this is more the language of poetry as in Western Humanism than philosophy or theology. Where accurate language is used we find rather a sort of reverent agnosticism or a series of affirmations balanced (and sometimes neutralized) by a corresponding series of negations to indicate the belief in Absolute Being which transcends all powers of man to comprehend. Unfortunately this reverend agnosticism sometimes has a reflex influence on the ethical and other ideal values by which man is to live his practical life, for if the distinctions man makes between the true and the false, the good and the evil have no real meaning in Ultimate Reality then there follows an inevitable doubt as to whether they can have real validity for human life. That is the haunting doubt which has afflicted Buddhist philosophy through the centuries and which has often undermined the vitality of its otherwise lofty ethics. To be sure, popular Buddhism has been positive enough in its affirmations and beliefs about the divine but usually where it has been positive it has been also all too human in its conceptions. Buddhists are, of course, not alone in this for the same may be said of others, including many modern Christians.

Thus in the East as in the West we find today this common attitude towards religion so that the first example we discussed in this section, namely Professor Dewey's "A Common Faith" is indeed rather typical of a very "common faith" in many lands. It remains, therefore, to say a few words in conclusion as to the validity of this widely held view.

As we have seen, the advocates of this general view of religion look upon religion as being above all else the discovery and the promotion of the good life for man. They agree in general that whatever else may make up the good life such e.g. as the whole rich content which modern physical science yields, it must include and give prominence to ethical and other ideal values. There may be differences in formulating these values in detail but in general by these are meant the ideals of truth, goodness and beauty as these have been repeatedly formulated by the higher ethical religions and idealistic philosophies and which are more or less accepted by the cultured classes all over the world. They agree further that these ideal values are not mere subjective values but that they are grounded in objective reality. They are, to begin with, grounded in human nature as such. Human life is so constituted that to live in harmony with these ideals is to experience the truly good life. All the more is this the case when these ideals are accepted by society in general and not merely by a few isolated individuals. Furthermore these ideal values, it is held, vindicate themselves to the one who lives by them. They need no further vindication and, in fact, can have no truer vindication, for he who does not know e.g. that truth should have the right of way over falsehood, right over wrong, because of the inherent quality of the true and the right will not be really convinced in any other way.

Now in all this we are in full agreement and we hold that this position is essentially valid. It is what is said beyond this point that we question the validity of the position taken.

Some representatives, as we saw, will not go beyond this point in their affirmations or beliefs because they hold that this would be purely speculative and not certitude. That seems to us a rather untenable position for the simple reason that human life is part of a wider reality and it is inevitably bound up with this wider reality. That this is the case for man's physical life is, of course, too obvious to be mentioned. But why should it be limited purely to the physical aspect? If it be granted that ethical and other ideal values are objectively real and that they are grounded in human nature then surely the inquiry is natural and legitimate as to whether these ideal values may not be grounded also in Reality beyond the strictly human sphere. Now we have seen that according to the views of most of those whom we have discussed above, these ideal values to be objectively real in the fullest sense must be grounded somehow in Reality as a whole or in Ultimate Reality and not simply in human nature.

But here arises the real crux of our problem. Granted that these ideal values are grounded in Reality as a whole or in Ultimate Reality as far as we can know it, how shall we think of the nature of this Ultimate Reality or the way these ideal values find their grounding in Ultimate Reality?

It must be granted that Ultimate Reality may far transcend anything man can experience or know even on the highest plane of ethical and other ideal values and for this reason there is a respectable place for the reverent agnostic as over against the cock-sureness and dogmatism of little minds, but there are some considerations which make the position of even the reverent agnostic not the most reasonable one to take. In so far as man experiences these ethical and other ideal values most adequately as he himself achieves the highest levels of human personality it would seem most reasonable to hold that Ultimate Reality is itself best conceived of in terms of Ideal Personality. However much it may transcend this in its full nature, since this is the most adequate and illuminating conception that we can form of it, it would seem to be the most reasonable one to hold. Of course, the pronoun "It" would then be a personal pronoun.

If ethical and other ideal values are accepted as objectively real and grounded both in human nature and in reality beyond the human it is reasonable to conclude as Confucianism, some Buddhists and certain of the above mentioned Western philosophers have concluded that there is a moral and an ideal order of cosmic proportions. But we would press the point further. Just what is meant by a cosmic moral order unless this stands for the relationship between moral beings? If this relationship is not simply one between man and his fellowmen but one which holds between man and the Beyond Man and Ultimate Reality, as must be the case if these ethical values are really grounded beyond the strictly human sphere, then how shall we conceive of the nature of Ultimate Reality better than in terms of Moral Being? The same question can be put regarding the other ideal values which are said to be objectively real and grounded in Ultimate Reality. The ideal of truth has little sense apart from a Being that thinks the truth. Thus the position of the great ethical and theistic religions which conceive of Ultimate

Reality, or the heart of Reality, in terms of Ideal Personality is certainly one which seems to follow most logically from the general position we have discussed in this section which professedly accepts the primacy of ideal values in human life. It will seem even more valid as we proceed in our further discussion with other aspects of the religious experience and the religious consciousness which we have not considered thus far.

We conclude, then, that this theory of religion which holds that religion is valid in so far as it stands for the highest ethical and other ideal values is itself valid in this affirmation but that when it would restrict religion's validity to this and deny that religion can have any insight whatever into the nature of Ultimate Reality it is guilty of an unwarranted skepticism, and in the last analysis this skepticism tends to undermine the real validity of ethical and other ideal values in practical human living. For unless we can believe that our ethical and other ideal values are objectively real in Ultimate Reality itself then they can not be altogether objectively real even in finite human life. We would, however, put this truth the other way around by saying that if our experience teaches us that these ideal values are objectively real for practical human living then it is more reasonable to hold that they are grounded also in Ultimate Reality and that through them we know the true nature of Ultimate Reality at least in part rather than to hold that they are not thus grounded or that we must be wholly agnostic as to the nature of the Ultimately Real.

B: VIII RELIGION AS ETHICAL IDEALS AND WITH A DIVINE POSTULATE

IN THE preceding section we discussed a theory of religion which sees religion's validity primarily in its identification with the highest ethical and other ideal values and which regards these values as grounded in human nature as such and also in a measure in reality beyond the human. We saw further that when it comes to making any definite affirmation about the nature of the transhuman sphere in which ideal values are said to be grounded the representatives of this general position are either wholly agnostic or exceedingly hestitant and vague. We therefore proceed next with a view of religion which also starts with the primacy of ideal values and which sees in these the very core of what is essential in religion but which at the same time takes one step further in the direction of the position held by the great ethical and theistic religions by affirming that the ethical values grounded in human nature have their ultimate grounding in a moral order which is itself the expression of a Supreme Moral Being though this latter affirmation is more of the nature of a necessary postulate than a datum based on direct experience of Divine Being. The best representative of this theory of religion is, of course, Kant.

As we saw in the section entitled "Towards a Norm of Truth," Kant was essentially right in insisting that man's awareness of moral magnitudes belongs to the most ultimate data of his experience beyond which we can not go. There is grounded in man's very being what Kant called the "Categorical Imperative" which bids him do the right as he sees the right irrespective of his desires growing out of his physical impulses or the consequences of his moral actions. Though man's physical life is closely conditioned by the external world, in his moral choices and conduct man knows himself bound not by the laws of the contingent world but by a sense of things that ought to be, by ideal values. Only as he lives in obedience to his ideals does he have a sense of being true to his own highest nature. And furthermore in this striving for the ideal he gains a sense of freedom, a sense of really transcending in his own inner life the realm of mere contingent things however much in his bodily life he is still bound by the laws of the external world. This does not mean that the realm of ideal values is wholly different from the realm of factual existence external to man or that man can gain this sense of freedom by cutting himself off from the factual, external world in a sort of Stoical indifference to it. Man can not gain mastery over either the inner or the outer world by running away from the latter or by insulating himself against it. It means rather that he becomes a free moral being and a real ethical personality when and only when he can use the things that make up the content of his life in the interest of the ideal values for which he feels that he must strive if he would be true to himself. That is the demand which the moral law, the Categorical Imperative, which is imprinted upon his own being makes of him. And this is an ultimate datum of the awakened moral consciousness which can not be reduced to lower or other terms.

Thus far Kant's position is essentially the same as the one discussed in the preceding section; or it would be more correct to say that the position of most of the Western representatives discussed is that of Kant since they so largely build on his insight. But it is from this point that Kant goes a step beyond these others since he holds that the moral consciousness makes necessary as a postulate the belief in a supreme Moral Being as the heart of the moral order. In fact, Kant makes a double postulate, namely, a belief in personal immortality for the individual who strives for the achievement of an ethical personality, and a belief in a supreme Moral Being, or God.

The conflict between the real and the ideal in human experience, Kant reasons, can not be a permanent state but the two must be somehow harmonized. This is the demand which man's moral consciousness stands for. But this implies really two things. One is that man's own nature be made completely moral. That is, the goal to which the moral ideal points in man's own nature is the achievement of a truly ethical personality. The other is that Reality as a whole must somehow support ultimately ideal values as these are embodied in a fully developed ethical personality. In other words, our sense of what is right demands that ultimately the truly moral life find complete satisfaction or bliss and that only such a life find this.

But the task of making man over into a completely developed ethical personality seems a rather unending task and one which requires more than the short span of man's life in this world. If, then, this is to be achieved a future life seems a necessary postulate. Of course, the future life is not a necessary postulate simply to allow time for completing our ideal task. It is rather that the moral ideal demands that the highest values worth striving for in this life must be conserved to give human life its full worth and meaning. To make the supreme task of life consist of the achievement of an ethical personality and then have this effort end in zero by the death of the individual would seem to rob the effort itself of all deeper meaning.

It is this consideration which leads to Kant's second postulate, the belief in God. Even though man might achieve in his own strength the ideal imprinted upon his own being he can not shape the whole of reality so that it will be favorable to the ideals for which he feels himself compelled to strive. That reality should support the ideal values is what the moral law in man's nature seems to demand, for that is the very meaning of ideal values, "things that should be." The facts of man's immediate experience seem, however, against this for often the good and the righteous suffer when the wicked "flourish like the green Bay tree." The moral consciousness protests against this view of reality as being the last word about it. It does not do away with the ugly facts of life by explaining them away but it insists as a necessary postulate of its own deepest insight that Reality must ultimately be brought under the regency of the ideal. This can, however, be only the case if at the heart of Ultimate Reality is a supreme moral Being who can and will subject the world of phenomena and contingent reality to the ideal known in moral consciousness.

This may at first sight seem like a purely arbitrary postulate and one, too, whose reasonableness seems to be contradicted by factual existence which often seems wholly indifferent if not actually hostile to ideal values. That is, however, not the case when one remembers Kant's theory of knowledge.

He maintains, as will be remembered, that man does not gain his deepest insight into reality through the theoretical reason since this gives him only the relationship between phenomena and not a knowledge of reality as it is in itself. This latter kind of insight man gains only through his experience as moral will in which he knows himself as a free being and above the realm of mere contingent things even though his bodily life is wholly subject to the laws of the latter. Through his moral intuition, his experience in moral choices and ethical conduct, he knows himself as akin to Noumenal Reality and hence he feels certain that in spite of the evidence to the contrary in factual existence Ultimate Reality is such that it will support the moral ideal. The existence of a supreme Moral Being at the heart of reality who will guarantee ultimately the triumph of the ideal and the conservation of an achieved ethical human personality in a future life is then, according to Kant, a necessary postulate of man's moral nature. It is not an arbitrary one but a necessary one growing out of man's truest and deepest insight into the nature of the ultimately real.

Now in this emphasis on the primacy of the moral ideal Kant has certainly stressed an element of religion which must be regarded as permanently valid. Even though religion may not find its full expression in terms of the moral life, no religion worthy of man's allegiance can be other than ethical in its emphasis. Essential Christianity, as well as the other great ethical religions, would be unthinkable apart from this emphasis. And we might add that the average man on the street who may have no formal connection with any organized religion would say that any religion worthy of man's respect must stand for "what is right." According to a questionnaire conducted among Anglo-American soldiers in World War I a very large majority had no formal connection with the Christian church but almost every one subscribed to this minimum of faith that "it is right to do the right thing" however difficult it may be to know just what the right thing is. So Kant, in building religion's validity upon its emphasis of the primacy of the moral ideal builds on what is solid ground for all but the most shallow sophists. And further, when Kant insists that in our moral intuition we have our deepest insight into the nature of Ultimate Reality and that a belief in the existence of a supreme Moral Being at the heart of things is a necessary postulate of man's moral nature he seems on fairly solid ground.

There are, however, several aspects of the Kantian theory of religion which make it inadequate. One is that however true it may be that in our moral intuition we have a deep insight into the nature of reality and that any worthy religion must build on this insight, it is not the only insight and therefore not the sole basis of valid religion. Religion at its best has to do with the whole of man's nature and while Kant may have been right in rejecting the old rationalistic arguments for the existence of God, a well-balanced religion will always have deep interest in what man can know about the physical universe. To be sure, modern religious leaders often make themselves ridiculous by quoting in season and out of season what some authority in astro-physics says about religion but it is nevertheless true that religion can not be indifferent to what competent scientists find to be true of the physical universe. In other words, religion should not build wholly on the inner life and the ideal values which we experience in our moral intuition even though these must ever be among the major elements of essential and valid religion. The truth of the matter is that in actual life we do not wholly separate our approach to reality into separate compartments such as the theoretical reason for which science stands, the moral intuition, the aesthetic appreciation or whatever other approach there may be. These are but aspects of our whole approach as they represent different aspects of the human personality which is a unity even though in different psychic states one or the other of these aspects may predominate over the others. Kant was right in saying that each of these aspects stands for something real but hardly right when he made the theoretical reason an instrument with which we handle only the phenomena of the physical world and the concepts derived from these while the moral intuition he regarded as the sole instrument through which we can approach the noumenal world. While religion is not primarily a philosophy of nature and while it concerns itself chiefly with the inner values of human life, particularly moral values, it can not be indifferent to the problems with which a philosophy of nature must deal, for in a broad sense man is himself a part of nature and what nature is apart from human nature is vital for an understanding of human nature itself. And the converse is equally true, namely, that what human nature is in all its aspects, including what man is as a moral and religious being, must be a real factor in arriving at any fair and sane philosophy of reality as a whole.

But there is a second point about the Kantian theory of religion which makes it inadequate, namely, the way he grounds man's belief in God. He was essentially right when he held that through man's moral intuition he becomes aware of moral magnitudes and that these constitute a moral order. But when he held that the belief in the existence of a Moral Law-giver, or God, is but a necessary logical inference which man draws, i.e. that the belief in God is only of the nature of an inference and nothing more direct than that he was not quite true to the religious consciousness which always claims a more direct awareness of divine being. To be sure, the existence of a moral order implies the existence of moral beings, and if the moral order is really a unity and of cosmic proportions and not merely a human moral order, then it is almost logically necessary to infer that at the center of this cosmic moral order is a supreme Moral Being. In fact, since we know moral magnitudes only in terms of the experience of personal beings and since these magnitudes seem to transcend the nature of any individual human being the belief in a supreme Personal Being whose nature is moral is a most rational belief even though it may not be an absolutely necessary logical inference. In this Kant seems nearer the truth than is the modern Humanist or the early Buddhist and typical Confucianist who also believed in a moral order and one even of cosmic proportions but who did not clearly infer from this that at the heart of the moral order is a supreme Moral Being, or who did so only very hesitatingly. The religious consciousness demands, however, more than a belief in God based on a mere logical inference. It finds it's more adequate interpretation if we say that in man's experience of moral magnitudes he can have a direct awareness of God since these magnitudes are never exhausted in their meanings as authoritative for human relationships but always carry with them a transcendental reference. The religious consciousness finds a truer interpretation in the words of Jesus, "Blessed are the pure in heart for they shall *see* God," not "they shall *infer* that God exists whose nature is moral."

If the belief in God rested only on a logical inference, even though this inference were based on man's moral intuition, religion in its very inner core would then still rest only on the theoretical reason, the very thing Kant had said it can not rest on since the theoretical reason according to his theory of knowledge gives us only the things of the contingent world and never an insight into the noumenal world. Thus to be really consistent and to recognize man's moral intuition as really standing in its own rights and as giving us true insight into the nature of ultimate reality, it would seem that we have a right to say that man can have in this very insight a direct awareness and experience of God. In other words, belief in God is then not merely a necessary postulate of man's moral nature but grows rather out of a direct experience of the divine through man's experience of ideal values.

Now this double defect of the Kantian theory of religion finds at least a partial correction in certain Neo-Kantians who build directly on the Kantian philosophy but who recognize more clearly than he seemed to have done that the religious consciousness in contradistinction from the merely ethical stands above all else for a direct awareness of transcendental reality, or the

Divine, conceived of in terms of ethical and other ideal values. The meaning of this should become clearer in the succeeding sections.

B:IX RELIGION AS A DIRECT AWARENESS OF AND DEPENDENCE ON TRANSCENDENTAL REALITY OR GOD

WE COME THEREFORE in this section to a view of religion and its validity which builds more directly on the religious consciousness itself. It agrees with the views expressed in sections seven and eight that religion is, of course, interested in promoting the good life of man and also that the very core of the good life consists of ethical and other ideal values which are grounded in human nature as such; but it sees more clearly that man is not a self-existent or self-sufficient being and so that the truly good life can never be had except as it is truly grounded in the divine and the ultimately real. In fact, the good life of man is not even the starting point or the primary consideration in this viewpoint since man is not the primary reality. The religious consciousness rather bears witness to the fact that man knows himself in contact with a reality other than himself and on which he feels himself utterly dependent for his life on any terms as well as for what he knows as the good life. Of course, the non-religious man also knows that his life is conditioned by forces other than himself and over which he has no ultimate control but rather in whose grip he feels himself. Where the religious consciousness differs from the non-religious is that in the former there is a conviction that man is in contact with a superhuman and ultimate reality which is somehow spiritual and transcendental in nature. Just how this awareness of transcendental reality or this consciousness of the divine arises may differ somewhat with different individuals, and likewise is it to be expected that there would be a rather wide range in the specific conceptions which men have formed of the divine but these differences do not necessarily invalidate each and every experience of this sort, as it is sometimes said. As in all other human experiences here, too, it is a question of what in the experience is valid and what not. And it is a question as to what concept of the objective reality which gives rise to the experience is the more adequate. In the very nature of the case any and every conception man can form of ultimate reality can never be wholly adequate in the sense of there being an exact correspondence between the idea and the reality for which the idea stands. One can only strive for an ever more adequate conception realizing all along that man can know, as it were, only "the hither side" of the real and that at the end of his furthest reach on every level of his experience there will be a mystery that transcends him. It is peculiarly the religious consciousness which insists that man can have an experience of the ultimately real but that the ultimately real, or the divine, is nevertheless a mystery that transcends all that man can know or experience and that therefore the befitting attitude of man towards this reality is one of wonder, awe, and worship. This is true whatever approach man makes to reality, be it by way of sense experience and the concepts based on this experience, as is the characteristic way of the physical sciences, or be it by way of the inner life and in terms of ethical and other ideal values. Whatever road one takes, to the thoughtful and the sensitive there arises somehow the conviction that man is in contact with a reality which he can know in part but which at the same time transcends his own nature and his power of comprehension. In spite of the fact that with the advance of scientific knowledge and skill on the various levels of experience man is able increasingly to shape his immediate physical and social environment more or less to his own liking and purpose he nevertheless realizes that in every aspect of his being he is ultimately utterly dependent upon this encompassing and this transcendental reality and that in the last analysis he must adjust himself to this if he would be truly wise. This is fundamentally the religious consciousness. If there is any common ground on which all religions meet it is here. It is, of course, also here that one can see best how religions differ from each other, namely, in the specific conceptions which they form of the nature of the divine or the ultimately real on which man feels himself dependent and also the way in which they express the relationship of man and the divine and the resultant life ideal.

It was Schleiermacher who among modern Western thinkers first formulated this theory of religion. He pointed out first of all that if one would understand the true nature of religion one has to look at religion from within the religious consciousness itself and so discover what actually goes on in the inner life of the pious soul. Religion's true nature and hence its validity can never be adequately expressed in terms of things that are not in themselves essentially religious. Thus it is not a correct understanding of its true nature or of its validity to point out what religion may do in the way of supporting the higher cultural interests of man, not even its support of ethical and other ideal values. To be sure, true religion affirms and promotes these ideal values but it does so because central in the religious consciousness is first of all an awareness of the divine and the ultimately real on which man feels himself wholly dependent and which, as it were, impresses itself on man with its own nature. If religion stresses e.g. the validity of ethical ideals it does so not simply on the grounds that these ideals can be shown to promote the best interests of human life, or merely on the grounds that these ideals as objectively real in themselves constitute the good life, but in addition to these and even more primary than these reasons it stands for an intuitive awareness and experience of the divine and the ultimately real as moral in character, and man's own life as bound up with and utterly dependent upon such a Being. Thus the norm of what constitutes the best interests of human life comes not from what man himself desires but rather from the conviction as to what is ultimately real and to which reality he must adjust himself.

In fact, the religious consciousness, as Schleiermacher knew it, revolves, as it were, around two poles. One pole is the divine on which man feels himself so utterly dependent in every aspect of his being, and the other pole is the self in which this consciousness arises and which always is aware of a measure of freedom and power of self-determination. These two foci appear, perhaps, most clearly in moral choices and moral action though they are also present in the rest of man's experience. In every act of man there is an affirmation of his freedom and his power to shape reality to his desire and purpose, but the deeper and more far-reaching fact of human experience is that man's activity and freedom in shaping reality, even the reality of his own inner life, are limited and conditioned rather by the way he adjusts himself to what is given and what is the ultimately real. Thus even man's freedom of self-determination which is one of the ultimate data of his consciousness and which finds its best expression in his moral consciousness is seen to be ultimately grounded in and dependent upon the divine and the ultimately real.

In Schleiermacher's interpretation of the religious consciousness as being a feeling of man's utter dependence upon the divine the term "feeling" is not to be identified with mere feeling. It is both a perception (Anschauung) and a feeling (Gefühl) and then the "feeling" is sometimes modified by the adjective "pious" (fromme Gefühl) so that it is akin to Kant's "moral intuition." His writings show something of the different conceptions which might be formed of the divine and the effect which such differences have on the religious life itself. Thus in his "Reden" he tends to conceive of the divine rather vaguely and simply as the ultimately real without any further characterization. In opposition to Hegel and the Hegelians who made the Real identical with man's clearcut logical definitions and neat ideas and who then made religion nothing more than a system of ideas and doctrines, Schleiermacher held that no ideas of the Infinite can give any adequate representation. Definite ideas deal with the finite, the phenomenal world of our sense experience but there is a more comprehensive world, the Infinite. To be religious is to have a sense and taste for the Infinite and Eternal, (Ein

Sinn und Geschmack fürs Unendliche), but experienced through the things of the natural world. It is an intuitive awareness of reality as a whole. One opens one's soul to it in a passive mood and one is active only in the sense of contemplating the real. The conception is very much like the conception in mysticism, especially what in Part One we discussed as Impersonal Mysticism. However in Schleiermacher's "Der Christliche Glaube," where he deals more with the characteristic Christian consciousness and where he builds more definitely on the moral consciousness, his conception of the divine is more definitely personal and also the character of the religious life is pictured as one of activity, more in terms of freedom and moral action working for moral ends. Schleiermacher's conception of the ultimate human destiny differs also considerably in his two major writings. In the former immortality seems to be a sort of return of the finite into the Infinite and man is immortal in so far as his nature is a part of the ultimately real without any further determination of what this really means. In the latter, on the other hand, where there is a conception of the divine as personal man's immortality is also conceived of in terms of a personal existence. Undoubtedly Schleiermacher's real views are best expressed in the latter while those in his "Reden" are more of the nature of stepping stones by which he sought to lead his readers from a general religious attitude towards the more definite Christian conception. But be this as it may, Schleiermacher rendered an invaluable service towards a more correct interpretation of religion's true nature and its validity when he stressed the thought that religion can be known best in the religious consciousness itself and when he showed further that the core of this consciousness consist of man's direct awareness of the divine or the ultimately real on which he feels himself utterly dependent. It is into this general framework that the great religions of the world, and to some extent also the minor ones, can be fitted, for in every vital religious consciousness there is this affirmation of an awareness of the divine and man's dependence upon it even though there is a great variety in the historic religions as to the conception of the divine and man's relationship to it.

B: X RELIGION AS A SENSE OF MORAL VALUES AND THROUGH THEM A DIRECT EXPERIENCE OF THE DIVINE

FROM KANT and Schleiermacher one passes naturally to Ritshcl and the Ritschlians who in their theory of religion build directly on both. They agree with Kant that valid religion must be ethical in content and emphasis and they see with Schleiermacher that the core of the religious consciousness is a direct awareness of the divine. Thus by including both elements true religion must consist, they say, of a moral life lived in conscious communion with God.

Ritschel held that in religion man is not primarily concerned with "the given factual existence of the world as a coherent and intelligible unity" but rather with the world of values, especially the values of which man is directly aware through moral intuition. Or as it has been succinctly expressed, religion deals with "value judgments" and not with "existential judgments." This distinction between value and existential judgments has, unfortunately, given rise to a misunderstanding of Ritschel's real position. He is frequently represented as saying that in religion man concerns himself with values that are largely subjective and that are not really grounded in objective existence. Nothing could be farther from what he meant by that distinction. It is true that he held that religion does not concern itself directly with "the given factual existence of the world." This he held was the province of science which seeks to discover what these facts are. In connection with this "factual existence" there may arise a feeling of value but such values are merely "accompanying values" dependent upon how man adjusts himself to this "factual existence." Thus e.g. there is the "factual existence" of fire and water and the relationship between the two in which fire or heat applied to water in a certain way converts water into steam and this may become a "value" to man but whether it is a value to man or not in no way changes this "factual existence" of fire and water and the relation between the two. So we might say that whatever "value judgment" arises in man's experience of this "factual existence" is of the nature of an "accompanying value" dependent wholly upon man's adjustment of himself to it.

There is, however, another order of existence, according to Ritschel, in which when one experiences the reality, or the "factual existence" one experiences at the same time its value. In fact, the sense of it as real and of it as a value are indistinguishable so that one can not have the one without the other. This is the case with man's awareness of moral magnitudes. To experience such magnitudes as real is to experience them as values; yea, as the supreme values of life. They are subjective values only in the sense that they can not be experienced as real or as values except as they are appreciated by the experiencing subject; i.e. their reality can in no other way be made evident to one. They can not be shown to have existence in terms of anything else and so if one is insensitive to moral magnitudes one cannot be convinced of either their value for human life or their reality by reference to something else. But they are not "subjective values" in the sense that their existence depends upon man's recognition of them. They are, on the contrary, objectively real, and to have a sense of moral values at all is to know them as objectively real.

Now Ritschel realized that the world of "factual existence" and the world of moral values seem to come into conflict in human experience. The former often seems wholly indifferent to the latter. But even though this seems to be the case, he did not propose to solve this conflict by saying that man's moral values are merely subjective whims and therefore must be subordinated to the insight man gains of reality in other ways. In good Kantian style, he held rather that in our moral experience we have an ultimate datum of consciousness back of which we cannot go and through which we have our deepest insight into Ultimate Reality, or God. To be sure, Ritschel avoided the ordinary type of metaphysical speculation holding that it was too barren for the religious life, but he nevertheless affirmed that in man's moral experience he has real insight into the nature of the ultimately real. This ultimately real was for him not something attained through intellectual speculation, quiet contemplation or mystical feeling but rather through living the practical moral life in man's relationship to his fellowmen. In this type of life man gains not only a conviction as to the objective reality of moral values but also of their grounding beyond the human in the divine. This latter is not a mere inference or postulate as it was with Kant but a direct awareness. Thus Ritschel agrees with Schleiermacher that in religion man has a direct awareness of the divine. He differs from the latter in that he limits the approach to the divine so largely to this one avenue of man's moral intuition whereas Schleiermacher held that man's total experience of reality should issue in his awareness of the divine and in a feeling of utter dependence upon God; though as we saw, Schleiermacher, in his "Christliche Glaube" also stressed more the ethical values as the supreme content of the religious experience. We should also add that Ritschel as a Christian theologian, like Schleiermacher turns to Jesus and the New Testament for the more specific content of his ethical values rather than to Kant's general "categorical imperative" which latter only tells man that he must do the right to be true to his better self but does not tell him further just what the right is. In Christianity, Ritschel held, man is guided by the view that moral values are real values grounded not only in man's nature as such but in God and his eternal kingdom of values and that these are supremely embodied in the life and teaching of the historic Jesus. Whosoever acts on these values as real will gain an unshakable conviction of their permanent validity and through them experience the source from which they spring, namely, God. It is as Jesus himself put this truth, "If any man's will is to do

R

his will, he shall know whether the teaching is from God, or whether I am speaking on my own authority." (John 7:17) Probably only one who is already more or less aware of moral magnitudes will act upon them as objectively real. He who has such an awareness may be haunted at times with the feeling that moral values may, after all, be only subjective values but if he persistently acts upon them as real he will gain the conviction that they are real and constitute the firmest grasp that man can have on the ultimately real.

That there may still be a lingering doubt as to whether moral values, acted upon as objectively real, give one a direct experience of God and that something more than this is needed, is well expressed by Hermann. He, too, holds that in man's moral action he gains his deepest conviction as to the objective reality of moral values. "It is indeed true," he says, "that in the moment of moral action one is always seized by the almightiness of the good and to that extent enjoys religious experience." (Quoted by Baillie, Interpretation of Religion, p. 293) But Hermann feels that this is not quite sufficient to give one the absolute assurance that a Supreme Good Will, or God, rules at the heart of the Kingdom of Goodness. There is needed something more and this, he holds, comes adequately only through man's experience of God's explicit revelation of himself in the supreme moral personality of the historic Jesus. He writes, "Under the impression that Jesus makes upon us, there arises in our hearts the certainty that God Himself is turning towards us in this experience. If we now ask, 'How is it possible that so mighty an utterance should be spoken to us in the fact that Jesus stands before us as an undeniable part of what is real to ourselves?' or 'How can this fact become for us the intimation wherein God discloses Himself to us in His reality and power?' these questions can be answered only by the fact itself, and by what it undeniably contains." (Ibid. p. 295) In another place Hermann gives really a double basis for man's belief in God. He says, "The Christian's consciousness that God communes with him rests on two objective facts, the first of which is the historical fact of the person of Jesus .... The second objective ground ... is that we hear within ourselves the demand of the moral law." (Ibid, p. 296).

This "second objective ground" is substantially the reaffirmation of the position held by all who accept moral values as objectively real and as grounded not only in human nature as such but also in ultimate reality, or God upon whom man is dependent. The first mentioned objective ground goes, however, beyond this position in that it introduces the thought of God's revelation of himself and so the center of religion is shifted from man's quest for the good life through God to God's quest for or grace to man. This latter view of religion and its validity we shall consider in a special section below. It is enough to say here that even though Hermann introduces this factor of God's self-revelation through the historic Jesus he would still make central in religion moral values, for it is the supreme moral personality of the historic Jesus and his unique God-consciousness that gives rise to the conviction in others that in Jesus "God discloses Himself to us in His reality and power." After all, the most convincing argument for the objective reality of moral values is in the embodiment of such values in an actual moral personality; and when central in the consciousness of such a personality we find a persistent consciousness of God as the driving power of the moral life, as was the case with Jesus who could say that it was his very meat and drink to do his Father's will, it is only natural that those who see in Jesus the supreme embodiment of the moral ideal should also see in him the supreme revelation of God, in whom moral values must be ultimately grounded to have unquestioned validity for human life.

Now the general position of Riteschel and the Ritschlians may be accepted as essentially correct in so far as they insist that valid religion must be identical with the highest ethical values regarded as objectively real and as grounded not only in human nature as such but also in Ultimate Reality or God. And they seem further right in holding that in man's moral life he can have a direct awareness of the divine. The weakness of their position is that they make this the sole approach to the divine. While it is true that valid religion must be a moral life lived in conscious communion with the divine it is not wholly limited to this. Furthermore the Ritschlian tendency towards a dualism between the interests of religion and ethics, on the one side, with science on the other, cannot be accepted as permanently valid. To be sure, there is room for a sort of division of labor and there is a wide range of so-called "factual existence" with which science deals which has little bearing on the problems of religion and ethics, but the wider and deeper interpretation of the data with which science deals must also be included in one's comprehensive view of reality, or in one's attempt to know and to adjust one's life to the ultimately real, or the Divine. This is not only the requirement of a comprehensive philosophical view of reality but also of the higher religions whether they be pantheistic or theistic, for the very core of the religious consciousness implies man's contact with the ultimately real and, therefore, every approach to the real and the experience on every level of reality, whether we call this science, ethics or religion, has its place.

We turn, then, in our next section to a view of religion which does greater justice to this broader approach.

B: XI RELIGION AS A LIFE OF IDEAL VALUES AND AN EXPERIENCE OF THE DIVINE THROUGH SUCH VALUES

WE COME IN this section to a view of religion which in a way gathers up the elements we have accepted as valid in the theories discussed in the four preceding sections. It is, howeveer, not a mere summary of these but represents also an independent insight.

Briefly stated, this theory holds that religion is above all else the living of one's life under the sway of ideal values and with the conviction that these ideal values are grounded not only in human nature but in ultimate reality and that through our experience of these values we can have a direct experience of the divine. It is not merely one type of ideal values such as the ethical which we saw constituted the heart of religion in the Kantian and Ritschelian view but the whole range of ideal values as experienced in the realm of the true, the good, and the beautiful. And again, it is not these ideal values as experienced merely in connection with the immediate problems of life in terms of science, human ethical relations and art but it is to know these in their metaphysical implications and to have through them a direct experience of transcendental reality and God.

Now this general view of religion has many representatives both ancient and modern. Wherever philosophical idealism in one form or another prevails some such view of religion will find its ablest interpreters. It finds, perhaps, its best modern expression in the so-called Baden School of NeoKantians and possibly the best representative of this school is Wilhelm Windelband. ("Praludien", "Einleitung in die Philosophie.")

As a Neo-Kantian, Windelband accepts the general position of the "critical philosophy" with its threefold *a priori* of the theoretical reason, moral intuition and the aesthetic judgment which are seen as the psychological bases of the three great cultural expressions of science, ethics and art and which have as their ideal content the true, the good and the beautiful. This threefoldness of human culture does not, however, exhaust the whole content of man's normal experience of reality for beside these three, and expressing itself in a measure through them, stands religion. Religion is neither wholly different from nor wholly identical with science, ethics and art. It expresses itself in and through them but at the same time it enhances them since it also transcends them. It enhances them not simply by making a harmonious whole of their separate findings, as philosophy might do, but rather by extending the implications of their ideal content to metaphysical reality. Or as Windelband puts it, "religion is transcendental life; its essence is that it enhances life beyond (routine) experience, it is to be conscious of belonging to a world of spiritual values, to recognize the insufficiency of empirical reality." (Präludien p. 305) To be sure, man does not in religion transcend the realm of the true, the good and the beautiful. But while he is thus limited to these three avenues the full content of the true, the good and the beautiful is not exhausted in what man finds through the positive sciences, ethics and art. In religion, Windelband holds, man goes beyond this for he does not stop with his experience of what might be called immediate reality as this is found through science, ethical human relationships and art but he knows these ideal values also in their metaphysical aspect and through this aspect he has an awareness of and insight into the nature of transcendental or Ultimate Reality. To live one's life in the consciousness of this transcendental reality, or the divine, is to be religious.

Now this distinction between "empirical" and "transcendental" reality Windelband and the Neo-Kantians in general gain from the distinction between the "ideal" and the "real" or "existent" in human experience. This distinction is, however, held with the conviction that the "ideal" is the ultimately real and that what is ordinarily regarded as the "real" or "existent" must be worked over by the power inherent in the ideal before it can be accepted as the permanently real. In other words, the ideal norms of man's psychic life are accepted as the measure of the truly real and as the forms into which experience must be cast to be intelligibly real at all. This is seen, perhaps, best in man's moral life where to the awakened conscience there is always a sort of antinomy between things as they *are* and things as they *should be*, but where the latter is given the right of way over the former just because of the conviction that it is identical with the ultimate ground and goal of reality. In ordinary ethical living the individual may accept things as they *are*. He conforms to whatever is the accepted standard of right and wrong in the group to which he belongs. Such standards often have their sanctions for him in mere custom and as such may be called "empirical reality" in the field of moral magnitudes. But all true ethical living must go beyond this. There is something more in man's sense of right and wrong than merely that which has its sanctions in human customs however valuable such conformity to customs may be. To the really moral man, not that which *is* but that which *should be* is the good and the right and this latter derives its authority from something higher than that which has proved itself workable or useful in the past experience of the given group. All real progress in moral living and all higher ethical values have been achieved by the partial or complete rejection of the accepted standard on the part of some heroic individual who has appealed to a higher principle. The courage which prompts such individuals to break with the accepted standard and to bring in the higher law comes not from mere personal inclination, self-interest, nor even from a motive of a possible gain for the group but rather from the consciousness of a higher reality with which the individual feels himself in contact and which bids him go forward, sometimes in direct opposition to all personal inclination and self-interest. In short, the awakened conscience knows itself in contact with and under the sway of an ideal reality which transcends what hitherto had been accepted as the real. Though the new links up with what has gone before it nevertheless transcends the old and it has its compelling authority over the individual just because of its transcendental aspect. To live one's moral life, then, in the consciousness of the transcendental aspect of moral values and through this experience transcendental or divine reality, is to be religious.

And what is true of moral values is equally true of all other ideal values. One may live one's life in terms of these values and as bound up simply with immediate reality or the narrowly empirical. But one may, on the other hand, go beyond this and follow these ideal values into their metaphysical implications and through them live in the consciousness of transcendental reality in which they have their ultimate grounding and whose nature they express. These ideal values are, as it were, the "hither side" of reality which in its full nature transcends us but which we nevertheless know best, in so far as we know ultimate reality at all, in terms of the ideal true, the ideal good, and the ideal beautiful. Or as Windelband puts it, "They are the highest and the last that we possess in the sum total of our consciousness; above them we know nothing. They are holy to us because they are neither the product of the individual's soul life nor the product of the empirical social consciousness but because they are a value of a higher spiritual reality which we are privileged to experience in ourselves." ("Präludien" p. 305)

Now if religion is above all else an experience of transcendental reality it may be asked whether it is possible to define more closely the nature of this reality. Does not the very fact that it is a transcendental reality preclude all possibility of further characterization except to say that it is a reality which transcends all empirical reality?

Windelband and other Neo-Kantians recognize this obvious difficulty. In fact, some of them prefer some other term such as "super-reality." But there is little gained by changing the expression when the thought is essentially the same. And after all, the meaning of "transcendental reality" as used by Windelband is not that it is a reality which wholly transcends man's powers of comprehension but rather one which he can know in part and yet which in all its fullness forever transcends him, for as he says, "mystery belongs to the very nature of religion." If man had no real knowledge of that reality, religion could hardly survive; certainly would it be impossible to gain recognition of its validity. Neither could religion live if the divine did not transcend man. The extremes of an absolute agnosticism and a banal anthropomorphism or a shallow humanism are alike deadening to vital religion. A living religion takes its stand somewhere between such extremes.

Windelband approaches this difficult task of defining more specifically what religion means by that ideal and transcendental reality under three main lines, namely, in terms of feeling, forming concepts, and willing or acting. Thus the object of the religious consciousness is surveyed from the standpoint of the "transcendental feeling," "transcendental concepts," and "transcendental willing or acting."

For man's experience of the divine in terms of "transcendental feeling," he accepts Schleiermacher's insight that religion is a feeling of man's utter dependence upon a reality other than himself in whose grip he knows himself to be. It is man's consciousness of his own littleness and weakness in the face of that overpowering reality which ultimately shapes and controls his life and destiny. However much man may be the architect of his own life he nevertheless realizes in his quiet moments that he is ultimately bound up with a reality which conditions him and determines him so that there is nothing for him but to seek some way by which he may come to terms with this reality. This is the primary religious feeling, the feeling of man's utter dependence.

But while religion is a feeling of dependence upon a reality which transcends man, it is always more than a mere dark feeling. In fact this feeling is more of an intuitive awareness of a reality and as such it carries with it some sort of a conception of its nature. At any rate, this "transcendental feeling" is always accompanied by an attempt to form some conception of the nature of this transcendental reality. It is not strange that the conceptions which men have formed of this reality and which find expression in the different religions of the world should vary rather widely. Since it is a reality which in its fullness transcends man's powers of comprehension and yet which man may know in varying degrees, it naturally follows that there should be such differences. In general, the differences grow from the differences in the approach men follow. There are two major approaches. One is by way of the physical cosmos, the other is by way of the inner life and the sense of values.

When the approach is primarily through the external world the outcome is again conditioned by which of two possible ruling concepts one makes primary. These two ruling concepts are the concept of substance and the concept of causality. If the concept of substance is regarded as the primary one then transcendental reality is conceived of as the "divine substance" and we get our familiar forms of pantheism. The divine is that which is in all things and of which all things are but specific forms or manifestations. It is the underlying and permanent reality of which all things consist in so far as they have real existence. It is the changeless in the changing world, that which is permanent in the flux of things and which at the same time transcends things since it is infinitely more than what man experiences in terms of them. Where, on the other hand, the ruling concept is that of causality the conception of this transcendental reality is more of the theistic type, i.e. the divine is that mysterious, creative power which somehow causes and maintains the cosmos but which is nevertheless other than the cosmos even though it is its ultimate source. Since this creative power works apparently according to rational principles and towards a purposeful goal it is conceived of in terms of what man knows himself to be as a creative will working towards rational ends though the divine must at the same time far transcend anything that man is or even anything he can conceive of in terms of ideal personality.

The other main approach to the nature of transcendental reality is by way of the inner life and the experience of ideal values, particularly moral values. Man's feeling of dependence becomes what Schleiermacher had called "das fromme Gefühl," the feeling for moral magnitudes. As Windelband expresses it, "the recognition of our insufficiency as over against the norm manifests itself as a feeling of helpless weakness, and the deepest need of redemption." But in man's experience of moral magnitudes and in his attempt to conceive of transcendental reality in terms of this experience he must inevitably think of this reality as personal, for man has no empirical knowledge of moral values other than values which express the character of or relationship between person and person. Or as Windelband states it "In ethical feeling man's relationship to the Infinite is one of spiritual life-communion. But such a communion we know empirically only as a relationship of person with person. Therefore must the object that gives rise to the feeling of ethical values be conceived of as personal." Of course, when the divine or transcendental being is conceived of in personal terms, it is by raising the personal to the highest and most ideal qualities conceivable. God is "the personal being in whom really exists all that should be and nothing that should not: the reality of all ideal values. Therein consists the holiness of God."

Now through this second approach to the nature of transcendental reality the resultant is again some form of the theistic conception. When we combine this with the resultant of the causal interpretation of the cosmos we get the familiar conception of God as found in the great theistic religions where God is the ultimate and supreme being conceived of in terms of ideal personality and who in some way that passes man's comprehension is the creative power and ultimate source of all things both physical and spiritual but who nevertheless is not identical with these things but transcends them. This conception Windelband accepts as being on the whole the most rational though it leaves much unanswered and, in fact, gives rise to perplexing problems.

The major difficulty which the theistic conception has to wrestle with is the problem of evil. If God is good and the ultimate source of all things why is there so much evil in the world? Even though physical evil might be interpreted as a hidden good, moral evil can not be explained away so easily. It will not do to say it is only "seemingly real" or that it is only the "absence of the good," for religion itself, and most of all ethical religion, insists on the reality of moral evil. To say that the good God "permits" moral evil and does not cause it still leaves it a substantiality which implies an ultimate dualism in reality that seems inconsistent with the theistic conception. As a matter of fact, all religions, and particularly the great ethical religions, have operated on the basis of a practical dualism in the sphere of the moral life. And yet an absolute dualism has never been able to maintain itself in the face of the mind's insistent demand for some monistic answer. Religion, too, especially in its higher forms has shared in this quest and has on the whole stood for a monistic—pantheistic or theistic—answer, even though such an answer leaves unanswered riddles.

Religion, says Windelband, is not only "transcendental feeling" and a forming of concepts about the transcendental reality but it is also "transcendental acting and living." To be sure, the religious man's activity is in a large measure conditioned by his natural environment and so it has much in common with the activity of others who may not be particularly religious. Nevertheless what is outwardly alike may have very different meanings for different individuals depending upon the conceptions which they may hold as to what is ultimately real and the relation of this to man's immediate activity. Even within religion great differences exist as to the meaning and value of man's ordinary activity. Thus some types of religion virtually empty the natural life and man's activity as a citizen of this world of all real value and meaning because of the absorbing interest in transcendental reality. This is the case with the markedly ascetic religions where the natural life is looked upon as either essentially illusory or as the enemy of the spiritual life. Some religions, on the other hand, greatly enhance man's natural life and see in it an expression of the divine or at least a means through which man can achieve spiritual values. However, in this latter view the enhanced natural life is usually regarded as pointing beyond itself and as having its fulfillment in and with that transcendental reality of which the ideal present life is, as it were, but the "hither side."

The most direct form of what Windelband calls "transcendental action" is where the meaning and the content of the action express man's direct relationship to the divine as this is found most markedly in such acts as prayer, sacrifice and the other distinctive religious expressions. Of course, these acts may degenerate into dead forms; even prayer may become mere words. However where religion is a living thing these acts express man's conviction of being in contact with the divine. Prayer is the most direct affirmation of this. Other religious acts are more symbolic in character and the acts need sublimation to find their full meaning. It is by way of the symbolic that art e.g. becomes a vehicle of the religious consciousness. The sculptor, the painter, the musician uses each the medium familiar to him to express his consciousness of the divine and transcendental reality. It may be for him a direct affirmation of the reality of the spiritual world though it is expressed in terms of the material. Of course, religious art may stop far short of that and be mere art where the meaning may be simply in the aesthetic gratification which the object of art calls forth. In fact, every worthy activity of man may become a religious activity having its complete meaning only in its relationship to the transcendental world. Most of all is this the case with man's activity as a social being, i.e. the life he lives in relationship to his fellowmen. Since religion is above all else "transcendental living", i.e. living one's life under the sway of ideal values which are regarded as having their grounding in and as expressing the nature of ultimate or divine reality, this finds its most normal expression in action when man really lives out those ideal values in his relationship with his fellowmen. The activity of an enlightened ethical conduct has for its purpose the development of those ideal qualities and characteristics in the human personality—self and other selves—which are believed to express most truly and fully the nature of ideal being. Thus religion in its normal forms always holds out the ideal of "the blessed community," "the fellowship of kindred spirits," "the church," "the kindgom of God on earth," or whatever formula may be used to express the conviction that the reality of the "transcendental life" must find its expression in man's actions towards his fellowmen. It is through this social expression that the individual gains his deepest certainty as to the reality of the "transcendental life." "For while it can not be doubted," says Windelband, "that there are wholly individualistic religious characters, these never theless develop only from the subsoil of that which is common in the historical development of the religious life of mankind." And that which is most persistent in the development of the religious life of mankind, especially in the higher religions, and which has permanent validity is the acceptance and promotion of ideal values as constituting the truly good life. Religion at its best is thus an experience of ideal values in human life and this experience carries with it the conviction that these values are grounded both in human life and in reality that transcends the merely human. As grounded in ultimate reality man gains through his experience of ideal values a direct experience of the divine, or God.

Now this characterization of religion must be accepted as essentially correct in regard to the higher forms of religion. There may be little in primitive religions that fits this picture though even the lower religions show at least a dim recognition of the fact that man knows himself in contact with a reality which conditions his life and which in some way transcends him. Certainly all the higher religions insist that reality is more and other than the things of sense-experience, that man is essentially a spiritual being and as such lives by ideal and spiritual values through which he comes into contact with a spiritual and divine reality which transcends both his own nature and the nature of the world that constitutes his so-called natural environment. Religion at its best is thus living one's life in the consciousness of these ideal values and this spiritual reality which man can know in part but which at the same time always transcends all his power of comprehension. That this is a fact of the religious consciousness cannot be seriously questioned. It is only a question as to the validity of this experience.

The validity of ideal values in human experience we need not discuss further than what has already been said above under sections seven to ten. That through these ideal values man may experience a transcendental and divine reality or Being is the real question here. There are two outstanding facts of human experience which seem to establish the essential validity of this deep conviction of the religious consciousness.

There is first the fact that all man's experience of reality has in it an aspect of "transcendency." As we have already pointed out in our discussion of the norm of truth, man experiences reality on different levels, as it were, and each of the succeeding higher levels in a true sense transcends the level below it. Each succeeding higher level is not totally different from the level preceding it for there is always a common element running through all of them but there is at the same time in each succeeding level an element that is new and different from what is found in the level just below it, something which could not be deduced from the lower. These levels, it is true, gradually shade off one into the other so that they constitute a real continuity but in spite of this fact of continuity there is also the fact of a real difference in each succeeding level so that the so-called higher levels really transcend what is found in the lower. In fact, we are justified in using the terms higher and lower just because of the presence of this "transcendency" in the successive stages. This fact becomes clear when we choose two realities which are rather far apart in the ascending scale such as, let us say, an inanimate object like a stone and a scholarly saint. It is quite true that the stone and the scholarly saint have some things in common. The modern physicist can show that in his last analysis they are the same sort of reality for by the physicist's analysis both are made up of atoms which in turn consist of protons, neutrons and electrons. Neither the stone nor the saint is what he appears to be, for the hard solid stone is really a "host of tiny electric charges darting hither and thither with inconceivable velocity," (Eddington, New Ways of Science p. 1) and the saint sitting in silent meditation is likewise made up of these tiny electric charges which are "like a swarm of gnats." But no sane physicist would claim that when he has reduced the stone and the scholarly saint to the same common elements that he has told us all that is true about the two or that they are in all respects the same sort of reality. There is at least this difference between the two that the scholarly saint *knows* that he is made up of "protons and whirling electrons" and the stone neither knows nor cares. There is therefore obviously something about the saint in which he "transcends" the stone however much he may have in common with it. And will anyone seriously maintain that this "transcendental" element in the saint is less real than the element which the saint and the stone have in common? The whole hierarchy of modern science from physics up through chemistry, biology, psychology and philosophy —to name but a few of this hierarchy—is an incontestably scientific proof of the fact that while experienced reality hangs together in a real continuity the real is far more and in some aspects far other than what we experience it to be on any one level such as e.g. the level of physics. No one would admit this fact more readily than the leading physicists themselves. "I do not think," says Edington, "that with any legitimate usage of the word it can be said that the external world of physics is the only world that really exists." (New Ways in Science p. 26). And what Eddington says about reality when viewed from the level of Physics can equally well be said from the level of the other sciences. Each insight into the real is partial and points to an element in reality however well known which can only be described as transcendental in character. When, then, an enlightened religious insight insists that the higher levels of human experience dealing with ethical and other spiritual values are real and that in terms of these spiritual values man can experience a Spiritual Reality which in its full nature transcends all that man experiences on the various levels of sense experience and all that man himself is even as a spiritual being, we have an affirmation which is philosophically most decidedly tenable. To be sure, the validity of this experience may still be questioned by those who have not themselves had the experience or who deliberately confine themselves to what they regard as the more obviously real but that might only prove that such people have blind spots and not that the enlightened religious consciousness is seeing things that are not real.

This brings us to the second outstanding fact of human experience which seems to validate the religious consciousness which affirms that man is in contact with a spiritual reality which transcends him. This is the indisputable fact that in man's experience of the real, the upper end of the scale deals with spiritual realities and that man himself is fundamentally spirit and can know no aspect of reality more directly than the spiritual. Nothing is more real to man or can be more real than his direct awareness of himself in the act of self-consciousness. This is far more direct than any knowledge of the external world. However real the external world is, it remains a fact that it is not real to man until he becomes conscious of it and this becoming conscious of anything is itself a spiritual act. This is, of course, a fact which philosophers have long since pointed out but it is easily forgotten and thus it is well that some of our leading physicists remind us of it as Eddington does when he says, "Let us not forget that mind is the first and most direct thing in our experience; all else is remote." (Science and the Unseen World p. 24). And in speaking of the true nature of our knowledge of the external world he points out again what Kant long ago showed so effectively. "It is the inexorable law of our acquaintance with the external world that that which is presented for knowing becomes transformed in the process of knowing." The reality that transforms the raw material in the process of knowledge is the mind itself which has its own fixed laws of thought. That these laws of thought are consonant with the laws of being is one of the assumptions of idealistic philosophy which always must remain an assumption. To assume that they are not consonant would be to deny all possibility of knowledge at the outset. The point we wish to make here is simply that even in our knowledge of the external world the mind and its laws are a primary reality and this reality man knows direct thorough self-consciousness. To try to explain the nature of the mind or the nature of man as a spiritual being in terms of the physical aspect of reality would therefore be an absurdity. And further, to regard the external world of physical reality as more real than what man knows himself to be as a spiritual being would be equally absurd; and by a spiritual being we mean a being to whom ethical and other ideal values—the good, the true, and the beautiful—are real.

Now since man is himself so obviously a spiritual being and lives by spiritual values and yet at the same time knows himself dependent upon a reality other than himself he has a perfect right to think of this Reality in terms of the spiritual values which make up the content of his own spiritual life. In other words, the conviction of the religious consciousness that man is in contact with a spiritual reality, or God, who is best conceived of in terms of ideal spiritual qualities but who at the same time transcends man's highest nature is a most reasonable conviction. It may not be an absolutely necessary conviction in every man's life; in fact, there are those who seem to live their life without such a conviction, though there are probably very few atheists anywhere, especially few among those to whom life's chief content consists of ethical and other ideal values. But be this as it may, the belief which man has in religion that he is in contact with a spiritual reality other than man and that transcends him, is philosophically not only tenable but it is on the whole a reasonable position and one that withal gives real meaning and true value to human life.

B: XII RELIGION AS GROUND IN A
"RELIGIOUS A PRIORI" & MYSTICISM

IN THE PRECEDING section we saw religion as living one's life under the sway of ideal values and with a conviction of being in contact with a transcendental or divine reality known best in terms of ideal values. And we saw further that where the conception of the divine reality becomes more or less definite the most adequate conception is in terms of ideal personality though with the recognition that God as the ultimately real must transcend man's highest conception of spiritual being.

Now the view of religion under discussion in this section seeks to go a step beyond this position and this in a double way. It affirms, on the one hand, that man has a peculiar faculty through which he senses the divine as the ultimately real and that because of this he can, on the other hand, know the divine as more and other than what he experiences in terms of the true, the good, and the beautiful or whatever other ideal values man may know through his ordinary experiences of reality. In short, this view has much to say about the so-called "religious *a priori*" through which it is claimed man has his only true and adequate experience of the divine and transcendental reality.

This raises naturally a double question. Is there, first of all, such a thing as a "religious faculty" or a "religious *a priori*"? And in the second place, does man have through this unique faculty a valid experience of God or one that is more nearly valid than what he may have in other ways?

It is often assumed that if it can be shown that man is endowed with a "religious faculty" or a "religious *a priori*" this would carry with it a validation of man's religious experience. The existence of such a peculiar faculty, we grant, would argue at least that religion is a normal expression of man's nature but it would hardly prove more than that. To claim that it would of itself validate man's religious experience would be like saying that because man is a thinking being therefore all his thoughts must be true, or because man is a moral being all his motives and actions must be good. Thus even though it could be established that man is endowed with a religious *a priori* it would still leave unanswered the question as to what in his religious experience is valid and what not.

One chief difficulty about this so-called "religious *a priori*" is the vagueness of the meaning given it by those who sponsor the view. Of course, if by it is meant simply that man has a capacity for religion then there is little room for argument. The very existence and persistence of religion in all ages and among all sorts and conditions of men would seem sufficient evidence. Or again, if the "religious *a priori*" means that in the religious experience the whole of man's nature is involved so that religion is always more than merely man's thought life, motives, purposes and deeds, or more than man's feelings of one sort and other; in short, that in religion we have something like man's total response and a sort of intuitive and direct insight into spiritual realities and values, then, too, the view could be accepted as essentially correct. If, however, by the "religious *a priori*" is meant that in addition to the three well recognized *a priori* of the theoretical reason, the moral intuition and the aesthetic appreciation or judgment through which man discern the true, the good and the beautiful there is a fourth and co-ordinate *a priori* through which man in a unique way experiences the divine and the ultimately real, or through which alone he can adequately have such an experience, then there seems room for differences of opinion.

It should be remarked in passing that while this term, the "religious *a priori*," is of rather recent origin, the conception for which it stands has a rather long history. It is, in fact, a conception common among mystics of all ages and of all shades. Wherever religion has tended to become too narrowly rationalistic or where its ethical ideals and values have been too closely tied up with what man finds practically workable there usually has appeared sooner or later a reaction which affirmed that man's neat yardstick of the rational is inadequate and that his "practical and workable" ways of righteousness are not commensurate with divine holiness. And because the divine as the ultimately real must forever transcend all that man can think or know, the mystic usually insists also that the way of experiencing the divine most adequately must be more direct and other than through thought processes, moral insight and such ordinary human experiences. Man's experience of the true, the good and the beautiful, say many mystics, is but a ladder that enables him to climb towards the divine and the ultimately real but that the divine as such he can only experience in the "mystic state." And since the divine as experienced in the mystic state is so far more and even other than what man can experience in terms of the true, the good and the beautiful, this experience can not be expressed in terms of these ideal values and so there is nothing left but to indicate what it is like by resorting to paradoxes, negations and, still better, absolute silence. Those who have not had the mystical experience can therefore never really know what its real content is, say the mystics. And this, of course, puts an end to all argument about validity and non-validity in religion.

But leaving aside for the present this nigh claim of the typical mystic, let us turn to those modern representatives of the "religious *a priori*" who seek to explain in terms of modern psychology what they mean by it and who then in turn seek to make good the claim that man can have an experience of the divine and the ultimately real which goes beyond what he can experience as the ideally true, good and beautiful. Probably the best representative is Professor Rudolf Otto in his widely read volume entitled "Das Heilige." (English translation, "The Idea of the Holy")

In his opening chapter entitled "The Rational and the Non-Rational," Otto points out that in Christianity and the other great monotheistic faiths God is conceived of in terms of rational concepts but he holds that such concepts are usually too narrowly "rationalistic" to be adequate. "Religion is not exclusively contained and exhaustively comprised in any series of 'rational' assertions." (p. 4) This may readily be granted, especially when the rational is taken in the restricted sense given to it by seventeenth and eighteenth century rationalists and culminating in the Hegelian philosophy. In fact, one can agree that the whole idealistic philosophy from Plato on down to the present has all too easily identified the real with what to man seems the rational and it is well that we be reminded occasionally to take a second and more penetrating look at reality as it actually is. From this position as a sort of base line Otto proceeds in chapter two entitled "Numen and the Numinous" to get at the real object of the religious consciousness and the ultimately real. He holds that this object is best designated as "the Holy." "The Holy" stands in part for what man experiences through moral intuition as a moral magnitude and as such it already transcends the merely rational. Otto builds thus on the Kantian insight that in man's moral intuition he has a deeper insight into noumenal reality than through the theoretical reason. But Otto then insists that "the Holy" is also more and even "other than" what man experiences in terms of ideal ethical values. To indicate this "more and other" he resorts to Latin terms and speaks of "Numen and the numinous," the noun "Numen" standing for the divine as such and the adjective "numinous" expresses the quality which man experiences in his contact with the divine. He also speaks of a "numinous state of mind" to indicate the peculiar faculty through which man apprehends the divine. "This mental state" he says is perfectly *sui generis* and irreducible to any other; and therefore, like every absolutely primary and elementary datum, while it admits of being discussed, it can not be strictly defined. There is only one way to help another to an understanding of it. He must be guided and led on by considerations and discussions of the matter through the ways of his own mind, until he reaches the point at which "'the numinous' in him perforce begins to stir, to start into life and into consciousness." (p. 7)

The crux of the problem is, of course, in stating more definitely what this "numinous state of mind" is through which one experiences the "numinous" quality in the "Numen." After all, a mere use of Latin words, though impressive to the unlearned, is not very convincing to the student of the philosophy of religion. Otto realizes this and so he proceeds to explain his terms though he never can quite get away from sonorous Latin phrases. The "numinous state of mind" he describes as the "creaturely feeling," thus echoing and perhaps supplementing Schleiermacher's famous definition of religion as a "feeling of absolute dependence." The "Numen" he describes as the "Mysterium Tremendum" and the "tremendum" he explains as standing for the elements of "awefulness," "over-poweringness," "energy" or "urgency" which are characteristic of the "Mysterium" but which in spite of having qualities that give rise to these feelings, or perhaps because of this, is nevertheless best described as the "wholly other," i.e. it is "wholly other" than what one finds in ordinary experience. With this latter Otto simply takes his stand with certain mystics who hold that the divine is so "wholly other" that its nature can not be adequately expressed in terms of ordinary human experience and so must be spoken of in paradoxes and negations. Otto, is, of course, not willing to leave it at this point and so he seeks to indicate by further analysis and associated feelings what the mystical experience is and what is the true nature of the "Mysterium Tremendum."

One may, however, question whether Otto in his further analysis of the "numinous state of mind" and the "Numen" makes good the claim that the former is *sui generis* or that the latter is so "wholly other" than what man experiences in terms of ideal values as the qualities which best represent the divine or the ultimately real known in the religious consciousness. To be sure, the divine as ultimate reality may well be spoken of as the "Mysterium Tremendum" in the sense that no concept which man can form is ever wholly adequate or exhaustive. Even the simplest object of sense experience seems to transcend man's capacity for fathoming its full nature and so it is only natural that the divine or the ultimately real should quite transcend all man's powers of apprehension and comprehension. We have already said in the preceding section that there is a transcendental aspect to reality on every level of our experience and that at the upper end of the scale we are still faced with a transcendental reality which we know only in part and which seems far more and even "other" than what we can fully grasp. But this does not necessarily prove that the divine and the ultimately real which thus transcends us and which can not be fully comprehended through our powers of thought, our moral intuitive insights or our sense of the beautiful can nevertheless be more adequately apprehended and comprehended through a unique "religious *a priori*," nor that when the divine is thus known it is seen more adequately as the "wholly other."

In so far as the mystics and the advocates of the "religious *a priori*" stress the thought of the "immediacy" of man's experience of God in the religious consciousness we accept their claim as warranted. In fact, in all vital religious experience this seems to be the case. All real prayer e.g. implies this, for prayer, if it is anything more than auto-suggestion, is a direct communion of man with the divine. And in the second place, in so far as the mystic claims that in all man's true experience of the divine there is an in-effable quality we can agree. These two points, the immediacy of man's experience of God and the ineffable quality of this experience may well be ac-cepted as essentially correct. But neither of these makes good the claim that man has a unique "religious *a priori*" or that through this he knows the real nature of the divine and the ultimately real to be "wholly other" from what man experiences in terms of the true, the good, and the beautiful. Certainly Otto's analysis of the "numinous state of mind" in no way shows that there is a more direct awareness of God than one can have through thought processes, through awareness of moral magnitudes, through our sense of aesthetic values or whatever faculty we have for apprehending the things and values of our ordinary human experience. Neither does his analysis of the "mysterium Tremendum" give much encouragement in the direc-tion of a truer insight of the nature of the divine or the ultimately real. To be sure, in the religious experience there are feelings at times too deep for ut-terance and desires of the heart that cannot be fully expressed in words, but it nevertheless remains a fact that the world's highest religions and those that have succeeded best in promoting the higher life of man have been those which have found it possible to express their experience of the divine in terms of truth, in terms of ethical ideals and values, or in terms of those qualities of the physical and the spiritual best described as the beautiful. If thought values, moral sensitiveness and aesthetic appreciations are the chief ways of approach to ordinary reality with which man deals from day to day, it would seem that these raised to their highest terms would also be the most adequate approach that we have to the divine and the ultimately real. Reality would, indeed, present an irreconcilable dualism if one's experience in terms of the true, the good and the beautiful could not be relied upon in whatever one may experience of the divine as the ultimately real. To be sure, there is always the danger of restricting the rational or the true to something that is too narrowly human, the good to merely what we happen to find practicable or workable for achieving our all too low aims, and the beautiful to what our own limited experience has found pleasant. Because of these restricted and limited experiences it is well that we be at times reminded that our neat measures of the real may be utterly inadequate. But while we freely grant this we must nevertheless insist that man's further experience of reality and his insight into the nature of the divine as the ultimately real must be really continuous with his ordinary experience rather than that it should rest on a way of approach which is so wholly different in its nature and in the results which it achieves that it can not even be expressed in terms of our ordinary and natural experience.

We have been speaking of mystics and mysticism as if these were agreed in all they affirm about their experience. Most mystics are perhaps agreed in a general way on the two points we have mentioned above, i.e. on the matter of immediacy in man's experience of God and also on the fact that this experience is in a way ineffable. But beyond this mystics differ considerably. There is especially the difference in their conception of the relationship between the strictly mystical experience to man's thought life and the life of moral action and moral values. One type sees in this latter no more than things of a provisional nature, mere rungs of the ladder by which man climbs up towards true reality to its threshold but to be kicked away as no longer necessary when he has taken his ecstatic leap into the mystic state and has found his union with the ultimately real. All that he has experienced in his thought life and in his moral awareness and moral action is to be left behind so that his enjoyment of true reality might not be marred. From the noise and fullness of sense experience and his thoughts the mystic of this type claims to enter "the white silence" of "the great void." The nature of this silent void is such that it can not be expressed in terms of human thought or ethical values and ideals. This type of mysticism we had in the West in Neo-Platonism and in some of the mediaeval Christian mystics who were more nearly Neo-Platonists than Christians. It is the type most generally found in Hinduism and Buddhism. In these religions the thought is quite common that man climbs the ladder to true reality in three ways. The philosopher climbs the ladder of true thoughts, the moralist ascends by way of moral intuition and right conduct, and the average religious devotee goes up by way of his devotion to and trust in a divine being conceived of in terms of ideal personality. All three lead equally to the threshold of the ultimately real but all three ladders must be abandoned as being merely provisional and not taking one into the truly real. This can only be reached in the mystic state. What this state is and what one experiences in it is so "wholly other" that one can not express it in terms of thought, moral qualities or any ideal values.

The other main type of mysticism which is usually associated with the great monotheistic faiths does not regard true thoughts, moral values and acts of devotion as merely provisional in character. It holds that while our thoughts of God are only fragmentary, as it were, and while our moral intuitions and ethical conduct leave much to be desired in man's approach to the infinite and perfect God, man has nevertheless in his fragmentary knowledge a real knowledge of God and in his moral intuition he has a true awareness of the nature of the divine holiness.

Now it is the mystic of this latter type who seems to build his experience of the divine upon his other experience of reality. The divine is to him the harmonious whole and the fullness of Being. Instead of being the "wholly other" God is the perfection of all that is true, good, and beautiful. The divine becomes the fulfillment of the best in the human rather than being its absolute opposite. Along this line one can make real sense of the mystical experience as the experience of a knowable but transcendental reality. Thus one can concede that the divine as the ultimately real transcends man's measure of the rational. But to say that it is the "wholly other" than the rational would mean, if it meant anything, the "irrational;" or to say that it is the "union of the rational and the irrational" would seem to be a self-contradiction. Or again, to say that the goodness of the divine surpasses man's measure of the good means something, but to hold that the divine is "wholly other" than what man experiences as moral values would leave man in moral darkness. In short, it makes sense when we say our experience in terms of the true, the good and the beautiful has validity in our experience of the divine as the ultimately real and that this reality transcends our powers of complete comprehension. But it does not make much sense to say that these categories are valid for ordinary experience but that they are not valid beyond this and so that man must resort to a unique faculty, and that when he does so he has an experience of the divine or the ultimately real as the "wholly other." Of course, the mystic who takes this stand may be allowed to stick to his conviction. His position is really unassailable as seen from his own standpoint for the very core of his contention is that he has an experience of a reality that is beyond the categories of the true and the false, and therefore beyond all reason and all reasoning. That is why he talks to the rest of us in paradoxes and negations. His best argument is really absolute silence, for in this way he is really quite consistent. Or as a Buddhist philosopher has put it, "Silence is the ultimate truth for the wise." But we, too, are consistent when we maintain that we have a right to think of the divine and the ultimately real in terms of what we experience as the true, the good and the beautiful. While we recognize that this leaves some problems unsolved, especially the problems of moral evil, we can face this problem fully as honestly and with as much hope for a solution as can the mystic who talks about the divine as the "union of all contradictions," "the reality which is beyond good and evil" or "the reality which is the wholly other." To say that our deepest insight into reality is to know it as "the wholly other" creastes an irreconcilable dualism and makes forever impossible the integration of man's religious experience with the rest of his valid experience.

Without such an integration, we maintain, there can be no real solution of man's thought problems. This dualism forces one either to regard ordinary experience of reality as essentially false and meaningless, as happened so frequently in Indian mysticism, or it throws doubt on the validity of the mystical experience itself and in turn on the religious experience as a whole. This irreconcilable dualism is shown by one of the outstanding characteristics of many mystics. Many mystics have reported that in their life periods of great exaltation and certainty have been followed by even longer periods of deep despair, doubt and utter emptiness. Such periods have alternated throughout their life right down to the end. This is a significant fact and should help to place the mystic in his proper place in the scheme of things. One might therefore accept the typical mystic as a sort of spiritual scout who in his extreme way seeks to expand the range of man's spiritual reach but it would seem rather unwise to accept his findings too uncritically. We who climb to the higher levels of life by the rungs on the ladder made of truth, goodness and beauty may well refuse to leave these solid foundations by taking the mystic's ecstatic leap into the thin air of the "wholly other." We grant as we have said repeatedly that the divine as the ultimately real transcends man and man's power of comprehension but in so far as we do comprehend we can express it best in terms of values such as are found valid in our ordinary experience of the real.

B:XIII RELIGION AS GROUNDED IN A
SELF-REVELATION OF GOD

WE HAVE SEEN that at the core of the religious consciousness is an awareness of God or the Divine. However in the views of religion discussed thus far the emphasis has been largely on the thought that the God-consciousness arises as a result of man's own quest for ideal values and meanings. Man seeks and therefore he finds God in and through the spiritual values of life. Even in Section XII where we discussed the theory of a "religious *a priori*" the emphasis was still on man's own quest for the divine though this view maintains that a successful quest is possible only because man is endowed with a unique spiritual faculty. We come now in this section to a theory which sees religion's validity grounded chiefly in a self-revelation of the divine rather than in man's own successful quest. Here, too, a God-consciousness is made the inner core of religion; in fact, it is made peculiarly so, but this is seen as arising from a self-revelation of God, or at least as having its highest authentication in such a revelation. Where there is no such self-revelation, it is held, there can be no really valid religious experience, for God is Transcendental Being and so can not be known adequately except as he reveals himself to man.

This interpretation of valid religion raises a double question. One is as to what is really meant by revelation and the place revelation actually occupies in the religious consciousness. The other question is as to how revelation validates religion even though it can be shown to be integral to the religious consciousness.

That the belief in revelation plays a rather big role in religion is easy enough to show. In fact, since vital religion always involves man's relationship with the Divine, it must naturally be more than merely man seeking the Divine but also the Divine activity reaching man; and this latter aspect may be defined as revelation. On almost every level of religion we find integral to the religious consciousness this conviction that man is aware of a divine reality disclosing itself or revealing itself to him. Of course, the meaning of revelation is far from uniform in the different historical religions and even within the same religion the meaning varies as does the conception of the Divine which reveals itself. It would take us too far afield to trace here step by step the varying meanings of revelation from the different forms of divination in primitive religions up to what it means in the mature religions. It is perhaps enough for our purpose if we confine ourselves to the meaning in the latter, especially to the meaning in the higher pantheism, mysticism and theistic religions.

In the higher pantheism the revelation concept is rather elusive since it is usually so all-inclusive. The pantheist sees the Divine in all things and so nothing can be peculiarly an act of Divine self-disclosure. Of course, the pantheist does not mean that every object in nature is the Divine as such but only that when it is seen in its true relationship to ultimate reality, or seen in its ultimate nature, is it the Divine. In fact, as we saw in Part One, the higher pantheism looks upon the universe as a spiritual reality. The most deeply real is seen first within man's own spiritual nature and then this is somehow transferred to reality as a whole. Thus e.g. the Mahāyāna Buddhist holds not only that "every man has the Buddha nature" but also that "in every particle of dust there dwells a Buddha;" And an Angelus Silesius could sing, "Kein Stäubchen is so schlecht, kein Stüpfchen is so klein; Der Weise siehet Gott ganz herlich drinnen sein."

When revelation is given such an all-inclusive meaning it is naturally impossible to distinguish it from what man may find in the way of spiritual values and meanings in things through his own quest. It can hardly be regarded as a special self-disclosing of the Divine. There is, to be sure a little of this latter aspect in that the typical pantheist does not, like the scientist, seek to understand reality through a penetrating analysis of individual objects as such but rather by an intuitive insight into the interdependence and unity of things. It is a heightened sense of the ultimate oneness of things and this oneness is felt to be essentially spiritual in nature. And the pantheist does not discover this spiritual reality so much through his own active questing as through a passive and receptive mood in which he lets reality make its own impression or reveal itself to him. But, as we have just said, this sort of revelation is too vague and general and not sufficiently distinguishable from what man finds of the real through his own quest to serve the purpose of those who would base religion's validity primarily on man's experience of a divine self-revelation. We can therefore dismiss this mode of the God-consciousness from our discussion in this section since whatever truth value it may contain is conserved in the doctrine of "Divine immanence" which is found in philosophical theism and which we shall mention below.

While the pantheist sees the Divine in all things the mystic usually seeks God within his own soul. So much is this the case that mysticism is often condemned as being little more than a dangerous subjectivism and a self-deception. It is true that much that passes for mysticism is often little more than this but it would be absurd to say that all mystical experience is a mere subjectivism. After all, the heart of the mystical experience is in its sense of a direct awareness and experience of the Divine. As such it is only a strong affirmation of what is a characteristic element of all vital religion. The mystic depends less upon what might be called indirect ways of knowing the Divine such as one might gain through external nature and which is such a characteristic of the pantheistic mood. He really turns his back on nature. He empties his consciousness as far as possible of all the distracting things of sense, quiets his own soul and so makes way for the Divine presence. Instead of stressing his own desires and questings, as is the case with the average man's quest for the real, the mystic is passive in mood and lets the Divine reality speak. He would hold that by striving too hard we often over-reach ourselves and this constitutes really a blinding subjectivism since it tends to make man's very desires the measure of the real. Only as man is truly receptive can he attain the deepest things. As Baron von Hügel puts it, "man attains in religion as truly as elsewhere—once given his wholehearted striving—in proportion as he seeks not too directly, not feverishly and strainingly, but in a largely subconscious, waiting, genial, expansive, endlessly patient sunny manner." (Essays and Addresses in the Phil. of Reg. Second

Series p. 60) So heightened is this sense of receiving as distinguished from finding through strenuous effort that the mystic sometimes seems overwhelmed by the incoming flood and that he loses all sense of self. However, at least in what we have called Personal Mysticism, the self is never completely blotted out. The experience is more a sense of communion between man and God but with God giving and man receiving in this communion.

Twas not so much that I on thee took hold,
As thou, dear, Lord, on me.

Or as Mechlit of Magdeburg put it:

Ich dachte einst wenn ich dich sehe droben
Will ich dir viel von Erdenschmerz und Jammer Klagen:
Nun hat mich, Herr, dein Anblick ganz und gar geschlagen;
Denn du hast mich hoch über mich und über meine Endlichkeit erhoben.
(SCHOLTZ: *Religions-Philosophie p. 10 F1*)

We have thus in Personal Mysticism a rather definite meaning of Divine self-revelation and one that offers a possible basis for the theory of religion which would rest its validity on God's self-revelation. When we turn, however, to what we have called Impersonal Mysticism where the Divine is represented as being so "wholly other" from all that man experiences in other ways that it cannot be expressed in terms of the latter, we are confronted with a perplexing problem. This sort of mysticism may be accepted as valid in so far as it stresses the thought that the Divine as the ultimately real transcends man's powers of complete comprehension. But when it is claimed that in the mystic state the Divine is experienced as so "wholly other" that the experience can not be expressed at all in terms of other forms of experience then the mystic puts himself beyond all possible validation except such validation as is contained in the mystical experience itself but which by definition has nothing in common with other forms of experience. It may not be legitimate on philosophical grounds to deny the validity of what such mystics claim as valid but neither can one build with much confidence on such claims.

When we turn to Theistic religions we find that the revelation concept is usually more clear-cut than in either pantheism or mysticism. In fact, it has several rather distinct meanings. First of all the natural order is usually accepted as being somehow an expression of God's activity and as such it is regarded as a kind of revelation of God's nature, especially God's wisdom and power. (O.T. Religion, Psalm 19; N.T. Religion, Nature parables of Jesus, Paul's affirmation in Romans 1:20 etc.) It is also at this point that philosophical theism and the higher pantheism are in substantial agreement for both see the Divine as immanent in things. The theist, however, would hasten to add that God is always more and other than what the natural order reveals; or rather that while the natural order is an expression of God's activity, God is not the natural order but transcends it.

A second meaning of revelation in theistic religions and one that is more specific is that God has revealed himself to and through certain individuals such as the great prophets and spiritual seers. By this is meant not merely that such spiritually sensitive individuals have found ethical values and spiritual meanings more successfully than others but that God has disclosed his will and himself to them in a direct way and that because of this they gained a clarity and certainty about spiritual values and God himself which they would not have had otherwise. In this affirmation theistic religion is in agreement with Personal Mysticism, or rather, Personal Mysticism is one aspect of theistic religion. The great historic monotheistic religions are in general agreement on this point though they would differ somewhat as to the particular individuals they recognize as having had such a revelation and also as to the exact content of the revelation.

In Christianity revelation is given its most specific meaning when it is held that God has revealed himself in a supreme and unique way in Jesus Christ. Even this is given two major interpretations. One links up definitely with the preceding meaning, namely, that Jesus represents a supreme and unique revelation because he stands, as it were, at the upper end of the long line of prophets and seers in that he had the truest insight into life's values and meanings, lived out these values in his own life as no other has done, and above all else, lived his life in conscious communion with God. Because of these things he revealed to man what the ideal human life is and how it may be lived in conscious fellowship with God. The other interpretation is that while all the above is true of the historic Jesus he is nevertheless more than that and he does not simply stand at the upper end of the long line of prophets and spiritual seers but belongs to an exclusive category of his own. In him, it is held, God himself has come into human life and revealed himself to man in a unique and final way.

Now from even such a summary statement it should be clear that in vital religion man knows himself not only as seeking and more or less successfully finding spiritual values and meanings in life but also as being in contact with a Divine Being who is seeking him and is revealing himself to him. As such this fact of the religious consciousness seems to bear direct witness to the existence of an objective spiritual reality which gives rise to this consciousness and thus it helps to establish religion's validity. It is, however, equally clear that while the sense of revelation seems to be an integral part of the religious consciousness in its various forms the meaning given to revelation differs too widely to draw any definite conclusion from the general fact.

Now as a matter of fact the theory of religion which would base religion's validity primarily upon a self-revelation of the Divine and which is really under discussion here is definitely based upon the revelation concept as held only in the great monotheistic religions and even more specifically as held in Christianity. In other words, the revelation concept in pantheism and in mysticism of the impersonal type can hardly be called a self-revelation of the Divine for only where there is truly a Divine Self is there any sense in talking about the Divine Self-Revelation. It is, after all, not an accident that the revelation concept is found with a clear meaning only in connection with theistic religions, being peculiarly prominent in such great monotheistic faiths as Judaism, Christianity and Islam. This fact stands out the more clearly when contrasted with what one finds e.g. in such a religion as early Buddhism in which there is little or nothing about a Supreme, Personal Being or Divine Self and therefore little or nothing corresponding to the revelation concept. On the other hand, in later Mahāyāna Buddhism where there emerges the conception of the Eternal Buddha conceived of in terms of ideal personality there emerges also a corresponding doctrine of a Divine self-revelation. That is to say, the conception of the Divine as a SupremePersonal Being and the doctrine of a Divine self-revelation go together. Of course, the presence or absence of a clear doctrine of Divine Grace and Divine Providence is a reflection of the same thing.

Let us look, then, more closely at the meaning of revelation in theistic religion and specifically in Christianity with a view of determining how far religion's validity rests upon revelation.

As we saw above, one meaning of revelation is that the natural order is an expression of divine activity and therefore the divine may be said to reveal itself through this order to those who have eyes to see. It is, however, a fact that this seldom stands alone but is usually put in the form that those who know God in some other and more direct way may see the hand of God also in the natural order. Furthermore, when in theistic religion the attention is fixed on the natural order as such it becomes more a case of man seeking and finding the Divine through his own quest rather than the Divine revealing itself specifically to man. The natural order is seen rather as responding to man's search for values and meanings and man concludes that these values and meanings are in the natural order not because he reads them into it but that they are there as an expression of the Divine whose nature is thus in a measure revealed. Since the manifoldness of the experienced natural order somehow hangs together in a unity more or less rational in character he concludes that it must be somehow the expression of a Supreme Intelligence and Power working towards rational and meaningful ends. This is the substance of the time-worn Cosmological and Teleological arguments for the existence of God so characteristic of the great theistic religions. It is also the thread that runs through philosophical Idealism both ancient and modern, particularly the type which derives from Plato and his school. It is true that a Kant questioned the validity of the older type of cosmological and teleological arguments for the existence of God holding that along such lines one can neither prove nor disprove anything but that was due to the fact that he regarded the natural order too much as a closed system and seemed blind to what modern thinkers try to express by such phrases as "creative evolution.' Furthermore man himself is part of the natural order and in the Kantian theory of religion, as we saw above, religion's validity rests above all else upon man's moral intuition which he held pointed beyond man and to God as its ultimate source. But whatever validity the Cosmological and Teleological arguments may have, it is quite true that belief in God and in his self-revelation rest largely on other grounds than simply on man's enlightened experience of the natural order in the stricter sense of this term.

We turn, therefore, to the more specific meaning of the revelation concept and where it is more than merely man's discovery of values and rational meanings in things but where it is rather a sense of having been found of God.

Now it is an indisputable fact that down through the centuries there have been certain individuals who have had a strong sense of having been the object of God's self-revelation. It is not merely that these individuals found spiritual values and meanings in life and that from this they concluded that at the heart of reality there must be a Supreme Spiritual Being in whom these values are ultimately grounded but they had rather a sense of an immediateness of the Divine presence and of God revealing himself to them. Here belong all the great prophets and seers of ethical monotheism, all the true mystics who were certain that God "laid hold on them." Probably one could arrange these individuals in an ascending scale indicating the degree of intensity or duration of their experience. There are also shades of differences in the actual content of the experience. With some definitely ethical values predominate while with others there is more the element of general truth insights and with still others the predominant element is more of the nature of the entrancingly beautiful. Whatever shades of differences there may be, the point is that these individuals undoubtedly had at times, if not steadily, a sense of a divine presence which was more real to them than anything else and which was real in a way which can only be described as a self-revelation of God. And because of such experiences these individuals became either the founders of religions or the great exponents of religion. Then, in turn, others building on the initial experience of these great prophets and seers, have gained a sense of spiritual values and meanings and through this, or perhaps more directly, a sense of the divine which enabled them to live their life in a God-consciousness that literally transformed them. That this is a fact of religious experience and religious history no one can seriously question. There is only one point that may be open to question and that is as to the real validity of this experience. Just because it is such an inner experience is why it is so very difficult to be certain whether it has a real objective reference or whether it may not, after all, be only a subjectivism and self-delusion.

What, then, is the criterion by which we can decide this question, for this is naturally the real crux of the problem.

Those who believe themselves to have had such an experience and others who base religion's validity primarily on Divine self-revelation usually reply that the Divine self-revelation is its own vindication to the one who has experienced it and that there can be no more direct or authoritative vindication than just what is contained in the experience itself.

Philosophically this position is unassailable and cannot be shown to be false. In fact, if there are independent grounds for accepting a spiritual interpretation of human experience at all, and if it seems on the whole reasonable to believe in the existence of a transcendental reality that is conceived of best in terms of ideal spiritual personality then it seems also quite reasonable to hold that such a spiritual being would reveal himself especially to those who are spiritually sensitive and also that such a self-revelation would naturally vindicate itself to the one who is the object of it. There could, of course, be no more direct or authoritative validation.

The question therefore takes on a new form, namely, as to how such a revelation can validate itself to others? Even if it can not do so in an absolute manner except to those who have experienced it directly, can it be made a matter of a reasonable faith by which others can live? And furthermore, since there are varying experiences which purport to be grounded in a self-revelation of the Divine, how is one to decide which of these is really valid or most nearly valid? The positiveness of the conviction on the part of the one who claims to be a recipient of such a revelation is usually very impressive and as such carries much weight with others but mere positiveness can hardly be accepted as conclusive for along that line may lie only a blind religious fanaticism. Neither would it be very convincing to say that all experiences of "revelation" so-called are true and valid however much they differ from each other since they seem objectively grounded to the one concerned. That answer might easily lead to religious obscurantism and ultimately reduce all religions which rest their claim on revelation to a mere subjectivism. In fact, such a solution would be rejected by no one more emphatically than by those who base religion's validity on revelation. In a world of more or less conflicting "revelations" how, then, can we know what is really valid?

Philosophically there seems no other answer to this question than to say that the content of what purports to be a revelation must be somehow integrated into the rest of man's valid experience. (Compare what was said in the section on "Towards a Norm of Truth"). We do not say that the former must be subordinated to the latter or that the latter must be made the absolute yardstick by which the truth value of the former is measured. Such an answer would preclude the very possibility of a Divine self-revelation containing anything which man can not gain through his own quest. This is the error which seventeenth and eighteenth century Rationalism made and we do not care to repeat the error. By "integration" we mean rather that the content of an experience which purports to be one involving a Divine self-revelation must be made at least continuous with what man experiences as the true, the good and the beautiful in his own honest quest however much the revelation enhances or even transcends this. What we said under Section XI belongs here as part of our answer. Especially would it seem to follow that the content of a Divine self-revelation must be continuous with man's experience of truth values, moral magnitudes and other ideal values if the Divine is best conceived of in terms of ideal personality, as is the case in monotheistic religions in which the claim about Divine revelation is made most persistently. Those who hold that the Divine is the "wholly other" of all that man has experienced on even the highest levels of a questing spiritual personality and that man can know the Divine only as it discloses itself to man in some mystic state naturally repudiate all attempts at integrating the content of revelation into man's other valid experience. To be sure, as we said, if the Divine is the "wholly other" then no real experience of it can be made continuous with man's other experience of reality. Perhaps such a position can not be shown to be false for it puts itself beyond the categories of the true and the false, but neither can it vindicate itself to any one who does not already accept its validity and who, of course, would need no further validation.

But as we said above, an experience purporting to be one which involves a Divine self-revelation could validate itself in a measure at least if it can be integrated into the rest of man's valid experience so that it is both continuous with the latter while yet transcending it. This is exactly what seems to be the case with some of the world's great ethical prophets and spiritual seers. They have actually opened up new vistas of ethical and spiritual values which, on the one hand, are continuous with the rest of man's valid experience but which, on the other hand, also enhance and even transcend this experience. Even where there may not always be an actual transcendence these great spiritual figures at least have clarified and made more certain what was only dimly discerned before. Now a striking fact about most of them is not only their clarity and depth of insight into life's values and meanings but what accompanies this insight, namely, a consciousness of God and a sense that it is God himself who has revealed himself to them. The Buddha and to a less extent Confucius seemed to be exceptions, but it is true of most others. One may not be able to prove that this inner core of their consciousness is absolutely valid, but neither can one show that it has no objective reference. In fact, since the content of their insight into ethical and other spiritual values can vindicate itself to any one who honestly undertakes to live his life by them, it seems reasonable to hold that this inner core of the prophet's experience, this sense of being in contact with a self-revealing Divine Being is objectively grounded. At least for many has it been the case that as they lived their life by such ethical and other ideal values they gained an awareness of God and a conviction that such values are grounded in him. Or rather should we say, that they gained a conviction of their life being caught up into and made over by a spiritual world which they themselves did not create but which is of God. Thus far at least can one go in validating philosophically this experience which purports to be one of a self-revelation of the Divine.

But what about the claim in Christianity that in Jesus Christ God has in a supreme and unique way revealed himself to man and that religion's highest validity must rest upon this revelation?

It would be easy enough to show that Jesus, as he said of himself, is continuous with the great prophets that preceded him. He came not to destroy but to fulfill. This holds not only with the great prophets of Israel but with all who have had a similar insight into life's true values. But Jesus was not only continuous with the best that went before him, he claimed also that he came to fulfill this best and thus transcend it. In what way can that claim be justified?

There is first his supreme insight into life's values and meanings. It is an actual fact that Jesus' ideals for human life are acknowledged as normative not only by his professed followers but by many others. One of the striking facts of the modern world is just this fact that many leaders in the great non-Christian religions are today measuring themselves and their ideals of life by the standards of Jesus Christ. Gandhi is simply the most conspicuous case. There are numerous others in India and East Asia. Equally striking is the fact that many ethical thinkers in the West who have little regard for or connection with the Christian church nevertheless acknowledge the ethical ideals of Jesus Christ as supremely valid. It is not too much to say that the world's most mature moral judgment accords the supreme place to the moral ideals of Jesus Christ.

In the second place the New Testament records which give us the ideals of Jesus are equally clear in representing Jesus as having himself lived out those ideals in his own life so that he himself is the very embodiment of his teachings. Sometimes it is claimed that the ideals he proclaimed can be found more or less definitely formulated in the teachings of the great ethical teachers who preceded him or who, though coming after him, had no connection with him. Be this as it may, the fact remains that is would be difficult to find any other man who both proclaimed such high spiritual values of life and at the same time embodied them so completely in his own life as Jesus Christ did. In fact, it is just because he was himself the best demonstration of his ideals that his ideals are accepted as so supremely valid. As long as ideals are merely a matter of words and ideas they fail to be wholly convincing but when they are once embodied in a living personality it is otherwise for as Dean Inge has so well said, "a character can never be refuted."

A third outstanding fact about Jesus Christ is his supreme God-consciousness. If one penetrates his inner life to discover the secret of his unique spiritual life one finds at the very core of his being that supreme consciousness of God. Nothing was more real to him than God, and to know Jesus Christ is to come, as it were, face to face with God. Possibly the world's great mystics have at times reached an overwhelming awareness of the Divine Presence; Jesus seemed to live his whole life in that consciousness.

Now this much seems quite clear from the New Testament records and it would in fact seem impossible to account for such records ever having come into existence unless such a one as is pictured there had actually lived and made his impress on men. The picture, in other words, is so indubitably real that it can not be other than that of a real historic personality. These facts about Jesus Christ and his way of life must then be accepted by any candid and open-minded philosphy of religion. As such these facts help establish even more firmly the objective reality of spiritual ideals for which religion at its best stands as well as the grounding of these ideals and values in God as the ultimately real. In short, Jesus Christ more than any other lived as one to whom these were the great realities of life and because of this fact he makes them real or reveals their reality to man. To quote again Hermann's way of putting this fact, "It is indeed true that in the moment of moral action one is always seized by the almightiness of the good," but this alone does not necessarily assure one that at the heart of goodness is a Good Will, or God. However as Hermann goes on to say, "under the impression that Jesus makes upon us, there arises in our hearts the certainty that God Himself is turning towards us in this experience." If we seek further why this is the case we cannot get beyond the fact of the experience itself. We may develop as Christian theology has repeatedly done, various doctrines about Jesus as being the unique and final revelation of God and valid for man because he is such a revelation but all such conclusions can have philosophically no deeper or more convincing validation than the impress which Jesus Christ in his life and teachings makes upon the mind and heart of the individual: or shall we say on successive generations of individuals, for it is not simply the impress on the individual as such that counts in the validation of religion but equally the fact that Jesus has for centuries and under the most varying conditions of life and human culture made this impression. Even to this day, with all our progress in so many ways, we have no deeper insight into life's values and meanings than what he gave and no greater certainty that these values are grounded in ultimate reality or God than the conviction we gain through our contact with him.

Thus the validity of religion which would ground itself in a belief in revelation must ground itself ultimately on the inherent content of that which purports to be a revelation. And however true it is that the religious consciousness on its highest and noblest levels bears testimony to what is best designated as a sense of a divine self-revelation, religion even then can validate itself philosphically only as the content of a "given revelation" can be validated. This, as we have already seen, involves some sort of continu-

T

ance with what man finds as the true, the good and the beautiful through his own honest questing into the real. That is to say, granted that Divine self-revelation is a fact of human experience there still remains the task of discriminating between what is an actual Divine self-revelation and what only purports to be one. Of course, if one is willing to accept on mere external authority anything purporting to represent a revelation he may do so. If it happens that the content of such a "revelation" is of a high order the individual accepting it may in this way enter a rich and satisfying life and withal be spared a lot of painful thinking and doubting. But even then, unless the actual content of that which purports to be a Divine self-revelation makes its own appeal through its inherent truth value and brings the individual into an awareness of and communion with the Divine it is hard to see how it could give the individual concerned anything like the free life of the spirit and that enrichment of the inner life for which religion at its best stands.

As a matter of fact it is unnecessary and really unwise to draw too sharp a line between truth values and spiritual realities which man gains through his own honest and persistent quest and that which comes to him through what is a Divine self-revelation. It may well be questioned whether there is ever a self-revealing of the Divine where there is not a questing for spiritual values and meanings. Nor can one believe that where there is such an honest and persistent quest there will be no response. The great religious figures have usually made the second part of the relationship the major factor but even then the other aspect remains. It is as Jesus himself put it when he said, "Ask, and it will be given you; seek, and you will find; knock, and it will be opened to you: for every one who asks receives; and he who seeks finds; and to him who knocks it will be opened." (Matt. 7:7-8).

SECTION C
NORMATIVE RELIGION

IN THE PRECEDING SECTION WE HAVE DISCUSSED VARIOUS THEORIES of religion, each setting forth its estimate of religion's truth values. These estimates differ rather widely, ranging all the way from those that see in religion little more than a naive and primitive philosophy of nature to theories that see in religion the very core of man's highest cultural values and the grounding of these values in the divine and the ultimately real. Of course, these estimates cannot all be equally true whatever elements of truth each may contain. One reason for this wide difference is that their respective authors obviously have different religions in mind or different aspects of what may be nominally one and the same religion. Another reason for this divergence of opinion is that different yardsticks of truth are employed. Thus with the material so varied as we have shown it to be in Part One and with such varying measures applied, it is not strange if the results are far from uniform.

But while the outcome of our survey may have been somewhat confusing we have nevertheless gained real insight into what in religion has permanent value and what might be said to constitute Normative Religion. Possibly for a philosophy of religion we might well let the matter rest at this point. However it may help clarify matters a little further by giving a summary statement of what in our opinion are the outstanding elements in religion that have more or less permanent validity.

As we saw in Part One, central in the historic religions has always been some belief in a super-human and divine or transcendental world with which man feels himself in contact and with which he must come into satisfactory relationship if he would have life at its best. In our survey of the various theories of religion it became evident that while most of the modern students of religion recognize that such a belief has been central in traditional religion of every type, it is this aspect of religion that many question as having any real validity for the enlightened man of today. Even though such critics admit that the god-idea has functioned in the past they question whether it has any objective reference and look upon religion's interest in it as a misplaced emphasis. What they do recognize as having permanent validity in religion is its quest for and promotion of the good life of man in the here and now. It is, therefore, well that we begin our summary statement of religion's validity with this latter aspect.

C: I THE GOOD LIFE AND NORMATIVE RELIGION

IT IS QUITE true that religion, on every level of its development, or every kind of religion from the primitive to the most mature, has usually stood for a real quest for the good life of man in the here and now. This is true even of the religions of pessimism, for though they despair of building up a truly good life in the here and now they at least hold forth something that makes life here more bearable. And whatever else Normative Religion includes it must ever have as one of its major objectives this matter of promoting the good and better life in the here and now, for if valid religion cannot help man in the practical problems of life as he must live it in the here and now, it may well be questioned whether it can be of much help in any other way.

On the lower levels of culture where man has little understanding of his own nature as spiritual and little appreciation of spiritual values and meanings and where life is so largely a sheeer "struggle for existence," the content of the good life for which his religion stands is largely a matter of material goods. Religion on this level concerns itself chiefly with such things as the increase of the food supply, shelter from the hostile elements, the warding off of disease and restoration to health, the prolongation of life, a numerous and vigorous progeny to help in acquiring the necessary material goods and defending these from the enemy—in short, in primitive religion man concerns himself largely with the things essential for existence and for his physical well-being. Ethical and other ideal values are only dimly recognized though there is even here a realization that material goods are really a communal good and there is also a sense of man being in contact with a reality other than himself and other than the physical environment which conditions his life and with which he must come into satisfactory relationship if he would have life at its best.

When the student of religion fixes his attention largely on this type of religion—and many do so in the fond belief that it is peculiarly in primitive religion that one can see most clearly religion's true nature—he readily grants that the religion of primitives had real validity for these primitives since it helped them in the acquisition and defense of the material goods of life. However since these goods can he had by the modern man at the hands of science, religion may well be dispensed with for it is, after all, only a primitive philosophy of nature which the enlightened have long since outgrown. Or again, when this type of critic bears in mind that the goods so essential for physical well-being are largely conditioned by the type of social organism that prevails, he is ready to grant that religion has had and may continue to have validity in so far as it provides social cohesion and stability to the social organism through the dissemination of certain common beliefs even though these beliefs are centered in a superhuman world and as such have no validity for the critic. The beliefs function effectively and in that sense are accepted as valid. Religion is thus seen as having had a sort of provisional validity for certain stages of human culture since it has promoted social values. However, proceeds this type of critic, when man reaches a higher level of intelligence he realizes that the Grand Etre that controls human life is really man himself or Humanity idealized, and then religion's traditional belief in the divine can be dispensed with or rather, must be given up as no longer valid.

While these views of religion are true in a way, especially if one limits one's inquiry wholly to primitive religions, they are hopelessly inadequate in their estimate of what is valid in the mature religions of mankind. In fact, even primitive religion is nearer the truth in its belief that there is some power other than man that shapes man's destiny than this view that the Grand Etre is Humanity itself.

The more truly scientific student of religion naturally turns his attention to religion as a whole and looks to the more mature religions of the world rather than to primitive religions for the elements of validity. And when he does so he readily discovers what must be obvious to all but the willfully blind that religion has promoted the good life of man; both in the matter of his physical well-being and in discovering and developing those spiritual values and meanings which must forever constitute the inner core of the good life of civilized man, and which spiritual values, in turn, are basic for the good life even on its physical level.

This does not mean that all types of the more mature religions are equally valid in this respect. In fact, some religions which have in a way the marks of maturity utterly despair of ever building up a truly good life in the here and now. Looking upon physical nature as inherently evil they offer their adherents a good life as consisting of an inner life of the spirit which is almost wholly independent of or indifferent to man's physical needs and which through a rigid asceticism gradually brings release from this "incurably evil world." And it is also true that even those higher religions which make a real place for physical well-being have frequently been none too zealous in providing for an adequate production and just distribution of the necessary material goods of life. But all in all the long upward struggle of Man as expressed in the higher religions of the race is an earnest quest for the good life on all its possible levels, and many of the insights gained have permanent validity. It may be granted that until the development of modern science there has often been a gross misunderstanding of man's physical nature and of the true relationship between bodily functions and psychical processes and health of spirit. That is even the case today with all the progress made in recent years in the biological and psychological sciences. Man is still largely the "Great Unknown," as Alexis Carrel points out. (Man the Unknown) But in spite of the fact that even the highest religions have often failed seriously in promoting man's physical well-being and that the modern man naturally turns to science for a truer insight and a more effective technique in this matter it nevertheless remains true that religion at its best has given us insights into human nature and into life's values and meanings which have permanent validity. And no insight is more valid than just this that the good life of man in the here and now must ever consist in its inner core of a quality of spirit and of cultural and spiritual values, however true it is that man's life is deeply grounded in the physical and that the truly good life ideal must include also physical well-being.

The validity of religion in its insistence on the primacy of the spiritual can be seen more clearly today than ever before. It is perhaps only when there is an adequacy of material goods or in an "economy of abundance" such as the physical sciences now make possible that one can see most clearly that the truly "abundant life" does not and never can consist primarily of material goods but rather of a qualitative spiritual life and the use one makes of material goods in the interest of cultural and spiritual values. As long as human life was so largely a struggle for sheer physical existence religion's emphasis on the primacy of ideal values may have seemed a bit unreal and impractical. Especially was this emphasis open to that suspicion when it only promised man a good life in some future world and when it often unwittingly pictured its paradises in terms of the material joys which man seeks in this world but which he so seldom attains in any degree of abundance. Under such conditions there is perhaps some point to the critic's jibe that religion is too much of a "bogus check on the future" or "an opiate" for the underprivileged. This is, of course, a superficial criticism but it has in it the element of the plausible just so long as man lacks the necessary material goods for physical well-being and religion does not bestir itself to lend a helping hand. When man's whole energy has to be devoted so largely to the acquiring of the bare necessities of life and when even then millions have no margin to spare, the cynic may perhaps be forgiven if he is a bit suspicious about religion's emphasis on the primacy of spiritual values or when it points to a life beyond in which the injustices and inequalities of this life do not obtain.

However the serious student of human nature and the unbiased critic of religion's emphasis on the primacy of spiritual values will know that this emphasis is not a mere subterfuge for something it can not really give but that it is something that is permanently valid under all conditions of life, including also the life of man in an age of scientific progress and achievements. In fact, it is peculiarly in an age such as ours in which for the first time in human history it is now possible to produce in adequate measure the material goods of life which are so basic for physical well-being that one sees most clearly that the good life of man in the here and now must nevertheless have as its inner core what are essentially spiritual values as religion at its best has maintained. This is the case not only because of what these spiritual values are in themselves but also because of their indispensability for even physical well-being in its fullest sense.

Let us consider first this latter aspect, namely that man's physical well-being is largely conditioned by the quality of his spiritual life.

First of all is the fact that our modern scientific understanding and mastery of the physical world on which so much depends for the good life in its physical basis is itself a great spiritual achievement and is possible only in a society where man has attained a high degree of mental and moral qualities. Though the fruits of the physical sciences are now available for all types of human beings, including the mere sensualist who wallows in the luxury of material comforts, the high priests of science who have unlocked nature's secrets have usually been persons with a questing spirit and with a passion for the true and the real; that is to say, with qualities of spirit which far transcend mere physical impulses and bodily desires. In fact, it often happens that the great scientist on whose basic work so much depends finds his deepest satisfaction, not so much in the material goods his work makes possible for his own well-being, but in the quest for the true and the real itself and in the knowledge that his work is a help to his fellowman.

A second fact about the good life on its physical level however achieved is that it receives its main content and yields its richest satisfactions, at least for civilized man, largely from the spiritual qualities with which it is suffused. Man, just because he is man, seldom if ever lives wholly on the plane of the physical but finds the highest good in physical well-being only as it is instrumental to spiritual values and meanings of one sort or another. To be sure, there are experiences where physical well-being pure and simple is a great good. This is especially the case when one has passed through a period of physical deprivation and suffering. Illness and its accompanying pain, hunger, thirst, exposure to the hostile elements, fatigue and other forms of physical hardships and suffering—in all experiences of that sort the mere cessation of pain and the satisfaction of the basic needs of the bodily life are and always will be seen as a great good. And it is quite natural that for the millions who live so near the borderline of starvation and whose life is one long struggle for the bare necessities of life, the good life is primarily one in which these things can be had in abundance. But it is nevertheless true that when the basic needs of the bodily life are met physical well-being depends for much of the real satisfaction it yields upon the associated spiritual activities and values. Just because there is "a spark that disturbs the clod" called Man the physical must ever be sublimated into something more. "The impetus of life, traversing matter," to use a Bergsonian expression, wrests from matter an ever richer meaning and value, and especially is this true at the furthest point which the stream of life has reached, namely Man.

It is, however, not only that the associated spiritual values give physical well-being many of its deepest satisfactions but also the fact that physical well-being is often directly conditioned by the individual's spiritual insights and attitude towards life's values. If modern science has given us any really new insight into human nature it is just in this matter of the intimate relationship between the physical and spiritual aspects of life. Science rightly stresses the organic unity of man's pyscho-somatic nature. Where the older views tended to over-emphasize the dualism of man's body-spirit nature and where traditional religion frequently set the physical into an antithetical relationship to the spiritual, modern science affirms the essential unity of man's nature even though it must continue to recognize that there is a dual aspect. To be sure, the physical sciences dealing so largely with man's bodily life tended at first to regard the physical as the more basic and even the psychological and social sciences, using at first so largely the technique of the physical sciences, also made it seem as if man's true life were almost wholly a matter of the harmonious functioning of the physical organism with the psychic and spiritual reduced to a sort of epi-phenomenon. A more mature science, while still maintaining that there is a real physical basis to much of man's psychic life, realizes that the psychic and spiritual can never be reduced to a mere resultant of bodily functioning; and furthermore that a man's spiritual life and ideals have a most direct bearing upon his physical well-being. Thus modern medical science at its best takes cognizance of this fact for it realizes that in illness a man's outlook on life may affect even the biochemical processes; and it must, of course, recognize the fact that a man's moral and religious ideals affect most decidedly the type of life he normally lives and so condition in a large measure his chances for physical well-being. In fact, there is a rather large percentage of illness and bodily disorder directly traceable to psychic causes for which there is no cure except a spiritual one and in a change of attitude towards life's true values. In spite of the great progress made by medical science, its almost complete eradication of many diseases which formerly decimated whole populations, its preventive measures and its wonderful alleviation of pain, and in spite of the fact that other forms of modern science have contributed so greatly to man's physical comforts, it is nevertheless true that the modern man often breaks down physically just because he lacks spiritual poise and because he pursues so madly values that can never truly enrich his life or give him true well-being.

It is, however, when we turn to the question of man's relationship to his fellowmen that we see most clearly how physical well-being is conditioned so largely by spiritual values and ideals. Even the simple savage living in spacious solitude can not live wholly by or for himself. He has enough wit to realize that the material goods of life are even for him largely a communal good and that his success in obtaining these is very much conditioned by his observance of certain customs and rules of conduct; in short, conditioned by rudimentary ethical ideals and spiritual values. How much more true it is that in our modern crowded and ever shrinking world and with our innumerable interdependencies even the barest necessities of the physical life are for many absolutely conditioned by a regard for what are essentially spiritual values. A breakdown of the social organism speedily brings in its train physical suffering and death on a large scale.

Then further, even though modern science and technology have now for the first time in history made possible what we call an "economy of abundance" there are, nevertheless, still millions in the economically undeveloped areas of the world who are ever near the borderline of actual starvation. And even though modern medical science has enormously improved man's chances for physical well-being there are still vast sections of the population in even the most advanced nations which have little or no medical care. Any one with even a little imagination and elemental human sympathy that enables him to identify himself at all with these neglected millions will rejoice over what modern science can accomplish in the way of healing man's physical ills and in providing so lavishly the material goods so essential for physical well-being. However, it should be equally clear that with all that modern science and technology can do in providing more adequately the things needed for man's physical well-being something more than science and technology is needed if the world's underprivileged millions are to have a bigger share in our "economy of abundance." That something more is a sense of justice, goodwill, kindliness and a regard for human values; in short, these age-long virtues and qualities of spirit which religion at its best has always stressed as constituting the very core of the truly good life and the motivating power that leads man to care for his fellowman so that all may share in the good and better life on all its levels.

How absolutely essential for the good life even in its physical aspects spiritual ideals and values really are is seen perhaps most clearly in the very areas in which the physical sciences have achieved their most astounding success, namely, in the field of nuclear physics and atomic energy. To be sure, we have barely passed the threshold of the Atomic Age and so do not know very clearly yet to what various uses atomic energy can be put to enhance man's life. The irony of modern life is just the fact that man's amazing achievement in science has produced a situation in which his very success has at the same time become his greatest danger, for any extensive use of modern nuclear weapons could bring death to both sides in any future war and, in fact, might result in wiping mankind from off the face of the earth. There seems to be no possibility that scientists can develop any adequate counter weapon of defense and so man seems doomed to live his life in deadly fear unless some other way than what science offers is found by which he can save himself from this precarious situation.

A glimmer of hope may be seen in the realization that an extensive use of nuclear weapons could be as fatal to those who first use them as to those against whom they are used since the latter could speedily retaliate. That is, undoubtedly, one major reason why some suggest that nuclear weapons be prohibited by international agreement. But who will see to it that international agreements are kept? That is the real crux of the problem and there is no solution to this problem other than one which is essentially a moral and spiritual one. No agreement is worth the paper on which it is written unless there is confidence on both sides that such an agreement will be kept. But such confidence must rest on what are basically moral and spiritual values, the very things which religion at its best has always stressed. And it should be added that when we speak here of moral and spiritual values we mean something more than mere rules for playing the game of life and which one may observe or break as suits one's convenience. We mean rather rules that are grounded in an eternal moral order and which man breaks at the risk of his own destruction. It is just because modern man's life is not thoroughly grounded in moral and spiritual values that he can not put much trust in agreements he makes with his fellowmen. Even among those who profess to be adherents of the great ethical religions there are all too many who do not take their religion very seriously, and Communists not only openly scorn all belief in the Divine but apparently also all moral values grounded in an eternal moral order.

Now it is just because of this uncertainty about or positive rejection of moral and spiritual values that modern man seeks something else on which he can center his interest and to which he can give his devotion and loyalty. That something else is for many their own nation. Instead of the kingdom of moral and spiritual values for which religion at its best has always stood, modern man tends to look upon the state as supreme in all things. He sees it as a sort of Mystical Absolute which has the right to demand of its citizenry a blind loyalty and unquestioning obedience. The state becomes more than the people that constitute its citizenry and more than all which they as individual human beings may regard as values, for the state is seen as having transcendental value of its own. As such it is placed above all rational criticism. It can do no wrong and gives ethical sanctions to any and every command made in its name. Every sacrifice made in its behalf is sanctified but all opposition to it is sacrilege. While some states are more nearly totalitarian in their claims than others it is a fact that all modern states tend to become "Totalitarian States," especially in time of war or national danger.

Of course, the totalitarian state seeks to justify its right to control every aspect of its citizenry's life on the grounds that this is to the best interests of of all concerned. But when this is carried to the point where it would deny the citizen his freedom of thought and freedom of conscience it forfeits its rights to demand obedience. There can be no valid totalitarianism which is is not one that is based on values that are universally valid and which values are to be accepted, not at the point of the sword, but voluntarily and because they make their own appeal to the spiritually mature. It is only the kingdom, of truth, the kingdom of moral and other spiritual values that has the right to man's absolute loyalty everywhere and at all times. And it is only when man lives his life as a loyal and devoted citizen of such a kingdom that he can have the truly good life.

C: II THE NATURE & GROUNDING OF THE SPIRITUAL

IN THE PRECEDING section we stated in a summary way what constitutes the truly good life of man in the here and now and we concluded that while physical well-being is a highly desirable aspect of the good life its real core is nevertheless a matter of the inner life of the spirit. Now if the truly good life is so largely a matter of a qualitative spiritual life—the life of the kingdom of truth, the kingdom of righteousness and goodness, and the kingdom of the beautiful—what is the real nature of these values themselves and how are they grounded in the ultimately Real? In other words, when man lives his life by such values is he living in a real world or in a mere make-belief world? If it is a real world is it one which is only provisionally or temporarily real, a sort of epi-phenomenon to something that is basically different and more basically real, or is it objectively real and actually grounded in Ultimate Reality so that man can accept it with all his soul as really valid? It is really impossible to think at all seriously about the good life of man in the here and now without facing up to questions such as these, questions as to metaphysical Reality. However much we may avoid such questions in the name of the immediately "practical" or out of an intellectual modesty in dealing with the transcendental world, nothing has greater bearing on the truly practical life than one's conceptions and beliefs in this field; and even an avowed agnosticism about the Ultimately Real can never in actual life be really maintained. The things we live by in our "practical life" are inevitably also an index to our metaphysical conceptions and beliefs. If that was so in the days when religion made a rather sharp division between the natural and the super-natural worlds it would seem to hold even more so for the modern man who insists that he lives in a universe and not in the lower storey of a two storey affair.

Now there are in general three major types of answers given to these basic questions. These three types find expression in the theories of religion which we have discussed at some length above. The first type and the one which underlies practically all the theories discussed under the first six sections virtually regards all spiritual values as more or less ephemeral and not as belonging to what is basically most real. They are seen as pleasant self-delusions which soften somewhat the hardness of real life or at best as merely instrumental to other ends. To be sure, the ideal of truth, goodness and beauty are recognized as a part of the life of a cultured person and also as rather important for the social organism to which the individual belongs, for no society can long endure or function smoothly unless people are fairly truthful in dealing with each other and are at least reasonably good and kind, but there is no deep conviction that these ideal values are in themselves the supreme values for which all else must be sacrificed when there is a conflict or that they are deeply grounded in the ultimately Real so that however much the individual may ignore them or live his life in opposition to them he can not change or destroy them but only himself.

The second type which finds partial expression in the fifth and sixth theories of religion and comes to full expression in the seventh clearly sees that the ideal values of life not only constitute the real core of the truly good life of man but that they are at the same time objectively real and carry within themselves their own validity. They are valid not simply because they are instrumental to other good ends but because of their own inherent nature. Thus e.g. the true on every level of human experience vindicates itself as over against the false. The good and honest man is so not simply because "honesty is the best policy" in that it creates confidence and so makes one's business prosper but because honesty is a quality of spirit which is its own vindication. In fact, if honesty were only a matter of policy it would indeed be poor policy to trust that sort of honesty. The only kind of honest man that it is good policy to trust is one who will be honest even when it does not pay. What is true of these ideal qualities of spirit is equally true of all ideal values. They carry within themselves their own vindication.

But while those who hold this view are right in insisting that the ideal values have their objective reference in human nature itself and are not to be regarded either as pleasant self-delusions nor as merely instrumental to other ends, they fail in seeing the metaphysical implications of these ideal values. They see them as grounded in human nature as such but they become all too hesitant in making any affirmations beyond this.

Now this hesitancy about the metaphysical implications seems to us a bit overdone. Obviously man is an actual part of the real world. And equally obvious is it that man is neither a self-creating nor self-sustaining being but owes his being to something other and more than himself. If, then, man lives his life best in terms of the ideal values and if these are accepted as not mere self-delusions but as truly real and as having their objective reference in the real world then it is hard to understand why those who hold this second view should not see the real implications of their view, namely, that these ideal values must inevitably point beyond the strictly human sphere and have their real grounding, as man himself has, in an ultimate Reality which is more than the merely human.

This is the position of the third main view about the ideal values of life, namely, that they are objectively real, have their grounding in a real way in human nature as such but that they are at the same time also grounded beyond the merely human sphere in the ultimately Real in which man himself has his true being. This is the view which underlies the theories of religion which we discussed in sections VIII-XIII. It is, of course, also substantially the view that is consonant with the more mature religions of the world themselves as well as all idealistic systems of philosophy. To be sure, the day is long past when the intelligent man is much impressed by the cock-sure affirmations of little minds when it comes to a discussion of metaphysical and ultimate reality. Probably a little more modesty and a certain degree of hesitancy has long since been overdue in this field. As we said in our survey of the God-concept in Part One, there is an honorable place for those who are "reverently agnostic" before the "mystery of Reality." In such a spirit there may be more real religion than in many an affirmation about the Divine. Religion in its noblest and highest forms frequently insists that the Divine as the ultimately Real is a mystery before which man may well bow in silence and about which he will not speak too facilely.

But while mystery lies at the heart of all true religion and while the Divine in its full nature must forever transcend man's powers of comprehension so that a certain degree of hesitancy in making affirmations is befitting, there is no valid reason why man should be regarded as having no insight whatever in this matter. In fact, it is just a bit surprising that so many modern thinkers who have completely discarded the old dualism of the natural and the super-natural and who proclaim in season and out of season that man lives in a Universe, should nevertheless virtually deny that man's tested experience gives him any real insight into the ultimately Real. Of course, if there is an absolute gap between the reality that man experiences and metaphysical Reality then no human knowledge or experience can have validity in the latter. But neither can there be, then, any validity in the belief that there is a metaphysical Reality which is wholly different. If however this is really a *universe* in which we live then it would seem that we have a right to hold that our tested experience of the real is a valid key to what is truly and ultimately Real. And if we can trust the ideal values of life as objectively real and as grounded in human nature then have we a right to think of the ultimately Real in which human nature itself is grounded in terms of these ideal values. To deny this right or to question its essential validity is to sink back into a paralyzing doubt and a relativism which undermines also the validity of truth in the human realm and reduces all ideal values to little more than pleasant self-delusions or at best to mere implements for other ends which may be used or rejected as the individual's convenience or whim may dictate. It is this sort of relativism and doubt as to the metaphysical validity of the ideal values of life which opens the way for all sorts of pseudo-absolutes and fanaticisms such as our modern doctrine of the "totalitarian state" which demands a blind faith in some external authority resting on physical force or fanatical religion demanding an equally blind faith and repudiating all reference to what is valid in man's natural life.

These considerations should force every serious student of human life to realize the tremendous importance of what has always been so central in true religion, namely, the question about the Divine as the ultimately Real on which man knows himself dependent and with which he must come into correct relationship if he would have life at its best. To seek the truly good life in the here and now without any reference to the Divine may be, after all, the worst sort of illusion. If religion in some of its forms can at times be rightly accused of indulging too much in mere "wishful thinking," normative religion is nevertheless far more realistic in so far as it would ground the good life of man in man's relationship to the Divine as the ultimately Real than are its critics who would build up the good life of man without any reference whatever to that Reality.

While religion is thus fundamentally right in its emphasis on the primacy of ideal or spiritual values and also in holding that it is in terms of these values that we gain our deepest insight into the nature of the ultimately Real or the Divine in which man's life has its ultimate grounding there is still left unanswered the question as to what more specifically is the most adequate conception of the Divine that man can have.

C: III THE GOD-CONCEPT OF NORMATIVE RELIGION

a *The God-concept in Mysticism*

AS WE SAW in Part One, man's conception of the divine has covered a very wide range. Many of the conceptions found in the historic religions are pathetically childish. Even in the more mature religions one finds affirmations which are all too human and limiting to be at all adequate or convincing. But, on the other hand, there are conceptions which have commanded the respect of the greatest minds and which still challenge our attention. We have mentioned three major types which have made their appeal to the spiritually mature. These are the Mystic, the Pantheistic and the Theistic or Monotheistic.

The God-concept of Mysticism is of course, more a mode of the god-consciousness than a god-concept for it is a major contention of the typical mystic that while man can have a direct awareness or experience of the Divine in the mystic state the Divine as thus known can not be expressed in any intellectual concept. Thus when the mystic expresses his experience at all in terms of thought values he resorts largely to paradoxes and a series of affirmations and negations. However even the mystic's "paradoxes," "negations" and his "silences," after all, give some indication as to the direction in which a more or less valid concept of the Divine might be found. As a matter of fact there are really two major types of mysticism, as we pointed out, namely, the personal and the impersonal. Personal Mysticism links up with the Theistic conception for it agrees with Theism that the Divine is experienced most truly on the highest levels of spiritual personality and in terms of the ideal values of life so that if one would speak in human concepts one can do this most validly in terms of an ideal spiritual personality. Only the mystic even of this type would hasten to add that the Divine transcends the human so utterly that no conception can adequately convey the truth. Impersonal Mysticism, on the other hand, links up more closely with the Higher Pantheism or Panentheism, for while it also approaches the Divine through man's inner experience and by way of the ideal values experienced best on the highest levels of spiritual personality it nevertheless hesitates to speak of the divine even provisionally in terms of an ideal and perfect superhuman Personal Being but uses rather the vague language of an impersonal spiritual *something* or takes refuge in an Absolute which is seen as being somehow the source of all that is real but concerning which no definite affirmations can be made. Thus Mysticism in its two major types throws very little light on a valid god-concept beyond what is found either in Theism or in the Higher Pantheism except perhaps that it persistently reminds us that the Divine as the ultimately Real forever transcends the human and can never be fully expressed in concepts that have evolved from human experience.

It comes, then, really to two major types of the God-concept with which a philosophy of religion must reckon, namely, the Theistic and the Higher Pantheistic. In the more worthy formulations of these two there are naturally certain areas which they have in common and up to a certain point the differences seem more a matter of words than actual substance.

Thus there is agreement that the Divine is somehow the unitary ground of all existence including man so that it is in the Divine that "we live, and move and have our being." (Acts. 17:28) The relationship of the natural order to the Divine as its ultimate source is often formulated in terms that are acceptable to both for when Theism expresses its doctrine of creation in terms of a divine "immanence" it seems fairly near the Higher Pantheism which sees the Divine in all things or all things grounded in the Divine. Even when Theism adds that the Divine though immanent, nevertheless, transcends the natural order, it is understood by the pantheist who says that while the Divine is in all things it is, nevertheless, far other in its true nature than what it appears to be in terms of man's ordinary experience of the natural order.

But while Theism, particularly "Immanental Theism," and the Higher

Pantheism have much in common as long as they express themselves in general philosophical concepts there are, nevertheless, deep-going differences in the actual meanings that lie back of these apparently similar general concepts. These vital differences pertain both to the more specific conceptions of the Divine as well as to the relationship of man to the Divine and its practical working out in the religious life. It is these more specific conceptions and the practical consequences that must be determining in our estimate of the two. At least is this the case if one looks upon religion as a real philosophy of life and not as a mere speculative system of thought whose only test of validity is its logical consistency. Logical consistency is, of course, important but if this is achieved either by ignoring or suppressing relevant facts about the real world in which man must live his life or by resorting to a vagueness of terminology which conceals rather than solves difficulties, the result is little more than a form of self-deception however stately the self-consistent system of thought may appear to be.

Let us come, then, more specifically to what is really meant by the Divine and man's relationship to the Divine as this is characteristically envisioned by the Higher Pantheism and by Theism.

b *The God-concept in Higher Pantheism*

WE HAVE GIVEN at some length in Part One the conception of the Divine characteristic in the Higher Pantheism. In a summary way this may be stated as follows: The Divine is that unitary substance that somehow underlies and gives existence to the pluralistic world of man's experience in so far as this world has any real existence and is not illusory. It is that mysterious power that expresses itself in the dynamic aspect of the natural order including also the psychic powers in man and other finite beings. Or again, the Divine is the universal life in which all living beings have their life. But whether expressed in terms of substance, power or life the Divine is somehow more of the nature of things spiritual than material. At times this emphasis on the Divine as spiritual is carried to the point where it becomes practically acosmic or at least where the world of sense-perception is treated as more or less illusory. This is especially the case with Indian Pantheism while in East Asian Panthesim the physical world is given a more substantial existence even though it is maintained that the spiritual aspect is more basic and the best key to the Ultimately Real.

Now while the pantheistic conception is quite characteristic of much in Oriental thought and is a matter of long standing, among Western thinkers there have been comparatively few real pantheists. Even where one finds a pantheistic strain it is more the right wing of an Immanental Theism than an out and out Pantheism. Thus we find some of the Mediaeval mystics speaking in a pantheistic strain as when Meister Eckhart says that "the soul is not only equal with God but it is—the same as He is." And yet even Eckhart and the other Christian mystics usually speak of the Divine much more in Theistic terms than in the vaguer terms of Pantheism. This was also the case later in connection with the Romantic Movement and in Aesthetic Idealism. There was a marked pantheistic strain running through that mode of thought. Some of the great nature poets of that period, especially a Wordsworth and even a Goethe saw the Divine in and through Nature and they conveyed to their readers a sense of a "spiritual something" pervading all things but without stating more specifically what that "spiritual something" is. The language of poetry is peculiarly fitted for stimulating the imagination about spiritual things while leaving each individual free to put as much or as little specific content into the meaning as the mood of the moment may dictate. Among Western theologians it was, of course, Schleeiermacher who spoke the language of Pantheism in his famous "Reden" but even he, in his "Christliche Glaube," spoke more the language of typical Theism. With all this pantheistic strain in Western thought it was, after all, more of the nature of a mood than a reasoned conviction, and it practically never stood by itself but was closely linked with its older theistic background.

Possibly the philosophy of Spinoza was an exception and stood more nearly for a really pantheistic interpretation. When he spoke of the ultimate as a unitary Substance with its infinite attributes and when he said more specifically that "individual things are nothing but modifications of the attributes of God, or modes by which the attributes of God are expressed in a fixed and definite manner," he spoke like a pantheist. Even more was this the case when he said that "our mind, in so far as it understands, is an eternal mode of thinking, which is determined by another eternal mode of thinking, and this other by a third and so on to infinity; so that all taken together at once constitute the eternal and infinite intellect of God." This undoubtedly would make all finite, spiritual beings integral parts of divine being, as is so characteristic of real Pantheism.

But let us come back to the typical Higher Pantheism which has had such a long history in the Orient. If the Divine as the ultimately real is fundamentally a unitary spiritual reality, how more specifically shall we think of it?

We have seen that the pantheist agrees that man makes his most successful approach to the Ultimately Real in terms of the ideal values of life and as he achieves the highest levels of spiritual personality possible to him. Even the physical aspect of reality when seen in its true nature is somehow spiritual, says the pantheist. Now if that is really so, may we, then, not think of the Divine most adequately in terms of a spiritual Being in whom are resident in an infinite and perfect form or degree those characteristic qualities or attributes of spirit which man knows in himself as a personal spiritual being? May we not conceive of the Divine as the supreme and perfect Mind or Intelligence, the free and self-directing Power or Will working creatively towards some purposeful and good end?

But these conceptions so characteristic of the theistic way of thinking the pantheist will not accept as really valid however much he may use such conceptions in dealing with the practical religious life. The pantheist admits that mind or intelligence is a basic characteristic of the Divine as far as man can know, and also that the divine is a psychic power akin to what man knows in himself as will and which works creatively in and through all things. But instead of saying that the Divine is the supreme and perfect Mind or Intelligence, the self-directing Will working freely in all things towards a purposeful and good end, the pantheist merely affirms that the Divine is mind or intelligence as it is such in finite minds and that it is personal as it becomes so in finite personal spirits. Possibly Spinoza put it a bit too baldly when he said that "all (finite minds) taken together at once constitute the eternal and infinite intellect of God" and yet that is a fairly approximate way of stating the pantheist's position. He would especially endorse the statement that "finite minds are but modes of the Divine."

But, if the Divine is really coterminous with the natural order and with finite spiritual beings like man so that "all (finite minds) taken together at once constitute the eternal and infinite intellect," one may well wonder how the Divine can, then, be in any real sense a unitary spiritual reality.

As a matter of fact when such questions are asked the pantheist meets them with a double line of answers. One line leads back from the pluralistic world of man's experience to the Divine as the "unknowable Absolute" in which all distinctions man makes in his thinking have no application. The other line deals with the world of finite things which is regarded as being somehow the expression of the Divine but about which all conceptions and affirmations are seen as only "provisionally true" or as merely "practical accommodations" to human ignorance and finite intelligence.

In the first line of answers the pantheist will thus affirm that the Divine as the Ultimately Real is a spiritual unitary something in which all differences and contradictions are mysteriously reconciled. It is the "dharma of non-duality" which is beyond "truth and error," "good and evil," "being and non-being," or any other distinction man makes in his thinking. If any affirmations are made then these must be balanced by the corresponding negations. The divine is the absolute Mystery before which man can only bow in silence.

But if the Divine is so wholly beyond all distinctions and affirmations, if it is wholly beyond even truth and error, one may well ask whether even this affirmation can, then, have any validity and whether it does not issue in an utter agnosticism. Such a Divine seems all too much like Schelling's Absolute of which Hegel so cleverly remarked that it is "the night in which all cows are black." It is all too much "the lion's den to which all tracks lead but from which none return."

But though the Higher Pantheism seems to be utterly agnostic the individual pantheist does not really live his actual life in this arid void of the "unknowable Absolute." He has thus his second line of answers. In this the Divine is given a very full and all too realistic content, for the Divine is made identical with what man is in himself and with the rest of the natural order. In this respect, Pantheism becomes virtually an out and out Naturalism. It is, of course, not a Naturalism of the older type which is basically materialistic but it is more like the newer Naturalism which recognizes the spiritual aspect of existence as equally natural with the physical. It thus brings the Divine very near to man's natural life; in truth, all too near. At times man himself is seen as a concentration point of the Divine. At other times everything else that makes up the natural is equally the Divine. This is, of course, a little too much like an inflated currency, for when all is equally divine, nothing can be very much so.

In all fairness to the pantheist it must be added that while what we have just said is theoretically his position, in actual practice he does not usually solve his problems in quite such a cavalier manner but makes real distinctions. In fact, in practical religion the pantheist usually forms a close alliance with religions that have rather definite conceptions about the divine as a super-human spiritual being (or beings) and of man's relationship to the Divine. As we pointed out in Part One, Pantheism is always linked in practice with various types of empirical religions ranging all the way from the crudest types of polytheism up to semi-theistic faiths. Each specific conception is accepted as normal for the level of intelligence on which it has arisen and each is seen as "provisionally true." But while each and every conception is thus endorsed the pantheist philosopher will always add that none of them has real validity when applied to the Divine as the Ultimately Real.

The practical upshot of this easy-going compromise with each and every conception of popular religion, on the one hand, and yet this utter agnosticism on the other hand, is what one might expect. It leaves popular religion with its unworthy conceptions of the Divine just where it finds them and does little or nothing to promote a more worthy conception. The pantheist is naturally equally generous towards the more worthy conceptions and probably lives his practical lfe more in terms of these. But even so, he does not throw his weight very heavily on the side of the worthier but usually lets things drift in an easy-going indifference and futile relativism resulting often in spiritual chaos. Unfortunately that also pertains sometimes to the ethical life and the other ideal values of life. Even though the cultured pantheist may live his own life in terms of the higher cultural values, his utter relativism tends to cut the nerve of ethical endeavor.

Now the pantheist may seem to satisfy the intellectual's thirst for a unitary explanation of all things by his identification of the Divine with the natural order and then by reconciling all differences with his "Dharma of non-duality" that is beyond all distinctions man makes. But this is too much a mere juggling of words. When he deals with the real world of man's experience he, too, finds himself compelled to accept as at least "provisionally true" the distinctions man makes. But the gap between what is "provisionally true" and what is really true, the Pantheist never even attempts to bridge. In fact, his characteristic distinction between what is philosophically true and what is "provisionally true," or true for practical human living, is of all dualisms the most radical. If man has his best approach to the nature of the Divine in terms of the ideal values of life—the true, the good and the beautiful as man experiences these in his practical life, and if man gains his insight into these ideal values most fully as he achieves for himself the highest levels of spiritual personality possible—or even if these approaches and insights are only provisionally the best and the truest—can this approach, we ask, and can these insights be in any sense even "provisionally true" unless these ideal values have at least some degree of validity when applied to the Divine as the Ultimately Real? If they have no validity whatever then there seems little sense for the pantheist or any one else to talk about a Divine at all or for that matter about truth in any form. But if, on the other hand, they do have a degree of validity—and we have a right to assume that they do in a real universe—then is not the most adequate conception man can form of the Divine that of an infinite spiritual Being in whom are resident in an ideal and perfect form or degree those ideal values of life and those qualities or attributes of spirit which commend themselves in man's practical experience as real and valid? To accept these as real and valid for our practical life and yet to say that they have no meaning as applied to the Divine or the Ultimately Real, is an unwarranted dualism between the real as man experiences the real and the truly Real. If we would avoid this radical dualism which is really intellectual suicide, we must accept our valid experience in our practical life as having also a degree of validity just as far as we can pursue the true and the real. Even though we readily grant, as we have repeatedly done, that at the end of every road of human inquiry there is a mystery which transcends man's powers of complete comprehension, we have a right nevertheless to maintain that man can have a partial understanding and that there are degrees of validity in the conceptions of the Divine that man has had. Furthermore if we accept as valid the ideal values of life which we have mentioned in our discussion of the truly good life of man then it would seem that no conception of the Divine can have a greater degree of validity than one which bases itself on these ideal values and sees the Divine as the supreme, spiritual Being in whom are resident in an ideal and perfect form these same ideal values.

c *The Theistic God-concept*

IN THE LIGHT of our whole discussion it seems to us that the conception of the Divine as found in the more worthy formulations of the great Theistic Faiths is the most adequate and is essentially valid. Briefly stated this is as follows: God is the Ultimate Reality and in so far as man can know, God is the infinite and perfect Spirit in whom are resident in an absolute or perfect degree the ideal values and qualities of spirit which man experiences most fully on the highest levels of spiritual personality possible to him. God is therefore one with whom man can come into personal relationship and through such personal communion find the truly good life. Then, further, God is seen as the creative source and sustaining power of the natural order. But while God is seen as immanent in the natural order as a creative intelligence and a self-directing power or will working freely towards some meaningful and good end, He nevertheless transcends this order and is not dependent upon it for his own free existence.

This conception of God and his relationship to the natural order and to man has, of course, its peculiar difficulties. Thus it is frequently said that the conception of God as personal is too anthropomorphic and limiting. The theist would, of course, admit that there are characteristics of human personality which can not be attributed to God but he nevertheless maintains, and we believe rightly so, that to conceive of God as the infinite and perfect personal spirit is more adequate than any other conception which has really a positive content. The theist would not quarrel with those who hold that God must be super-personal if by that is meant that God as the infinite Spirit transcends the characteristic limitations of the finite human spirit. But the theist would utter a word of caution here, namely, that the attempt to conceive of God as super-personal all too easily sinks back to the lower level of the sub-personal or the vaguely impersonal. When the theist speaks of God as the perfect and infinite yet personal Spirit he means that the qualities or characteristics of spirit which man knows best in his own consciousness as a personal spiritual being exist in God without the human imperfections and limitations. In using such adjectives as "perfect" and "infinite" he seeks to indicate ways in which God transcends man and man's powers of complete comprehension but in which the transcendental is nevertheless given some real content which is continuous with what man can know or experience in his own life as a personal being.

Now if one accepts the ideal values of life which man experiences most adequately as he attains the highest levels of spiritual personality possible to him as at all real and if man's life is in any real sense grounded in the Ultimately Real—and our whole discussion makes these two propositions eminently reasonable—it would seem to follow that there can be no more valid conception of God as the Ultimately Real than one which is formulated in terms of these ideal values and qualities of spirit. Thus when the theist affirm that God is the infinite Mind or Intelligence and means by this what man knows in self-consciousness as mind, he challenges those who reject this to show what conception of the Ultimate would be more adequate to express that aspect of reality which responds to man's rational thought and which we know as the true. One does not have to agree wholly with those of our modern astro-physicists who seem to hold that even the physical cosmos is in the last analysis a sort of "Mind Stuff" but one must agree that this marvellous universe is infinitely more like the creation or manifestation of an infinite Mind than the product of blind force or that it is a chaos without rhyme and reason. Or if one would express the same thing from the standpoint of Will, the universe seems far more like the work of an intelligent and purposive Will working in an orderly way towards some meaningful end than the resultant of a mere energy unguided by intelligence. To be sure, the dynamic process is too complex and the goal towards which it moves is too vast and distant for man to grasp fully but still he can comprehend enough of it to get at least an inkling of its general trend. This is especially true if there is any meaning at all to what modern science describes as the evolutionary process. What is specially striking in the development of the evolutionary concept itself is the ever increasing emphasis on characteristics which imply the presence of a creative and purposive intelligence in the evolutionary process. Even the older formulations could not quite eliminate spiritual conceptions when they contained such expressions as "natural *selection*" and "survival of the *fittest.*" The newer formulations frankly speak of a "creative" and an "emergent" evolution affirming thereby that there is operative in and through the natural order a Power that is more and other than the natural order itself and that the working of this Power shows unmistakable evidence of a guiding intelligence and purpose.

Now the theist does not, of course, base his belief in God wholly or even chiefly upon the nature of the physical cosmos. In fact, historically the nobler forms of the theistic faith have grown primarily out of man's ethical life. When one accepts the ethical as an ultimate datum of human experience which can not be resolved into lower terms and when one sees in man's moral intuition a valid approach to the Ultimately Real then the theistic conception of the Divine is almost the inevitable conception. Man's practical life is lived on the basis of moral values and ethical distinctions, but man's empirical knowledge of ethical values arises primarily from the relationships of person with person. As man recognizes the ethical as having universal validity and cosmic significance and yet as being in its very nature a relationship between person and person it follows that as he thinks of his relationship with Infinite Being he must think of it as a personal relationship i.e. a communion between himself and God as the Infinite and Perfect yet Personal Spirit.

Thus the theist thinks of God as the infinite Mind and creative Power working freely in and through the natural order but also as the Cosmic Moral Will known primarily through man's ethical life. But these characteristics the theist maintains are characteristics of personal Being. Any attempt at a more adequate conception in the direction of a super-personal Spirit, as we said above, usually issues in a conception which is either void of all real content or sinks to the level of the sub-personal. That, at least, seems to have been the case in the long history of religion as seen especially in the great Oriental religions; and there is little reason to believe that our present day Western thinkers who reject the theistic conception as inadequtae will fare any better.

Now as we saw in our discussion of the more worthy theories of religion in sections VIII-XIII, almost all accept, at least by implication, the theistic conception as the most nearly valid. This was perhaps only natural since these theories centered so largely on the ethical in religion. Possibly the Kantian and most of the post-Kantian theories, built too exclusively upon man's moral intuition and ethical experience for an all-rounded philosophical validation of the theistic faith. While, as we have just said, the ethical approach issues almost inevitably in a theistic conception it is not necessary to rest the case of theism so exclusively on this foundation. Kant and his followers may have been right in regarding the traditional philosophical arguments for the theistic faith as no longer quite convincing. The age-old Ontological argument may be valid enough in holding that God is truth itself or as Augustine put it when he said "Where I have found the truth, there I have found my God, the truth itself." But this is a bit too vague and does not really answer man's personal needs for which he seeks an answer in religion and in his personal relationship with God. Likewise the threadbare Cosmological and Teleological arguments could have little weight at a time when the pronouncements of the developing physical sciences and the resultant cosmologies were almost wholly materialistic and mechanistic in interpretation. Belief in God as held by theists, or for that matter any spiritual interpretation of metaphysical Reality, had little support from the prevailing philosophies of nature, for Nature was seen all too much as a closed system of mechanical necessity, a huge self-running Machine with the spiritual aspect of man's life reduced to an accidental epi-phenomenon. It is not surprising that religious thinkers tended more and more to accept the all too simple division between the sphere of science and the sphere of religion, each going its separate way, and that religion saw its philosophical validation wholly in the inner life of ethical values or rested its case wholly on a supernatural revelation accepted in simple faith and without any reference to the rest of man's valid experience. That is about all that can be done if the pronouncements of the physical sciences are accepted as wholly valid and if such pronouncements are characterized by a wholly materialistic and mechanistic conception of reality.

Fortunately for both science and religion modern thinkers have recovered a little more balance. Many of our first rate scientists including also leading physicists who presumably know more about the ultimate constituents of the physical cosmos than others, are far more modest about their own insight into the nature of Ultimate Reality; and furthermore, in so far as they do venture to make pronouncements as to the nature of metaphysical reality these are often amazingly favorable to religion's insistence on the primacy of the spiritual. We do not hold that religion in general or the theistic conception in particular must look to the physical sciences for their chief philosophical validation, for that would be tantamount to saying that the external world and the physical is as such the deepest reality or that it is more like Ultimate Reality than what man himself is as a spiritual being or what man may experience in his own inner life of self-consciousness and awareness of moral magnitudes or other ideal values. In fact, it seems to us a bit absurd to have so many of our religious leaders today hang almost breathlessly upon the latest utterances of any one who claims to speak in the name of science for a validation of spiritual things. And it is thus rather refreshing to have, on the other hand, leading scientists themselves stress the limitations of the different sciences even in the sphere of their true relevancy, not to mention the wider sphere of philosophy and metaphysics. Thus, e.g. Eddington in an epilogue to his volume on "New Pathways in Science" writes: "The first question asked about scientific facts and theories, such as we have been discussing in this book, is 'Are they true?' I would emphasize that even more significant than the scientific conclusions themselves is the fact that this question so urgently arises about them . . . .

"*We are that which asks the question.* Whatever else there may be in our nature, responsibility towards truth is one of its attributes. This side of our nature is aloof from the scrutiny of the physicist. I do not think it is sufficiently covered by admitting a mental aspect to our being. Concern with truth is one of those things which make up the spiritual nature of Man. There are other constituents of our spiritual nature which are perhaps as self-evident; but it is not so easy to force admission of their existence." (pp. 310f.)

But while the pronouncements of the physical sciences should not be accepted too uncritically and should be limited to the sphere of their real relevancy, and while it must be recognized that there are different levels of reality and different approaches to the Ultimately Real, it is nevertheless worthy of note that the newer cosmology which is emerging at the hands of modern scientists is surprisingly favorable to a spiritual interpretation of metaphysical reality and in some ways gives a strong support to a theistic conception of God as the creative Intelligence and purposive Power manifesting itself in the physical cosmos. The older materialistic and mechanistic cosmologies are no longer intellectually respectable. To be sure, the concept of mechanism will continue to function for certain aspects of the physical cosmos but to accept it as adequate for reality on all its levels or for reality as a whole is regarded as naively childish.

"Today there is a wide measure of agreement, which on the physical side of science approaches almost to unanimity, that the stream of knowledge is leading towards a non-mechanical reality; the universe begins to look more like a great thought than like a great machine. Mind no longer appears as an accidental intruder into the realm of matter; we are beginning to suspect that we ought rather to hail it as the creator and governor of the realm of matter . . . .

"The new knowledge compels us to revive our hasty first impressions that we had stumbled into a universe which either did not concern itself with life or was entirely hostile to life. The old dualism of mind and matter, which was mainly responsible for the supposed hostility, seems likely to disappear; not through matter becoming in any way more shadowy or insubstantial than heretofore, or through mind becoming resolved into a function of the working of matter, but through substantial matter resolving itself into a creation and manifestation of mind. We discover that the universe shows evidence of a designing or controlling power that has something in common with our own individual minds—not: so far as we have discovered, emotion, morality, or aesthetic appreciation, but the tendency to think in the way which, for want of a better word, we describe as Mathematical." (Jeans: The Mysterious Universe pp 137f).

"Nature's great book is written in mathematical language." (Galileo, quoted by Jeans, p. 111).

Eddington seems even more insistent than Jeans that Mind is the primary reality. In answer to the question "whether the nature of reality is material or spiritual or a combination of both" he explains his view in terms of the ocean and its waves letting the water stand for the spiritual and the shape of the waves for the physical. Then he adds: "Similarly I assert that the nature of all reality is spiritual, not material nor a dualism of matter and spirit. The hypothesis that its nature can be to any degree material does not enter into my reckoning, because as we now understand matter, the putting together of the adjective 'material' and the noun 'nature' does not make sense.

"Interpreting the term material (or more strictly, physical) in the broadest sense as that with which we can become acquainted through sensory experience of the external world, we recognize now that it corresponds to the waves not to the water of the ocean of reality. My answer does not deny the existence of the physical world, any more than the answer that the ocean is made up of water denies the existence of ocean waves." (New Pathways in Science p. 315).

It is, in fact, most striking how many modern scientists and philosophers give recognition to the mental and spiritual aspect of the physical cosmos.

It is as Eddington puts it when he says rather whimsically, "There *is* an external world . . . . But I think there can be no doubt that the scientist has a much more mystical conception of the external world than he had in the last century where every scientific 'explanation' of phenomena proceeded on the assumption that nothing could be true unless an engineer could make a model of it." (Ibid p. 323).

Even in dealing with the most ultimate physical constituents such as atoms and electrons the modern physicist realizes tht he must make room for the principle of indeterminacy and an element of spontaneity which seem more akin to the spiritual than to the older physic's mere "matter and motion." Then when it comes to the level of living organisms the scientist is dealing with realities where the psychic is increasingly manifest as one ascends the evolutionary ladder from the simpler and lower to the more complex and higher. Not only is the conception of organism given a constituent place in the scientist's understanding of the cosmos, since living organisms are so obviously a part of the cosmos and so obviously represent a different level of reality from the strictly inanimate level, but the nature of a given organism is seen as determining in a measure at least the character of the physical constituents themselves making thus an electron in an organism differ from an electron in an inanimate object. In fact, Whitehead makes Organism a ruling concept in his philosophy; probably more so than is warranted since he tends to think of the whole physical cosmos as an organism and which seems a bit fantastic. But he is right, and in this is supported by others, when he holds that a living organism is a whole which as a whole can determine the parts that compose it fully as much as that the parts condition the whole. He writes: "The concrete enduring entities are organisms, so that the plan of the whole influences the very characters of the various subordinate organisms which enter into it. In the case of an animal, the mental states enter into the plan of the total organism and thus modify the plans of the successive subordinate organisms until the ultimate smallest organisms, such as electrons, are reached. Thus the electrons within a living body is different from an electron outside it, by reason of the plan of the body." (Science and the Modern World p. 111).

Now this trend towards a due recognition of the mind aspect of reality becomes even more marked as modern biology takes up the task of describing the evolution of living organisms and accounts for the evolutionary process as a whole. Beginning with Bergson's *Elan Vital* which he regarded as a creative energy ever working towards new forms of life, biologists stress increasingly not only the creative factor but also the evidence of a guiding intelligence and purpose. To be sure, there is much in the process which looks like mere blind activity and a movement in a meaningless circle and yet both the nature of individual organisms on every level and the scheme of the evolutionary process as a whole give an overwhelming impression of being the expression of a creative intelligence working towards some purpose. It is as Hobhouse has summarized it when he writes: "Mind is the permanent—we may venture to say the substantive—basis of purposive conception or activity. Where we trace germs or filaments of purpose we infer the rudiments of mind. Where a purpose of a given scope is plain there is to be inferred a mind of no less scope. If, as we now conclude, a purpose runs through the world-whole, there is a Mind of which the world-purpose is the object. Such a Mind must be a permanent and central factor in the process of Reality. (Hobhouse: Development and Purpose pp 364f).

One might quote at great length from the writings of modern scientists and philosophers who base their philosophies primarily upon the findings of science to show that there is today this strong trend towards a due recognition of mind and the spiritual not only as constitutive of the natural order as man more and more explores this but also as being a necessary characteristic of metaphysical reality in so far as man may know the Ultimately Real. It is true that with some the conception of metaphysical reality tends rather towards a vague Panpsychism not unlike the older Pantheism of Oriental philosophies. With others, however, the conception moves definitely in the direction of Theism.

Now Cosmic Theism may be regarded as a wholesome corrective of the Kantian and certain post-Kantian theories of religion which, as we have seen, rested their case almost entirely on moral intuition and man's ethical life. It is likewise a corrective to theories of religion which rest their case almost wholly on a self-revelation of the Divine accepted in simple faith and some times with an open repudiation of what man may know of God through the natural order. But while this more favorable trend in modern scientific thought is a wholesome corrective it is equally one-sided if limited to itself and needs the corrective of the older insights, for Cosmic Theism tends to build too exclusively on the findings of the physical sciences. It would seem, then, that the most valid conception man can have of the Divine as the Ultimate Reality is one which is based on a synthesis of his total valid experience. Such a synthesis will recognize as valid the evidence in the cosmos of a creative Mind working purposively towards some meaningful end. It will accept also as valid the insight man has gained through moral intuition and his practical life of ethical values and distinctions and thus see the

Ultimate in terms of a Cosmic Moral Will. Such a synthesis is essentially consonant with the theistic faith, the belief in God as the infinite, personal Spirit in whom are resident in perfection the qualities of spirit and ideal values which man knows best as he achieves the higher levels of spiritual personality and lives on the plane of the true, the good and the beautiful.

In this total valid experience of the race we must ever recognize as normative also the insights into moral values and spiritual meanings gained by the great prophets and seers, for these have vindicated themselves by their own inherent worth. But in doing so we must also note that these great figures of history have usually had an overwhelming sense of having gained their insight and certitude, not so much through their own quest as through a self-revelation of the Divine. That fact adds tremendously to the validity of the Theistic God-concept.

But what gives the Theistic God-concept its supreme validity, especially for Christians, is Jesus Christ and the life he lived among men. That he achieved the deepest moral and spiritual insight can hardly be questioned. That he embodied in his own life the ideals he proclaimed is equally plain. It is just because of this that he is in a real way the norm not only for Christians but for any man who seeks the truly good life in terms of moral and spiritual values. But as we have said before, there is a third fact about Jesus Christ which is even more significant, namely, that he lived his life in conscious communion with God. It is this which so impressed many who came into close contact with him that they saw in him the very revelation of God Himself. It is true enough that there have been others, especially some of the great mystics, who at times seemed to have a direct awareness of God, but this was usually a temporary experience and these mystics seldom could communicate to others what they experienced in the mystic state. Jesus Christ, on the other hand, seemed to live his whole life in union with God, the Heavenly Father, and in almost everything that he said he directed men's thoughts to God.

Now it was just this fact about Jesus Christ which the New Testament, especially in the Fourth Gospel and in some of Paul's letters tries to express in various ways. Thus the opening chapter of the Fourth Gospel, using concepts by which Greek philosophers sought to express the nature of Ultimate Reality, speaks of Jesus Christ as the divine *Logos* by which "all things were made" but which "became flesh and dwelt among us, full of grace and truth." This same Gospel reports Jesus as saying of himself: "I proceeded and came forth from God; I came not of my own accord, but he sent me." (John 8:42). And again we read: "He who believes in me, believes not in me but in him who sent me." (John 12:44). "He who has seen me has seen the Father." (John 14:9). Paul says much the same thing when he writes about Jesus Christ as having been "in the form of God" but as one who "emptied himself" and was "born in the likeness of men." (Phil. 2:5,6). Paul also says that "the God who has said, 'Let light shine out of darkness,' has shone in our hearts to give the light of the knowledge of the glory of God in the face of Christ." (II Cor.4:4,6). In these and in similar ways the New Testament seeks to express what Jesus Christ had to say about himself and his relationship to God.

If we ask now as to what light this throws on the God-concept, for that is our major concern here, the answer is that Jesus Christ always spoke of God in personalistic terms. Granted that in much of what he said he spoke in parables and in symbolic language. And granted further that no conception of God can fully express what he is in his true and full Being so that an attitude of reverence and worship of the Divine Mystery is most befitting. But it, nevertheless, remains true that no conception of God which has a really positive content and is not a mere vague abstraction is more adequate and valid than one which is cast in essentially personalistic terms, that is, in what man knows best on the highest levels of his own spiritual life.

In short, then, the theist accepts truth on every level of human experience. He welcomes any light which modern science may throw on the nature of Ultimate Reality and notes that even the physical sciences seem to speak more and more in terms of Mind and things Spiritual as constituting the nature of Ultimate Reality. But the Christian Theist, nevertheless, finds the supreme vindication of his faith in God through his fellowship with Jesus Christ, for it is in this fellowhip that God becomes most truly real to him.

C: IV NORMATIVE RELIGION & THE DESTINY OF THE INDIVIDUAL

As WE HAVE seen in Part One, a most persistent trait of religion is the belief in the immortality of man. However final death may appear there is nevertheless the recurrent and persistent conviction in the heart of man that death is not the end of things. On every level of human culture and as an integral part of almost every form of religion this belief in a future existence is found.

The philosophy of religion must therefore, as in the case of other cardinal beliefs of religion, seek to determine what validity this widespread belief of the race can have. Is it true that when the body dies and is dissolved into its component physical elements this is not the end of man's life but that in some real sense he continues to exist? By this is not meant a mere "immortality of influence" but a real existence in which there is at least a degree of continuity and identity of man's present essential being.

Now in the very nature of the case the question of survival after death is one regarding which dogmatic assertions seem peculiarly out of place, for if life itself is still a great mystery death and what lies beyond death is even a greater mystery. But while this is so, can the belief in an existence beyond death be nevertheless regarded as reasonable, or on the whole more reasonable than that the death of the body ends all?

It should go without saying that many of the conceptions and beliefs about the future existence found in the various religions are too crude to be very convincing. The heavens and paradises of popular religions seem often little more than the creation of the pious imagination and wishful thinking. Even in the formulations of the more worthy conceptions wishful thinking seems to have played an all too prominent role. But after due allowances have been made for the excesses of the romantic imagination there still remain certain facts about the nature of human life and man's encompassing and sustaining reality which make the belief in immortality more than a mere product of the pious imagination or the fabrication of wishful thinking. Granted that even the noblest conceptions and beliefs in this field are colored with what man wants of life or would like to have true, this very passion for a life beyond death and this all but universal belief in survival is itself a factor that deserves consideration as throwing light on man's real nature. To be sure, the universality of a belief does not prove its validity but the fact that man everywhere and at all times has hoped for and believed in a future life tells us a great deal about the real nature of the human spirit and its possible worthiness to survive the death of the body.

After all, the question as to the destiny of the individual is a cardinal question in religion just because it is one which every thoughtful person must face sooner or later. Physical death is one of the absolute certainties of life and so the question as to whether death means the end of the chapter or not arises inevitably in man's mind. The answer, however, which one gives to this question will depend in a very large measure upon one's conception of human nature and the nature of the world in which man lives, including also one's conception of metaphysical reality or the Divine and the Ultimately Real. As we said in Part One, the three cardinal elements of religion, namely, the Divine or transcendental world, the good life in the here and now, and the future life mutually condition each other. It is especially true that the conception of the third and the grounds upon which the belief in a future existence rest are bound up most intimately with what one believes about the Divine and what one regards as constituting the true nature of man's present life. Belief in immortality, therefore, does not and can not stand alone but is more of the nature of a projection of faith which is buttressed on a spiritual conception of human life and on a recognition of the Divine and transcendental world upon which man knows himself dependent.

Thus e.g. if one holds a materialistic or mechanistic view of human nature and of reality in general, it follows quite naturally that death will seem like the end of the individual. All that survives can then be merely the chemical elements that compose the bodily organism. But as we have seen, such a conception of human life is utterly inadequate and grotesque. However true it may be as far as it goes, it tells us little of what makes up the real life of man. It tells us nothing of what constitutes man's life as a spiritual being—a being who thinks and to whom the distinction between truth and error is important; a being who is aware of moral magnitudes and who lives by moral values and even surrenders the physical life in pursuit of a spiritual ideal; a being in quest of beauty on all levels of the beautiful including also "the beauty of holiness;" yes, a being in quest of the Eternal in the midst of Time and who cannot be content with all that earth offers but who at the end of a full and mature life longs for an ever better life and who has gained his deepest conviction as to the possibility of such a life from his experience of a qualitative life of the spirit which by its inherent nature vindicates itself as a partial glimpse of the Life Eternal. All this and more the materialistic interpretation of human life ignores and because it does so it naturally draws the conclusion that the death of the body is the end of man's life.

But if these things are the things that really make human life what it is and what differentiates man from the mere animal, then the conclusion that physical death ends all is not such an obvious conclusion. In fact, the death of the body seems then more like a transitional phenomenon in the life of the spirit.

Let us, however, look more specifically at some of the more reasonable conceptions of a possible future life and the grounds for believing in such an existence.

As we said above, any reasonable conception and belief must in the very nature of the case grow out of what constitutes the true nature of man and the nature of man's encompassing reality upon which his life is dependent. There are for that reason two major lines of thought in the higher religions advanced in support of the belief in man's survival beyond death. One line

W

bases itself primarily upon the spiritual nature of man, i.e. on the inherent nature of the human spirit as a reality which transcends the bodily life however much it is at present linked with the physical organism. Because the spirit is even now transcendent in nature it can and does survive the death of the body. The other line of thought bases itself more upon the spiritual nature of existence as a whole and particularly upon the spiritual nature of Ultimate Reality or the Divine upon whose creative and sustaining power man's life is dependent and therefore may be trusted to sustain the spirit also beyond the transitional phenomenon we call death. These two major lines of thought are, of course, mutually complementary and the higher religions usually base their faith in immortality more or less on both.

In developing the first line of thought a basic problem that arises immediately is, of course, the problem as to what is the real relationship between the two obvious aspects of man's life, namely, the psychic and the physical. As we said in our discussion of the Good Life, man is a psychosomatic being and the trend in modern thought, particularly in medical science, is towards an emphasis on the organic unity of these two aspects of man's nature. While we can accept this view of man's nature and recognize for practical purposes this inter-relatedness and inter-dependence of the two sides of man's life, we must not blind ourselves to certain other facts which make one hesitate in taking this theory of a psycho-somatic organism in an absolute sense.

Nothing brings out more sharply the question as to the real nature of the relationship between the psychic and the physical than does the phenomenon we call death. If the psychic aspect of the psycho-somatic organism is as truly real as is the physical aspect, what becomes of the psychic when death occurs? Only the chemical elements that compose the body seem to survive. The psychic aspect, if it continues to exist certainly no longer continues in organic union with the physical elements that compose the body.

Now as a matter of fact there are four types of answers given to the question as to the real relationship between the two aspects of man's life and what actually follows the death of the body, only one of which it seems to us is at all adequate.

There is first the extreme position of the materialist already mentioned above. The materialist must, of course, recognize the psychic aspect of life for even the materialist thinks and is conscious of his inner life. He is quite ready to accept the view that man is a psycho-somatic organism and that this constitutes an absolute unity but it is a unity in which one of the two constituent parts is completely swallowed up by the other, for the materialist maintains that the psychic aspect of life is in the last analysis merely a temporary epiphenomenon resulting from the peculiar structure of the physical organism. Consciousness and the inner life of the spirit is nothing more than a sort of nerve and brain activity. And thus when the physical organism runs down and the nerve and brain structure ceases to function consciousness and the whole psychic life cease to exist. This simple interpretation of man's life and this verdict as to life's issue will probably always commend itself to simple minded people, especially to those whose life is primarily a matter of the physical senses. But as we have already shown in our discussion of the Good Life such an estimate of life is too naively simple. If e.g. thought or consciousness is reduced to mere brain functioning what is it that determines the difference between a true thought and a false one? The materialist's statement is then a mere brain functioning and has no more validity than one which denies it for the latter is also brain functioning. That leads, of course, to intellectual suicide and the materialist apparently has not enough wit to see this. But if there is a real difference between truth and error and if this distinction really makes a difference then we must also find some more adequate conception of the nature of man's psychic life and the possibility of spiritual survival.

A second view of human nature, and one which is almost the exact opposite of the Materialist's view, holds that man in his true being is pure spirit and that the bodily life constitutes really an imprisonment of the spirit from which he must be freed. This view finds more or less of an echo in the ascetic trend of various religions but has its most emphatic expression in the Sankhya philosophy of Hinduism. Undoubtedly such a view of human nature would seem to do full justice to man's spiritual nature and the certainty of his survival beyond the death of the body, but it is so extreme in what it has to say about man's present psycho-somatic life that it does not inspire much confidence in what it has to say about man as pure spirit.

A third view of human nature is the one we have already mentioned incidentally, namely, one which not only affirms the psycho-somatic character of man's present life but which stresses the thought that these two aspects constitute a real unity. Both aspects are regarded as equally real. Neither is subordinated to the other nor are they regarded as standing in a cause and effect relationship. They are seen as wholly inter-related and interdependent. Expressed in terms of modern psychology, this view has much to say about a thorough-going parallelism between the psychic and the physical. It is a parallelism of a double series but without either series affecting in a causal way the other for the two are seen as but two *aspects* of what is fundamentally one and the same reality. Thus it is often said by those who hold this view that the perplexing problems of the relationship between the psychic and the physical cease to be problems since the psychic and the physical are but two phases of one and the same thing, two ways in which the mystery of reality manifests itself.

Now this emphasis on the complete unity of the psycho-somatic organism called man has its practical advantages. It is a wholesome corrective of the two extremes mentioned above. Man's present life in a real sense constitutes a sort of organic unity between the two obvious aspects of the psychic and the physical. Modern medical science operates rather successfully on the basis of this conception and our modern social philosophy has also profited from this view. Religion, too, as a practical philosophy of life has gained much by this emphasis as we said in our discussion of the Good Life.

But while this view of human nature may be accepted in a general way it should not be pushed too far. If the psychic and the physical are but two phases of one and the same reality then one should think that where one aspect is present the other aspect must be equally present. Without entering into this wider aspect of the problem and confining ourselves to the problem as it presents itself in man's nature, it is evident that there are certain experiences which can not be explained in terms of this view. It fails most signally, of course, in giving any satisfactory account of what happens to the psychic aspect when the death of the body occurs.

But this theory fails not merely in dealing with the phenomenon of death, it also fails in accounting adequately for much of man's present psychic life. After all, there is much of our psychic life which indicates that it completely transcends the bodily life. In some phases of our experience, it is true, there seems to be a rather close parallelism between the psychic and the physical but there are others where it is more than doubtful whether this is the case. In all sense-perception it seems quite obvious that the physical plays an important part; in fact, it seems as if it played the major role. But the moment one turns one's attention to the mind's activity in forming concepts and ideas built up from sense data and in elaborating great systems of thought; especially when one turns to the inner and contemplative life and the consciousness of spiritual values and meanings, it seems that the purely psychic becomes increasingly dominant if not wholly independent of all cerebral activity. Even though it could be demonstrated that cerebration always accompanies every psychic state or consciousness it would still seem a bit absurd to equate one with the other even though such equation is not the crude thing of the old fashioned materialist but the more subtle "two phases of one and the same thing."

There are, as a matter of fact, first rate scientists and philosophers who reject all strict parallelism on scientific grounds and who affirm that the psychic or spiritual in much of its activity wholly transcends all bodily functioning and which therefore makes the belief in a spiritual survival a most reasonable belief. "If, as I have tried to show," writes Bergson, "the mental life overflows the cerebral life, if the brain does but translate into novements a small part of what takes place in consciousness, then survival becomes so probable that the onus of proof falls on him who denies it rather than on him who affirms it; for the only reason we can have for believing in the extinction of consciousness at death is that we can see the body become disorganized, that this is a part of experience, and this reason loses its force if the independence of almost the whole of consciousness with regard to the body has been shown to be also a fact of experience." (Time and Free Will, pp 72-73).

Eddington, in discussing the wider question as to the relationship between the physical and the psychic aspects of existence also questions the validity of any strict parallelism theory. He writes, "We have evidence that your consciousness is associated with a certain portion of your brain; but we do not go to assume that a particular element of your consciousness is associated with a particular atom in your brain. The elements of consciousness are particular thoughts and feelings; the elements of the brain cells are atoms and electrons; but the two analyses do not run parallel to one another. While therefore I contemplate a spiritual domain underlying the physical world as a whole, I do not think of it as distributed so that to each element of time and space there is a corresponding portion of spiritual background. My conclusion is that, though for the most part our inquiry into the problem of experience ends in a veil of symbols, there is an immediate knowledge which lifts the veil in places; and what we discern through these openings is of mental and spiritual nature. Elsewhere we see no more than the veil." (New Pathways in Science, p. 322).

It is this "immediate knowledge" which we have in self-consciousness that gives man his deepest insight into his own nature as a spiritual being and which as such transcends the "veil of symbols" that makes up the physical aspect. There are two aspects of self-consciousness in particular which indicate how the spirit transcends the physical aspect and why it can not be equated with the latter. One is the fact that in self-consciousness man knows himself as a Oneness. In spite of the varied aspects of our psychic life there runs through it all a thread that binds this variety together into a real unity. In every psychic state the self knows it as its own. It is for each of us "my experience" no matter how varied this experience is. And this consciousness of an "I", "My" or "Mine" binds our psychic life together into a sort of real unity. On the other hand, the nerve and brain structure with which the psychic is associated is made up of an infinite number of atoms which however closely connected they may be with each other for the time being are nevertheless always external to each other and always constitute a pluralism and never a real oneness. Even if we think of them as constituting a unity in a physical organism there is still a radical distinction that we must make in our thought between such a unity and the unity of our self-consciousness.

The second outstanding fact about man's self-consciousness is an awareness of the identity of the self over a period of time in spite of the change which growth or a developing self involves. The atoms which, on the other hand, make up the brain and nerve structure are a constant flux and are always being replaced by others. There is nothing in this flux of atoms which even remotely corresponds to the consciousness of identity in the developing spiritual self. In other words, in the physical series which is supposed to parallel the psychic series at all points, the elements are an almost infinite pluralism and wholly external to each other while in the psychic series there is a real oneness. And again, in the physical series there is a complete change of elements from time to time so that there is not a shred of identity between the elements at the beginning of a certain period and those that are present at the end of that period whereas in the psychic series there is a real continuity and identity. In fact, if this latter were not the case all logical thinking and sequences would be impossible for unless the self that formulates the premise is the same self that draws the conclusion all thought processes would seem invalid.

The truth of the matter is that the nature of the psychic or spiritual self is fundamentally so different from the physical organism that it becomes quite meaningless to equate one with the other in any sort of strict parallelism. It seems much more accurate to regard the bodily organism as a kind of instrument of the spirit through which the latter operates on the physical environment but which is not necessarily involved in all psychic processes. To quote again from Bergson, "Besides the body which is confined to the present moment in time and limited to the place it occupies in space, which behaves automatically, and reacts mechanically to external influences, we apprehend something which is much more extended than the body in space, and which endures through time, something which requires from, or imposes on, the body movements no longer automatic and foreseen, but unforseeable and free. This thing, which overflows the body on all sides, and which creates acts by new-creating itself, is the 'I,' 'Soul,' 'Mind,'" (Mind and Energy, p. 39).

When one thinks of the lives of great spiritual personalities and their creative activity of one sort and another this transcendental nature of the spirit stands out most clearly. To be sure, there is a physical aspect to such activity but what makes it significant and differentiates it from mere animal life is its qualitative and spiritual character. Thus e.g. a great mathematician and astronomer is able in pure thought to envision the orbits of the heavenly bodies and their relationship in space to each other, not only as these are at the time of actual observation but as they were at different periods in the distant past or as they will be at some distant future date. Such construction in imagination, though based in part upon data gained through sense-perception and thus dependent upon the bodily organism, is nevertheless far more the product of the creative spirit and as such seems little dependent upon the bodily organism. It seems rather absurd to say that the psychic series which represents this great thought structure which the scientist has thus built up in imagination and in which he is present in spirit in the outer reaches of space and by which he passes freely from the present into the distant past and forward again into the remote future, has and must have a corresponding series in the brain and nerve structure. And if it is true that the creative activity of the spirit manifested in the work of a physical scientist transcends the bodily organism or any conception that we can formulate of a physical series paralleling the psychic series, what shall we say of those psychical processes which deal with moral magnitudes and spiritual meanings? Undoubtedly the moral prophet and the spiritual seer can be spoken of as psycho-somatic organisms the same as any other human beings. They too live by eating and drinking, and when they evaluate moral magnitudes interpret spiritual meanings and values there may be some cerebration going on, but to equate one with the other or to insist that one must at all points involve the other, seems a decided over-statment of the facts.

But not only in the lives of great spiritual personalities do we have evidence of the essentially spiritual nature of man as something which transcends the bodily organism or which "overflows" the channels of a strict "parallelism," there are experiences in the life of every normal human being which are so predominantly psychic in character and which seem to have little or no corresponding expression in the physical organism. Thus the universal sense of duty that often drives an individual onward in his course against all bodily inclinations, all moral striving in the face of temptations induced by bodily desires, all creative activity inspired by man's capacity for anticipating or envisioning the future and through which he can make real to himself the things that are not but that *should* be and that can be brought into being by the creative spirit; in short, all creative activity of the spirit originating from within as distinguished from those psychic states which are more of a response to external stimuli, demonstrate the fact that man is fundamentally a spiritual being and that the spirit transcends the limitations of any strict parallelism. And it is just because man in his inner consciousness knows himself as a spiritual being even though much of his life is intimately bound up with the bodily organism that he can not accept the verdict that the death of the body means the end of things but he persists in believing in some form of spiritual existence after death.

This, then, it seems to us is the more valid view of human nature and the individual's destiny, namely, one that recognizes the psycho-somatic character of man's present life and that sees that these two aspects of his nature constitute a sort of organic unity but not in the strict sense of an absolute parallelism in which the psychic always involves a functioning of the bodily organism. It regards the bodily organism rather as an instrument of the spirit and the spirit as inherently of such a nature that it transcends all bodily functioning. And since the spirit thus transcends the body even now it seems quite reasonable to believe that the spirit can and does survive the death of the body.

But the belief in the survival of the spirit rests not merely upon the conception of the spirit's own inherent nature; in the higher religions it rests even more upon man's relationship to the Divine as the Ultimate Reality. As we have repeatedly pointed out, the very core of religion is the conviction that man's life is grounded in or dependent upon the Divine and it naturally follows that man's destiny must also be bound up with the Divine. The ultimate issues of the individual human life are naturally determined by the nature of Ultimate Reality.

Now we have already discussed in the preceding section what to us are the more worthy conceptions of Ultimate Reality or the Divine. We spoke of three major conceptions, namely, the mystic, the pantheistic and the theistic. These three, we saw, really resolve themselves to two as far as the more specific conceptions of the Divine are concerned, namely, to the latter two since in mysticism the Divine is always regarded as so wholly transcendental that no conception of its true nature can be formulated, but in so far as the mystic does formulate his conception he follows either the pantheistic or the theistic pattern. This same thing holds also for the conception of the nature and grounds of the future life of man.

Thus the mystic usually insists that just as the Divine is a spiritual reality which wholly transcends any conception man can form even though he can have an immediate awareness of the Divine presence, so the nature of man's future life is wholly beyond any conception that can be formulated. But it is nevertheless a spiritual existence since it is an existence in complete union with the Divine and which man can experience even now in the mystic state. That, in fact, is the very essence of the mystical experience, according to the mystic, namely, that man can even now be caught up, as it were, into the divine life which is the life eternal.

The pantheist with his conception of the Divine as a vague spiritual Something which is somehow in and through all things naturally affirms the immortality of man for man is an expression or mode of Divine Being. But just as the pantheist develops two almost wholly opposite conceptions of the Divine when pressed for a more specific interpretation so does he also solve the problem of the individual's destiny along two almost contradictory lines. Thus, on the one hand, he affirms that the Divine is a spiritual Something concerning which no further affirmations can be made since it is really the unknowable Absolute, the Dharma of Non-Duality etc., etc. And so about the future existence of the individual the pantheist holds that nothing further can be affirmed than that man survives in so far as he is a mode of Absolute Being. Since the Divine is not regarded as personal man, too, when he returns to the source of his being ceases to be a personal being. The familiar figure with which the pantheist seeks to express the relationship is that of the relationship between the wave and the ocean. As the wave has a temporary existence as wave but sinks again into the ocean's depths, so the individual human spirit has a merely temporary existence as a self-conscious personal being and at death is absorbed back into the depths of the undifferentiated Absolute.

But just as the pantheist for practical purposes allies himself with popular religions in which there is a more or less definite belief in the Divine as personal and which beliefs the pantheist accepts as "provisionally true" or true for "practical purposes," so likewise does he accept as "provisionally true" or "practically true" the paradises and heavens and hells of these same popular religions.

The upshot of this all too sceptical or agnostic spirit, on the one hand, and this all too easy-going compromise with the half truths of popular religions, on the other hand, is that the common believer envisions man's future life all too much in terms of his present life while the more thoughtful find it next to impossible to give it any real content.

Now as we have shown above, the pantheistic conception of the Divine involves, in its practical working out in life, really a radical dualism between what is the real of man's experience and what is assumed to be the truly or ultimately real. But such a radical dualism is, philosophically speaking, intellectual suicide. And we have also said that if we are to think of the Divine or the Ultimately Real as spiritual in any real sense, which the pantheist claims to do, then we can form no more adequate conception of it than that of a Supreme Spiritual Being in whom are resident in an ideal and absolute form those qualities and ideal values of life which man experiences best on the highest levels of spiritual personality possible to him. Now this same thing holds equally for the most adequate conception of the nature and ground of man's spiritual survival beyond death. If man survives at all as a spiritual something, as the pantheist affirms, it would seem that there must be at least some degree of continuity and identity with what man is now as a spiritual personality. And thus the grounds for believing in the possibility of a spiritual life that is essentially the life of a spiritual personality is not simply the inherent nature of man as a personal spiritual being who even now transcends the life of the bodily organism, but even more the fact that the Ultimate Reality is God, the Supreme Personal Spirit, who is the source and sustaining power of man's spirit in the present life and who therefore may be depended upon to satisfy that deeply implanted desire for a better life and bring it to perfection in the Life Eternal. Therefore to believe in a personal God is to believe in the immortality of man; at least the man whose life is linked with God even now. "For to know Thee, is perfect righteousness; yea, to know Thy power, is the root of immortality." (Wisdom of Solomon, 15:3). And Jesus himself gave the classic answer to the Saducees, who claimed to believe in God and yet denied man's immortality, when he said, "Have ye not read that which was spoken to you by God saying, I am the God of Abraham, and the God of Isaac and the God of Jacob? God is not the God of the dead but of the living."

In short, one can not believe in the great evolutionary process by which the Supreme Intelligence and Purposive Power of the universe has developed ever higher forms of life and at the upper end of the scale produced man, who alone of all creatures can in a measure "think the thoughts of God after him" and who has capacity for endless growth in the things of the spirit, and then conclude that such a being ends with the death of the body. One can not believe in the full validity of man's moral and spiritual struggle which has as its goal the development of an ethical and spiritual personality and then write zero as the final outcome of it all. It simply does not make sense. It makes far better sense if we say that this effort looks towards the achievement of abiding values. It is as we participate in this type of life that we gain our deepest conviction not simply of its reality and authority for us in our present life but also of its transcendental character. It is a life in which we are privileged to share rather than of our own making. It somehow vindicates itself as the Life Eternal.

But just as man's faith in God can rest not simply on man's general experience of the essentially spiritual nature of things or upon the indubitable reality of ethical and other ideal values which constitute the core of the truly good life, but more specifically upon the supreme revelation of God in the person of Jesus Christ, so also does faith in personal immortality find its supreme reason in Him who as no other has really "brought life and immortality to light." At the grave of a good man one instinctively feels that the death of the body can not be the last word. The real man was so infinitely more than the bodily life which thus comes to an end. We have a right to believe that this "infinitely more," this nobility of spirit must survive. But this instinctive feeling grows into a certitude of faith and knowledge in the presence of the living Christ, the Lord of Life and Death. It is He who had the right to say, "because I live, ye shall live also."

BIBLIOGRAPHY

AMES, E.S.: *The New Orthodoxy,* University of Chicago Press, 1918
BAILLIE, G.: *The Interpretation of Religion,* T. & T. Clark, Edinburgh, 1929
BERGSON, Henri: *Mind and Energy,* Macmillan & Co., 1920
BROWNE, Lewis: *The World's Great Scriptures,* Macmillan Co., 1946
CLARKE, James Freeman: *The Great Religions,* Houghton Mifflin Co.
COMTE, Auguste: *Positivistic Philosophy,* L. Trubner, 1853
CREEL, H.G.: *Confucius, the Man and the Myth,* The John Day Co., New York, 1947
DEGROOT: *The Religion of the Chinese,* Macmillan Co., 1916
DEWEY, John: *A Common Faith,* Yale University Press, 1934
EDDINGTON, Sir Arthur Stanley: *New Pathways in Science,* Macmillan Co., 1935
——: *Science and the Unseen World,* Macmillan Co., 1929
ELIOT, Charles: *Hinduism and Buddhism,* Edward Arnold & Co., 1921
——: *Japanese Buddhism,* Edward Arnold & Co., 1935
FAIRBAIRN, Andrew Martin: *The Philosophy of the Christian Religion,* Macmillan Co., 1923
FUNG, Y.L.: *History of Chinese Philosophy,* Henry Vetch, Peking, 1937
GENSHIN: *Collected Essays on Birth into Paradise (Ojo Yoshu),* Transactions of Asiatic Society of Japan, Second Series, Vol. VII, 1931
GILES, Herbert A.: *Confucianism and its Rivals,* William and Norgate, London, 1915
GLASSENAPP, Helmuth von: *Die Fünf Grossen Religionen,* Eugen Diedrich Verlag, Düsseldorf, Köln.
GODDARD, Dwight: *The Buddhist Bible,* Pub, Dwight Goddard, 1938
GUNDERT, W.: *Japanische Religionsgeschichte,* D. Gundert Verlag, Stuttgart, 1935
HOBHOUSE, Leonard Trelawney: *The Theory of Knowledge,* Mathuen & Co., London, 1896
——: *Development of Purpose,* Macmillan & Co., 1913
HOCKING, William Ernest: *Types of Philosophy,* Scribner's & Sons, 1929
——: *The Meaning of God in Human Experience,* Yale U. Press, 1963
HOLTOM, D.C.: *The National Faith of Japan,* Kegan Paul, Trench Tubner & Co., 1938
HÖFFDING, Harold: *The Philosophy of Religion,* Macmillan Co., 1906
HÜME, Robert Ernest: *The Thirteen Principal Upanishads,* Geofrey Cumberlege, Oxford U. Press, 1931
——: *Treasure House of the Living Religions,* Charles Scribner's & Sons, 1932
JAMES, William: *The Varieties of Religious Experience,* New Hyde Park N.Y. University Books, 1963
JEANS, Sir James Hopwood: *The Mysterious Universe,* Macmillan Co., 1930
JELKE, Robert: *Religions-Philosophie,* Verlag von Quelle & Meyers, Leipzig, 1927
JURJI, Edward J.: *The Great Religions of the Modern World,* Princeton U. Press, 1946
LEGGE, James: *The Chinese Classics,* Lane, Crawford & Co., Hongkong, 1872
——: *The Four Books,* The Chinese Book Co., Shanghai, 1930
KRAEMER, H.: *The Christian Message in a Non-Christian World,* Harper & Brothers, 1938

LIN YUTANG: *The Wisdom of China and India,* Random House, New York, 1942

LIPPMANN, Walter: *A Preface to Morals,* Macmillan Co., 1929

LYMAN, Theodore: *The Meaning and Truth of Religion,* Charles Scribner's & Sons, 1933

MORGAN, Kenneth W.: *The Religion of the Hindus,* The Ronald Press Co., New York, 1953

MOORE, George Foot: *History of Religions,* Charles Scribner's & Sons, New York, 1949

MÜLLER, F. Max: *Editor, Sacred Books of the East,* The Clarendon Press, Oxford, 1894

NATORP, Paul: *Religion Within the Bounds of Humanity,* 1894

NOSS, John B.: *Man's Religions,* Macmillan Co., 1949

OTTO, Rudolf: *The Idea of the Holy,* Oxford U. Press, 1924

PRATT, J.B.: *The Pilgrimage of Buddhism,* Macmillan Co., 1928

REISCHAUER, A.K.: *Studies in Japanese Buddhism,* Macmillan Co., 1917

RICHARD, Timothy: *The New Testament of Higher Buddhism,* T. & T. Clark, Edinburgh, 1910

SAMSON, G.B.: *Japan-A Short Cultural History,* The Cresent Press, London, 1931

SCHOLTZ, Heinrich: *Religionsphilosophie,* Verlag von Reuther & Reichard, Berlin, 1922

SUZUKI, Daisetsu Teitaro: *Outlines of Mahayana Buddhism,* The Open Court Publishing Co., 1908

——: *Zen Buddhism: Selected Writing of D.T. Suzuki,* Doubleday & Co., N.Y., 1956

TAKAKUSU, Junjiro: *The Essentials of Buddhist Philosophy,* University of Hawaii, 1947

WHITEHEAD, Alfred North: *Science and the Modern World,* Macmillan Co., 1925

WINDELBAND, Wilhelm: *An Introduction to Philosophy,* London Unwin, 1921

WINTERNITZ, M.: *Geschichte der Indischen Literature,* C.F. Amerlangs Verlag, Leipzig, 1920

WIEMAN, Henry Nelson, and MELAND, Bernard Eugene: *American Philosophy of Religion,* Willet Clart & Co., Chicago & N.Y., 1936

WRIGHT, Arthur F.: *Studies in Chinese Thought,* The American Anthropological Association, 1953

INDEX